W9-DGR-672

Walter Gordon and the Rise of Canadian Nationalism

From the 1950s to the 1970s Walter Gordon was the voice of English Canadian nationalism, first as chair of the Royal Commission on Canada's Economic Prospects, then as a minister in Lester B. Pearson's Cabinet, and
finally as founder and honorary chair of the Committee for an Independent
Canada. In the late 1960s many Canadians heeded Gordon's call for limits on
the level of American investment in Canadian industry and joined with him to
form a broad movement to limit American influence in Canada.

Walter Gordon and the Rise of Canadian Nationalism examines the origins
of Walter Gordon's nationalist ideology and its impact on Canada. It traces
his ideas from his family influences and the intellectual currents present in
his early years to his work as a chartered accountant, public servant, and head
of a small conglomerate. Drawing on extensive interviews and impressive research, Stephen Azzi provides not only a biography of an important political
figure but a significant study of the political and intellectual controversies
that Gordon and his ideas created, shedding light on the larger political and
economic questions of the post-war era.

STEPHEN AZZI teaches history at Carleton University.

STEPHEN AZZI

Walter Gordon and the Rise of Canadian Nationalism

McGill-Queen's University Press
Montreal & Kingston · London · Ithaca

Legal deposit second quarter 1999
Bibliothèque nationale du Québec

Printed in Canada on acid-free paper

This book has been published with the help of a grant
from the Humanities and Social Sciences Federation
of Canada, using funds provided by the Social
Sciences and Humanities Research Council of Canada.

McGill-Queen's University Press acknowledges the
financial support of the Government of Canada
through the Book Publishing Industry Development
Program for its activities. We also acknowledge
the support of the Canada Council for the Arts
for our publishing program.

Canadian Cataloguing in Publication Data

Azzi, Stephen, 1965–
    Walter Gordon and the rise of Canadian nationalism
    Includes bibliographical references and index.
    ISBN 0-7735-1840-1
    1. Gordon, Walter L., 1906–1987. 2. Canada – Politics
    and government – 1963–1968. 3. Canada – Economic
    policy. 4. Nationalists – Canada – Biography. 5. Cabinet
    ministers – Canada – Biography. I. Title.

    FC621.G67A99   1999   971.064'3   C99-900304-6
    F1034.3.G67A99   1999

This book was typeset by Typo Litho Composition Inc.
in 10.5/13 Times.

To my wife, Megan Sproule-Jones

Contents

Preface / ix

Acknowledgments / xiii

Illustrations / xvii

1 The Making of a Public Figure, 1906–1955 / 3

2 The Gordon Commission, 1955–1957 / 34

3 Man and Superman, 1958–1963 / 66

4 It Was Walter Gordon's Budget, 1963 / 95

5 A Lion in Winter, 1963–1965 / 111

6 The Dilemma of Canadian Affluence, 1966–1968 / 133

7 The New Nationalism, 1968–1987 / 167

8 Conclusion / 189

Notes / 195

Bibliography / 255

Index / 293

Preface

When he first came to national prominence in the late 1950s, Walter Gordon was a lonely voice. As chair of the Royal Commission on Canada's Economic Prospects, Gordon warned Canadians of the country's heavy reliance on foreign capital and urged the government to enact measures for greater domestic control of Canadian industry. But few Canadians were ready for his program; Canada had locked itself in a Cold War alliance with the United States, and the Liberal party, which had governed Canada for more than twenty years, was pursuing a policy of close economic, political, and military collaboration with the Americans.

Gordon's distress over foreign investment coincided with a growth in Canadian affluence. Between 1939 and 1979 the real income of the average Canadian more than tripled.[1] The major source of this wealth was the United States, which had the largest economy in the post-war world. The Americans bought most of Canada's exports, supplied many of the consumer products that Canadians enjoyed, and provided millions of dollars in direct investment to help fuel the boom in Canadian industry and develop the country's natural resources. For Gordon, however, this affluence had a limited appeal: it provided Canadians with a high standard of living but meant that ultimately they did not control their economic destiny.

These ideas were firmly rooted in Gordon's early years. His family distrusted American society, and the imperial sentiment that was ever-present in his home, church, and school further challenged American values. His brief experience as an accountant in New York and his later dealings with American businessmen and politicians cemented his misgivings about the United States. Though he was inclined to see most problems in economic terms, his views differed sharply from those of professional economists, partly because he had no formal training in the subject, benefiting instead from a thorough knowledge of the practical economics of the business world. On trade issues he was a protectionist, an approach that originated in his work for the Tariff Board and his early business dealings, particularly as an owner of a textile company and several auto-parts manufacturers. During the Great Depression, Gordon developed a deep concern for the less fortunate and a *dirigiste* approach to the economy, traits that were solidified by his marriage to a woman of strong social conscience, Liz Counsell, and his wartime work for Clifford Clark, deputy minister of finance.

On the issue of foreign investment Gordon enjoyed little success in the decade following his royal commission report. As minister of finance in Lester Person's government he moved quickly to implement his ideas, introducing several ill-considered measures to discourage foreign investment in Canada. Faced with widespread opposition and hostility in the House of Commons, where the Liberals were a minority, he reluctantly withdrew many of his key budget proposals. For the remainder of his term as finance minister he continued to speak against foreign control of Canadian industry, but he could not achieve his goals because the budget fiasco had damaged his friendship with Pearson, and most of his colleagues disagreed with his approach. In 1965 Gordon resigned from the government after leading an election campaign that failed to produce a majority for the Liberal party. Out of Cabinet, he wrote a book on public policy, made a series of speeches across the country, and provoked a confrontation with Finance Minister Mitchell Sharp at the 1966 Liberal party conference, where Gordon was soundly defeated. His friends pressed a reluctant Pearson to bring him back into the government as president of the Privy Council, but he no longer enjoyed the influence that once had been his. He supervised the work of the Watkins Task Force on foreign investment, but the government would not adopt its proposals, some members of the Cabinet even opposing publication of the report.

If Gordon appeared to be a spent political force when he resigned from the Cabinet in February 1968, he seemed to have even less chance to win approval for his proposals as a private citizen. Canadians would not likely flock to this man who had lived a life of privilege and pursued policies that reflected his position as owner of a small conglomerate. Clad in chalk-striped English grey suits, with his back erect and his moustache neatly trimmed, Gordon spoke to Canadians in a bland, unemotional way. He seemed an unlikely leader of a nationalist movement.

Yet Gordon was successful in raising public concern over the level of foreign investment in Canada. In the late 1960s and early 1970s the war in Vietnam, the battle over civil rights, and the assassination of prominent Americans revealed a fraying of the social and political fabric in the United States. Many Canadians became suspicious of their southern neighbour and began supporting measures to reduce the American presence in Canada. The federal government reluctantly responded to the pressure, adopting several policies designed to deal with American influence. The Canada Development Corporation created a large capital fund to encourage domestic enterprise, and the Foreign Investment Review Agency began screening outside investment, while Petro Canada and the National Energy Program ensured a Canadian presence in the oil and gas industries.

Much of the credit for these measures must go to Walter Gordon. Working to encourage concerns about Canadian reliance on the United States and to focus them on economic rather than cultural issues, he was the leading figure in creating the movement that became known as the "new nationalism." On economic issues he was not particularly profound, but he advanced a clear set of ideas with vigour and persistence for more than a quarter-century. His views changed over time, but on the main issues he remained constant. Unlike other prominent nationalists – such as James Coyne, George Grant, and Mel Watkins – Gordon's critique of foreign influence remained in the public eye for decades. From the mid-1950s to the early 1980s he was Canada's main critic of the United States, and his successes and failures tell us much about the way Canadians viewed their place in the post-war world.

Acknowledgments

I have profited greatly from the help of numerous people who shared with me their time, hospitality, and wisdom.

Roughly one hundred of Walter Gordon's friends, colleagues, and associates welcomed me into their homes and offices, provided coffee, lunch, or dinner, and recalled their experiences. Tom Kent spent a day with me and responded to many subsequent requests for information with detailed, precise, well-considered replies. Paul Hellyer gave me several pages from an early draft of his memoirs and answered the many questions that I posed after our initial interview. Douglas Fisher allowed me to look at the clipping files in his office. Gerald Stoner and David Stanley provided me with documents from their personal collections; Mr Stanley also provided extensive commentary on an early version of the manuscript. Margaret and Jack Pickersgill were generous with their time and their memories, and rented their home to me for two summers while they were in Newfoundland.

Mr Gordon's family deserves special mention. I met with his wife, Elizabeth Gordon, and his sister Kathleen Griffin. I also spoke at length on the telephone with his children, Kyra Montagu, Jane Glassco, and John Gordon. They all responded with honesty and good humour to my prying questions. John Gordon also granted me access to his father's papers before they were opened to researchers. Walter Gordon's sister-in-law, Helen Venables, had me to lunch with Mr Gordon's cousin Mary Robertson, and family friend Dorothy Gill. Without his family's help Mr Gordon would have emerged in these pages as a colder, drier, and more distant man than he clearly was, and with his genuine sense of humour less than intact.

The staff at archives and libraries across Canada offered assistance. I am particularly grateful to George Henderson at Queen's University Archives, and Loretta Barber and Maureen Hoogenraad at the National Archives of Canada.

In the period that I was researching and writing this book I was blessed to have two employers – John English and Harold Culbert – who were generous and supportive, as was Murray Calder, for whom I worked while I was completing the final revisions.

Several scholars have unselfishly shared their insights and the results of their own work. Gerald Wright and Ruth Smith have allowed me to use their notes from interviews with several key figures. Greg Donaghy, Frank Clarke, and Steve Schumann generously gave me copies of chapters, articles, and essays that they had yet to publish. Denis Smith openly recounted his own experience in writing the biography of Walter Gordon, and welcomed me into his home to look at his research notes. George Urbaniak and Keith Eagles broadened my perspective, teaching me much about historical practice.

Professors John English and Norman Hillmer are the two key figures in my intellectual development. Professor English suggested this topic to me, helped me with his unrivalled knowledge of published and archival sources on post-war Canadian politics, and thoroughly read the many drafts I gave him. More than anyone, Professor Hillmer gave me the confidence to complete this project, guiding me, often not so gently, in the right direction. He read every word of the manuscript, offering countless helpful and perceptive comments. I could have asked for no better role-models or mentors than John English and Norman Hillmer. They are fine scholars and finer human beings.

I was lucky to have chosen McGill-Queen's University Press as a publisher. I am grateful to Philip Cercone, who makes everything seem possible, and to Joan McGilvray, who guided the book through the many stages of production. A very talented editor, Susan Kent Davidson, was able to decode many of the weaker passages in the manuscript.

My family has been my anchor throughout my life. My parents instilled in me a curiosity, a love of learning, and an interest in discovering the truth. My brother David helped with research at a key time in this project. My cousins Leanora Churchill-Smith and Silvia Levy, and their families, welcomed me into their homes on holidays and whenever I needed a break.

I met Megan Sproule-Jones shortly before I started this project. We were married while I was in the middle of writing the manuscript. She applied her skills as a professional editor to the task, and helped to shape the entire work. Throughout the tension that often accompanies a project of this nature, she maintained a positive attitude, accepting the presence of a third person – Walter Gordon – in our home. The book's dedication is only a small measure of my debt to her.

Colonel Harry Duncan Lockhart Gordon, father of Walter Gordon, in the mid-1950s. The Colonel was charming and had a good sense of humour, but was also impatient, decisive, and determined, all traits inherited by his son. [Archives of Ontario, C-306-0-0-581]

Walter Gordon at age twelve, a member of the football team at Upper Canada College. Gordon was a student at UCC from 1918 to 1922, and there was exposed to the ideas of Canadian imperialists who believed that a strong tie with Britain would prevent the United States from absorbing Canada. [Upper Canada College Archives]

Gordon in the uniform of a Royal Military College cadet. Gordon attended RMC from 1922 to 1926, studying engineering and science. The school did not encourage verbal expression, but did teach basic leadership skills. [Massey Library, Royal Military College]

Gordon in 1946, the year he chaired the Royal Commission on Administrative Classifications in the Public Service. In the 1940s and 1950s Gordon was well known as a government consultant in both Ottawa and Toronto. [*Toronto Star*]

Walter Gordon, Molly Towers (wife of Bank of Canada governor Graham Towers), Lester Pearson, and Elizabeth Gordon in the early 1950s. Liz and Walter Gordon had a remarkably strong marriage. Liz shared her husband's social conscience and was active in Toronto's artistic community. [Gilbert Milne, Bank of Canada Archives, GFT75-47-13]

The first meeting of the Royal Commission on Canada's Economic Prospects in July 1955. From left to right: A.E. Grauer, Omer Lussier, Walter Gordon, Douglas LePan, Ray Gushue, and Andrew Stewart. The commission issued controversial reports in 1957 and 1958, recommending measures to limit foreign investment in Canada. It established a foundation and legitimacy for economic nationalism in post-war Canada. [Duncan Cameron, National Archives of Canada, PA-184342]

Lester Pearson, Louis St Laurent, and Paul Martin at the Liberal leadership convention in January 1958. Pearson won the leadership, defeating Martin by 1074 votes to 305. Gordon chaired Pearson's campaign, and later helped his friend to restructure the Liberal party. [Duncan Cameron, National Archives, PA-110785]

Gordon returning from his 1959 tour of China. Gordon visited the Far East in 1954 and 1959 and was critical of American policy on his return. Later, Gordon was the first Canadian Cabinet minister publicly to denounce American involvement in the Vietnam War. [I. Lavery, *Toronto Star*]

Pearson and Tom Kent, in the opposition years. Kent was Pearson's senior policy adviser and Gordon's ally in the struggle to improve Canada's social safety net. [Bill Cadzow, National Archives, PA-117098]

Gordon and Pearson pose with the 1963 budget speech. The budget was a turning point in Gordon's political career and in the history of Canadian nationalism. [Duncan Cameron, National Archives, PA-117104]

Gordon in November 1965, shortly after resigning as minister of finance. Gordon felt betrayed when Pearson accepted his resignation, despite having promised before and during the election campaign that Gordon would remain in finance. [*Toronto Star*]

Walter Gordon at the 1966 Liberal policy conference. Gordon appealed to delegates to adopt a resolution to limit foreign investment. [Duncan Cameron, National Archives, PA-201544]

Finance Minister Mitchell Sharp at the 1966 conference. Sharp succeeded in his efforts to have Gordon's resolution shelved by a vote of 650 to 100. According to journalist Bruce Hutchison, the conference "was the final destruction of Walter Gordon." [Duncan Cameron, National Archives, PA-201543]

Toronto Mayor Philip Givens, Mitchell Sharp, and Walter Gordon, 7 January 1967, only days after Gordon returned to Cabinet. The broad smiles mask a developing tension between the two Cabinet colleagues. On the photographer's request, they stood together and smiled. As soon as the photograph was taken, Gordon and Sharp walked away from each other without having exchanged a word. [R. Innell, *Toronto Star*]

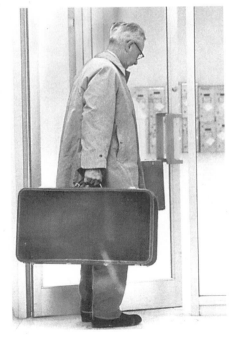

Gordon returning from Jamaica, March 1967. Gordon cut his vacation short because he had heard that Finance Minister Mitchell Sharp planned to change the Bank Act bill while he was away. There was, in Gordon's words, "a flaming row in cabinet" a few days later. [F. Lennon, *Toronto Star*]

Mel Watkins and James Laxer, the leaders of the Waffle group in the New Democratic Party, pictured here in June 1972. Gordon hired Watkins to head the Task Force on the Structure of Canadian Industry, which issued a 1968 report recommending moderate measures to deal with the foreign investment issue. The next year Watkins and Laxer helped to write the Waffle Manifesto, which called for the widespread nationalization of industry. [R. Bull, *Toronto Star*]

Gordon's portrait from the 1969 annual report of Canadian Corporate Management Co. Ltd. Founded in 1945, CanCorp was a highly successful conglomerate. As head of the company Gordon was willing to compromise his political views by selling Canadian firms to American buyers. [Intercity Reproduction]

Gordon at the University of Toronto Teach-In on the Americanization of Canada, March 1970. By the early 1970s Canadians – particularly young Canadians – had heard his call for limits on foreign investment. [D. Griffin, *Toronto Star*]

Claude Ryan, Jack McClelland, and Gordon at a press conference announcing the launch of the Committee for an Independent Canada, September 1970. Gordon was the organization's first honorary chair, while Ryan (editor of *Le Devoir*) and McClelland (president of McClelland and Stewart publishers) served as the first co-chairs. [F. Lennon, *Toronto Star*]

Abraham Rotstein holding the *Canadian Forum* issue that contained a leaked version of the Gray Report, a government study that called for the creation of the Foreign Investment Review Agency. Gordon's long-time ally, Rotstein was a University of Toronto economist, editor of *Canadian Forum*, a member of the Watkins Task Force, and a co-founder of the Committee for an Independent Canada. [Canapress]

Walter Gordon at his seventieth birthday party, January 1976. More than 800 people showed up to pay tribute to Gordon, who was now seen as an elder statesman and the father of the new nationalism. [F. Lennon, *Toronto Star*]

Gordon with Beland Honderich, editor of the *Toronto Star*. Honderich had a deep admiration for Gordon, and his paper consistently gave prominent and sympathetic coverage to Gordon and his activities. [F. Lennon, *Toronto Star*]

Walter Gordon and the Rise of Canadian Nationalism

CHAPTER ONE

The Making of a Public Figure
1906–1955

Walter Gordon's ideas were a product of his environment and experience. In this sense Gordon was unexceptional, but he denied the importance of his early years. A startlingly self-deceptive comment in the first paragraph of his memoirs illustrates his view: "So far as I can recollect, nothing that occurred during my school and college days had any bearing on the happenings, policies, and ideas with which this political autobiography has to deal."[1] Using this statement as justification, he began the account of his life with the day he started his professional career, shortly before his twenty-first birthday. Gordon's unwillingness to recount his early life illustrates much about his personality. His family was private and discreet, traits that were further strengthened in Gordon by his training as an accountant, a profession that prizes confidentiality. Reluctant to share his background with reporters or historians, Gordon always distrusted "people who remember things forty years ago."[2] Journalist Christina McCall recounted an unusual occasion when Gordon, after telling a story from his childhood, "looked distinctly uncomfortable, as though he had committed some kind of unacceptable gaffe."[3] For Gordon, not only were his early experiences irrelevant to his public life; they were also profoundly personal and not the proper subject of journalistic or scholarly investigation.

Despite his views to the contrary, Gordon's personality, ideas, and approach to problems were strongly rooted in his social milieu and his early experiences. From his family and schooling Gordon developed his patriotism, a belief that Canada and the United States were fundamentally different societies, a distrust of American influences, a strict sense of discipline, and deeply held and unrefined concepts of loyalty and honour. His education at the Royal Military College accounted in part for Gordon's weakness in expressing his opinions and his rudimentary understanding of economic theory. His personal and professional relationships with many members of the financial establishment taught him to view problems in economic rather than social or cultural terms, and led him to believe that Canadian business-people tend to act in the country's best interests. Through his work as a management consultant Gordon gained a thorough understanding of organizational structures and power.

The most exceptional factor in Gordon's life was his birth into a world of privilege, into a family that was a member of Canada's economic elite from the time of his grandfather, W.H. Lockhart Gordon. Born near Edinburgh in 1845, Lockhart Gordon graduated from Cambridge with honours and was admitted to the bar of the Superior Courts in England in 1869. The next year he moved to Canada and set up a legal practice.[4] Having established himself in Toronto, Gordon returned to Britain to marry Emily Gordon Smith (who then bore the unfortunate name of Emily Gordon Gordon). Lockhart Gordon had known her since childhood, and had proposed by mail from Canada. After his marriage he returned to Canada, where he prospered both in the law and in commerce. In 1883 he and James Irwin, a Peterborough lumber baron, became commissioners for the Canada Land and Emigration Company, a firm owned by several British investors. Under the terms of an agreement with the shareholders, Gordon and Irwin were given eight years to pay off the company's liabilities and to make a profit. In return, each gained a quarter of the shares of the company, renamed the Canada Land and Immigration Company of Haliburton. Lockhart Gordon became the managing director of the new company, which harvested lumber from the unsold lands of nine townships.[5] When he died in 1929, he had an estate valued at nearly $400,000, roughly equivalent to $4 million in today's terms.[6]

The most successful of Lockhart Gordon's nine children was his eldest, Harry Duncan Lockhart Gordon. Born in Toronto in 1873, Harry was educated at Upper Canada College and the Royal Military College in Kingston. In the mid-1890s he went to London, England, to train as an accountant. Returning to Canada in 1898, he received his designation as a chartered accountant and began to work for Clarkson & Cross, a well-established accounting house, founded in 1864. In 1905 Harry Gordon married Kathleen Cassels, the daughter of Sir Walter G.P. Cassels, a member of one of Canada's most prominent families, which claimed descent from Alfred the Great and William the Conqueror. Kathleen's father was a senior partner in the law firm that still bears his name, now known as Blake, Cassels & Graydon. A leading Toronto lawyer and an expert in patent and trademark law, Cassels became in 1908 the only judge of the Exchequer Court of Canada. With the appointment of additional judges, the court grew, and Cassels became president of the court.[7] Cassels was a close friend of Lockhart Gordon, and they had lived together on George Street when Gordon first came to Toronto. In later years the two families had tea together every Sunday afternoon. As a child Harry often took Kathleen, his future wife, for a walk in her pram.[8]

After they married, Harry and Kathleen settled in the south end of Toronto's affluent Rosedale neighbourhood. As a wedding gift Lockhart Gordon had given them a plain, red-brick house at 4 Maple Avenue, and it was here that their first two children were born: Walter Lockhart Gordon in 1906, and Hugh Lockhart Gordon in 1907. When Walter was about three years old, his parents sold the house and purchased a home three blocks away at 10 Dale Avenue, where the family lived until Walter was nine. Harry and Kathleen's three other children were born at this address: Isabelle in 1910, Kathleen (Kitty) in 1912, and Duncan in 1914.

The family's affluent surroundings reflected Harry Gordon's success. After his marriage he left Clarkson & Cross to start his own practice, and then, in 1907, he and R.J. Dilworth formed the partnership of Gordon & Dilworth. In the following eight years Harry Gordon built up a practice larger than Clarkson & Cross. In 1913, upon the retirement of W.H. Cross, G.T. Clarkson, then in his sixties, asked Gordon to return and manage the business. Gordon accepted on the condition that both firms be dissolved and a new partnership created under the name of Clarkson, Gordon & Dilworth. His old employers readily agreed.[9]

The new firm found a home at 15 Wellington Street West, on the top floor of the Merchants Bank building. Over time the partnership, commonly known as Clarkson Gordon, expanded to occupy the entire premises, first taking over the second level from the Anglican bishop of Toronto, eventually purchasing the building and occupying the first floor as well.[10] Erected in the 1840s, the building was constructed of grey Waterdown stone and surrounded by a cast-iron fence. A golden globe rested at the building's apex, and at the centre of each of the large wooden doors was an immense brass knocker in the shape of a lion's head. The edifice suited perfectly the established, solid, successful accounting firm that would be its major tenant for half a century.[11]

Months after the founding of Clarkson Gordon, Harry Gordon's work with the new firm was interrupted by the outbreak of the Great War. Upon graduating from the Royal Military College in 1894, he had joined the militia, slowly rising through the ranks until he became in 1913 lieutenant-colonel in command of the Ninth Mississauga Horse Regiment. From then on, his employees – and most other acquaintances – addressed him as Colonel Gordon and referred to him as "the Colonel." With the onset of war the Colonel enlisted in the Canadian Expeditionary Force (CEF) as a squadron commander in the Fourth Canadian Mounted Rifles, an infantry battalion. In July 1915 he sailed with his regiment from Quebec to Plymouth, travelling by train to Shorncliffe. A few months later he had an attack of appendicitis and was forced to undergo surgery. His wife travelled to England to care for him, bringing their two older sons, while she sent the three younger children to live with their maternal grandparents in Ottawa. Kathleen Gordon set up residence in Folkestone, where she sent Walter and Hugh to the Grange preparatory school.[12]

Though he had hardly recovered from his operation and needed help to board the ship, Colonel Gordon travelled to France with his regiment in October 1915. He was with the Fourth Canadian Mounted Rifles when they first experienced the filth and terror of trench warfare. In April 1916 the Colonel was transferred to the headquarters of the Third Canadian Division, where he served as divisional claims officer and permanent president of courts martial. Two months later he was appointed to command his old regiment, which had been crushed at the Battle of Mount Sorrel. Upon his return Gordon discovered that the Fourth Canadian Mounted Rifles had been reduced from 680 men to 73, from 22 officers to 3. He reorganized the regiment, and was in command at the Battle of the Somme in September and October of 1916, and at the Battle of Vimy Ridge in April 1917.[13] His service was exemplary: he was mentioned in the dispatches of Sir Douglas Haig, the British commander-in-chief, for "distinguished and gallant Services and devotion to duty," and was later awarded the Distinguished Service Order. A fellow officer remembered Gordon as a good disciplinarian and a person with special qualifications as an organizer and administrator.[14]

Like so many children, Walter Gordon only realized his own identity when he met others who did not share it. At his school in Folkestone students taunted him, ridiculing his Canadian accent and choice of words. After several weeks Walter finally lashed out, fighting with his classmates on the playground, eventually finding himself at the bottom of a heap of boys. In possibly his only published comment about his boyhood, Walter recounted his reaction to this incident: "There was nothing funny about being a Canadian. In fact, I would bloody well sooner be me than one of them, and that idea stuck with me for a long time."[15]

Gordon's nascent Canadian identity was also shaped by a growing sense that Canadians differed from Americans, that the two had fundamentally distinct values and priorities. This feeling came from his parents, who, seeing the human cost of the war every day, began to resent American neutrality. They became convinced that the war would have ended much earlier had the United States entered in its initial stages. This hostility towards American neutrality was common among Canadians.[16] In the case of the Gordons the resentment was particularly strong because of their physical proximity to the war, and, unlike many Canadians, they held on to their bitterness long after the war. Walter's sister Kitty later recalled constant anti-American remarks in the Gordon household in the 1920s.[17]

The impact of the war on Walter would be difficult to underestimate. When Colonel Gordon returned to England in May 1917 to take command of the Eighth Canadian Reserve Battalion, the family tried to rent a house in Folkestone. Not able to find one to their liking, they rented a house in Hythe. According to the Colonel, "One disadvantage about the house was that the German bombing planes, returning from London, used to drop any bombs they had left, at or near the house, before they recrossed the channel. As the house was mainly built of glass, it was not too pleasant."[18] The Gordons would have been frightened also by the German raid on Folkestone in 1918. These months must have been particularly upsetting for Kathleen Gordon – whom her daughter remembered as "highly strung" – and for the two young boys.[19] Terrified by the raid and by the bombs exploding nearby, the boys would easily have adopted their parents' view that the war had dragged on because of the United States, and blamed the Americans for their fears.

The war years also had a profound physical effect on Walter. One morning at his boarding-school he found himself unable to get up. His fellow students pulled him from his bed and left him on the floor while they went to eat breakfast and prepare for class. An hour and a half later Gordon was still immobile on the floor, and was soon diagnosed with polio. For the rest of his life he would have to wear thick eyeglasses, and was nearly blind in the left eye. He lost muscle control over the left side of his face, including his left eyebrow, meaning that when he wished to raise his eyebrows to emphasize a point or to express surprise, he instead made an expression that Peter Newman described as "superior amusement," a look that may account for the common perception that he was arrogant.[20]

For Walter the war years ended in April 1918, when his father was granted three months' leave and the family returned to Canada. Before his leave ended, the Colonel applied to be discharged from the CEF, arguing that Clarkson Gordon's survival required his return because many of its partners and clerks had left to enlist in the armed forces. The firm was conducting work "of National importance" for the government, including an investigation of the newsprint industry and an audit of the Hydro-Electric Power Commission of Ontario. The Colonel also reported that his health was weak and that he would have to undergo an operation in the near future.[21] His request was granted, and in July he returned to his prestigious and lucrative position as senior partner at Clarkson Gordon.

Discovering that tenants had neglected their house on Dale Avenue, the Gordons decided to move to a new residence. In 1918 they sold the house for $30,000 and rented Vincent Massey's home at 71 Queen's Park Crescent. As Colonel Gordon remembered, "after living there for one year, we liked the locality so much, I bought 43 Queen's Park for $23,000, and spent $12,000 on altering it."[22] The new home was a large four-storey, red brick house with a grey stone entrance and a view of the provincial legislature from the front windows. It had been built in 1890 by a prominent banking family whose business had gone bankrupt a few years later. The house had high ceilings, decorated with raised patterns in the major rooms. There was beautiful wood-work in virtually every room. Many of the half-dozen fireplaces had a wood surround, and all the bay windows had elegant wood trim. A walnut bookcase in the sitting-room had doors with leaded-glass windows. Facing a stained-glass window, the main staircase had an impressive wood bannister. The home also had a conservatory with a copper roof and a detailed tile floor, underneath which was a basement vault with a massive metal door. It was in these comfortable surroundings that Walter lived for much of his adolescence and early adult life.

The house at 43 Queen's Park Crescent reflected the Gordons' wealth and their position within the economic elite. The years following the war were full of opportunities for a chartered accountant. The unprecedented industrial development in Ontario and the introduction of income tax brought new clients to Clarkson Gordon.[23] The Colonel's affluence gave him membership in a special society, one that was conservative – both socially and politically – and dominated by white men of British descent. Members of the privileged class were more likely than most Canadians to have been born in Britain and to be supporters of the Conservative party and adherents of the Anglican Church, ties that were particularly pronounced among members of the accounting elite.[24]

Colonel Gordon exemplified that elite. Although not born in Britain, he was the son of a British immigrant and showed a considerable affection for the land of his ancestors. He travelled with the family to England or Scotland every year, and, as his daughter Kitty recalled, he "fought the 1914 war for his king."[25] He was, as were a disproportionate number of his colleagues, Conservative and Anglican. Colonel Gordon's father was a lay representative to the annual synod of the Diocese of Toronto for thirty-two years, and he himself was a representative to the synod thirty times.[26] The Colonel also served as church warden of St James Cathedral from 1922 to 1924, and again from 1929 to 1931.[27] The names of two of his brothers, lost in the war, were engraved at the base of the Memorial Cross on the cathedral's west lawn, and in 1919 he deposited the colours of the Fourth Canadian Mounted Rifles in the church.

His family's prominence in the church ensured that Walter would be exposed to the pro-British and anti-American sentiment common among Anglicans in those days. Many members of the church were imperialists, espousing a pan-Britannic nationalism coupled with a strong loyalty to Canada.[28] Before the war the church's official organ, the *Canadian Churchman*, spoke of Canada's "duties and responsibilities as one of the strong arms of that great Imperial body which clasps so large a portion of the world in its free, just, beneficent embrace."[29] Canada was a member of the "joint Imperial family," bound to the empire by "ties of blood, of sentiment, of government." The *Churchman* was clear in its rejection of the United States and of American culture and values: "Surely when men of Canadian birth, but of United States adoption, indulge themselves in laudation of their adopted land coupled with intimations that Canada would be wise to haul down the Union Jack and hoist in its place the Stars and Stripes – it is intensely gratifying that the 'Daughters of the Empire' ... are instructing the youth of our country in the solemn obligations of loyalty to the constitution and the crown, and patriotic devotion to their flag and country."[30] Gordon later considered himself an atheist, but the imperialist sentiment of the church continued to have an effect on the way he viewed Canada's place in the world.[31]

The ideas of the imperialists also played a strong role in Gordon's education. Both Walter and his father attended Upper Canada College (UCC), which John Kenneth Galbraith has called "the most unabashedly elitist of Canadian preparatory schools."[32] Gordon was a student at UCC briefly in 1915 before the family moved to England, and then from 1918 to 1922.[33] These were years when imperialism was in the air at UCC, strengthened by the school's strong ties to Canada's four most prominent imperialists: George Grant, George Parkin, George Denison, and Stephen Leacock. Denison had founded the college's Old Boys' Association and was a member of the board of governors, serving as its chairman for twelve years. He was a presence at the school and was constant in his attendance at Prize Day.[34] Leacock had been educated at the college, was later a teacher when Parkin was principal, and was a close friend of William Lawson "Choppy" Grant, the principal during Gordon's stay and both the son of George Grant and the son-in-law of George Parkin.

Choppy Grant's views were typical of the imperialists, who felt a strong loyalty to Britain and prized British values and institutions. "Canada stands by the Empire," Grant once wrote, "and has full confidence in her power to work out a self-respecting and a brilliant destiny therein."[35] The imperialists feared that independence from Britain would lead to the absorption of Canada by the United States, a country that Grant believed was "falling into horrible depths of degradation."[36] Before the First World War this anglophilia and anti-Americanism combined to fuel the movement for imperial federation. Many imperialists hoped that Canada could develop beyond colonial status within the empire, arguing for an imperial Parliament to deal with common matters of defence and foreign policy. Gordon later remembered that until the 1930s he, like most Torontonians, was pro-British.[37]

In the 1920s UCC students shared many of the views of their imperialist elders. The student editor of the *College Times*, Wynne Plumptre, believed "It is a fine thing now to be a member of the British Empire, as it was in the time of St. Paul to be able to say 'I am a Roman Citizen!' "[38] Plumptre's comments reflected the imperialism that grew in the half-century following Confederation, a feeling that arose from pride in Canada's membership in the world's greatest empire and from the belief that the British connection was necessary for Canada to remain independent of the United States.

Articles in the *College Times* in the 1920s show a suspicion of American economic influence in Canada. In 1924 W.H. Bilborough expressed an early version of Gordon's attitude towards trade with the United States, arguing that a tariff wall should be put up to prevent the "most unfair competition" from American manufacturers and to "give the Canadian manufacturer a fair chance." Though the tariff would raise the cost of manufactured goods, "it would do away with a great deal of unemployment, and above all keep Canadians in Canada."[39] In his desire to raise the tariff Bilborough reflected the ideas of his imperialist elders, who did not see free trade – or unrestricted reciprocity, as they called it – as a simple commercial arrangement. Instead, they thought that it would mean the eventual absorption of Canada by the United States. The students also showed concern over American investment in Canada. "It is whispered that this country is being gradually economically sold to the United States," wrote student Lionel Gelber, later a historian of the Anglo-American relationship. "The trouble in Canada is either inertia or a total non-existence of a politically vigorous body of public opinion."[40] Gelber's editorial showed a recognition that the 1920s were a crucial turning-point in Canada's economic relations with the United States. To increase business with Canada, many American companies began setting up branch plants in Canada, which enabled them to avoid Canadian tariff barriers. The result was an enormous increase in American capital in Canada, which first surpassed British investment in 1922. American investment grew fourfold from 1914 to 1929, rising from $881 million to $3.8 billion in a mere fifteen years.[41]

Though the UCC boys recognized the American economic penetration of Canada, the *College Times* never acknowledged the rising cultural influence of the United States, an issue that concerned many Canadians. In the decade after the Great War, American popular culture flooded across the border. A *Toronto Telegram* poll in September 1925 found that the city's seventeen most popular radio stations were American.[42] As one commentator noted, "Radio thrust the United States into Canadian life in a way that had not been possible before, bringing American politics, sports heroes and jazz into the Dominion's homes."[43] The situation for magazine readers was comparable. Economies of scale gave American periodicals an advantage over their Canadian competitors, and American magazines consequently dominated the Canadian market. By the mid-1920s Canadians bought eight times more American magazines than Canadian.[44] "The news-stands in all the big cities," noted *Saturday Night* in 1925, "fairly teem with magazines from the U.S. which are fit only for the centre table of a house of ill-fame."[45] Similarly, *Maclean's* feared the arrival of serious competition from American periodicals, from "the silent and insidious penetration of alien thought, alien ideas, alien practices."[46] The 1920s were also the years of the collapse of the feeble Canadian movie industry and the onslaught of American cinema. Canada had little theatrical tradition and a shortage of capital to participate in the expensive and risky movie business. It was impossible for small Canadian companies to compete with MGM and other American giants without some form of government intervention, which was not forthcoming.[47] None of this, however, was recognized in print by the UCC students. Their suspicion of the Americanization of Canada was concentrated on economic rather than cultural matters.[48]

The ideas of the UCC boys were no doubt shaped by Choppy Grant, who dominated the college and was a force in the intellectual development of many students. Not confining himself to the role of administrator, Grant taught history and spoke to the boys every Sunday at evening prayers. A superb orator, Grant often captivated his audience.[49] Robertson Davies recalled the force of one of his regular Sunday night addresses: "After that evening I was his slave – a tiresome, cheeky contradicting slave, but assuredly a slave, and there are times of pressure in my life when I am still his slave, though I hope in a more enlightened way."[50] Gordon shared Davies' high opinion of Choppy Grant and maintained his connection to the Grant-Parkin family through his lifelong friendship with the principal's daughters, Alison Grant Ignatieff and Charity Grant.[51]

The primary emphasis at UCC was on teaching the pupils to be individuals and gentlemen. Though Grant was a successful scholar, academic training was not his first concern. According to Davies, "character and moral principle" were Grant's first priority, followed by "propriety of conduct ... such conduct as became a gentleman." Intellectual ability placed only third.[52] "For his staff," wrote historian William Kilbourn, "he sought out teachers of passionate conviction usually combined with remarkable personality traits, who could both discipline and inspire the students."[53] His students remember being excited one night in prayer hall by his shouting, "Live in the large! Dare greatly, and if you must sin, sin nobly!"[54] Leacock recalled that the task of the school was to turn boys into gentlemen: "No gentleman cares to talk about himself; no gentleman talks about money, or about his family, or about illness, about the inside of his body or about his soul."[55] Grant would have been proud of Gordon. In his political life Gordon displayed an individualism very rarely seen in Canadian politics. The gentleman's code, which forbade any discussion of one's personal life, governed Gordon's conduct in interviews and in his writings; it also helps to explain his deep sense of privacy and his reluctance to use emotional arguments to gain support for his policies.

Gordon did not chafe under the heavy discipline at Upper Canada College, which bore some of the characteristics of a military institution. All students were members of a cadet battalion that held regular drills, and the teachers used caning as a form of punishment, occasionally taking it excessively far.[56] Gordon had become used to stern discipline, both in boarding-school in England and in his own family. Though the Gordon children had grown up in large houses with servants, Walter's sister believed that they were never spoiled. Their parents were strict but fair, insisting "if you started something, you finished it."[57]

Severe discipline, largely enforced by the students themselves, was the most striking feature of the Royal Military College (RMC), which Gordon attended from 1922 to 1926. Cadets were called "recruits" throughout their first year at the college, and their initiation rites, carried out by fourth-year cadets, were labelled "recruiting." The leader of the initiation ritual was the battalion sergeant-major (BSM), the top cadet of the senior class. In Gordon's first year the BSM, H.A. Richardson, was particularly brutal and thought nothing of slapping cadets in the face to show his displeasure with them.[58]

The initiation rites took many forms. The daily swim in Lake Ontario was one example. Although the morning swim stopped at the Thanksgiving break, George Monk, one of Gordon's classmates, remembered a morning when it was so cold that the tracks of water from the cadets' feet froze on the dock. Another form of recruiting was the "shit meeting," held in a small space in the basement boiler-room, where senior cadets yelled abuse at recruits while they stood at attention until they collapsed from exhaustion. The game "burnt meat" was common, the winner being the cadet who had sat the longest on an overheated radiator. The seniors required that recruits run everywhere they went "on the double." Any recruit who did not obey the commands of his seniors could be put on Defaulters Parade, at which cadets marched around the square in full pack for half an hour, starting at 6:00 A.M., or could be confined to barracks for as long as twenty-eight days. Senior cadets could also cane recruits who had broken the regulations. More than seventy years later Monk still remembered the yells of one cadet who was being caned with a scabbard stick.[59]

The excesses in discipline came to a head when Gordon was in his second year. In February 1924 first-year cadet F.L.M. Arnold lied to a senior about failing to attend a hockey game. The BSM decided to punish Arnold with a twenty-stroke caning, which another cadet administered with such vigour that the cane broke. Three nights later Arnold fled the college, crossing over the ice on Lake Ontario to the United States.[60] Arnold's father revealed the incident to the press, shocking the public and causing the minister of national defence to strike a committee, chaired by General Sir Arthur Currie, to investigate the case and to evaluate the administration of discipline at the college. Reporting in April, the committee found that conditions at the college were "generally satisfactory." According to the committee, "Any irregularities were in direct violation of the Standing Orders of the College and belonged to the life of the Cadets when not in class and off parade. They arose from the practice of leaving the administration of discipline largely to the senior Cadets." Even so, the report recognized that there were serious problems at the school: "The senior Cadets carried on fagging and recruiting to such an extent as to endanger the health of some of the recruits and also enforced menial and objectionable duties and discipline by corporal punishment contrary to the regulations of the College." The committee believed that the commandant had taken the necessary measures to deal with the situation – such as stopping the practice of caning – and recommended no further action.[61]

Despite the occasional brutality of the school, Gordon cherished his years at RMC.[62] The discipline in his family and at UCC had been rigid, and "Gord," as he was known, adapted easily to the college's severe regimen, despite being a year younger than most of his classmates.[63] As a fellow cadet recalled, "Walter was cool as a cucumber. He never got excited about anything."[64] In his fourth year Gordon was commander of one of the college's four platoons and was responsible for administering discipline to the younger cadets. Those under his command believed that he was a very severe senior but thought that he did what was expected and was no harsher than many others. Indeed, some remembered him as being fair and well-liked by the other cadets.[65] Gordon was also popular because he excelled at sports. Physical training was an important part of life at RMC, and Gordon was a strong long-distance runner, the school's 100- and 220-yard-dash champion, the captain of the football team, and an excellent boxer.[66] Years later, Gordon's stories of RMC centred on sports.[67]

At RMC a cadet could best impress his teachers and classmates with acts of boldness and courage. "You showed guts" was the greatest praise a cadet could receive.[68] As one graduate recalled, "The greater the obstacle, the more glory in overcoming it."[69] Walter Gordon certainly showed guts. In his third year at the college he broke his jaw in a boxing tournament but finished the round. The cadets in his corner tried to convince him to quit, but he refused. He returned to the ring to start the next round, but the referee ended the fight.[70] Gordon was sent home to Toronto to nurse the broken jaw. Away from RMC, with his mouth wired shut, he was miserable. His sister remembered that he was in a bad temper and kicked her when she went near him.[71]

RMC cadets all studied the same curriculum, heavily weighted towards engineering. By fourth year, cadets spent more time in engineering than in all other classes combined. English, French, and history were the only humanities taught at the college, though there was no history in the first two years and little in the final two. Social sciences, including economics, were absent from the curriculum. Other than engineering, most of the courses were devoted to the sciences or to military subjects, such as artillery, tactics, equitation, and military law.[72] Unlike other schools, RMC did not encourage verbal expression. Whenever a cadet was challenged, whether he was at fault or not, the only possible reply was "no excuse."[73] Former cadet Robert Bennett remembered that this unthinking response resulted "in an expressionless, unresponsive façade when confronting authority in its various guises."[74] In later years the curriculum changed, and many RMC cadets became outstanding writers and speakers, including historians J.L. Granatstein and Desmond Morton. In Gordon's day, however, an RMC cadet did not learn how to express his thoughts in detail. Some of Gordon's classmates communicated well both orally and in writing, but these skills were acquired outside the college.

Though the college did not value verbal expression, the professors did teach leadership skills. One of Gordon's professors was Lieut.-Col. Leroy F. Grant, for whom the cadets had great affection and respect. Grant, a professor of civil engineering, taught the cadets how to succeed as managers, telling them that the most successful managers usually displayed "a characteristic of firmness coupled with a sort of austere dignity. The best manager is never 'one of the boys.' ... The best shield that a manager can wear is distance. His little foibles – and all men have them – may thus be concealed."[75] Grant's teachings were reinforced when Gordon watched his father run the family firm.

To his classmates Gordon seemed to have no ambition, but as graduation approached he did have one goal: "to go to the University of Toronto, where I thought I just might make the football team." Because of his RMC training, the university would have admitted him into the fourth year of its engineering program, and, as Gordon remembered, "that's what I would have done from then on." Colonel Gordon, however, wanted his son to join the family firm, an option that did not appeal to Walter. When Walter graduated, the Colonel gave him a sum of money, saying that he could use it to finish his education at the University of Toronto or to spend in any other way he wished. Faced with this option, Gordon chose to travel to Europe, and once he ran out of money, he returned to Canada. Having no funds to continue his education, he decided to enter his father's business.[76]

On 2 January 1927 Gordon became an accounting student at Clarkson Gordon. The partnership was small but had a strong local reputation, much of it due to the Colonel's high standards. Clarkson Gordon did not have a structured organization, relying instead on the Colonel's forceful leadership. At the office Walter's father was a stiff, fierce, abrupt man with a clipped voice and decided views. One former partner remembered him as "a very tough bugger." The members of the firm, and no doubt most of their clients, held Colonel Gordon in awe; the next generation of Clarkson Gordon employees would have a similar admiration for his son.[77]

For the continuity of the firm, it mattered that Walter had inherited several of the Colonel's traits.[78] The Gordons, father and son, were intelligent and shared a good sense of humour. Both were private and reserved but could be charming in small groups. They were decisive and demanding, but neither unreasonably so. Determined and tenacious, both suffered from bad tempers. Though Walter later learned to control his, one colleague remembers an incident when he broke a telephone by throwing it against a wall.[79] Walter differed from his father in that he could express himself in a more pleasant manner, and had a deep interest in politics that was foreign to his father. Still, in important respects the two had much in common. Both were idealistic, with an insistence on high standards that bordered on arrogance. When the United States Securities and Exchange Commission wrote to ask about generally accepted accounting principles in Canada, the Colonel replied, "Canadian accounting principles are whatever Clarkson Gordon does."[80] Colonel Gordon, remembered one partner, "would tell his clients what he thought, whether they would like it or not," and he started the firm's practice of serving not just as accountants but as general advisers to clients.[81]

By the 1920s Clarkson Gordon had a strong reputation and was retained regularly by the provincial government at Queen's Park. G.T. Clarkson, a member of the firm's founding family, conducted so much work for the province that, as Walter Gordon commented, "there were times when he seemed to spend more time at the Parliament Buildings in Queen's Park than he did in the firm's offices on Wellington Street." Indeed, at one point the sensational newspaper *Hush* published an article on Clarkson's influence under the headline "Clarkson known as Jesus Christ around Queen's Park."[82] Gordon's father also carried out work for the province. In 1918 he helped with an investigation of the newsprint industry and an audit of the Hydro-Electric Commission, and in the midst of a scandal in 1925 the government turned to Colonel Gordon to investigate the Provincial Secretary's department.[83]

Early in his training at Clarkson Gordon, Walter was asked to help with work the firm was conducting for the federal government. These assignments sparked Gordon's interest in public affairs, and changed the course of his life. The first such task, accepted shortly after he joined Clarkson Gordon, was minor. The Royal Commission on Customs and Excise retained the firm, as Gordon remembered, "to examine the books and records of a wide variety of enterprises which the commission proposed to investigate." Gordon served as a "glorified office boy" to Albert Nash, the partner in charge of the investigation. His job "was to see that copies of reports were available on time for the commission's sittings, and to do odd jobs," including fetching liquor for the commissioners.[84]

An intriguing incident occurred shortly after Gordon qualified as a chartered accountant in 1931. He moved to New York City and accepted a position at one of the large accounting firms. After working there for just ten days, he decided to quit and return home. His justification, given in his memoirs, was perfunctory and unsatisfying: "For one thing, the idea of spending two hours or more a day commuting was not exciting. I preferred to remain a Canadian and, if possible, help demonstrate that Canadian professional men, if given the opportunity, can be just as competent and imaginative as their counterparts in other countries."[85] None of Gordon's surviving relatives and friends recalls this event, and none is able to offer a more convincing explanation for his decision to leave New York. One close friend, B.B. Osler, believed that Gordon "had a row with someone he thought was behaving dishonestly" and lost his temper.[86] Whatever the reason for his quick decision, the time spent commuting was probably less important than Gordon's realization that he disliked the American commercial climate. The New York business community in the early years of the Great Depression was no doubt a mercenary place ungoverned by the Rosedale niceties to which Gordon was accustomed. As his daughter Kyra noted, "He found American bankers and businessmen to be smooth and not morally conscientious about the effects of their decisions on people other than themselves."[87] His brief experience in New York likely cemented Gordon's impression, gained from his parents during and after the war, that Americans and Canadians were fundamentally different people with a divergent set of values.

Soon after he returned to Toronto, Gordon married Elizabeth Counsell, whom he had met in 1926 at the RMC June Ball. Liz's mother was the formidable Marjorie Counsell, the daughter of Sir George Gibbons, president of London & Western Trusts.[88] Liz's father was Jack Counsell, a wealthy, eccentric lawyer. Born in Hamilton of affluent parents, Counsell was educated at UCC and at the University of Toronto, graduating in 1897. In that year he joined the Hamilton Tigers football team, and as captain in his first season he led the team to the Ontario championship. Called to the bar in 1900, he became known as "the workingman's best friend" for his work in injury-compensation cases. Counsell, who loved caviar and alcohol, became what he called a "theoretical communist" and a "student of socialism."[89] In 1925 he was elected vice-president of the Canadian Labour Defence League, a front organization for the Communist Party of Canada.[90]

Although not as extreme in their views as Jack Counsell, Walter and Liz shared many of his concerns. As a young man in his twenties Gordon himself had been intrigued by communism. His sister Kitty recalled finding him and his friends in the basement of their home, secretly reading and discussing the

many communist pamphlets that they had laid out on a table.[91] Gordon remembered that the Great Depression stimulated his social conscience: "I was
very concerned about unemployment – it wasn't their fault they were unemployed. I remember that men used to sleep out in the ravines behind our
house. I told my father that if I was one of those men I would come in here
and steal everything we had."[92] In the mid-1930s Gordon was a part owner of
Canadian Forum, a periodical that advocated leftish policies and was often
concerned with American influence in Canada.[93] He was also a close friend
of several members of the League for Social Reconstruction, an influential
organization of left-leaning intellectuals, whose membership included many
prominent writers and social critics.[94] Gordon's childhood friend, Hartland
Molson, observed that as a young married couple, Walter and Liz "were
pretty impatient at the way the world developed."[95]

It would be difficult to underestimate the importance of Liz to her husband.
Their relationship was remarkable; even after decades of marriage the Gordons could be seen walking through Rosedale holding hands. Long-time
friend and colleague Dave Ferguson once warned, "You mustn't ever talk
about Walter Gordon without talking about Liz Gordon." Liz was a tall, ele-
gant, charming woman, often remembered for her spectacular hats. She had a
tremendous wit, and an ability to laugh at herself. Walter also had a pleasant
sense of humour and could be engaging in small, intimate groups, but, as Ferguson said, "he was not easy with strangers or outside his immediate
milieux." Though shy at heart, Liz was gracious and outgoing, and built
many social bridges for her husband. Without her Walter would have seemed
much more coldly patrician, formal, and distant.[96]

In 1934 Gordon was assigned to work for the Commons Committee on
Price Spreads, which later became a royal commission. Again, Gordon
worked under Albert Nash, a senior partner in the firm, which had been
retained to conduct several inquiries and audits for the committee. Although
he briefly studied the farm implements industry, Gordon's major contribution was an investigation of the merchandising and labour policies of the
T. Eaton Company. Gordon filed a four-hundred-page report and, for five
exhausting days, answered questions before the committee.[97] Afterward,
Norman Sommerville, counsel to the committee, wrote to Colonel Gordon
praising his son:

For a young man, the presentation of so complicated a case as that of the Eaton organization was in itself a courageous undertaking. It must be very gratifying to you to
know that he not only acquired an intimate knowledge of all the details of the busi-

ness, but that knowledge was so well founded that he was able to present the subject matter to the eleven members of the Committee in a clear, simple and complete manner. His very pleasing personality added to the presentation. I congratulate you on Walter's success. I have very high hopes of his future in the profession.[98]

Eaton's was pleased enough to retain Clarkson Gordon as its auditors, a surprising achievement for Nash and Gordon.[99] The House of Commons had established the committee because of attacks by its chairman, H.H. Stevens, on the business practices of department stores. Eaton's, entirely a family-owned firm, was likely deeply sensitive to the committee's investigation, which uncovered the shocking use of sweat-shops and price-fixing by big business, particularly when the investigation of Eaton's was partly carried out by an inexperienced young accountant. Gordon, however, conducted himself with professionalism and care, upsetting neither Eaton's nor the members of the committee.

Another individual who made a name for himself on the price-spreads inquiry was Lester "Mike" Pearson. Though they may have met earlier, Gordon and Pearson first became friends while working on the commission.[100] In early 1935 Prime Minister R.B. Bennett had worried about the slow pace of the inquiry. He called on Pearson, a thirty-seven-year-old foreign service officer, to serve as secretary to the commission and to bring the investigation to a close. Pearson laboured every day from nine in the morning until midnight, eventually succeeding in helping the commission to complete its work. In recognition of this achievement Bennett gave Pearson a pay raise and saw that he received the Order of the British Empire.[101] Gordon and Pearson remained friends after the commission finished its work, though their relationship was not particularly close until the late 1940s.

Gordon's success on the price-spreads investigation led to a partnership in Clarkson Gordon and a string of government assignments. In 1935, again under Nash's supervision, he assisted in the Tariff Board's investigation of the automobile industry.[102] Clarkson Gordon's report to the board gently warned that the removal of the duty drawbacks based on the amount of Canadian content would mean that "there will be no incentive to the Canadian automobile manufacturers to qualify their cars as to 50% Canadian content."[103] In the spring of 1936 Gordon sent a confidential memorandum to the board, arguing that "manufacturing in Canada and employment will be reduced if the content requirements are eliminated, unless the rates of duty on automobiles and parts are considerably increased."[104] The chairman of the Tariff Board, Judge George Sedgewick, responded that Gordon's services had been retained to provide the board with statistics, not to decide the tariff, which was the board's responsibility.[105] Nevertheless, the vice-chair of the board, Charles Herbert, who was responsible for drafting the report, liked Gordon's proposals. As a result, the Tariff Board followed Gordon's suggestions and advocated a new automobile tariff, a recommendation that Parliament soon adopted. Gordon later observed with satisfaction that one of the results of the new tariff "was the growth of machine shops throughout Ontario, many of which were called upon to expand rapidly during the war to produce munitions."[106] Many years later Gordon's company, Canadian Corporate Management, owned several of these shops and benefited from their success.[107] The experience showed the future politician a positive side of the tariff, and for the rest of his life he was suspicious of proposals for free trade.

Gordon's interest in public affairs was greatly reinforced by his work in Ottawa during the Second World War. As an RMC graduate, a former lieutenant in the non-permanent militia, and a member of a family with a distinguished history of military service, Gordon was expected to enlist in the army at the outbreak of war.[108] As he often joked, however, the only thing his grandfather had left him was a severe case of gout, which made a military commission impossible.[109] Instead, Gordon furthered the war effort in the best way he could, as a dollar-a-year man in Ottawa.

Gordon's first wartime position was with the Foreign Exchange Control Board. Under the War Measures Act the government introduced extensive exchange controls a few days after the outbreak of war. The newly created Foreign Exchange Control Board, an agency of the Bank of Canada, was responsible for stopping the flow of capital from Canada, inspecting all foreign-exchange transactions by Canadians.[110] The board's chairman, Bank of Canada Governor Graham Towers, called G.T. Clarkson, seeking assistance with the board's work. In the past the firm had turned to Albert Nash when the federal government needed help. With the outbreak of war, however, the English-born Nash had enlisted in the army.[111] In his stead, Clarkson asked Gordon, Nash's assistant on several government assignments, to go to Ottawa in response to Towers' call. Gordon agreed and became chief of the Examiners Section of the board (later renamed the Commercial Section), which dealt with the problems of import and export trade. Among other duties, Gordon's section was responsible for all applications for foreign exchange by Canadian subsidiaries of foreign-owned firms.[112] In late January 1940 Gordon left the Foreign Exchange Control Board to return to the family firm, which had begun to face serious difficulty as more and more staff members joined the armed forces.[113]

Back in Toronto, Gordon helped to found a new company using the management expertise of Clarkson Gordon. For decades Clarkson Gordon had served clients not just as accountants but as general business advisers. Increasingly, however, the firm found itself giving advice on issues related only remotely to financial matters. Members of the firm felt confident consulting on a wide range of topics, but many clients needed help with production and merchandising, areas where Clarkson Gordon had little expertise. Gordon turned to the industrial engineering firm of J.D. Woods & Co. for help. The Woods company had originated in the York Knitting Mills (later Harvey Woods), a company that had an extensive industrial engineering department under the leadership of Ralph Presgrave.[114] Presgrave pioneered the development of wage-incentive plans based on time-study, a field in which he would gain an international reputation. Realizing that a market existed for consultants who could improve plant efficiency, the president of York Knitting, J. Douglas Woods, created J.D. Woods & Co. Ltd. in 1932, with himself as president and Presgrave as vice-president. In 1938 Walter Gordon proposed to merge Clarkson Gordon's consulting work with that of the Woods company, but the Woods people feared being swamped by the larger firm and declined Gordon's offer. Despite this setback, Gordon persisted in trying to create a management-consulting company using the skills of both firms. In 1940, after he promised that the Woods company could keep its name and identity, the two companies agreed to merge their consulting practices.[115] Clarkson Gordon purchased a 50 per cent interest in J.D. Woods & Co., and three members of the Clarkson firm joined the company's board of directors, including Walter Gordon, who became vice-president.

Though he had returned to Toronto, Gordon had not severed all ties with Ottawa. On Towers' request he went back briefly in the summer of 1940 to research and report on the implications for Canada of a British surrender. In December 1940 he received a call from the minister of finance, James Ilsley, who had first met the young accountant while serving as a member of the price-spreads inquiry in the mid-1930s. The minister asked Gordon to join his department: "He said they had some eminent academics on the staff but needed someone with some practical experience in business."[116] Gordon accepted Ilsley's offer and was appointed special assistant to Clifford Clark, the deputy minister of finance.

Though Gordon's wartime work in Ottawa was too brief to supplant many of the attitudes he had acquired in business, it had an important influence on his thinking. Gordon saw Clark as "the dominating genius of the department and, in fact, of wartime Ottawa." He was, intellectually, "the most exciting man" Gordon had ever worked with. Clark was an active deputy minister and had an enduring impact on Canada, particularly in his proposals for social policy. He believed that the government should play an active role in helping the less fortunate and, as Gordon observed, "I soon became a convert to this philosophy if I was not one already."[117] Gordon was also influenced by the great change in philosophy for Clark and the Department of Finance. At the outbreak of the war the department had abandoned the classical view of fiscal policy and begun to play a more vigorous role in managing the economy.[118] Proposing a comprehensive approach to the country's troubles, Clark was at the centre of this transformation. His office, according to J.W. Pickersgill, "was the balance wheel of the administration and the spearhead of innovation in the new art of influencing and directing the national economy in a free society."[119]

Gordon was at the centre of the highly interventionist Department of Finance. Under Clark's supervision he designed the basis for the tax-rental agreements, under which provincial governments would allow Ottawa to collect their taxes and which the *Financial Post* called "the most important deal ever transacted in Canadian public finance."[120] A telegram from Ilsley to Alberta Treasurer Solon Low illustrates Gordon's important part in negotiating the agreements. Ilsley agreed to meet with Low, but "as Mr. Gordon is away it would be difficult to settle much."[121] Gordon also played a key role in reorganizing the Wartime Prices and Trade Board so that it could implement wage and price controls, and later served as a member of the board.[122] He was offered the position of general manager of the Foreign Exchange Control Board in October 1941, and after consulting with his father, he responded that he would accept on two conditions: that he hold the title of vice-president, and that Towers be made a member of the board. He declined the offer after the government agreed only to his first condition.[123] Gordon's experience in this period – when the government was managing the economy instead of merely tinkering – strengthened the *dirigiste* approach that he showed throughout his life.

Gordon performed well in Ottawa, and Clark hoped to turn him into a career bureaucrat. Clark soon discovered, however, that he could not keep Gordon on track. Robert Bryce, who worked closely with Clark, believed that Gordon "had his own interests and when he got into a key position he developed the things that were on his mind rather than [what] was on the minister's mind or the deputy minister's mind."[124] Gordon also suffered from a poor knowledge of macro-economics, not understanding, for example, the term "balance of payments" when he joined the department.[125] Though he could handle many responsibilities expertly and impressed many of his colleagues, Gordon's interests and expertise were too narrow for him to serve as a deputy minister.

Gordon's gout had become so excruciatingly painful that he found it difficult to carry on in Finance, and in February 1942 he returned to Toronto.[126] He was incapacitated at ever-increasing intervals, usually, he remembered, "when it was most inconvenient to be laid up."[127] Clarkson Gordon was significantly short-staffed, and the Colonel, now almost seventy, was having trouble running the firm. Gordon settled back into the partnership, slowly taking the reins from his father, though he continued to visit Ottawa on special undertakings. He also pledged to continue to help the war effort by expanding J.D. Woods & Co. and placing the company at the service of the Wartime Prices and Trade Board on a non-profit basis, while not charging for his own services.[128] In a short period the Woods company grew from five to more than thirty employees and began a wide variety of studies for the government, centring on the conservation of materials and human resources.[129] The agreement with the Wartime Prices and Trade Board ended in January 1943, after assignments had slowed to a trickle.[130]

Through his work in Ottawa, Gordon had met and impressed many senior officials, and, not surprisingly, they continued to ask for his help after the war. His first major post-war appointment came in 1946, when Clark asked him to chair the Royal Commission on Administrative Classifications in the Public Service. Because he was already busy with the post-war reorganization of the family firm, Gordon accepted the position on condition that he would devote only part of his time to the commission. As a result, the final report was dominated by the views of Sir Thomas Gardiner of the British civil service, the only one of the three commissioners who worked full time on the inquiry.[131]

In this assignment Gordon displayed traits that resurfaced in his professional and political careers. He rushed the commissioners' work and later expressed pride that they had spent only three months on the job.[132] With so little time, however, the research was bound to be superficial. The commissioners, for example, conducted no in-depth studies of personnel systems in other countries. Gordon's two colleagues travelled to Washington, but they went without Gordon or the commission's secretary, and stayed only a few days. At best they could carry out only a rudimentary examination of the American bureaucracy.[133] Furthermore, the commissioners met with the senior officials of the Civil Service Commission (CSC) just once, for about an hour. After the royal commission published its report, two representatives of the CSC, Chairman Charles Bland and Stanley Nelson, convinced the prime minister that Gordon had made up his mind before beginning his investigation and had not given them an adequate opportunity to present their views.[134]

At twenty-eight pages, the commission's final report was terse and reflected the shallowness of the investigation. The report made nineteen major recommendations but expressed each one abruptly. In the words of political scientist J.E. Hodgetts, it "failed to sketch out in adequate detail the concrete steps which would have to be taken to realize the substantial changes recommended."[135] It was too brief and facile to function as the basis for a reorganization of the civil service, and having met the hostility of the CSC, it virtually disappeared without action by the government. As one CSC official remembered, "I did not feel the impact of his report at all."[136] Indeed, the only measure adopted was the recommendation that senior public servants receive well-deserved raises, including Lester Pearson, who received a 50 per cent raise, and Clifford Clark, whose salary increased by 46 per cent.[137]

Few noticed Gordon's first royal commission, and as a result the report's weaknesses did not diminish his reputation in Ottawa or Toronto. The prestige of the consulting firm, renamed J.D. Woods & Gordon Limited in 1944, continued to grow in the post-war years, and Gordon, who was managing director of Woods Gordon from 1944 until he became president in 1959, was called on to diagnose the problems of many government departments and agencies. In 1947 Premier George Drew fired the chairman of the Hydro-Electric Power Commission of Ontario and offered the job to his squash partner, Walter Gordon. Busy with the reorganization of his own firms, Gordon refused, but agreed to restructure the commission and recommend a new chair.[138] In 1948 the minister of defence, Brooke Claxton, asked Gordon to help decentralize his increasingly inefficient department.[139] The next year, on the recommendation of Vincent Massey, chair of the Royal Commission on National Development in the Arts, Letters and Sciences, the government retained Gordon to report on the structure of the National Film Board.[140] When a scandal shook the Ontario Highways Department in 1954, Premier Leslie Frost asked Gordon to investigate the department.[141] The same year, on the joint request of Frost and Prime Minister Louis St Laurent, Gordon helped to devise a new fiscal arrangement between Ottawa and the Ontario government.[142] In 1954 Gordon also assisted in the revision of salaries for senior federal civil servants.[143] By the late 1950s Gordon's firms had so many contracts from the provincial government that, in the words of one civil servant, "there seemed to be a man from Clarkson Gordon or Woods Gordon behind every pillar in Queen's Park."[144] Walter Gordon was indisputably at the top of the management-consulting field.

Gordon did not confine himself to advising others on how to run government departments and private businesses; he was also a successful entrepreneur in his own right. In 1945 – together with Hartland Molson, later president of Molson Breweries; James Murdoch, president of Noranda Mines; and R.A. Laidlaw, a lawyer and member of a wealthy lumber family – he founded Canadian Management Company, which became Canadian Corporate Management Co. Ltd. in 1949. The idea of creating a conglomerate had occurred to Gordon before the war. In 1939 he went to Britain and raised £5 million, the equivalent of $280 million today.[145] With the approach of war, however, the Bank of England discouraged the export of cash from Britain, and effectively scuttled the deal. After the war British capital was not available on the same scale, so Gordon relied on Americans when he raised $2 million to start Canadian Management Company.[146] Originally, roughly 70 per cent of the company was held in the United States, though after thirty years this had declined to 15 per cent.[147]

In his memoirs Gordon claimed that the creation of Canadian Corporate Management, commonly known as CanCorp, resulted from a desire to prevent Americans from gaining control of Canadian companies: "In the late 1930s, I began to think about the tendency, which was just beginning, for the owners of Canadian businesses to sell out to American corporations. It seemed to me this trend could be offset by forming a Canadian holding company with adequate capital which would be available as an alternative purchaser."[148] This passage likely reflects Gordon's concern over foreign investment in the late 1960s, when he wrote his memoirs, rather than his attitude in the late 1930s. Several factors suggest that CanCorp was not created to stem the tide of American direct investment. It is unlikely, for instance, that many of the directors and shareholders shared this objective. Larry Bonnycastle, CanCorp's president in the 1970s, believed that "the purpose of the company is to grow internally by acquisition."[149] R. Douglas Stuart, the American president of Quaker Oats, believed in the free movement of capital between countries and saw the company merely as an investment vehicle.[150] Other Americans on the board of directors, including Winfield Ellis, Glen Lloyd, Irving Pratt, and Godfrey Rockefeller, likely shared Stuart's views. In later years the company would invest in businesses that operated out of the

United States.[151] Most significantly, the company's transactions in the late 1950s show that Gordon's concern over foreign ownership was secondary to the goal of accumulating capital.

Gordon's experience in business had a considerable impact on his political views. One of Canadian Corporate Management's largest investments was a controlling interest in Canadian Cottons, the country's second largest textile company.[152] The 1950s were, with the possible exception of the 1990s, the worst decade in the industry's history, and as a result Canadian Cottons posted a loss every year after 1952.[153] Canadian textile companies were not competitive because of the small size of the Canadian market and high costs, including the expense of transporting heavy cotton bales, heating large mills, and setting up looms for small production runs. Though the company was losing money, it remained in business until the Tariff Board could complete an inquiry into the industry.[154] During these years, in the words of President Larry Bonnycastle, "it was hoped that conditions in the industry would improve either as a result of improved world conditions in the textile industry or as a result of the acceptance by the Canadian government that the industry required increased protection in its home market."[155] The government, however, refused to give further protection to the industry, and in 1959 Canadian Cottons closed its doors. Henry R. Jackman, a director of the company, believed that Gordon's experience with the textile industry influenced his political ideas.[156] This view was confirmed years later by an oblique reference in one of Gordon's letters to a colleague. Discussing the possibility of Canadian and American tariff reductions, Gordon explained his views by describing himself "as an ex-businessman who has been hurt in the past."[157]

As Gordon's fortune and reputation grew, so did the strength of his friendship with Pearson. Both men were witty and engaging, and they enjoyed each other's company, but they had little else in common. Pearson, the son of a Methodist minister, never developed Gordon's interest in business and finance, not even when it related to his own money, which was managed by his wife. And though public policy was Gordon's chief concern in the 1950s and 1960s, he had little knowledge of foreign affairs and could not speak on the subject at Pearson's level.

The two men also had contrasting skills and limitations, a fact that strengthened the friendship at first. Pearson was a historian and a diplomat, professions fraught with uncertainties. He had become successful by delaying decisions, fostering ambiguity, and trying to please everyone. He hated being disagreeable and avoided confrontation at almost any cost. He often gave the impression that he agreed with people, only to surprise them by acting in an opposite manner. Pearson could see both sides of a question and genuinely sympathized with others, but he found it difficult to make up his mind. Many observers had the impression that the last person who spoke to Pearson had the most influence on him.[158] Pearson "was a man of principle," according to his political colleague Jean Marchand, but "he thought that all principles were quite flexible."[159] In many ways Gordon had reached the top of his profession by displaying the opposite traits. Trained in engineering and accounting, two fields that deal in absolutes, Gordon was definite and decisive. He prized himself as a man of action and was unable to delay decisions or to accept ambiguous situations. He was always polite but never compromised his views to please others, and he made sure everyone knew where he stood. While Pearson often rallied support by appearing helpless, Gordon maintained an image of supercompetence and was reluctant to ask for assistance.

The two men had considerably different organizational skills, an area where Pearson was particularly weak. When he invited Jim Coutts to work for him in the Prime Minister's Office, for example, Pearson was unable to describe what he wanted Coutts to do: "I have eight empty offices ... and I have to fill them up. Would you like to sit in one of them?"[160] In contrast, organization was one of Gordon's exceptional strengths, and he had been responsible for reorganizing many corporations and government departments. Gordon also had a strict sense of loyalty to his friends, a characteristic fostered in his family and at RMC. Pearson did not seem to feel much personal loyalty, and was, according to his friends, true to the greater good, or, as his critics would say, loyal only to himself.

Another key problem was that the two men did not view their friendship in the same way. Their association had become strong only in 1948, when Pearson left the civil service to become secretary of state for external affairs. In the 1950s and 1960s Gordon thought of Pearson as his closest friend, but Pearson saw Gordon less as an intimate companion than as a trusted political friend.[161] Perhaps it would be more accurate to say that Pearson did not have intimate friends. He was, according to diplomat Arnold Heeney, "increasingly impersonal – a deep one whose secret self very few if any can know."[162] Tom Kent agreed: "Pearson was, essentially, a loner. He had countless friends in the hail-fellow-well-met sense. But he did not give himself to close relationships with men."[163] Walter Gordon was very different. "Beneath an independent and reserved surface, he was a man of warm feelings," said Kent.[164]

Initially, the differences between Gordon and Pearson helped to bring them together. Lacking any appreciation of organization or finance, Pearson relied heavily on Gordon. In 1948 Prime Minister Louis St Laurent offered Pearson the position of secretary of state for external affairs. Pearson was unsure whether he should leave the security of his civil service post, and hesitated to accept the position until Gordon stepped in, raising more than $100,000 from his wealthy friends for a trust fund that would ensure that the Pearsons would not suffer from the uncertainties of public life.[165] Gordon himself was probably the major donor.[166] The fund paid an annuity of $400 a month, roughly $3,000 in today's terms. A decade later, when Pearson had become Liberal leader, Gordon took responsibility for rebuilding the party, shattered in the election of 1958, when the Liberals won only 48 seats to the Conservatives' 208. Pearson would later recall, "there was no one to whom the party had greater cause for gratitude for the success it achieved … than Walter."[167]

By mid-century it already seemed inevitable that Gordon, a friend of the external affairs minister and Canada's top consultant on government efficiency, would be encouraged to enter political life. In 1949 he refused St Laurent's suggestion that he run as a Liberal candidate in Toronto.[168] Believing that he deserved a senior portfolio, Gordon was also reluctant to accept the prime minister's offer in 1954 that he join the Cabinet as a junior minister. His reluctance was only confirmed by a discussion with C.D. Howe, one of the Cabinet's strongest ministers, who made it clear that he expected new ministers to play a secondary and subordinate role. Gordon believed that his positions as senior partner of Clarkson Gordon and president of Woods Gordon and Canadian Corporate Management were more interesting and offered more freedom than a minor Cabinet post.

Gordon also rejected the inflexibility of a Cabinet portfolio because of his worsening gout. He had first discovered that he had the disease while competing in a race at RMC: feeling a stone in his shoe, he found none when he took the shoe off after the race. An accomplished athlete at RMC, Gordon later found that he was less and less able to participate in sports. During the war the gout caused him considerable pain and restricted his mobility. He often used crutches, and was forced to wear large round shoes that reminded his young daughter of Mickey Mouse.[169] By the late 1940s his condition was so bad that his doctor told him that he would likely not survive more than five years.[170] "I thought I might be dying from it," Gordon remembered; "I couldn't walk more than 50 feet."[171] In the 1950s, however, a new medicine was developed that helped to treat gout, allowing Gordon to pursue an active life and take on challenges that would bring him to public prominence.[172]

Gordon brought many traits to public life, his strict moral code being one of the most striking. The word "decent" was an adjective often used to describe him. He felt personal loyalty deeply, and seldom criticized others. He also displayed tremendous compassion and an immense sense of responsibility towards the less fortunate. Years later, journalist W.A. Wilson recalled Gordon's concern over unemployment: "To an extent that I have never encountered in anyone else, wealthy or poor, he had the enviable ability to think of the unemployed as real individuals not just disagreeable statistics."[173] Realizing that he had a privileged birth, he became a great philanthropist. His donations to worthy causes came not because he wanted attention or credit but because he believed he had an obligation to others. Indeed, he seldom allowed his gifts to be publicized, and only did so on occasions when he knew that the attention would encourage others to give. Few knew, for instance, that he helped to distribute food at soup kitchens.[174] He was also generous with his friends. When he sold Canadian Corporate Management, he gave $1,000 each to several friends with one condition: that they use it frivolously. He also did much to advance the work and careers of public servants and academics like Ed Safarian and Douglas Fullerton, even though they disagreed with many of his key ideas on Canada's economic relationship with the United States.

Gordon built a strong, loyal following through his generosity and his engaging personality. He was friendly and outgoing, particularly in familiar surroundings. Though it was hardly visible in his public persona, Gordon had a well-developed sense of humour. He could always see the funny side of life, and was often laughing or smiling. He possessed a rare ability to laugh at himself, and he enjoyed telling self-deprecating stories. This approachable aspect of his personality contrasted with a more serious side. He was disciplined and intensely private, so much so that many considered him shy. He found it very difficult to express his emotions, particularly in public.[175] As a man who never faced failure until he entered politics, Gordon had an abundance of self-confidence, which was often mistaken for arrogance, a trait that existed, but not to the extent that his critics believed.

Related to his self-confidence was Gordon's decisiveness, a characteristic that helped him in business but hurt him in politics. When faced with a problem, Gordon liked to think of a solution, implement it quickly, and only then apologize for any mistakes and correct them. "My inclination is to ask 'Why not?' if I hear what sounds like a good suggestion," he once observed.[176] Often, however, he did not give enough thought to the things he did. Gordon's decisiveness was also reflected in the way he spoke. Like his father, he did not enjoy small talk, preferring to get to the point quickly. He was not a man to waste words, never using two words where one would do. James

Coutts noticed that Gordon did not engage in political gossip: "You would never want to have lunch with Walter unless you knew what you wanted to talk about."[177] Gordon arrived at appointments with a list of topics he wished to discuss, and he expected others to do the same. He began these meetings by asking, "Should we start with your list or mine?"[178]

Because he was anxious to get things done, Gordon could also be impatient. He had little tolerance for people who dawdled or for those who preferred talk to action. "If somebody didn't have anything important to say, I didn't want to waste my time," he said.[179] Gordon had learned at RMC never to offer excuses, and he hated hearing excuses from others. He also exhibited an impatience with details. In Peter C. Newman's view, his main problem as a politician was that "boredom usually overcame him before the full implications of a complex issue were clear."[180] His biographer Denis Smith agrees: "He was impatient with complexity and detail, and almost always made his case in broad and general terms."[181] The characteristic was a considerable handicap in his public life. He performed badly in the House of Commons because he believed that the procedures and many of the debates were a waste of time. He once referred to himself as "a frustrated victim of our present [parliamentary] system."[182] "He didn't like political conflict," according to Denis Smith, "and didn't have the supple ability to build political alliances. He just bulled ahead."[183] As a result, Gordon did not get along with his chief advisers in the civil service; he thought they considered any proposal with excessive thoroughness. His impatience also led him to lose his temper on occasion. Many friends and colleagues never saw this feature of his personality because Gordon had learned to control himself, but on very rare occasions he was still prone to angry outbursts.

Related to his impatience was Gordon's tendency to decide before he had all the relevant information. Michael Mackenzie, a partner in Clarkson Gordon, remembered that he was a believer in the quick fix.[184] When heading a Woods Gordon team on an assignment, Gordon would often write an interim report early in the consultation. This report was useful for identifying the issues and problems that required the most attention, but Gordon often used it to arrive at conclusions before all the evidence was available. This trait was also evident in the work that Gordon did for the government. In his first royal commission he was accused of making a priori judgments, and in his second he released a controversial preliminary report that did not reflect the commission's research.

A similar weakness, also less important in his professional life than it became in his political career, was Gordon's weak grasp of theoretical economics. After graduating from RMC, where he had no exposure to the subject, Gordon learned about the practical side of the economy through his work as an accountant and a businessman. He was a voracious reader and often read books on economics, but he had a weak grasp of certain issues, particularly international economic problems such as trade and balance of payments.

Gordon also suffered from an inability to explain adequately his policy proposals, both in public and in private. He had become successful by emulating his father, and had learned to express himself concisely. He never developed the ability to make a strong, detailed, thorough argument, and when challenged, he usually reacted with a shrug or a laugh, responses that were as unexpressive as "no excuse," the phrase he had used at RMC. "I don't go around trying to change people's views," he once said, a strange comment from a man who spent much of his life dealing with public policy. Allan MacEachen, Gordon's Cabinet colleague, observed that he "never wanted to debate his positions." Similarly, Peter Newman, who with Gordon co-founded the Committee for an Independent Canada, was eager to discuss the "new nationalism," only to be disappointed: "You couldn't have a philosophical discussion about it with him."[185]

Gordon balanced his weaknesses with many highly advanced skills, particularly in administration and organization. In these areas Gordon's competence was virtually unsurpassed. Under his leadership Clarkson Gordon and Woods Gordon grew from four offices with a staff of 200 to 900 staff members in twelve offices. "Walter Gordon," according to partner A.J. Little, "was responsible more than any other single partner for setting the policies of both firms and providing the initiative that sparked their expansion." Gordon also showed his organizational ability in rebuilding the Liberal party after the devastating defeat of 1958. Gordon Edick, the party's executive director in Ontario in the early 1960s, remembered the effect of Gordon's work on his organization: "I've never seen such a transformation in my life."[186]

For Gordon, the individual was at the centre of the organization, and he showed a knack for finding the best people for the job. "He had," remembered Ross Skinner, "a profound belief that if you found the right people, you could do almost anything." Gordon benefited from an ability to surround himself with strong men and women without feeling threatened. Dave Ferguson concluded that the success of Clarkson Gordon and Woods Gordon was largely due to Gordon's efforts at recruitment; he "attracted the best in the business ... [and] knew the environment that had to be created in order to get the most out of them." Gordon transferred this quality to his political life, where one of his lasting legacies was, according to Coutts, the individuals he had recruited: "He left several hundred, if not several thousand, people in public life who were imbued with his ideas."[187] Even so, Gordon's skill at assessing character led him at times to rely on individuals to such an extent that he neglected questions of organizational structure.

Gordon's competence and his attractive personality were important because they were traits that allowed him to occupy positions where he could promote his ideas. Perhaps his most important conviction was his faith in the ability of government. Gordon had learned from his brief apprenticeship under Clifford Clark that the state had tremendous power to improve people's lives. He continued to believe that government could solve many problems and, unlike many of his business colleagues, thought that a degree of public ownership was essential to the Canadian economy. His interventionism played a considerable part in his attitude towards American investment. Philosophically, he was willing to see the government play an active role in shaping the economy, including regulating the nationality of the owners of firms operating in Canada. As a result, he often proposed policies that seemed extreme and even dangerous to his more apprehensive colleagues.

Though Gordon's views on the role of government arose during his years as a civil servant, he had not spent enough time in Ottawa to temper his anxiousness to get things done, never developing the extreme caution exhibited by most bureaucrats. Mitchell Sharp, his successor as finance minister, has suggested that Gordon pursued an aggressive approach towards the economy precisely because of his background in the financial community.[188] Individuals in the business world, in Sharp's view, tend to be more willing to take risks because they have little to lose except money. "This is the world that Walter Gordon knows," said Art Child, president of Intercontinental Packers, "where risks are courageously taken in order to achieve a worthwhile end, where there is often no time to search for all the possible pitfalls. If something goes wrong, it will be fixed, and one still marches on to the ultimate goal. If Walter Gordon has made any mistakes, he will fix them, and he will not make the same one twice."[189] Sharp, trained as a public servant, was more cautious; a mistake could seriously damage the economy – it could put thousands out of work, spur inflation, or hurt the dollar.

Another significant aspect of Gordon's thought was his feeling that Canadians differed fundamentally from Americans. Gordon's outlook was rooted in social attitudes that he never tried to explain, perhaps because he was unable to do so. He liked Americans, finding them "essentially generous and warm hearted," but he also believed that they had a "volatile nature."[190] He had, in the early 1930s, tried to join the American business community, but had rejected it and returned to Canada. By the mid-1950s he had decided to work to contain the influence of the United States on Canadian society.

Gordon expressed his preoccupation with American influence almost entirely in economic terms. This sprang from personal experience. In his memoirs Gordon admitted his concern over the growth of American accounting firms in Canada: "It was during the early years of the war that we began to realize how much the accounting profession was changing. The large American firms, in particular, were expanding into other countries, and we concluded that when the war was over this trend would be accelerated. It was imperative for us to take steps to meet this competition."[191] Perhaps the biggest contrast between Canadian-owned companies and their non-Canadian counterparts was in the hiring of outside professionals.[192] Gordon's views were undoubtedly affected by direct observation of the tendency of Americans, when buying a Canadian enterprise, to change the accountants of their new subsidiary to those used by the head office in the United States.[193]

Though the United States had considerable, possibly greater influence in Canada through its culture, this did not seem to worry Gordon so much as the question of investment. His wife was active in the artistic community, but, as their younger daughter, Jane, recalled, "He didn't have a primary interest in the arts." Their older daughter, Kyra, agreed: "He wasn't hostile [to the arts]; he just didn't care."[194] Skilled as an accountant, a management consultant, and a businessman, Gordon saw the world through a financial prism. This is not to say that he cared only about the accumulation of capital. Throughout his life he displayed a social conscience that was foreign to many of his business associates. He could understand the problems of unemployment and poverty – much as he grasped the difficulties of American ownership – because they were issues with a strong economic component. He never fully recognized, however, that Canada could be threatened by American culture.

By the mid-1950s Gordon's personality, his strengths and weaknesses, and his approach to problems were set. He arrived on the national stage in 1955 when he became chair of his second royal commission, which, unlike the first, would receive considerable attention from the press and from politicians. This was not the beginning of the evolution of Walter Gordon. On the contrary, the traits he had developed over his first half-century were those that he would bring to public life. More importantly, the attitudes and approaches that Gordon developed in his early years would play an important role in shaping Canadian politics in the next quarter-century.

CHAPTER TWO

The Gordon Commission
1955–1957

In the post-war years Walter Gordon was one of the first Canadians to challenge the country's relationship with the United States. At the time, however, few others shared his concern over U.S. economic influence. Though unease about American power and influence has always formed a strong undercurrent in Canadian life, this ever-present undertow was particularly weak in the decade after the Second World War, when most Canadians were satisfied with the security and affluence that Canada's close relationship with the United States provided. The balance of power in the world had shifted dramatically, and Canada found itself strongly reliant on the United States. The southern neighbour was both a bulwark against the perceived threats of Soviet imperialism and an economic power capable of leading Canada to prosperity.

Canadian leaders for the most part seemed untroubled by the country's increasing closeness to the American giant. The often excessive suspicions of the Cold War, the fear of Soviet expansion, the terror of nuclear war – all contributed to Canada's eagerness to build a strong alliance with the United States. The Gouzenko spy affair, which brought the Cold War into the open, had unfolded in Canada, and in its aftermath Canadians showed considerably more distrust of the Soviets than did the people of other Western countries.[1] "The chief menace now is subversive aggressive Communism, the servant of power politics," warned Lester Pearson in 1948 while still undersecretary of state for external affairs. "In the face of the menace of aggressive communism, the democracies are brought closer together, *all* of them."[2]

If the United States was the only power that could resist Soviet global ambitions, it was also Canada's surest route to post-war prosperity. The

Canadian Cabinet, still remembering the devastating years of the Great Depression, embraced the overwhelming benefits of American affluence. The government saw no drawback that could outweigh the tremendous advantages of American trade and investment. In October 1949 Trade and Commerce Minister C.D. Howe, a key figure in Canadian-American economic relations, expressed a deep satisfaction with the level of foreign ownership in Canada. "We hope that more American companies will avail themselves of the favourable conditions for investment in Canada," he said. "It has been our habit to make the resources of one country available to the other country, and most of us feel that this has proven to be a good policy and one that we will do well to foster."[3] The government believed that a policy of welcoming foreign investment and encouraging trade was well justified by the result: a consistently high level of employment and income.[4]

The government's policies made Canada an attractive field for foreign investors. From 1939 to 1955 foreign capital in Canada rose from $6.9 billion to $13.5 billion.[5] This rise in American investment accompanied a much more dramatic increase in trade with Canada's neighbour. Exports to the United States grew from 42 per cent of Canadian exports in 1939 to 60 per cent in 1955. Over the same period Canada's imports from that country rose from 66 per cent of all imports to 73 per cent.[6] The increase in trade, coupled with foreign investment, helped to fuel Canada's post-war economic development. By the mid-1950s Canadians had a significantly higher standard of living than before the war, the country's gross national expenditure per capita increasing 77 per cent in real terms from 1939 to 1955.[7] This prosperity helped to forge a consensus about Canada's path, a consensus that showed few fissures in the decade following the war.[8] As Gordon remembered, "The public mood and the economic outlook were euphoric. It was a period of apparently unlimited self-generating growth, of little or no thought about the future in specific terms, combined with boundless optimism."[9]

Widespread doubts of American beneficence arose when it became clear that the anti-communist crusade of United States Senator Joseph McCarthy was little more than a witch-hunt. In late 1953 McCarthy was condemned in Canada, both in the House of Commons and in the media. Liberal MP David Croll equated McCarthyism with fascism and communism, arguing that all three philosophies had "the same end and the same means. Their end is to confuse, to divide, to conquer and ultimately to enslave. Their means are the big lie and the big smear. They were born in the gutter ... fascism has already died and been buried in the gutter. We hope sincerely that the other two will share the same fate."[10] Major Coldwell, leader of the CCF, criticized

McCarthy in similar terms, saying that if one thing threatened "the welfare, peace and democracy of North America, perhaps of the world, it is the kind of man that Joseph McCarthy is."[11] The media agreed, the *Ottawa Journal* calling McCarthy "irresponsible and vulgar" and *Canadian Forum* publishing a cartoon that showed Georgy Malenkov watching McCarthy on television, the Soviet prime minister saying, "Of course I have no sympathy with his objectives, but his methods – ahh!!"[12] Economist B.S. Keirstead aptly described the Canadian reaction to McCarthy as "a country-wide dismay and distrust of American leadership and a troubled sense that our closest and most trusted friends had been attacked by a spiritual illness that left us baffled as to how we were to conduct our affairs with them."[13] Walter Gordon was no doubt troubled by McCarthy's uncivilized behaviour, particularly when Lester Pearson became one of the senator's targets. Though McCarthy was gradually forgotten after he was censured by the American Senate in December 1954, Canadian resentment of McCarthyism lingered.

In the wake of McCarthy's excesses, some Canadians began to question aspects of Canada's relations with its neighbour. In August 1954, while the American Senate was holding public hearings on whether to censure McCarthy, historian Donald Creighton disparaged the American influence in Canadian affairs. Speaking at the Couchiching Conference, Creighton said, "Every minute of every day Canadians are reading or listening to words which have been written by Americans for American audiences, and almost exclusively in terms of American national interests, purposes, and ambitions." According to Creighton, "For the last eight years the nation which virtually invented modern advertising has been engaged in what can only be described as the greatest sales campaign in its history, the campaign to sell the Cold War, in an exclusive American package, to the rest of the Western world."[14] Most Canadians did not share Creighton's unease with the American alliance. John Diefenbaker, the Conservative foreign affairs critic who chaired the session at which the paper was presented, denounced Creighton's views, as did University of Toronto philosophy professor Marcus Long and Toronto economist Wallace Goforth. Walter Gordon, however, made a point of shaking Creighton's hand after the session.[15]

One month after Creighton's speech Gordon travelled to East Asia, where he began to doubt the wisdom of American foreign policy in that part of the world. At the Canadian Club in Toronto upon his return, Gordon blandly questioned the American refusal to recognize the communist government of Mao Tse-tung, saying that while in Asia he had not met one person who agreed with American policy: "They all thought the present communist government would remain in power in China for a long time. And accordingly that present United States policy is wrong."[16] Gordon still supported Canada's continued membership in the Western alliance, but was beginning, if only tentatively, to express doubts about the quality and substance of American leadership.

By the mid-1950s American visitors to Canada were surprised by the growing sense of unease over Canada's relationship with its neighbour. The United States vice-consul in Toronto, Frank Tinker, was glad to leave Canada in late 1954 because he sensed a growing animosity towards Americans. He had found that Americans living in Canada "feel like unwelcome interlopers" because many Canadians had traded "national pride" for "childish spite." American students from the University of Rochester's Canadian Studies Program discovered a similar antagonism when visiting Canada. "I was in Toronto," commented one student, "and the chief parlor game seemed to be panning Americans." Another wondered why "some Canadians seem to dislike us so much." Though there had always been Canadians who disliked or distrusted the United States, few complaints had been heard in the early postwar years. The misgivings only resurfaced on a wide scale in the mid-1950s.[17]

By 1955 Gordon had decided that the Liberal party – in power since 1935 – had grown stale and needed to put new life into its economic policies. Michael Barkway, Ottawa editor of the *Financial Post*, agreed with Gordon, observing that Louis St Laurent, seventy-three years old in 1955, was "exhausted, depressed and indecisive." C.D. Howe, then sixty-nine, was never notably patient, but now he was "more than ever intolerant of criticism, uncertain in temper, erratic in judgement and almost obsessively secretive."[18] Because a government led by these men seemed unlikely to travel down a new road, Gordon decided to push them. He drafted an article questioning Canadian economic policy, with a recommendation for a royal commission to forecast Canada's growth and examine the issues surrounding it. In his memoirs Gordon remembered that the draft article raised "the question of selling control of our business enterprises to foreigners and the effect this could have on Canada's independence."[19] But Gordon may have been projecting his later concern over foreign investment back to 1955. The draft article mentions the "desirability of encouraging Canadians to acquire greater financial interest in our resource industries" but says nothing about foreign investment in other sectors, or about the relationship between foreign investment and Canadian independence.[20]

Gordon, chair of the National Executive Committee of the Canadian Institute of International Affairs, intended to publish the article in the institute's *International Journal*. Before publication, however, he sent the manuscript to Ken Taylor, deputy minister of finance, to ensure that it would not be embarrassing to the minister – his friend Walter Harris – or to his former colleagues in the department. The result was a telephone call from Harris, who accepted Gordon's proposal for a royal commission, intending to announce it in his upcoming budget speech. Gordon was pleased with the result: "Instead of having to prod the government into taking action, they had been convinced by the draft article. My objective had been achieved with a minimum of effort."[21]

In Cabinet there were differences over the Royal Commission on Canada's Economic Prospects and its chair. C.D. Howe opposed the commission's appointment; after all, as Tom Kent, editor of the *Winnipeg Free Press*, put it, "an investigation of the Canadian economy was, in Mr. Howe's view, an investigation of C.D. Howe."[22] In later years Gordon often told the story that Harris had succeeded in obtaining Cabinet approval for the appointment of the commission only because Howe had been in Australia when the matter was discussed.[23] In reality, Howe did not leave Ottawa until after budget day, and was present when the commission was discussed.[24] After announcing the commission, the government considered three individuals for the position of chair: Gordon, W.A. Mackintosh, and Graham Towers, the recently retired governor of the Bank of Canada, whose name was put forward by Pearson.[25] In the end, the Cabinet settled on Gordon.

The other commissioners were men chosen, for the most part, from the academic community. Omer Lussier, more than a decade older than the other commissioners, was a professor of economics at the School of Surveying and Forestry Engineering at Laval University. A pleasant, shy man, Lussier was one of the most respected members of his profession. Though he had a strong knowledge of geology, agriculture, and economics, his background was in some ways limited. He had, for example, never travelled to western Canada. Lussier was not confident in his possible contribution, and considered resigning in the early weeks of the commission's work. A.E. "Dal" Grauer, president of BC Electric and its holding company, BC Power Corporation, was a former Rhodes Scholar and former professor of economics at the University of Toronto. Two university presidents, Raymond Gushue of Memorial University and Andrew Stewart of the University of Alberta, were also included in the commission's ranks. Stewart was a key member and played more of a role than any other commissioner save Gordon, especially on agriculture and matters pertaining to western Canada.[26]

In consultation with senior civil servants, Gordon selected Douglas LePan as the commission's secretary and director of research. LePan brought impressive qualifications to the job. Educated at the University of Toronto and at Oxford, he joined the Department of External Affairs after being discharged from the army in 1945. LePan was an accomplished poet who had studied writing on a Guggenheim Fellowship and had won the Governor General's Literary Award in 1954 for *The Net and the Sword*.[27] Since 1951 he had served as minister counsellor at the Canadian embassy in Washington. In character LePan provided a sharp contrast with Gordon, and relations between the two were occasionally tense. Reflective and sensitive, LePan had lengthy views on matters of importance, and as a perfectionist often had trouble making decisions. Responsible for writing the commission's report, LePan composed superb prose, but produced it slowly. Though Gordon had enormous respect for LePan and his skilful pen, he wanted the report written at a faster pace. LePan was twice hospitalized during the commission work – once for pneumonia, and once for exhaustion and a heart attack. On both occasions Gordon urged him to take enough time to recover fully, advice that LePan rejected the first time it was offered. Nevertheless, he blamed Gordon for the strain that had caused his health to fail.[28] The tension between the two appears not to have hurt the commission's work; on the contrary, it may have helped to sharpen the final product.

LePan recruited an impressive staff for the commission. As assistant directors of research he chose Jack Davis of the Department of Trade and Commerce; Douglas Fullerton, an investment consultant with Harris and Partners; Simon Reisman of the Department of Finance; and William Hood, a professor of economics at the University of Toronto. Andrew MacKay of the Department of External Affairs and Maurice Sauvé of the Canadian and Catholic Confederation of Labour served as assistant secretaries. Among the researchers were several professors of economics: David Slater of Queen's University, John Young of Yale, Anthony Scott of the University of British Columbia, and Edward English and Scott Gordon of Carleton University. At Gordon's request Maurice Lamontagne of the University of Ottawa also joined the commission in its later stages. Other researchers included Anthony Hampson of the Department of Finance; Robert Howland, economic adviser to the Nova Scotia government; Michael Mackenzie of Clarkson Gordon; and Edward Safarian of the Dominion Bureau of Statistics. Most of the staff members were young and just setting out on successful careers. From their ranks in later years would be drawn three federal Cabinet ministers (Sauvé, Lamontagne, and Davis), a provincial Cabinet minister (Davis), two deputy ministers of finance (Reisman and Hood), a Federal Court judge (MacKay), a president of York University and chair of the Economic Council of Canada (Slater), a chair of the National Capital Commission (Fullerton), a president of the Canada Development Corporation (Hampson), a superintendent of financial institutions (Mackenzie), and a chair of the National Energy Board (Howland). Safarian would soon be recognized as the leading expert on foreign investment in Canada. The staff, remembered Ted English, was composed of "standard, middle-of-the-road economists." Most had formal economic training and, according to Fullerton, were "brought up on free trade." Gordon, in their view, "didn't know much" about trade. The researchers worried about rumours that Gordon wanted to limit American investment in Canada and protect Canadian industry from competition from foreign imports.[29]

In May and June 1955, while LePan was recruiting the staff, Gordon prepared an outline of the commission's work. He called for a comprehensive survey of the Canadian economy – including international economic questions – and an examination of policy alternatives. There was little existing research into many areas of the economy, and Gordon proposed that the staff conduct more than twenty studies to assist the commissioners in their work.[30] Gordon's outline formed the basis of the discussion at the first full meeting of the commissioners in July.[31] At this session Gordon argued that the commission should aim to complete its work within eighteen months, before the next federal election. "From the outset," according to LePan, "the only commissioner in favour of such a tight schedule was Mr. Gordon himself. All the other Commissioners were opposed, as were all the members of the Commission staff."[32] To them a year and a half was not enough time to evaluate the Canadian economy seriously. Gordon, however, was accustomed to moving quickly, and thought unrealistically that the commission could examine all aspects of the economy in less than two years.

From the beginning, foreign investment and the tariff were, for Gordon, an important part of the commission's study. In his outline of the commission's work Gordon asked many questions about Canada's international economic relations: "Should we do more processing of our natural resources at home? ... What are the implications of large-scale foreign investment in Canada? ... How far is Canadian enterprise likely to be owned and controlled by the United States and what are the implications? ... What measures might be taken to reduce the dependence of Canadian industry on United States research facilities?"[33] Before hearings opened, Gordon outlined publicly the scope of the commission's inquiry. Speaking in Edmonton to the Canadian Federation of Mayors and Municipalities, he identified many questions that the commission planned to address, including Canada's increasing reliance on the American economy and the growing levels of foreign investment in Canadian industry.[34] Through this well-publicized speech Gordon in effect served notice to those who were to appear before the commission that he was willing to consider views on foreign ownership that contradicted the existing orthodoxy.

Gordon showed his early interest in foreign ownership when, in August 1955, he telephoned Leroy Grant, his old engineering professor from RMC. Grant had recently made several trips across the country for the Engineering Institute of Canada, and Gordon asked for his observations on American penetration into Canada. Grant's response, based entirely on anecdotal evidence, likely confirmed what Gordon already suspected: "Hardly a week passes that some old Canadian firm is not bought by American interests." According to Grant, "The American buys stock, elects directors and manages the enterprise. Many American companies with big Canadian interests do not give Canadians an opportunity to participate in the profits by buying stock." Grant made it clear, however, that the Americans were not the only villains: "The present situation is not so much the result of U.S. financial imperialism, as of the attitude of Canadian yankomaniacs."[35] These were views that Gordon would hear again during the commission's hearings.

Gordon also intended that the commission examine Canada's tariff structure. In July 1955 he had spoken about the commission's goals with his friend Arnold Heeney, Canada's ambassador in Washington. According to Heeney, Gordon intended to "produce a basis for a new national policy with a distinctly 'protectionist' flavour." Gordon believed that this would entail an abandonment of "pure liberal doctrines," and Heeney thought that it would involve a "certain stirring up of anti-U.S. feeling."[36]

The public hearings opened on 18 October 1955 in St John's, Newfoundland. Gordon had not wanted to hold hearings, but others had convinced him that they were necessary.[37] Gordon handled the proceedings briskly and politely. After a few days MacKay became upset that many of the witnesses left feeling that the commission had not listened to them; the commissioners had thanked all the witnesses for their submissions but often had not engaged them in any dialogue. MacKay told Gordon that the commission had been unfair to some of those who had expected a bit of discussion, and as a result Gordon began to show more interest in those appearing before the commission.[38]

According to Gordon, the commission heard more about foreign investment during the public hearings "than about any other single subject."[39] This view is not supported by the evidence. Most of the briefs submitted to the commission did not mention foreign investment, focusing instead on other issues, such as taxation and the tariff. Voices opposing government policy are usually louder than those in support, and this was true in the submissions to the commission. Though many supported foreign ownership, few actually expressed it in the hearings. Most of the comments on the subject were negative, often coming from the ranks of professional organizations, investment dealers, and organized labour.[40] They complained that American investment was direct, bringing with it control of Canadian corporations, and that it was concentrated in key industries. All three groups perceived that American ownership threatened their employment opportunities. Investment dealers and security analysts perceived a threat from wholly owned American subsidiaries that did not offer shares on Canadian markets. Professional organizations, such as those representing engineers or researchers, worried that American firms tended to employ American professionals and often relied on the head office for research support, seldom developing products in Canada. Organized labour, at the hearings the most vocal opponent of American capital, complained that foreign ownership meant fewer manufacturing jobs because American-owned companies imported components from their plants in the United States, discouraged their Canadian subsidiaries from seeking export markets for Canadian goods, and exported Canadian natural resources to the United States for processing. Part of this opposition to foreign investment arose because, to many members of the labour movement, the struggle between labour and capital had become a conflict between Canadian and American interests. When owners made decisions that did not benefit workers, union members often ignored the obvious profit motive, alleging that these decisions were made for reasons of nationality.[41]

In defence of the sale of natural resources to American buyers, Robert Fowler, president of the Canadian Pulp and Paper Association, bluntly stated a position likely shared by many of the corporate executives who had appeared before the commission: Canada could not force other countries to buy Canadian manufactured goods instead of raw materials. "They can, and will, turn elsewhere for the raw materials they need or find alternative materials to maintain their industrial development." Primary industries were "the basis of our prosperity and growth." Secondary industries would develop in

time, but "to push them artificially, by an attempt to limit primary production, is to limit what we can do best and to depress the living standards of
Canadians."[42] These comments provoked a sharp backlash. The British
Columbia Trade Union Congress wrote to Gordon, calling Fowler's views
"short sighted and economically suicidal." The members of the organization believed it was "little short of asinine" to argue "that we, as a Nation,
remain hewers of wood and drawers of water." The letter explained that
converting raw materials to finished products would help to reduce Canada's $800-billion trade deficit with the United States. To follow Fowler's
proposed course of action "would only result in a worsening of this present
unfortunate situation, and would lead to eventual economic suicide."

The BCTUC accused industrial leaders of being "more concerned with their
own immediate economic gain than with the economic welfare of our country
as a whole. Labour can only consider such statements as nothing more than
an attempt to sabotage our national economic aspirations. These aspirations
are to manufacture an ever increasing amount of our own raw materials in our
own country, and only by accomplishing this, can we restrain the most debil-
itating of all exports, the loss of our highly skilled people into the ever ready
opportunities of more industrialized nations."[43] The Association of Professional Engineers of Ontario expressed a similar view in a brief that also summarized Fowler as saying "that Canada's best future role is to remain a hewer
of wood and drawer of water," words that he never used. "It must be evident
to all that, in an age of nylon, plastics, jet engines, transistors, television and
nuclear fission, any such attitude, as that suggested by Mr. Fowler, can only
lead to industrial suicide and would stifle the growing research and development prowess which Canada is displaying in a very marked degree."[44] Both
sides in this debate were trying to protect their own interests while presenting
their views in the language of national self-interest.

The commission hearings, which ended in March 1956, sparked considerable debate in English Canada over the issue of foreign investment.[45] As one
American commentator noted, the hearings "played an important part in setting the stage for an extraordinary burgeoning of public comment about the
U.S. capital 'invasion' which was manifested from early 1956."[46] In January
1956 Michael Barkway wrote an article entitled "Memo to the Gordon Commission: How Far Are We from the Wood-Hewing Age?" Barkway questioned the government's belief that Canada was developing into a more
industrialized economy and asked whether the country was "still mainly
occupied in producing raw materials which the more 'advanced' countries
can make into finished products."[47] Similarly, in February an editorial in the

Hamilton Spectator entitled "Who Owns Canada?" noted "a growing suspicion in the mind of the average Canadian that his country is being devoured by United States industrial investors."[48]

Foreign investment also attracted attention from politicians. Before the hearings there had been no substantial discussion of the issue in the House of Commons. By early 1956, however, the matter was being raised with increasing frequency, inside and outside the Commons. On 19 March, Tory leader George Drew repeated some of the sentiments that had been voiced to the commission, arguing that "Canadians should declare their economic independence of the United States." In Drew's opinion, "political and economic independence go hand in hand ... We must decide that we are not going to be hewers of wood, drawers of water and diggers of holes for any other country."[49] Similarly, in a radio speech on 2 March CCF leader Major Coldwell asked why Canada should export its raw materials and buy them back as manufactured goods: "Should we not use our vast and rich resources for the benefit of the people whose heritage they are?"[50]

Lester Pearson presented the government's response to these questions in Montreal on 27 March. Speaking to the Canadian Club, he argued that Canada's post-war economic progress "could not have taken place in the way and in the time that it has, without outside participation, especially by investors from the United States, but also from Great Britain and other countries." Pearson scolded those who were sounding the alarm about American economic influence: "there is no excuse for the assertion – either careless or calculated – that the economic and political domination of our country by the United States is imminent; or for dragging up old anti-American prejudices ... The times are too serious and the problems too real for irresponsible exaggeration." According to Pearson, the choice was clear: Canada could accept capital investment from the United States, or it could restrict its own rate of development.[51]

Concern over foreign investment intensified in early April 1956, when the Dominion Bureau of Statistics issued *Canada's International Investment Position, 1926–1954*, a report that outlined the levels of foreign ownership in Canadian industry.[52] An earlier edition had been released in 1950, but in the days before McCarthy and the Gordon Commission few Canadians expressed any interest.[53] In 1956, however, the DBS figures on levels of foreign ownership caused a considerable stir. The press gave unusually prominent coverage to the report, and within days this book of tables, charts, and statistics had become a bestseller.[54] The *Financial Post* asked whether the pace of Canadian economic expansion was worth "the loss of ownership and control and the increasing emphasis on primary resources development. This is the biggest question facing ... the Gordon Commission."[55] The *Financial Post* also increased public alarm by misinterpreting the statistics: "Foreign ownership and control – now mostly American – extends to a far greater proportion of Canada's productive enterprise than at any time in the last 30 years."[56] A closer reading of the statistics would have shown that foreign capital, as a proportion of all investment in Canada, was at its highest level in 1930, not in the mid-1950s.[57] During the Great Depression few Canadians challenged the high levels of foreign investment, but the affluence of the 1950s provided a different context. The day after the report was issued, the Ottawa correspondent of the *Toronto Star* predicted that "in the weeks ahead, U.S. citizens – and some Canadians, too – may be surprised, even shocked at the anti-U.S. sentiments held and expressed by many of Canada's legislators."[58]

The prophesy proved correct. Speaking to the Alberta Conservative Association on the night after the study appeared, John Diefenbaker warned, "if the St. Laurent Government is re-elected, Canada will become a virtually forty-ninth economic state in the American union."[59] His attitude had clearly shifted from two years earlier, when he had attacked Donald Creighton for expressing concern over American influence in Canada, a change of view that reflected the new mood in Canada. Léon Balcer, member of Parliament and president of the Progressive Conservative party, made similar comments during the budget debate in the House of Commons. In the first sentence of his speech Balcer referred to the report from the Dominion Bureau of Statistics, and followed with his interpretation of the statistics: "What is happening before our very eyes is nothing less than economic invasion by our neighbours to the south." In Balcer's view, foreign investment posed a serious threat to Canadian independence: "We can well ask ourselves if this country is not falling into an economic colonialism which may be different from political colonialism but which can be one just the same, and have nefarious effects on the sovereignty and population of Canada."[60] During the budget debate another Conservative MP, E. Davie Fulton, echoed Balcer's views: "History shows us that economic domination, if not resisted, if not altered, inevitably leads by a process of absorption to ultimate political domination as well."[61]

One of the reasons for this response to a routine statistical publication was that few Canadians had a clear understanding of the level of foreign ownership in Canada and were surprised when they saw the figures. Most Canadians knew that foreign investment was on the rise, but had not realized the extent.[62] In the past C.D. Howe had estimated that 6 per cent of new investment in Canada came from foreign sources, and had not been seriously challenged on this statement.[63] The situation was made worse by the fact that the press sensationally reported the increase in American investment without mentioning that the ratio of foreign investment to Canadian investment had not increased at all, because the growth of foreign investment had been matched by a corresponding expansion of the economy as a whole.

Within a week of the publication of *Canada's International Investment Position*, high-ranking Canadian and American officials felt obliged to intervene in the debate. On 16 April retiring United States Ambassador R. Douglas Stuart, one of the original investors in Canadian Corporate Management, made a public statement in Vancouver defending the role of American capital in Canadian development. Without naming Drew, he quoted and criticized the leader of the Opposition's 19 March speech in Hamilton, highlighting the contradiction in the ideas of those who favoured the tariff while opposing American investment, for the tariff was one of the main causes of foreign investment. Branch plants in Canada were established "to surmount the already formidable Canadian tariff."[64] For Stuart, this contradiction showed that opposition to American capital in Canada was more emotional than logical.

Stuart's speech provoked a backlash from the opposition parties and helped to increase the level of anti-Americanism in Canada. Speaking to the Commons External Affairs Committee, Diefenbaker labelled Stuart's speech "an unwarranted intrusion by the Ambassador [and] ... an unwarranted reflection on the man who occupies the position of leader of the opposition." Coldwell agreed with Diefenbaker, saying the speech "was not only unusual but a highly improper thing for an ambassador to do." Coldwell urged Pearson to tell the American government that Canada objected "to the entry of an ambassador into what is at the moment a very hot and controversial subject in Canada."[65] At the next sitting of the committee Pearson defended Stuart's actions, saying that the ambassador had no intention of intervening in Canadian affairs and was merely "giving the frank and honest views of a sincere friend of Canada, which we all know him to be."[66]

Stuart's speech also provoked comment in the House of Commons. Fulton, for example, lashed out at the ambassador, saying that Stuart's intervention was "itself a measure of the seriousness of the situation." For Stuart to believe that he had the right to intervene in Canadian affairs showed "how far things have gone along the line of acceptance of American domination." A CCF member, George Castleden, criticized Stuart's speech in similar terms, calling it "a very grave error."[67] Castleden quoted extensively from the DBS report on foreign investment in Canada, and warned that American interests would gain further control of Canadian resources through the proposed Trans-Canada Pipeline.

On 23 April the controversy prompted Howe to defend foreign investment publicly. Speaking in Hamilton, he insisted that outside investors were "skilled and responsible," and brought "capital and often technical management which are not always available from domestic sources." He insisted that without the foreign investor Canadian development would have been much slower, because Canadians had not "generated enough savings to supply all the capital required for Canadian development in the postwar years ... Why put unnecessary handicaps in the way of our future by adopting narrowly nationalistic and emotional attitudes towards foreign capital?"[68]

Within a few days of the speech, Howe would become the central figure in the uproar in the House of Commons over the government's pipeline bill. Most of the opposition's rhetoric centred on the charge that the government was violating the rights of Parliament by applying closure, though fear of American economic influence also played a prominent role in the controversy. Conservative MP Donald Fleming was one of the most vocal opponents of Howe's bill. "Who is the author of this infamous proposal?" he asked. "I say to you that it is the same minister who ... will not lift a finger in the face of the growing concentration of Canadian trade in the American basket, who views with equanimity and indifference the growing United States economic influence over Canada, ... who wants to play fast and loose with a great national heritage." Fleming called on "free men in a free Canadian parliament to assert Canada's independence of United States economic domination."[69]

The opposition to foreign investment during the commission hearings and the pipeline debate was vocal and was reflected in a shift in public opinion. In July 1956 a poll showed that 17 per cent of Canadians disapproved of the foreign investment that had poured into Canada; 68 per cent approved, and 15 per cent had no opinion or advanced a qualified answer. The question, however, had asked about the role of foreign investment in the past; when Canadians were queried about the future, a different result emerged. Of those polled, 43 per cent thought that Canada now had enough or too much foreign capital; only 33 per cent wanted to see more, while 24 per cent were undecided or had qualified views. This poll provided an interesting contrast with one conducted only six years earlier. In 1950, 60 per cent of Canadians thought that Canada should continue to encourage American capital to develop its natural resources.[70]

In May 1956, with the public debate raging, Gordon circulated a memorandum to the commissioners in which he outlined in detail, perhaps for the first time, his ideas on foreign ownership. Gordon recognized the important contribution of foreign ownership to Canada: "The tremendous development which has occurred in this country since the war simply could not have happened without foreign capital, foreign skills and foreign know-how." Offering no explanation, he added that the interests of the foreign owners did not always coincide with the interests of Canada as a whole: "This is understandable and need not be commented upon further, except to say that, other things being equal, it would seem to be healthier, or at least more desirable, over a period of years for a greater proportion of this country's important industries to be controlled by Canadians." Repeating many of the views voiced during the hearings, Gordon's memorandum laid out a code of conduct for foreign firms operating in Canada:

a) They should employ Canadians in senior management and technical positions whenever it is possible to do so ...

b) They should sell an appreciable interest in the equity of the Canadian subsidiaries to Canadians, and provide for the direct representation of such Canadian investors on their boards of directors.

c) They should publish their financial statements and make full disclosure of their Canadian operations.

d) Whenever it is possible to do so, they should employ the services of Canadian engineering and other professional firms, Canadian service personnel of all kinds, Canadian contractors, and should purchase equipment, machinery and supplies from Canadian sources.

As head of the country's largest accounting firm and largest management consulting company, Gordon shared the concerns expressed in the commission hearings by professional organizations. As president of a small manufacturing conglomerate, Canadian Corporate Management, Gordon also wanted foreign-owned firms to purchase more equipment, machinery, and supplies from Canadian firms. He did not, however, acknowledge an important complaint of organized labour, that American firms exported raw material to the United States rather than processing it in Canada.[71] He viewed the problems of foreign investment from the perspective of management, not labour.

Gordon relied on the tax system to solve the problems associated with foreign ownership. He suggested tax concessions for companies that had at least 20 or 25 per cent Canadian equity participation, including a special depreciation provision that would allow these firms to write off their capital assets faster than wholly foreign-owned enterprises could. He proposed an increase in the rate of withholding tax on dividends paid to non-residents by firms that did not have at least 20 to 25 per cent Canadian ownership. He thought the government should introduce legislation to prohibit the sale of voting shares in Canadian banks to non-residents, a special tax to discourage the sale to non-residents of controlling interests in Canadian companies, and amendments to federal and provincial laws that would require foreign firms to publish their financial statements. For the most part Gordon's proposals aimed at reducing the level of foreign ownership rather than dealing with the problems associated with it. He specifically rejected legislation that would compel firms to employ Canadian professional and service personnel, or that would require their executives to live in Canada. While these were "important objectives," foreign-owned companies should merely "be encouraged to meet [them] in the interest of good public relations, if for no other reason."[72] Although he had voiced concerns about the behaviour of foreign-owned firms, Gordon's main goal was not to change their practices but rather to reduce their presence in Canada. This step, he believed, would solve the problems he had identified. In his view, foreign-owned firms behaved differently from Canadian firms because of their nationality and not because of the profit motive.

Having defined his views on foreign investment and other key economic issues, and realizing that a federal election would take place soon, Gordon decided that the commission could make more of an impact by publishing a preliminary report. He had originally thought that the commission could complete its work within eighteen months, and was not willing to spend more time away from his professional practice.[73] A preliminary report was not an unusual step: six previous royal commissions had issued reports before the end of their investigation, including the Royal Commission on Customs and Excise, which Gordon had served in the late 1920s. Even so, many of those working on the commission were against this move. LePan remembered, "There was strong opposition to Mr. Gordon's wishes ... I would say that a majority of the commissioners, as well as a majority of the staff, were strongly opposed to issuing a Preliminary Report." The researchers disagreed with the proposal because most had not completed their work and felt that the preliminary report would be premature. LePan himself disliked the idea and complained about the proposal to his friends in the public service.[74]

Most of the commissioners voiced similar concerns. Though Omer Lussier, the least assertive of the commissioners, quickly agreed with Gordon's proposals, the others expressed doubts. On 20 September, Gordon wrote to Stewart, Grauer, and Gushue, suggesting the interim report. All three opposed the idea. Grauer had misgivings and convinced Stewart that the preliminary report was a bad idea. Grauer then telephoned Gordon and asked for a meeting to discuss the matter, but he discovered that the chairman had already made the decision. In a conversation with Gordon, Gushue said that he opposed the idea because he believed it would detract from the final product, but added that if all the other members of the commission felt otherwise, he would defer to their views. Then, not realizing that Gordon had already made up his mind, Gushue wrote to express his views more formally: "I am not at all happy about this. I think that if it can be avoided it ought to be as it will undoubtedly spoil the final report. However, as stated before, if all the other members of the Commission feel otherwise I shall defer to their collective wishes. I assume from your references that this is the case. I should like to know definitely." The letter was too late. A few days earlier Gordon had issued the press release announcing that the commission would release a preliminary report. Gordon later wrote to Gushue to explain his actions, ending with this statement: "In any event, things have now proceeded to the point where it would be most difficult to reverse them."[75] Most of the commissioners opposed the preliminary report, but could do little when presented with Gordon's *fait accompli*.

While the commission worked on its preliminary report, debate over foreign investment continued. On 13 October Michael Barkway of the *Financial Post* rejected the Dominion Bureau of Statistics' study on foreign investment, which he said seriously underestimated the level of foreign control.[76] On the other side of the debate, C.D. Howe recognized the rising political importance of the issue when, under pressure from Deputy Minister Mitchell Sharp, he delivered a speech on 15 October, outlining a code of conduct for foreign firms operating in Canada.[77] The speech, drafted by senior officials in the Department of Trade and Commerce,[78] stated repeatedly that Canada welcomed foreign capital but acknowledged that rising concern over foreign investment meant that American corporations would have to accept greater Canadian participation: "Other things being equal, it is good business for a Canadian subsidiary of a foreign company to become as Canadian as it can, without losing the benefits of association with the parent country ... anyone who does business in Canada ... should reckon with the normal feelings of nationalism ... present in Canada, just as ... in the United States." Howe offered three suggestions for American firms in Canada: they should sell a minority of their shares to Canadians, hire Canadians in executive and professional positions, and provide regular information to the public about their operations.[79] Howe's proposals were mild; he never mentioned legislation to regulate the behaviour of foreign firms, and certainly never suggested that the tax laws should be used to discourage foreign ownership.

A few weeks after Howe's speech, a crisis in the Middle East brought many Canadians to the belated realization that Canada was firmly in the American camp. On 29 October, Israeli troops invaded Egypt to capture the Suez Canal, nationalized a few months earlier by the Egyptian government. The next day, while the United Nations Security Council was discussing the matter, Britain and France dispatched troops towards Egypt and issued an ultimatum to both Israel and Egypt to cease fire and withdraw from the canal area. Canada cautioned Whitehall that such action could damage the unity of the Commonwealth, but British officials ignored these warnings and lied to the Canadian government about their intentions. This signified, in historian John English's words, that "Canada was no longer a close part of the family."[80] The crisis ended when the United Nations accepted Lester Pearson's proposal for an international force to separate the belligerents. Pearson's diplomacy earned him the Nobel Prize, but to many Canadians it seemed that the government had deserted the mother country in favour of the United States, which had opposed the actions of the British, French, and Israelis. For other Canadians, Suez showed that Canada could no longer look to Britain to offset its reliance on the Americans.

Against this backdrop, the royal commission's *Preliminary Report* was released in January 1957. According to LePan, its recommendations "were those that Walter Gordon wanted to produce, broadened, tempered and deepened by the very capable research staff which the Royal Commission engaged."[81] Optimism underlay most of the 142-page report, which examined Canada's major industries, commercial policy, capital investment, municipal financing, immigration and human resources, and the problems of the Atlantic provinces. The sense of hope was most noticeable in the commission's prediction of a 67 per cent increase in the gross national product from 1955 to 1980, a forecast that proved remarkably accurate.[82]

The report's section on the tariff was typical in its use of generalizations and its failure to provide any substantive evidence in support of its recommendations. According to the commission, a reduction in the level of international tariffs would not likely occur soon. The report argued, therefore, that "it would seem sensible for this country, for the time being, to hold the tariff line, on the average, at about its present level." Even so, the government should "straighten out some of the anomalies which exist in the present tariff." In particular, the commission recommended the elimination of preferential treatment for "end use" items and items "of a class or kind not made in Canada."[83]

The section on foreign ownership began with a bland statement: "Canada has always welcomed the investment of foreign capital and has benefited greatly and will continue to benefit from the foreign capital that has been invested here." The commission could find "little evidence to suggest that foreign-controlled Canadian companies are being operated in a way which is at variance with the best interest of Canada." Still, the report warned that, in the future, foreign investment "may tend to create problems." The increasing concentration of foreign ownership could cause distress among Canadians, which in turn "could lead to actions of an extreme kind being taken at some future time." Using curious logic, the commission proposed mild legislation to limit foreign investment, not because it had found any problems with foreign ownership but to prevent a future demand for more extreme measures.[84]

Closely mirroring the views expressed in Gordon's memorandum to the commissioners, the report proposed three objectives for foreign concerns operating in Canada:

(a) Wherever possible, they should employ Canadians in senior management and technical positions, should retain Canadian engineering and other professional and service personnel and should do their purchasing of supplies, materials and equipment in this country.

(b) They should publish their financial statements and make full disclosure therein of their Canadian operations.

(c) The larger Canadian subsidiaries should sell an appreciable interest (perhaps 20% to 25%) in their equity stock to Canadian investors and should include on their boards of directors a number of independent Canadians.

To achieve these goals, the commission suggested tax incentives, again reflecting Gordon's ideas. These measures included a special depreciation allowance for Canadian-owned firms and a higher withholding tax on dividends paid to non-residents by firms that did not have "an appreciable percentage" of Canadian ownership. The commission also recommended laws to prevent "any substantial measure of control of the chartered banks and of the life insurance companies from coming into the possession of non-residents."[85]

Reaction to the report was mixed. Trained economists were the most negative, often labelling the report "woolly" or "half-baked." John Deutsch, head of the economics department at the University of British Columbia, expressed the views of many of his colleagues. He thought the report was "half-baked" and found himself "unable to follow or understand the logic and economic analysis." In particular, he found the discussion on the tariff and foreign investment "quite woolly in many places." The report's weakness was "all the more [a] pity because the Commission had available the services of quite a large number of able economists."[86] Similarly, Harry Johnson, a Canadian economist at the University of Manchester, criticized the report's understanding of economic theory: "Its discussion of policy problems is narrowly empirical and pragmatic, uninspired by any consistent philosophy of resource-oriented growth or even of economic policy."[87]

Professional economists aimed their sharpest criticism at the section on commercial policy. Johnson called this chapter "a model of under-developed economic thinking, really requiring a review of its own." Stefan Stykolt and Harry Eastman were particularly critical, arguing that the report was protectionist, despite its insistence that the tariff remain at its current rate. They contended that the proposed simplification of rates would result in a substantial rise of the tariff, perhaps double, on many commodities falling under the "end use" and "of a class or kind not made in Canada" classifications. Stykolt and Eastman also believed that there was a basic contradiction in the commission's concern over foreign investment and its rejection of free trade: "The Commission shows some symptoms of schizophrenia. On the one side it looks with favor on the protection of manufacturing and processing industry. On the other it resents the American investment in Canada which is largely a result of that protection." These views were repeated in the perceptive critique of the famous economist Jacob Viner, an American citizen who had been born in Canada. Like his colleagues, Viner opposed an increase in the tariff on commodities classified as "end use" or "of a class or kind not made in Canada." He noted also the failure of the report to discuss the many "agencies, international codes and symbols associated with that pursuit of the dream of freer and fairer world trade in which Canada, in close partnership with the United States, prominently participated from the late 1930s onward." Tom Kent, editor of the *Winnipeg Free Press*, agreed, saying that one of the report's oddest quirks was its only casual reference to the common market.[88]

Economists also criticized the report's section on foreign investment. Stykolt and Eastman rejected bluntly the commission's proposal to have different tax rates for companies with 25 per cent Canadian ownership: "The success of such a scheme might soothe the tender susceptibilities of extreme Canadian nationalists, but would do little to strengthen the control of Canadians over industries located here." Similarly, Johnson denounced the suggestion that 25 per cent Canadian participation in foreign-owned firms would ensure that they would act in Canada's interests. He thought it was the duty "of the government and not the minority shareholders to look after the national interest." In his view the proposal was nothing more "than another attempt to blackmail successful alien risk-takers into paying tribute to unenterprising but powerful local capitalists as the price for controlling the mob; so far, in contrast to other developing nations, Canada has gained by abstaining from such behaviour." According to Johnson, policies motivated by a "fear of foreigners" would result in a lowering of Canada's rate of growth.[89]

The press response to the report was more positive than that of the professional economists. The *Regina Leader-Post* was impressed with the scope of the report and the amount of work done in a short time. The paper considered the report a "blueprint" that "consolidates expert opinion on matters affecting Canadians of today and the Canadians of the future." Similarly, the *Vancouver Province* called the report "a forthright document which will provide an extremely sound basis from which to project our economic growth." According to the *Province*, "The deeper you get into the report the more remarkable it seems in its encompassing qualities ... The Commission appears to have done a first-class job in giving the government and the country this long-range blueprint." Comparable praise came from the *Toronto Telegram*, the *Montreal Gazette*, the *Montreal Star*, and *La Presse* of Montreal.[90]

Not all the newspapers were positive, however. The *Winnipeg Tribune* thought that the report was uneven, with some aspects of the economy having been discussed thoroughly while others were only passed over lightly. "The Commission does not hesitate to rush in with startling policy recommendations in some fields ... yet it makes no recommendations in other areas." Moreover, the report appeared "to have dealt with some aspects of the economy in isolation, neatly boxed off from the rest." The *Tribune*'s main competitor, the *Winnipeg Free Press*, voiced the same concern, saying that, despite some "good material," the report was "disappointing" and "a jumble." In a surprising editorial the *Vancouver Province* called the report a "bob-tailed, patched-up job put out in a hurry," only a few days after having lauded it. The editors admitted that they had initially praised the report before they had read it.[91]

The commission's recommendations on the tariff were ignored by most newspapers, except in the west, where critics condemned the report as protectionist. Grant Dexter of the *Winnipeg Free Press* echoed the criticism of the professional economists, pointing out that the report contained several proposals to increase the tariff despite saying that the tariff should stay at its current level. The result was "a definitely protectionist report." In particular, the elimination of the "end use" tariff class would mean that farm implements and fertilizers would cease to be duty-free. Writing in the *Victoria Times*, Dexter's friend Bruce Hutchison also criticized the report's protectionism, saying that the commission had "laid an egg."[92]

The newspapers were not unanimous in their assessment of the section on foreign investment. The *Calgary Herald*, the *Montreal Star*, and *La Presse* praised the recommendations on foreign ownership. Other papers criticized the chapter, with the most vocal and most effective criticisms coming from the *Winnipeg Free Press*. In an editorial by Tom Kent the paper argued that the commission's proposals would not solve the potential problems of foreign ownership. It would give Canadians a minority share of large American companies, but would not give them control: "If the fear is that American companies may put other considerations above Canadian interests, they remain equally free to do so after 25 per cent of their shares are held in Canada." The commission's suggestion, therefore, would not serve the population as a whole but rather would benefit investors on Bay Street, who would then "be able to dip into the profits of some successful American companies." For Kent, "the idea that the apparatus of the Canadian state should be used to secure this result, by a discrimination that is offensive to all the principles of justice and sound tax policy, is ludicrous. As the solemn proposal of a Royal Commission concerned about the long-term welfare of the Canadian people, it is humiliating." The *Toronto Star* made a similar comment, accepting that there was "cause for concern" over foreign ownership but insisting that the solution proposed by the commission was "neither fair or effective."[93]

The political reaction to the report was as varied as that of the press. The government had no comment to make in the Commons on the day the report was published. The next day, under pressure from the leader of the Opposition, the prime minister suggested that the report would have no impact on the government: "The government has nothing to announce on this matter and it may very well be that some of the projects that the government will place before parliament will – not because of the report but because of the consideration that had been given to the matters previously – coincide with recommendations of the report."[94] Howe at first dismissed the report with one word – "Bullshit!" – and later argued strongly against the recommendation that the Wheat Board implement a quota system based on production rather than deliveries.[95] Jimmy Sinclair, minister of fisheries, also disagreed with the recommendations on the Wheat Board and criticized the proposal that the government encourage the export of hydro power.[96] Public Works Minister Robert Winters was more positive, publicly praising some of the suggestions for the Atlantic provinces and saying that the report was "another step in focusing attention on Maritime problems and intensifying the national desire to help."[97]

In the House of Commons, members from the opposition parties attacked the report. Prairie members denounced the suggestions on wheat and irrigation, and on agriculture's future role. Coldwell said that farmers would suffer from the recommendation that the Wheat Board control production.[98] His colleague Hazen Argue was much blunter, calling the commission's treatment of agriculture "short-sighted, depressing and incompetent."[99] Maritime members were particularly negative. Conservative George Nowlan alleged a lack of attention to the region, saying that, of 65,000 words in the report, there were only "about 12½ words of comfort for the Maritimes."[100] Liberal Allan MacEachen, himself an economist, was also disappointed with the report, which provided "no integrated program for maritime redevelopment; ... no examination of the commercial and monetary policies pursued by the government that might have a favourable or adverse affect on the economy of the Atlantic region ... [and] no recommendations for stimulating the private sector of the economy in the Atlantic region."[101]

There was no consensus among provincial officials on the value of the report. William Griesinger, Ontario's minister of public works, was favourable.[102] British Columbia Premier W.A.C. Bennett criticized the recommendations on wheat, irrigation, export of power, and transportation, saying that the report "completely missed the boat."[103] Commenting from New York, where he had not had a chance to see the report, Premier Hugh John Flemming of New Brunswick said he was "shocked and disappointed" at the recommendation that the federal government give financial aid to Maritimers who wanted to move to other parts of Canada.[104] But after he had read the report, Flemming was more positive and urged the federal government to adopt the commission's recommendations on the Atlantic provinces.[105] Premier Robert Stanfield of Nova Scotia similarly criticized the section on offering assistance to individuals leaving the Maritimes, but praised the rest of the report.[106]

Senior members of the civil service were critical, believing that it had been a mistake to publish a preliminary report. Robert Bryce, clerk of the Privy Council and secretary to the Cabinet, voiced his concerns in a letter to his friend John Deutsch. He found the report "stimulating and provocative" but thought that "the most controversial aspects of it do suggest that Doug LePan was right in asking for more time to put things carefully and convincingly." Howe's deputy minister of trade and commerce, Mitchell Sharp, also enjoyed the provocative nature of the report but believed that it should not have been published: the report "provided some light reading and an opportunity for Mr. Howe to express himself pungently on a number of current issues." But Sharp was "surprised and rather disappointed by the interim report, which might well have been withheld until the analysis had been proceeded with to more reasoned conclusions. As it is, the work of the Commission has been damaged by hasty presentation of conclusions which are not supported adequately in the least."[107]

Perhaps the most serious criticism, though never made public, came from the commission's own staff. The researchers, particularly those working on international economic questions, did not feel that the report reflected their work, and this provoked a sharp confrontation. As David Slater recalled, "Reisman was a ringleader among those of us who were concerned about the difference between the evidence and the [report's] assertions on foreign ownership and control." In response to their complaints LePan organized a meeting with Gordon for those staff members researching international questions. Reisman spoke first, explaining that the interim report didn't reflect the staff's research. According to Slater, Gordon reassured the researchers, giving them the impression that there would "not be a repetition of the slap-dash approach that was characteristic of the interim report."[108]

Despite the criticism, and despite the government's failure to embrace its conclusions, the report was influential. Jack Davis recalled that the report tended "to crystallize ... a lot of the concern that was developing across the country."[109] Moreover, as Tom Kent argued, the report had an important psychological effect, helping "deepen and spread the impression that there was indeed something wrong but the Liberal leaders could not or would not do anything about it; that the Government had gone stale, needed new ideas, but wouldn't accept them."[110] The report also had an effect on the academic community. Before the Gordon Commission, Canadian economists did not consider foreign investment a proper topic for debate. For them it went without saying that governments should not limit the free flow of capital across national boundaries. The Gordon Report was seminal, triggering considerable political and academic discussion of the subject. The report gave Gordon's concerns over foreign investment an air of legitimacy.

The debate over Canadian-American relations was intensified by events in early 1957, developments that raised further doubts about the United States.

On 4 April Herbert Norman, Canada's ambassador to Egypt, committed suicide, not wanting to face the accusations of a United States Senate committee investigating charges that he had been a communist. For many Canadians, the American senators had murdered Norman.[111] In the House of Commons, John Diefenbaker declared that Norman had been "a victim of witch-hunting proclivities." Alistair Stewart, a CCF member of Parliament, agreed: "I believe Mr. Norman was murdered by slander. I believe he was killed as if someone had put a knife in his back."[112] These views were not confined to Parliament. An editorial in the *Globe and Mail* called Eisenhower's response to the suicide "imprudent and patronizing," and lamented the president's failure to "at least express some regret that a distinguished servant of Canada had been hounded to destruction by the irresponsible and slanderous attacks of a branch of the United States Government." The editorial reflected the changing mood in Canada towards the Canadian-American relationship: "A growing number of Canadians are beginning to question the nature of this 'friendship' ... It must be the most one sided love affair in international history."[113] Two days after the suicide students at the University of Toronto gathered at the centre of the campus clad in white sheets and burned effigies of McCarthy and the senators who had hounded Norman.[114] Arnold Heeney recorded in his diary that the activities of the American senators "infuriated Canadians and produced a wave of anti-Americanism at home which Mike [Pearson] says exceeded anything in his experience."[115] Norman's suicide fostered the growing doubts in Canada about the United States and played an important role in the federal election of 10 June.

Canadian-American relations were at the very centre of the election. The anger at Norman's suicide added to the concerns over other aspects of the friendship, including the question of foreign investment. The Conservative party responded effectively. In a speech on 7 April 1957, a few days before the election call, the party's new leader, John Diefenbaker, launched the Tory campaign by condemning the government's reaction to the hounding of Herbert Norman: "Let us tell the Americans they have no business condemning Canadians ... This government is afraid to stand up. It should have said to Washington, 'you look after your affairs and we'll look after ours.'" Later in the speech Diefenbaker said that he only supported foreign investment "if it is used for the benefit of Canadians in the years to come."[116] Throughout the election campaign Diefenbaker attacked outside investment and the development of the country's natural resources by foreigners.[117] A year later Gordon wrote, "There is a very definite feeling of nationalism in Canada – anti-Americanism if you will – and the Tories capitalized on this."[118]

While the debate over foreign investment continued and the commission-ers worked on their final report, the research staff struggled to complete many pioneering studies in Canadian economics. Though they were unhappy with the *Preliminary Report*, most of the researchers were pleased with the work-ings of the commission. According to Safarian, the commission had "the best working relations I've ever seen." Some of the researchers had worried at the outset that Gordon would try to skew the research, but this did not happen. As Safarian recalled, "It wasn't Gordon's style to intervene to try to influence a researcher." The staff members were pleased that the commission was back-ing a lot of expensive and fundamental economic research, producing, for ex-ample, the first comprehensive work in Canada on productivity, the stock of capital, and the use of input-output materials. According to Slater, "Gordon had a strong belief in the importance of careful analytical work."[119]

But Gordon had a double standard when it came to foreign ownership and the tariff. Gordon simply was not interested in research on these subjects. John Claxton, the commission's legal counsel, agreed: "Research for him was a like research for a legal brief. You looked for what supported your case."[120] Gordon largely ignored the work of the researchers on foreign investment. *Canada–United States Economic Relations*, the study by Irving Brecher and Simon Reisman, offered a different emphasis from that of the *Preliminary Report*. The authors listed the potential problems with foreign investment but concluded that they were far outweighed by the benefits. The few problems would be minimized not by nationalist policies but by "closer integration – financial and otherwise – of non-resident firms with the Cana-dian community."[121] Many of the problems with foreign firms arose not because of the nationality of the owners but because of economics, particu-larly "the economies of location, production, marketing and research, and by the uncertainties associated with United States commercial policy."[122] Brecher and Reisman implied that these problems could best be addressed by the government's focusing its attention on the general economic climate rather than on the question of ownership. Though the authors made no policy proposals, their conclusions suggested that Gordon's recommendation for the use of tax laws to discourage foreign investment was unnecessary.

Though Gordon could ignore the subtleties of the research on foreign investment, it was not as easy for him to overlook the commission's research on the tariff. The study was conducted by John Young, a professor of eco-nomics at Yale who held a doctorate from Cambridge. Young agreed to work for the commission after Reisman personally guaranteed that the commission would publish his work on the tariff, and on the understanding "that this would involve a close examination of its effects on secondary industry."[123] Young's work, according to Slater, was the best tariff study since W.A. Mackintosh's *The Economic Background of Dominion-Provincial Relations*, which had been prepared for the Royal Commission on Dominion-Provincial Relations.[124] Closely following neo-classical economic theory, Young suggested that, in 1956, the cost of the tariff to the Canadian economy would be roughly $1 billion, far higher than anyone had suspected.[125]

Young's ideas presented problems for Gordon. Although he indignantly denied being a protectionist, Gordon always defended the tariff with both political and economic arguments.[126] Simon Reisman, who spent much of his life negotiating trade agreements, believed that Gordon's position was clear: "If I've ever met a protectionist, he was a protectionist."[127] A May 1956 memorandum shows Gordon as a classic protectionist, wanting to restrict trade to protect local industries and jobs. If Canada were to enter into a free trade agreement with the United States, "the great majority of Canadian manufacturing industries would not be able to survive in their present form – or to survive on any appreciable scale." Any substantial step towards free trade would "have serious implications for the future of Canada, not only in so far as her economic independence was concerned, but also as to her ability to maintain for any extended time her independence as a separate political entity."[128] In these views Gordon had support from Grauer and Gushue. In a memorandum dated 4 June 1956 Grauer argued against tariff reductions: "The economic cost of the Canadian tariff, when secondary effects are taken into account, does not seem to be as high as economists generally supposed. There therefore seems little point in inviting the short-run costs of industrial dislocations by unilateral tariff reductions from the present relatively low levels."[129] On his copy of this memorandum Gushue wrote "Agreed!" beside this statement.

In January 1957 Gordon read a draft of Young's work, and outlined his concerns in a letter to Reisman. Young had argued for free trade, in direct contradiction to the commission's *Preliminary Report*: "How is it proposed to reconcile Jack's present draft with the conclusions of the Commission?"[130] In April, Gordon expressed similar views to LePan, criticizing Young for advocating free trade. According to Gordon, Young's proposal was "contrary to what the Commission has already said in the Preliminary Report and in any event offends the rule against advocating policy changes in the studies." He insisted that, to salvage the study, Young and Reisman would have to agree not to advocate policy, either directly or indirectly, and not to contradict the *Preliminary Report*: "We cannot very well authorize publication of a study which seems at times to be diametrically opposed to such conclusions."[131] Gordon then listed five pages of specific changes that he wanted Young to make to the manuscript. Gordon's comments show that his views on the tariff were firm and that he was not interested in research on this question. The integrity of Young's work was less important than Gordon's desire to have the research conform to the views in the *Preliminary Report*.

After some consideration, Gordon decided that he would not publish Young's work. Reisman, virtually co-author of the study, objected strenuously, saying that if the commission did not publish the manuscript, he would do it himself.[132] To settle the dispute, Gordon agreed to ask an outside economist to review Young's manuscript and advise whether the commission should publish it. Gordon's choice was Maurice Lamontagne, a University of Ottawa economist who, as chief economic adviser to the Privy Council from 1955 to 1957, had been one of the few senior French Canadians in the public service. Lamontagne, one of Gordon's close friends, had left the public service in 1957 because he had become closely identified with the Liberal party and intended to run in the upcoming federal election. In a memorandum to Lamontagne, Gordon said that his concern was "whether the Commission should authorize the publication of a study which, in essence and by inference, differs in its conclusions from those which the Commissioners have arrived at."[133] Originally, however, Gordon had wanted the study to examine whether the tariff's "general incidence seems reasonable" and whether "the existing pattern of rates needs revision."[134] Answering these questions clearly required Young to advocate a particular policy. Gordon's real objection, therefore, was not that the study had overstepped its bounds by recommending policy but that its conclusions ran contrary to his own. Gordon suggested four major changes: Young should give greater weight "to the dislocations which would result from any major reduction in the tariff"; he should be more enthusiastic "about tidying up the tariff"; he should not contradict the commission's view on dumping; and he should not disagree with the recommendation on free trade with the United States.[135] Ultimately, Lamontagne convinced Young and Reisman to make a few minor changes to the study, and told Gordon, "You have to publish this, but you don't have to assume responsibility for it."[136]

The commission did not assume responsibility for any of the thirty-two studies it published. Each had a brief disclaimer on the title-page: "While authorizing the publication of this study which has been prepared at their request, the Commissioners do not necessarily accept responsibility for all the statements or opinions that may be found in it."[137] For Young's volume, however, Gordon thought this statement was insufficient. Instead, he insisted on a longer note – "the shitty little disclaimer" in Reisman's words – which went to some length to discredit the report: "The study entitled 'Canadian Commercial Policy' by John H. Young makes a more abstract case for free trade – and does so more explicitly – than perhaps some people would expect or think justified in a staff study for a Royal Commission. We do not accept responsibility for or necessarily approve the statements or opinions which it contains … Our own conclusions about the tariff and commercial policy, insofar as Canada's economic prospects are concerned, are stated in our report."[138] LePan apparently opposed the inclusion of this statement. In the other studies the disclaimer appeared over the names of the commissioners and secretary. In this case, however, Gordon instructed the editorial consultant "that Mr. LePan's name is not to be included."[139] LePan's name eventually did appear in the book, though it is not clear if this was because of a printing error or because he had changed his mind.

The commission's *Final Report* advanced the same views on commercial policy that had been outlined in the first report. Gordon, not content to discredit Young's study in the disclaimer, also included an explicit rejection of Young's conclusions in the report. Commenting that the study "is of some interest" because it "purports to show" the cost of the tariff, the commissioners responded that there "is no satisfactory way of measuring or estimating the true cost of the Canadian tariff in economic terms." Their recommendation: "The best policy for Canada is to hold the present tariff levels." The *Final Report* again suggested that the government simplify the tariff structure, proposing once more the elimination of the classifications "end use" and "of a class or kind not made in Canada." Because it would have increased the tariff, economists had sharply criticized this suggestion when it appeared in the *Preliminary Report*. In response, the *Final Report* added that "care should be taken that any changes which are made … do not result in any material alteration in the general level of the tariff."[140]

As with the section on the tariff, the *Final Report*'s conclusions on foreign investment followed the main lines of the *Preliminary Report*. Though the *Final Report* contained a more detailed description of the structure of investment in Canada, the recommendations were the same, often using the same language.[141] The chapter on investment, written and revised by Gordon, outlined once more the objectives of greater Canadian participation in foreign-owned firms, and again recommended the use of the tax structure to achieve these goals.

The commission's *Final Report* was presented to the Diefenbaker government that had taken office in June 1957, but the new Conservative government was no more enamoured with the *Final Report* than the Liberals had been with the *Preliminary Report*. Gordon submitted the final product on 28 November 1957, but the government did not release it to the public until 12 May 1958, more than five months later. The government made no comment on the report in the House of Commons, and the opposition sought none.[142]

The press response to the *Final Report* did not differ significantly from the reaction to the *Preliminary Report*, though the comments this time were a little less vocal, reflecting both the moderation in the report and the sense of anticlimax caused by the earlier release of the commission's views. The most sustained, intelligent criticism came from Tom Kent, editor of the *Winnipeg Free Press*, who examined the report in an eleven-part series. Kent considered the recommendations on trade "arrant nonsense." The commission had stated that moderate changes in the tariff would not have any significant effect on the Canadian standard of living. Kent countered sharply, "With tariffs, the cumulative effect of moderate changes is very great. How could it be otherwise, given the importance of foreign trade to us?" Kent rejected the commission's argument that a reduction in tariffs would cause too great a disruption to the Canadian economy: "In these sentences the Commission out-does itself in naivety … All free-trade proposals are proposals for the progressive removal of tariffs over a period of years." This gradual process would lessen any economic upheaval. By implying that free trade, if adopted, would become effective overnight, the report was "merely dodging the real question." Labelling the commission protectionist, Kent acknowledged that its views on trade had a legitimate place in Canadian political thought: "But that surely is its traditional place – in the Conservative party."[143]

Kent's criticisms of the commission's views on foreign investment were even sharper than his examination of the section on the tariff. The report, in his view, indulged in a "remarkable piece of sophistry" by arguing that something should be done about foreign investment, despite the commission's inability to identify any problems with outside capital. Kent could imagine only one possible explanation for this contradictory argument. Gordon knew that the Conservative party would win votes in the next election by criticizing American corporations; the commission's recommendation was aimed at the Liberal party and, if adopted, "would prevent the Conservative party from making mileage out of anti-Americanism." Kent also repeated criticisms that he had levelled at the *Preliminary Report*, sharpening his language in the intervening year. The commission looked at foreign investment "not from the viewpoint of consumers, workers or traders but purely through the spectacles of Toronto-type financial interests." What would be the result of Gordon's proposal to force American-owned firms to sell a minority of shares to Canadians? In Kent's view, "Some people would do very well floating the public issue of shares in American-controlled companies. Some investors would get a dip into the profits of successful companies that are at present outside the stock market. And there would be some extra directorships open to the people of Bay Street, Toronto, and St. James Street, Montreal."[144]

Despite the harsh criticisms, and despite being ignored by the government, the commission made an important contribution to public debate in Canada. Concern over Canada's relationship with the United States, rooted in the Anglo-Canadian psyche, had been brought to the surface during the McCarthy years.[145] The Gordon Commission, by announcing that it would serve, in part, as a forum to discuss American economic influence, acted as a sounding board for those who opposed the government's policy of welcoming American capital. The coincidental release of statistics on foreign investment shocked many Canadians who had only recently become aware of the issue through press reports of the commission hearings. The resulting debate provided the foundation for the near-violent confrontation in the House of Commons over the pipeline bill. The showdown at Suez and Herbert Norman's suicide were unrelated incidents that also led to a heightened awareness of Canada's reliance on an often unattractive neighbour.

The Gordon Report played a central role in fostering and consolidating what had been disjointed and inchoate doubts about Canadian-American relations. The report's comments on foreign investment came from a commission appointed by the government and not from an opposition looking for partisan advantage, from an often-mistrusted press, or from self-interested individuals trying to improve their employment prospects. Gordon and his colleagues were well-respected, apparently impartial commentators. If they had doubts over the role of foreign investment in Canada, these feelings could no longer be dismissed as easily as economists and Cabinet ministers – particularly Howe – had done in the past. The work of the commission was a watershed in Canadian economic, political, and intellectual life. It established a foundation and legitimacy for the post-war concern over foreign investment.

The commission also brought Walter Gordon to national prominence. He had been well known in government and business circles for many years, but, despite having chaired a royal commission in the 1940s, he was still unknown to the public. After his well-publicized second royal commission, this was no longer the case. Occasionally controversial, Gordon was a prominent figure by the late 1950s. Though many disagreed with his views on Canadian politics and economics, it would not be possible for his opponents to ignore what he had to say.

CHAPTER THREE

Man and Superman
1958–1963

Through his royal commission in the mid-1950s Walter Gordon put the issue of foreign investment on the public agenda. In the next few years, however, other interests often overshadowed his concern over Canada's economic dependence on the United States. Though he continued to talk publicly about foreign investment, the issue was less important than his other activities, particularly his work in business and politics.

These were magnificent years for Walter Gordon. Between 1958 and 1963 his reputation as a businessman, a consultant, an expert in organization, and a policy guru reached its peak. He added to his family's fortune. He strengthened his relationship with the country's largest newspaper, the *Toronto Star*. He assumed a role as the *éminence grise* of the Liberal party, both in organization and policy. By the end of April 1963 Gordon was, in many eyes, the most powerful minister in a new Liberal government; he held the top economic portfolio and, more than anyone else, had the prime minister's ear. Gordon and his followers had conquered the Liberal party and the Canadian political scene. His policies were generally and widely embraced. The only exception was his position on foreign investment, which the party and the Canadian people had not accepted, a fact that Gordon never fully understood.

In the 1950s Gordon had a highly successful business record. After Grant Glassco left Clarkson Gordon in 1957, Gordon became the firm's only senior partner. He played an aggressive role in recruiting clients and was, according to partner Geoff Clarkson, "the best business-getter of his day, by a long shot." During this period Clarkson Gordon grew at a rapid pace, taking over local partnerships in Regina, London, Edmonton, Calgary, Windsor, and Vancouver. Clarkson Gordon's sister firm, Woods Gordon, also grew as the demand for consulting services rose. In 1953 it became the first Canadian management consulting firm to advise companies on the use of computers in business. Woods Gordon also continued to take on large jobs for the public sector. In 1959, for example, Canadian National Railways retained the firm to help in the reorganization of the company.[1]

The late 1950s were good years too for Canadian Corporate Management. In the spring of 1959 CanCorp, as it was often known, sold six companies to Canadian International Paper, a subsidiary of the American-owned International Paper Company. Among them were Canadian Vegetable Parchment, a major supplier of grocery bags and wrapping paper; Vancouver Pacific Paper, an important distributer of kraft papers; and Mid-West Paper, which the *Financial Post* called the "biggest wholesaler of paper to prairie printing firms."[2] Having argued strongly against foreign ownership in the royal commission reports, Gordon's decision to sell these companies to an American firm is surprising. Robert Fowler, Gordon's friend and president of the Canadian Pulp and Paper Association, later remembered that this was "a very sound and profitable deal for him to make, and I don't recall that he had any mental qualms about doing so."[3] Similarly, John Brunton – who was, in the 1960s and 1970s, vice-president of Larkin Lumber, a CanCorp company – recalled that as a royal commissioner and a politician Gordon had been concerned over foreign investment, "but business was something else."[4] Gordon justified the deal by saying that "we were forced to sell those companies against our will." Fully 40 per cent of the companies' supplies were coming from International Paper, and the American company had given CanCorp an ultimatum: "Sell to us or we'll take our business away and start up on our own." According to Gordon, the companies "were sold to Americans because we had a gun to our head."[5] He preferred to sell out to Americans rather than to risk losing money competing with them.

There was no gun to Gordon's head on another occasion when he helped an American firm expand into the Canadian market. In 1957 CanCorp entered into a deal with Motorola Inc. of Chicago. Under the agreement, Gordon's company would create and build a plant for Canadian Motorola Electronics and would own 85 per cent of this new firm, with Motorola Inc. owning the remaining 15 per cent. The American company would be entitled to purchase controlling interest in the Canadian subsidiary before the end of 1971, which it did at the end of 1968.[6] In essence, Gordon had helped Motorola, an American enterprise, attain a foothold in Canada, which the company later used to establish dominance over Canada's cellular telephone market.

As a result of its activities in the 1950s, Canadian Corporate Management showed impressive profits. In 1959 the company had a $2-million capital profit, no doubt largely a result of the deal with International Paper. From 1950 to 1959 the value of a common share in Canadian Corporate Management increased from 79¢ to $22.85, almost thirty times the original value.[7] "One of the ironies of Walter's life," recalled Alastair Gillespie, vice-president of CanCorp in the mid-1960s, "is that he made a substantial amount of money by selling Canadian enterprises to Americans." According to Gillespie, this "very basic inconsistency" was well known on Bay Street and likely accounted for much of the anger generated towards Gordon when, as a politician, he tried to limit American ownership in Canada.[8]

One of the most important factors in Gordon's rise as a politician and his ability to spread his ideas was his relationship with the *Toronto Star*. From its early days the *Star* had been a left-leaning liberal paper with a nationalist edge.[9] In 1948 the *Star*'s long-time publisher, Joseph E. Atkinson, passed away, leaving his 80 per cent share of the paper to the Atkinson Charitable Foundation. Atkinson, or "Holy Joe," as he was often known, had established the foundation in 1942 because he was concerned that the paper would fall into the hands of Conservative owners. Atkinson knew that after his death his successors could only pay his estate taxes by selling a large share of the paper. Because there were few wealthy Liberals interested in the *Star*, his heirs would have no choice but to sell the paper to a Conservative. Atkinson and his legal advisers were shrewd and engineered a strategy to avoid the succession duties. Bequests to charities were not subject to estate taxes. By leaving the paper to the Atkinson Charitable Foundation and appointing the trustees of his estate trustees of the foundation, Atkinson could avoid paying duties while, in effect, bequeathing the paper to the individuals of his choice. Clarkson Gordon had been the *Star*'s accountants for many years and would have been involved in this transaction at an early stage.[10]

This inspired scheme outraged Tory Toronto. The *Toronto Telegram* estimated the estate's worth as "at least $25 million," insisting that the people of Ontario were being robbed of $10 million in succession duties.[11] In response, Ontario Treasurer Leslie Frost introduced the Charitable Gifts Act, which prohibited any charity from owning more than 10 per cent of a business enterprise, meaning that the Atkinson Foundation would have to sell controlling interest in the paper. "The idea, clearly," in the words of journalist Doug Fetherling, "was to force the *Star* out of business – or at least to force its sale into hands more friendly to the government."[12] The potential buyers, such as Roy Thomson and Cyrus Eaton, did not share Atkinson's liberal views.

Indeed, the most likely buyer was a group of Toronto Conservatives that included E.P. Taylor, J.A. "Bud" McDougald, Wallace McCutcheon, and W.E. Phillips.[13]

The deadline for the sale of the Atkinson Foundation's shares in the *Star* expired in April 1956. Leslie Frost, now premier, found himself in a difficult position. Public opposition to the Charitable Gifts Act was much more vocal than he had expected, and most of the press was accusing him of trying to silence an opposition paper. Even so, as premier he could not allow the foundation to break the law. Frost, a consummate politician, searched for a compromise. He approached his friend Walter Gordon and asked him to work out an arrangement for the trustees to buy the paper, preventing the *Star* from being sold on the open market.[14] Gordon arranged for the Atkinson Charitable Foundation to sell the *Star* to Hawthorn Publishing Limited (later known as Toronto Star Limited). In early 1958 the Ontario Supreme Court authorized the purchase of the *Star* for $25.6 million.[15] The trustees put up about $1 million in cash and raised most of the rest from the public through bonds, debentures, and preference shares. The initial cash investment by Beland Honderich, the *Star*'s editor-in-chief, was roughly $150,000, which he raised with Gordon's help.[16] Over the next few years Honderich and the other shareholders repaid their loans from the large dividends that they paid themselves. Though they had assumed a very large financial risk, they had, in the end, got the paper for free. The deal made Honderich and the other shareholders very wealthy.

His relationship with the *Star* gave Gordon the ability to spread his ideas, particularly in Toronto. The *Star* had the largest circulation of any paper in Canada and had enormous influence in Toronto and the rest of Ontario. The paper had a particularly strong sway over Liberal party policy. As one editor said, "*Star* policy is Liberal policy. Or will be Liberal policy within two years." After Gordon saved the paper for the trustees, Honderich developed a deep admiration for him, described by *Toronto Telegram* publisher John Bassett as almost "an adoration." Though they were close friends, and Gordon asked to be called "Walter," Honderich never referred to him as anything but "Mr Gordon." Hartland Molson, a friend of both men, remembered that Honderich would speak of Gordon in "almost a religious tone." Honderich also imposed this admiration for Gordon on the *Star*'s editors. According to Charles Templeton, managing editor in the early 1960s, "Honderich insisted that, whenever Gordon made a speech, the story be carried on page one. Sometimes such a display was valid; Gordon often made news. At other times, the story was unimportant and trivialized the front page."[17]

In the years following the sale of the paper to Atkinson's trustees, Gordon and the *Star* developed a relationship that was exceptional and intense. When Gordon returned from a trip to China in 1959, the paper published a series of ten articles that he had written.[18] The *Star* also ran excerpts from Gordon's memoirs and his book *Storm Signals*.[19] According to Bob Nielsen, chief editorial writer in the 1950s and 1960s, Gordon was "by far the most influential person on *Star* policy."[20] To the *Star*'s critics the favourable coverage of Walter Gordon was his reward for having saved the paper.[21] In later years journalist and politician Douglas Fisher would call the paper the *Daily Walter Gordon*. Fisher considered Gordon "a creation – as a politician – of the *Toronto Star* and Mr. Honderich."[22] Though Fisher was exaggerating when he called Honderich the most significant influence on post-war Canadian policy, there can be little doubt that he was one of the most powerful members of the fourth estate.[23] In the post-war years the *Star* was, in the words of former editor Peter C. Newman, "the chief house organ of Canadian nationalism."[24] It was also the chief promoter of Walter Gordon. "One can wonder," remarked Alastair Gillespie, "if Walter Gordon would have been the major force he was without the *Toronto Star*."[25]

Gordon's political career benefited also from his relationship with Mike Pearson, who entered the Liberal leadership race after Louis St Laurent retired in 1957. As early as 1949 Gordon had mentioned to Pearson the possibility of his being the next prime minister.[26] In 1955 Gordon told his friend that the country needed him as prime minister: "I have a feeling that people would like to follow your star – in droves – if and when you decide the time is right to give them the nod."[27] After Pearson received the Nobel Prize in 1957, Gordon helped to organize a giant dinner attended by two thousand guests. He arranged the event, in part, "to help Pearson win the leadership convention and, if he did so, to help him re-establish the fortunes of the Liberal Party."[28] At the leadership convention in Ottawa in January 1958, Gordon acted as Pearson's campaign manager, and, having discovered that the campaign had no funds, he himself paid the bills, a total of $3,000.[29]

Pearson won the leadership handily – 1,074 votes to 305 for his opponent, Paul Martin – and a few months later, on 31 March 1958, faced a general election. He turned to Walter Gordon for help, asking his friend to run as a candidate in one of the Toronto ridings. Fearing defeat, Gordon refused: "I did not believe that in the current climate of opinion I could be elected ... I pointed out that, if I ran and lost, my potential usefulness to the Liberal Party would be finished." Instead, Gordon offered to help Pearson with his policy speeches, assistance that some Liberal party stalwarts resented.[30]

After the election, which the Conservative party won with a record 208 seats, C.D. Howe wrote to his former Cabinet colleague Walter Harris: "I took the liberty of telling Mike that advice from those who have never been elected to office, and are unwilling to be candidates for office, must be regarded with scepticism. I doubt if he believes that even now."[31]

For a year after the election Gordon played little role in Liberal party politics, largely because of his work for the Committee on the Organization of Government in Ontario, which required him to remain non-partisan. In early 1958, while the federal election was in progress, Leslie Frost had asked him to chair a committee studying the structure of the provincial government. Gordon declined: "I pointed out to him that ... I was a close friend of Mike Pearson's and would be embarrassed to take on anything while the [election] campaign was in progress."[32] Frost replied that he would gladly wait until after the election before announcing the creation of the committee, with Gordon as its chair. Appointed in May 1958, the committee investigated all aspects of government organization, concentrating particularly on the role of boards and commissions. Frost gave Gordon a free hand, saying that the committee would be "clothed with the powers of a Royal Commission" if the chairman desired.[33] The committee's report, released in January 1960, asserted the principle of ministerial responsibility for all government activities, including those of government agencies.[34]

In September 1959, after Gordon finished his work for the Ontario committee, he offered to reorganize the Liberal party. Gordon took this first tentative step into politics because of his friendship with Pearson, his interest in implementing his own policies, and his strong dislike of Diefenbaker.[35] "By this time he had acquired a very deep and strong feeling that Mr. Diefenbaker was going to ruin this country," Pearson remembered.[36] Gordon was not a partisan Liberal, but as he later told a reporter, "I had become disgusted at the way our country was being run. I felt the only means of correction was to get the present government out of office."[37] Gordon later showed his level of contempt for Diefenbaker in a letter to Douglas LePan, saying that the Tory leader "does remind me of Hitler who was far more dangerous."[38]

Pearson accepted Gordon's offer of help. After talking to the members of the Liberal hierarchy about the party's organization, Gordon reported to Pearson in a letter dated 5 November 1959. Gordon's suggestions focused on personnel, much as they did when he worked as a management consultant. He recommended that Pearson replace Mary Macdonald, the executive assistant who had worked in his office since 1947. Pearson should ask George Marler, the party's executive vice-president, and Henry Erskine "Bob" Kidd, the general secretary responsible for the day-to-day operations of party head-quarters, to submit their resignations "without delay." Pearson should also discharge several of the party's paid staff members, "again without delay." Gordon recommended that Kidd be replaced by James Scott, who would hold the title of national organizer and would report to a committee rather than to the party leader or president. The committee would be chaired by someone who would act as Pearson's deputy on organizational matters and who, preferably, would also be party treasurer. "I have not anyone in mind as yet – except myself," Gordon wrote, "but will hope to come up with a more satisfactory suggestion before I see you."[39] Gordon remembered that "Pearson agreed to these recommendations with considerable reluctance." But he delayed taking action, waiting more than a year before creating the proposed committee. On the staffing issues, Gordon took the initiative and fired Kidd himself. A member of the old guard, Kidd was upset at the new prominence of Gordon and his friends. "The inner councils of the party," he wrote, "now seem to be dominated by men from Toronto." He appreciated Gordon's fund-raising efforts, which included collecting $200,000 to repay a bank loan. "Yet the question may arise, whether this gives him the right to exercise absolute control over expenditures to the point where he may veto not only undertakings given by the president of the National Liberal Federation – but by the Leader himself?" In Kidd's view, the changes were "a palace revolution."[40]

While he was taking charge of the party apparatus, Gordon joined forces with a group of Liberals who went by the name "Cell 13." The leader of this group was Gordon Dryden, and its members included Royce Frith, Dan Lang, Richard Stanbury, Judy LaMarsh, Paul Hellyer, James Scott, Boyd Upper, Gordon Edick, and Keith Davey. A desire to return the Liberal party to power, not a common ideology, united Cell 13. After the 1958 election the group had taken over the party in Toronto, electing Davey as president of the Toronto and Yorks Liberal Association, Frith as president of the Ontario Liberal Association, and Lang as the provincial association's treasurer. In May 1961 Davey replaced Jim Scott as national director of the Liberal party. Edick remembered that, when he first got involved in the party in 1958, there was "talk and damned little action." Gordon and Cell 13 changed that. In Edick's words, "I've never seen such a transformation in my life."[41]

Gordon's role in the Liberal party extended beyond organization; he was equally interested in policy and its implementation. Writing to Pearson in March 1960, he outlined his position, saying that he wanted a party platform that was "leftish, imaginative, reasonably clear cut and that ... will discard as many as possible of the old theories and beliefs that are no longer relevant." He also laid out his own ambitions: "I can say without reservation that I would like to serve under you as Minister of Finance. The job would intrigue me both because I would enjoy participating as a senior Minister in Canada's international negotiations and because I would like to help you tidy up our present domestic policies or lack of them. At long last, I seem to have got my gout under control with the result that I feel better than I have for many years."[42]

Gordon knew that many members of the Liberal party would not accept his positions on foreign investment or defence. In his letter to Pearson, Gordon said that his views were unchanged from those he had expressed in the royal commission reports. On foreign investment, he explained that he was "unhappy about the gradual economic and financial take-over by the United States, or rather by the owners of United States capital, that is taking place and if I were in public life I would wish to urge some modest steps to counteract what is presently going on in this direction." Gordon's views on defence policy showed a similar concern over American influence. He believed that Canada should pursue an independent defence policy, possibly by cancelling the NORAD agreement, a step that would lead to a "full dress argument, or showdown, with the Americans."[43]

In February 1960 Gordon began to put his ideas on record in a series of public statements.[44] These speeches are crucial to understanding Gordon because, as he later admitted, his opinions did not change substantially afterward.[45] He outlined his views on many public policy issues, with particular attention to unemployment and monetary policy. He insisted that Canada could not remain a separate country if it did not take steps to halt the integration of the Canadian and American economies, a process he described as "tempting, insidious, considerable and continuous." Though a greater consolidation of the two economies "might conceivably result in a higher standard of living for Canadians eventually," Gordon rejected this option, partly because he thought that it would lead to considerable disruption in the economy and an increase in unemployment. "And quite apart from this, surely the loss of our economic independence, which to some extent would follow inevitably from economic integration with the United States, would sooner or later mean the end of our political independence also."[46] Gordon never provided any argumentation to support his assertion that free trade would lead to political union with the United States. Nor did he examine the relationship between the tariff and the high levels of foreign ownership in Canada. He never considered that the tariff was a cause of the high levels of foreign ownership and the branch-plant mentality that he so despised.[47]

In Gordon's mind, foreign investment, like free trade, threatened Canada's political independence. He recognized that limiting foreign investment and maintaining the tariff would require Canadians to pay "some sort of price in terms of a less rapid rise in our standard of living." He left no doubt, however, that he believed Canadians should accept this sacrifice: "I for one am prepared to say without any qualification that I hope Canadians will choose to regain a greater measure of economic independence than we now have." Beyond Gordon's unsupported assertions about the threats to Canada's independence, the speeches presented no substantial arguments against foreign investment. He did not – as he had in the royal commission reports – raise questions about the performance of foreign firms in Canada.[48]

On the issue of defence, Gordon began by expressing the mainstream view: "The Americans are our friends – our very best friends – even if at times we may find their attentions a little overpowering. And the Russian Communists are not our friends, let us remember. We do not like their system and do not want to be part of it." He believed that the United Nations and NATO were "the cornerstones of Canadian foreign policy, and should remain so." Gordon, however, had doubts about the NORAD arrangement, which he believed "was entered into so hurriedly and obviously without much serious consideration." In his view NORAD "seems to boil down to the fact that Canada has contributed a few squadrons to the American Air Force."[49]

Copies of his speeches from February, May, and June, as well as a draft of the speech he would deliver in August, accompanied a letter that Gordon sent Pearson on 12 July 1960. He told Pearson that the speeches, together with the royal commission reports, covered "practically everything on which I have any views that matter." Before he would become more involved in the Liberal party, Gordon was anxious to know that Pearson shared his views on public policy. As he later recalled, he was aware of Pearson's "habit of changing emphasis (or perhaps even direction) from time to time depending on the direction of the wind. It was a wrench for me to give up my professional practice and I did not wish to do this and then find that Pearson had become less enthusiastic than he appeared about my economic views."[50] Gordon's letter to Pearson outlined his position: "I need not emphasize the importance of this whole subject to both of us. It is imperative that there should be no misunderstandings ... I can easily go to Ottawa on Friday afternoon if you think a conversation would be useful."[51] Gordon noted Pearson's response two days later: "Mike called to say he … agreed *completely* with my ideas. He repeated this two or three times saying that this is exactly how he feels on these various issues with particular emphasis on the draft speech for Aug. 29."[52] Gordon remembered that this conversation resolved "any doubts I may have had about possible differences of opinion about policies." Gordon was now fully committed to Pearson and the Liberal party. Without Pearson's assurances, Gordon later recalled, "I would not have participated so enthusiastically in the effort to make him Prime Minister."[53]

Two months after his conversation with Pearson, Gordon attended the Study Conference on National Problems, usually known as the Kingston Conference. Pearson had asked Mitchell Sharp, a vice-president of Brazilian Traction, Light and Power Corporation and former deputy minister of trade and commerce, to organize the conference. Like the Port Hope Conference of 1933, the event was designed not as a Liberal party convention but rather as a gathering of liberal-minded thinkers, many of whom were close friends of Gordon, including individuals from the worlds of journalism, academia, politics, business, and labour. Gordon welcomed the conference, telling Pearson he hoped that, after the event, "the Liberal Party will produce a dynamic expansionist philosophy and programme which it will be prepared to go to bat for."[54]

Pearson had told Gordon privately that he agreed completely with his friend's views, and his opening speech at the Kingston Conference publicly reinforced this commitment. Pearson repeated Gordon's argument that economic interdependence threatened political independence, saying that Canada's dependence on the United States for trade and capital was "an increasing threat to our independence." "Have we escaped the colonial frying-pan merely to have jumped into the Washington fire?" Pearson asked. "Have we sold our birth-right for a mess of below-par u.s. dollars?" Though he avoided any specifics, Pearson insisted that foreign investment was "a major problem and I am equally convinced that there is something we, as a Party, can do about it and should – and will."[55]

On the first day of the conference Gordon was a commentator at a session entitled "How Independent Can We Be?" The speaker was Michael Barkway of the *Financial Post*, an early supporter of Gordon's views. While the Gordon Commission was doing its work, Barkway's articles had condemned the level of foreign investment in Canada, and his newspaper continued to express this view through the early 1960s. At Kingston, Barkway argued for several policy changes that would make Canada more independent of the United States. Canada should remain part of NATO, but the country's defence policies should be more detached from those of the United States: "Strategically, apart from our obligations to NATO, we should be in the same position as one of the Latin American republics." Barkway also advanced ten complaints against the practices of American-owned firms, including the tendency to ship raw materials to the United States for processing, to export less than Canadian-owned firms, to hire consulting services from the United States, to use research and designs developed in the United States, to pursue purchasing policies directed by the parent company, and to favour American suppliers. Barkway suggested that the government urge foreign-owned firms to change their practices, a policy "not necessarily involving immediate legislation, but always looking to the possibility of it."[56]

Gordon, the session's first commentator, agreed "that Canada should take steps to regain a greater measure of independence." He accepted Barkway's complaints about foreign-owned firms, mentioning in particular the lack of research work in Canada, but said that he was not interested in exerting pressure on such firms to change their practices. Instead, Gordon wanted to limit foreign ownership: "I would like to see changes in our tax structure designed to encourage U.S. and other foreign owners of Canadian subsidiaries to sell part or all of their companies to Canadians." Gordon agreed with Barkway's argument that Canada should pursue more independent foreign and defence policies because "in the long run we are likely to wield more influences in the world if, upon occasion, when we disagree with our friends and allies, we are prepared to say so."[57]

The two other commentators and the members of the audience were more critical of Barkway. William Hood, an economist at the University of Toronto and former assistant director of research for the Gordon Commission, criticized the paper, saying that its emphasis was "largely misplaced." Hood believed that the government could best help Canada's independence by fostering Canadian business rather than by discouraging foreign investment. The government, he thought, should help industry by retraining workers and assisting in their relocation, investing in education, and offering tax concessions to firms undertaking expenditures in research and development. Hood, however, did not support other measures "for dealing with foreign enterprises in Canada and the importation into Canada of the products of foreign enterprises." And he specifically rejected protectionist trade policies as detrimental to Canadian ownership: "Protection invites foreign enterprise to a country – our own history demonstrates that." Hood repeated what John Young had said in his detailed report for the Gordon Commission: "Protection is a costly policy."

Hood was followed by Montreal consultant Harry Wolfson, who raised serious questions about the assumptions that underlay the ideas of Barkway and Gordon. Wolfson questioned the difference between American and Canadian businesses, asking whether anyone seriously believed that Canadian shareholders or directors had a substantially different motivation from their American counterparts. He admitted that there were some instances of American firms operating differently from Canadian companies, but maintained that the government could pass legislation to deal with these cases rather than limiting the extent of foreign ownership in Canada. Even if legislation could not prevent these problems, American investment was a small price to pay for an increase in national production.

After Hood and Wolfson had finished, those attending the session were given an opportunity to participate in the discussion. Most disagreed with Barkway's paper. The historian Frank Underhill won an ovation for his comment that the Liberal party had traditionally been close to the United States and should leave anti-American preaching to the Conservatives. Underhill could not see how Canadians would benefit by substituting "the wolves of Bay Street" for the "wolves of Wall Street."[58]

At the session entitled "External Economic Policy" the main speaker was Harry Johnson, who had recently moved from the University of Manchester to the University of Chicago. Johnson was on his way to becoming a commanding figure among professional economists and a sharp critic of Gordon's ideas. At roughly six feet and weighing far more than two hundred pounds, Johnson was a big man, both physically and intellectually. William Kilbourn, one of the conference organizers, remembered that "Johnson dominated any room he was in." According to economist David Slater, "Johnson was regarded as the best Canadian-born economist of his generation." He published more articles in scholarly journals than any other economist, and was reputed to be the only one to have written two articles during one trans-Atlantic flight. In the words of economist J. Vandercamp, Johnson had "a vast capacity for reading, he had the unrivalled ability to provide a critical overview of a subject area." Though he had little direct sway over policy-makers, Johnson was influential in academic circles. He usually spent a few weeks each summer at Queen's University's Institute for Economic Research, where he met most of the promising young Canadian economists, many of whom felt a great debt to him. A very intense man and a heavy drinker, Johnson was not known to be tolerant; in the words of economist Bernard Bonin, he was "a debater" and "a fighter." Dismissive of the Gordon Commission's report, Johnson refused to accept foreign investment as a legitimate topic for public debate. In Johnson's speeches and articles, Walter Gordon was to become his favourite target.[59]

Johnson's presentation attacked the arguments that Barkway and Gordon had made the previous day. Johnson argued aggressively that protectionist policies and measures to control foreign investment reflected "not so much of the noble spirit of Canadian independence, as the small, smug mind and large larcenous hands of Bay Street." Johnson continued, insisting that free trade with the United States "would be of great economic advantage to both countries, and especially to Canada. It would give Canadian producers free and, what is perhaps more important, secure access to the American market. It would also lower the cost of living in Canada and raise Canadian real income towards the American level." There was, according to one witness, a "big ovation" when Johnson criticized Gordon's arguments against economic integration. He cited John Young's work for the Gordon Commission, accepting his "fairly reliable estimate" that the cost of the tariff was roughly $1 billion in 1956. "The cost of the present degree of protection to Canada is extremely high, and the gain obtainable by eliminating it correspondingly great," he argued. Accepting that some inefficient industries would suffer under free trade, Johnson pointed out that many Canadian enterprises and the Canadian economy in general would thrive with the elimination of both Canadian and American tariff barriers. The American tariff, according to Johnson, forced many American firms to locate in the United States when it might have made more sense to establish plants in Canada, where they would have close access to abundant raw materials and would benefit from lower wage levels. He ended his remarks by asking a simple question: "Why do you want inefficient industries to prosper at the expense of the public?"[60]

Most of the session's participants agreed with Johnson's arguments for free trade. Robert Fowler believed that neither free trade nor American investment threatened Canadian independence. Fowler worried, however, about the possibility of persuading Canadians and Americans to accept a policy of tariff reduction. Two economists formerly with the Gordon Commission also supported Johnson's views. Edward English favoured free trade, arguing that it would lead to increased specialization but would not affect the overall level of employment. Similarly, John Young had little quarrel with Johnson's analysis, though he did not think that there was a simple choice between Johnson's argument for free trade and Gordon's view that the government should hold the tariff at the same general level, a comment that won widespread applause. Young thought that Canada should work towards free trade, but should do so gradually. Only a few participants expressed strong reservations about Johnson's ideas. R.B. MacPherson, a Montreal economist with DuPont, argued that economic integration with the United States could lead to the exodus of Canadian manufacturing to the United States and to a large drop in Canada's income. In a similar vein, Gordon dismissed Johnson's views as extreme, and insisted that free trade would cause unemployment.[61]

Most of the economists at the Kingston Conference reacted to Gordon's ideas in the same negative, almost condescending way that they had responded to his royal commission's proposals on trade and investment. A comment by economist Ian Drummond illustrates their general attitude: "Nationalists are always getting their economic analysis wrong, and economists are always trying to set them right."[62] But in the 1950s and 1960s economists were often too certain in their convictions and too quick to dismiss ideas that originated from outside their closed circle. Many of the views they espoused with such certainty in the 1960s seem misguided a generation later. Gordon's weakness was not that he had challenged the professionals in their field of expertise, merely that he had often done so in an ill-considered way and without sufficient argumentation.

Most of the Kingston Conference participants, including many non-economists, opposed Gordon's views on Canada's economic relationship with the United States. Davidson Dunton, president of Carleton University, was one of those called upon to present a review of the discussions at the end of the conference. Most of the participants thought that "there wasn't much clear evidence of great harm being done" by foreign investment, Dunton said. "Certainly, there was not much evidence that there were greater disadvantages from that capital inflow here than there were advantages."[63] The *Winnipeg Free Press* agreed with this summary: "Not a single voice was raised in support of Mr. Gordon's or Mr. Barkway's views ... On the contrary both were severely criticized for a form of economic chauvinism."[64] In reviewing the debate on the tariff, Dunton suggested that it would be hard for any liberal-minded person "to go away from here and casually, or by mistake, argue for higher tariffs, or not work on every possible and practical occasion for tariff reform and reduction of tariffs."[65] George Brimwell of the *Toronto Telegram* observed that "the sentiment of the conference" was for lower tariffs "in the Liberal tradition."[66]

Perhaps the most important papers at the Kingston conference were those by Maurice Lamontagne and Tom Kent, calling for the completion of Canada's social security system. Lamontagne's paper centred on limiting unemployment, arguing that the government should expand the public sector of the economy, encourage the growth of resource and secondary manufacturing industries, and help to develop depressed areas such as the Atlantic provinces. Kent's paper called for medical and sickness insurance, employment training, regional development, urban renewal, public housing, education reform, and an increase in Unemployment Insurance benefits. The government would fund these programs by a substantial inheritance tax and by removing certain business tax deductions, including the deduction for advertising and promotion.[67]

Old-guard Liberals were wary of the new policies advocated at the conference. Paul Martin opposed the conference, believing that it gave a platform to non-Liberals.[68] C.D. Howe was particularly critical of Tom Kent's involvement, saying that he had "done more harm to the Liberal Party, both in Manitoba and Federally during his short stay in Canada, than anyone I know. Surely the Party can do better than that."[69] "I am afraid," Howe wrote to a friend, "that Mike is being advised by the wrong type of officers. The meeting of the 'Thinkers Club' certainly did not help him politically."[70] But Howe did not realize that John Connolly, a veteran Liberal, had first suggested the Kingston Conference, and that the idea's main proponent was Lester Pearson himself.[71]

At the Kingston Conference, Gordon formed a new alliance that would shape the Liberal party. Tom Kent was an English intellectual who had worked for the *Manchester Guardian* and the *Economist* before coming to Canada to edit the *Winnipeg Free Press*. He had an active and imaginative mind, and was a prolific writer. Kent had produced the sharpest, most sustained attack on the Gordon Commission reports and, before the Kingston Conference, still thought of Gordon as a "Bay Street type."[72] In the late 1950s Kent and Gordon had been competing influences on Pearson and had been suspicious of each other. But after Kent's Kingston speech, Gordon approached him and praised him for advocating policies that would help the Liberals to outflank the newly formed New Democratic Party, saying that he wanted to "shake the hand that has strangled the New Party before it's born." According to Kent, "that handshake was the beginning of an alliance that never afterwards faltered."[73] Gordon, chair of the policy committee for the upcoming National Rally, wrote to Kent asking him to join an informal group that would co-ordinate the policy resolutions. Kent accepted the offer and said that he was particularly pleased with Gordon's appointment as policy chair "because nowadays our views are reasonably close together on most matters!"[74] Though the two men had found common ground on social policy,

Kent continued to disagree with Gordon's views and his emphasis on the issue of foreign investment.[75]

The National Rally of the Liberal party took place in Ottawa in January 1961. Gordon had taken the position as policy chair knowing that it was not "a request for advice or new ideas" but simply "a means to trap me into publicly declaring my allegiance" to the Liberal party. Gordon was happy to accept because, as he explained, "since 1955 I have had a sneaking wish to see some political party adopt policies that, to me, would seem slightly less unwise than the ones they usually advocate."[76]

The National Rally approved several resolutions dealing with a wide range of issues. One of the policies came under the heading "For a Strong and Independent Canada." This proposal was clearly designed to please both sides of the foreign investment debate. Stressing the important role that foreign capital had played in Canada's development, it emphasised Canada's continued need for such investment. The resolution warned, however, that Canadians "must make quite sure that such industries are operated in a way that will contribute fully to a growing Canadian economy in accordance with accepted Canadian standards and with acknowledge[ment] of and regard for Canadian aspirations." The party did not advocate legislation to limit outside investment, instead favouring policies "to encourage greater Canadian participation in the ownership of Canadian enterprises." Measures to foster domestic investment would include tax incentives, a program to educate Canadians about the importance of investing their savings in Canada, and an amendment to legislation dealing with the investment of pension, trust, and insurance funds. The resolution never suggested that the government discourage foreign investment, except for investment in banks and trust companies, which by law would remain under Canadian ownership and control. Another policy dealt with international trade and showed little affinity with Gordon's ideas, saying, "A new Liberal government will promote world trade on the widest possible basis." The resolution avoided the issue of free trade with the United States, instead pushing for multilateral trade agreements.[77] The party also approved several strongly reformist policies, supporting health insurance, pension reform, a scholarship plan, and regional development funds.

The rally further cemented Gordon's position in the Liberal party. By the end of the conference Gordon was recognized, in the words of Maurice Sauvé, as "leader of the progressive and reformist element in the Party." Sauvé had been among a group of Gordon's supporters who had pushed to have him appointed party president.[78] They gave up when Pearson told them that Gordon would chair a committee to handle planning and strategy for the upcoming federal election. According to Tom Axworthy, Senator John Connolly was appointed party president to keep the traditionalists happy. Pearson would chair the new Leader's Advisory Committee and would appoint Gordon vice-chair, ensuring that his friend had effective control of the party.[79]

Pearson had created the Leader's Advisory Committee on the suggestion of Paul Hellyer, who noted that Gordon was causing resentment among the old guard because he was "a 'Johnny-come-lately' who hadn't yet earned his spurs on the political battlefield." Gordon, according to Hellyer, "would breeze in and make decisions, or at least give that impression, with little recognition that the senior members of the party even existed."[80] Hellyer had found that Pearson "didn't want to move without Walter Gordon," and he remembered that "all of us, but especially Martin and Chevrier and Connolly and Pickersgill, were all less than enthusiastic or perhaps a bit suspicious of his role in things."[81] Martin believed that the role of veteran Liberals had been diminished by Gordon's ascendancy: "I knew that if I intervened in matters to do with party organization, I would be sent away with a flea in my ear." In Martin's view, "our leader relied too much on the new captains of the party, who had scant political experience."[82] Pearson heeded Hellyer's advice and created a committee composed of Pearson, Gordon, the party president (Connolly), the past president (Bruce Matthews), the former Liberal Cabinet ministers who still sat in the Commons (Lionel Chevrier, J.W. Pickersgill, Martin, and Hellyer), the national director (Davey), and the top advisers from the office of the leader of the Opposition (Allan MacEachen, Maurice Lamontagne, Tom Kent, and Richard O'Hagan).[83] Under the new committee structure Gordon would continue as Pearson's pre-eminent adviser, but the veterans would have an opportunity to comment on his ideas.[84]

Having effectively taken over the organization of the party, Gordon continued to try to shape party policy. In the summer of 1961 he wrote *Troubled Canada: The Need for New Domestic Policies*. The book was researched by Dave Ferguson, a consultant at Woods Gordon. After Gordon and Ferguson went through many drafts, Gordon showed the manuscript to his brother Duncan, whose advice he often sought. As a result of Duncan's comments, Gordon substantially changed the tone of the book, moderating its partisanship.[85] Published in November, the book was a broad-based attack on the Diefenbaker government. By June of 1962 it had sold approximately two thousand copies, Gordon buying roughly one-quarter of this number.[86]

In *Troubled Canada* Gordon explained his ideas in cold economic terms but never offered any sustained analysis. He argued that lower interest rates and a devaluation of the Canadian dollar would encourage exports, discourage imports and foreign borrowing, and generate employment and growth. He admitted that Canada had profited from the presence of foreign capital, benefiting from American research and technology as well as "scientific, technical and managerial expertise."[87] Even so, he insisted, these benefits were outweighed by the tremendous disadvantages of foreign investment.

Troubled Canada was one of the first Canadian books to discuss the problem known as extraterritoriality: the application of foreign laws to foreign-owned firms operating in Canada. Gordon was particularly concerned with the extraterritorial application of American anti-trust laws and the Trading with the Enemy Act, which prevented American-owned companies from trading with China, Cuba, North Korea, or North Vietnam.[88] The first well-publicized case of extraterritoriality had been the controversial decision of the Ford Motor Company to prevent its Canadian subsidiary from exporting trucks to China in early 1958, a decision that came at a time of high unemployment in the Canadian automotive industry.[89]

The book's argument on foreign investment had first been expressed in the reports of Gordon's royal commission. He worried that foreign-owned firms were not promoting Canadian officers and that "technical and scientific personnel are not given sufficient opportunities to use their imagination and skills because the subsidiaries have access to the research being done by the foreign parent company." The subsequent sentences confused Gordon's intent: "Such instances may be the exception rather than the rule. Most companies probably prefer to promote people from within the organization … rather than bring people … from the parent companies. But when exceptions to this occur, they are talked about and at times exaggerated even when the reasons for them may be sound enough. And when so many of the bigger companies are controlled by Americans, this sort of thing can be harmful to Canadian-American relations. It is one of the inevitable results of absentee ownership."[90] Gordon acknowledged that most foreign firms hired and promoted Canadians. Using an odd line of reasoning, he argued that the problem was not the business practices of American companies but the Canadian perception. Many Canadians believed, incorrectly, that foreign firms tended to favour foreign employees over Canadians, a misconception that could lead to an anti-American sentiment that would damage Canada's relations with its southern neighbour. Though he admitted that the problem was perceived, not real, Gordon argued against foreign ownership rather than trying to educate Canadians about the true nature of foreign control in Canada.

In *Troubled Canada* Gordon exaggerated the instances where American firms engaged in business practices damaging to Canada. Having said that these cases were exceptional, Gordon none the less insisted that foreign ownership "inhibits the development and training of a large corps of experienced Canadian entrepreneurs, business managers, promoters and financiers." He also repeated what he had said in the royal commission reports, implying that foreign-owned firms tended to import parts and components from outside Canada, that they conducted less research in Canada, and that they were less likely to have Canadian officers. In a particularly revealing passage Gordon insisted that his views "cannot be analyzed scientifically or proved absolutely. But the fact that a judgment or belief is arrived at in part intuitively or through personal experience does not necessarily make it any less true."[91]

Some of Gordon's views, as expressed in his speeches and in *Troubled Canada*, could have been tested with the statistics then available. American-owned firms, contrary to Gordon's assertion, were not less likely to export than their Canadian counterparts. Exports by American-owned companies in 1957 accounted for 41 per cent of Canadian exports, though only 26 per cent of Canadian companies were owned by Americans. Furthermore, American-owned firms did not show an unreasonable tendency to employ American citizens. Only 1 of every 35 supervisory, professional, or technical employees came from the United States, and only 1 of every 241 other employees. The statistics available in the early 1960s also showed the large amount of tax revenue that Canada derived from American-owned firms. In 1957 American firms paid $799 million in Canadian taxes, of which $582 million was in direct corporate income tax, one-third of Canada's total.[92] This was a point that Gordon never raised.

Troubled Canada received a mixed reaction from Canadian economists, most of whom were critical of the section on foreign investment. They accepted Gordon's argument that lower interest rates and a devaluation of the Canadian dollar would create employment. "In describing a desirable monetary and foreign-exchange policy Mr. Gordon is on firm ground," wrote economist Ian Drummond. Drummond, however, was critical of Gordon for not showing any understanding of John Maynard Keynes and budget cycles. Though he accepted Gordon's concern over extraterritoriality, he noted that Gordon did "not provide any economic reason for Canadian employees and consumers to fear American capitalists."[93] Gordon, according to G.L. Reuber, professor at the University of Western Ontario, "invokes the bogey of national independence and appeals to intuition and belief – all of which is rather incongruous in a book emphasizing the need for a more rational approach to economic policy."[94]

Before the publication of *Troubled Canada*, Harry Johnson wrote a stinging rebuke of those who shared Gordon's views. "Canadian nationalism as it has developed in recent years has been diverting Canada into a narrow and garbage-cluttered cul-de-sac," Johnson asserted in his usual caustic style. Concern over foreign investment was distracting Canadians from the true nature of Canada's economic problems. Johnson believed that American investment and Canada's high level of American imports did not mean Canada was dominated by outsiders: "in some ways, on the contrary, they represent Canadian exploitation of the United States." Johnson illustrated his point with two examples. First, he noted that the roughly $500 million of corporate income taxes that Canada collected annually from foreign investments came "more or less directly at the expense of the United States Treasury" since corporations were allowed under American tax law to offset taxes paid in Canada against taxes owed in the United States. Second, he argued that through depletion allowances the United States government was heavily subsidizing Canadian resource development. Most importantly, Johnson denied that trade and investment carried any threat to Canada's economic independence. Americans doing business in Canada did not have the right to vote in Canadian elections, "so Canadian independence as embodied in the sovereignty of Parliament can hardly be threatened that way," a statement as dogmatic as any made by Gordon. Johnson attacked Gordon's frequent assertion that a loss of economic independence would lead inevitably to a loss of political independence. "I would expect," Johnson wrote, "that closer economic integration, by enabling Canadians to achieve a standard of living closer to that of the United States, would make them better able and more willing to use the political sovereignty of their country to pursue political and social policies appropriate to their own conceptions and requirements." Johnson also echoed Tom Kent's influential criticism of the Gordon Report, arguing that Gordon's policies would benefit certain groups in society at the expense of others. Forcing American-owned firms to sell shares to Canadians would mean "that some Canadian capitalists will obtain higher dividend and directorship incomes ... and some Canadian employees of American firms will be paid more." It would also result in "some reduction in the efficiency of the operations of already established enterprises" and "a loss to the country."[95] But it would do little to benefit the country as a whole.

The economists who criticized Gordon hardly noticed the book's failure to assess the impact of American culture on Canada. *Troubled Canada* included a fifteen-page chapter on foreign control of industry but not a word on culture. His next book, *A Choice for Canada*, contained a single page on radio, television, newspapers, and magazines, but the discussion was entirely about ownership, not content; Gordon discussed the cultural industry without considering culture.[96] Gordon mentioned culture briefly in *Storm Signals*, but explained, "These matters have not been touched on, because in dealing with domestic policies, this book has been restricted to economic issues."[97] In a similar vein, Gordon's speeches would occasionally mention aspects of culture, but always in terms of ownership, not content.[98] In general, Gordon's speeches and correspondence are remarkable for their failure to mention Canadian culture. One would expect Gordon, the most prominent Canadian to argue against American influence in Canada, to have been distressed over the dominating presence of American television, cinema, magazines, and novels. Yet he never saw nationality as an expression of culture, always examining the issue in economic and business terms.

Important thinkers would later advance the view that culture was more important to Canadian independence than ownership or trade. In 1962 Canadian novelist Hugh MacLennan dismissed the idea that the threat to Canadian identity came from the economic influence of the United States: "It comes from something far subtler in its effects and more difficult to recognize. It comes from the unplanned American domination of so much of our internal communications, with the result that, instead of looking at Canada through our own eyes, or interpreting her through our own speech, we look at her, and often we think about her, without realizing half the time we are doing so, through the eyes, values and interests of our neighbors, who are not thinking of us at all."[99] Canadian-born economist John Kenneth Galbraith agreed, arguing that economic autonomy was unimportant: "If I were still a practicing as distinct from an advisory Canadian I would be much more concerned about maintaining the cultural integrity of the broadcasting system and with making sure Canada has an active independent theatre, book publishing industry, newspapers, magazines and schools of poets and painters ... I wouldn't worry for a moment about the difference between Canadian or American corporations."[100] Gordon was most surely exposed to these ideas; he was a good friend of Galbraith, novelist Robertson Davies, and painters Molly and Bruno Bobak; his wife had a cultivated interest in the arts and played an important role in the acquisition of works for the Ontario Gallery of Art and smaller galleries across the country; their daughter and son-in-law founded Toronto's Tarragon Theatre, one of the first theatres to produce only Canadian plays.[101] Yet never did Gordon embrace the idea that American culture was a primary threat to Canada's identity.

Gordon's ideas had little appeal in Quebec, where culture was an important issue, and his book was not translated into French. The most likely publisher was Jacques Hébert of Les Editions du Jour, who declined the opportunity to publish the book, saying, "I am not sure that the book, in French, could interest a sufficiently large portion of our market."[102] In a memorandum to Pearson, economist Maurice Lamontagne explained why. For most French Canadians, he said, "the most immediate danger did not come from the United States but from English-speaking Canada." Increases in foreign capital did not affect French-speaking businessmen, who had never held a dominant position in the province's economy. American owners only replaced English Canadians, "already considered in Quebec as 'foreign' sources of capital." Moreover, American investment brought considerable economic benefits to Quebec, particularly high wages and increased employment opportunities. "The results were considered as being very desirable and contributed to create a favourable climate for American capital in Quebec."[103]

Gordon faced opposition in certain quarters of the Liberal party as well. In another memorandum to Pearson, Lamontagne indicated that not everyone in the party's ranks accepted Gordon's ideas on trade. Gordon had argued that free trade would disrupt the Canadian economy, but Lamontagne thought that "this contention is greatly exaggerated."[104] Lamontagne's view had also been the consensus at the Kingston Conference, where most participants supported the open flow of goods and capital between countries. Throughout the opposition years, key figures in the party, like Jack Pickersgill and Mitchell Sharp, did not believe that it was Liberal policy to limit foreign investment.[105] Kent agreed: "it was never officially Liberal party policy. It was Walter's view."[106]

But for a while it was also Pearson's view. He had assured Gordon that he "agreed *completely*" with his views and had told the Kingston Conference that a Liberal government under his leadership would do something about the "major problem" posed by U.S. capital. When he received letters opposing foreign investment, Pearson's response, likely drafted by a staff member, sounded a lot like Gordon, arguing that "it will be necessary to make a number of changes in our tax laws which will discourage Canadians from selling Canadian resources and Canadian-owned companies to foreigners; and at the same time encourage foreigners and foreign corporations to sell their assets here back to Canadians." Pearson suggested that, as a first step, foreign firms should sell a minority of shares to Canadians, "but the ultimate objective must be to buy back Canadian resources and Canadian companies to the maximum possible extent." He concluded by assuring the reader "that if the

Liberal Party is called upon to form a government under my Leadership, action along these lines will be taken."[107] How could Gordon be faulted for thinking that Pearson agreed with him?

But Pearson was not a strong economic nationalist. Rather he was, in the words of Jack Pickersgill, "a status nationalist. He wanted the flag, the Order of Canada, ceremonial changes so Canadians could stop feeling like quasi-colonials. But he wasn't interested in economic affairs."[108] Pearson's son Geoffrey agreed, telling a reporter that his father "wasn't an economic nationalist ... [H]e didn't have enough knowledge or grasp of monetary and fiscal policy or wasn't enough interested to develop a coherent view on that subject."[109] Pearson also did not share Gordon's general distrust of American influence. He had served in the Canadian embassy in Washington and had come to know most of the Americans in high government positions. He had many American friends and liked American culture, particularly baseball and musicals. Every year he enjoyed spending some time in New York.[110]

Heavily reliant on Gordon's skills as an organizer and fund-raiser, Pearson also found himself looking to Gordon for advice on economic policy. Despite his doubts about economic nationalism, he converted, albeit temporarily, to Gordon's view that the government needed to discourage foreign investment in Canada. But he never felt strongly enough about the issue to have it adopted as party policy over the objection of many senior Liberals. As a result, the Liberal party never defined its position on foreign ownership in the early 1960s. According to Tom Kent, "the nationalist issue as such was simply never faced up to. It didn't feature in all these statements of policy that I drafted and were approved by Mr. Pearson. We really just ignored that issue."[111]

Opinion polls tell an interesting story about the impact of Gordon's ideas on the average Canadian. The Gordon Commission played an important role in raising the level of public opposition to foreign investment. In 1950, 60 per cent of Canadians thought that Canada should continue to encourage American capital to develop its natural resources. By July 1956 this number had dropped substantially. Of those polled, 43 per cent thought that Canada had enough or too much foreign capital; only 33 per cent wanted to see more, while 24 per cent were undecided or had qualified views. This trend continued in the years immediately after the royal commission. By 1961, 52 per cent of Canadians thought that Canada had enough foreign investment; 32 per cent wanted to see more, and 16 per cent were undecided. As the economy grew, so too did opposition to foreign investment. But as memories of McCarthy and Herbert Norman's suicide began to fade and with the economic downturn in the Diefenbaker years, opposition to foreign investment began slowly to drop. A poll in 1963 showed that opposition to further outside investment had fallen to 46 per cent from 52 per cent in 1961.[112]

Much more telling, however, were polls of Ontario and Quebec conducted in 1962 and 1963 for the Liberal party. Though a Gallup poll showed that most Canadians opposed the growth of foreign investment in Canada, the party polls proved that this issue was not very significant to those in central Canada. In September 1962, when asked to identify the main issues facing Canada, less than 1 per cent of Ontarians and only 2 per cent of Quebeckers mentioned foreign investment. A similar poll in January 1963 showed that only 2 per cent of Ontarians and no Quebeckers expressed concern over foreign investment.[113] A poll conducted in March 1963 showed a comparable result: only 1 per cent of voters in Ontario and none in Quebec considered foreign investment a major concern.[114]

Though most Canadians worried little about foreign investment, Gordon's ideas won important converts. After Gordon, the most influential Canadian to express concern over foreign ownership in the 1960s was James Coyne, governor of the Bank of Canada. Coyne, like Gordon, had no formal training in economics; at the University of Manitoba he had studied history and mathematics, and as a Rhodes Scholar at Oxford he had studied law.[115] In a series of speeches beginning in late 1959 he warned the public of the dangers of inflation and Canada's heavy reliance on borrowed money. His first speeches contained little on foreign investment, but after Gordon began to speak publicly on the subject, Coyne also addressed the issue. Coyne argued that control of the flow of foreign investment in the post-war years would have resulted in a larger degree of Canadian control of domestic industries and resources, kept imports at lower levels, and held down the value of the Canadian dollar so that secondary industries would have expanded and employment levels would have been higher. He accepted that some foreign ownership was necessary, but insisted that Canada now had too much. "The necessity or usefulness of increased foreign investment in Canada since the war is sometimes greatly over-estimated," he said.[116]

Though Gordon disagreed with Coyne's views on monetary policy, inflation, interest rates, and the value of the Canadian dollar, the two had remarkably similar views on foreign investment. In speeches Gordon repeated Coyne's words that Canadians were "living beyond our means."[117] Coyne worried that foreign control of Canadian industry would lead to the loss of Canadian political independence, an argument that Gordon had used earlier.[118] Coyne also argued that foreign control restricted opportunities for

Canadian managers, scientists, and owners, lamenting that "Canadians are not encouraged to have new ideas, cannot put their ideas to the test, and cannot assume responsibility for proving and carrying out their ideas." He pointed, as an example, to the Canadian automobile industry, which had never built a product designed for Canadian conditions.[119] These comments expanded on Gordon's earlier remarks that foreign investment meant "less opportunities for Canadian scientists, engineers, economists, and other experts."[120] Like Gordon, Coyne never seemed to consider the broad implications of his proposals. In the words of A.F.W. Plumptre, the senior assistant deputy minister of finance, "Mr. Coyne concerns himself almost entirely with ultimate objectives. Nowhere does he really consider, in practical terms, how – the means by which – the objectives may be reached."[121]

Economists were almost unanimously opposed to Coyne's ideas. They believed that the level of savings was determined by the country's national income, not by the interest rates.[122] The way to increase domestic investment, therefore, was to encourage economic growth. This would require the Bank of Canada to lower interest rates, not increase them as Coyne had done. In December 1960, twenty-nine economists wrote a letter to Minister of Finance Donald Fleming, saying that they had lost confidence in the governor of the Bank of Canada.[123] One of the signatories, H. Scott Gordon, published a small book explaining why. The economists did not believe that Canadians were relying too heavily on borrowed funds. Canada had "one of the highest rates of saving in the free world," and the country's foreign indebtedness in 1960 was less than half what it had been before the war. Professor Gordon rejected Coyne's position that foreign investment threatened Canadian independence, suggesting that "the argument should be exactly the other way round. American direct investment in Canada should make the American businessman and his government more anxious to preserve our good will than otherwise. We are holding these large quantities of American assets inside our territory. They are subject to the policies of the Canadian government. If anyone is in a position to exert political power because of this it is surely ourselves."[124] Fleming dismissed the economists' letter, but within a few months he asked Coyne to resign.

The Coyne affair was one of many issues that led to the Conservative setback in the election of 18 June 1962. The governing party dropped from 208 to 116 seats, while the Liberals surged from 49 to 100. The NDP with 19 seats, and Social Credit with 30, would hold the balance of power in a Parliament of minorities. The biggest Liberal gains were in Ontario, where the party went from 15 seats to 44. Gordon was elected to Parliament for the first time, defeating his Conservative opponent in Davenport by 9,101 votes to 6,741.

The parliamentary session of 1962–63 was one of Canada's most interesting. The House of Commons was summoned to meet in late September, more than three months after the election. Though he knew little about the workings of the House, Gordon assumed the role of unofficial Liberal finance critic. In this role he seldom mentioned the issue of foreign investment in Canada. Indeed, according to one reporter, "He appeared more mild and uncertain than most political novices. Those close to him say he was frustrated and dissatisfied in the opposition role."[125]

During this session Gordon was shaken by Pearson's failure to consult him on a major policy shift. In January 1963 Pearson announced, despite a resolution of the National Liberal Rally against nuclear weapons, that Canada should keep its commitments to NATO and NORAD by allowing Bomarc missiles on Canadian soil to be armed with nuclear warheads. Gordon's reaction was "one of considerable dejection," and he considered resigning: "I was seriously disturbed to think that he would make a decision of this magnitude without consulting his closest friends and colleagues in the party." Pearson, in Gordon's words, "seemed to have overlooked the need to inform and convince his friends and colleagues in the party that a change in policy of this importance was imperative ... Some of us did not believe the leader of the party had the right, or should have the right, to reverse this policy unilaterally."[126] But Gordon at best was exaggerating Pearson's failure to consult on this issue. Pearson had talked to him ahead of time about the issue. "Walter knew the statement was coming ... There *certainly* was some kind of consultation on that," remembered his friend Keith Davey.[127] Gordon's complaint, therefore, was not that Pearson had failed to consult him, but that the leader had not heeded his advice.

Pearson's stand on nuclear weapons hastened the disintegration of the Conservative government, leading Diefenbaker to call an election for 8 April 1963. Gordon again chaired the Liberal campaign. As election day neared, the Liberal team became alarmed at the strong campaign Diefenbaker was waging. Gordon spoke with senior party officials Keith Davey, Royce Frith, and Dan Lang about what could be done to revitalize the Liberal appeal. The four decided that Pearson should outline specifically what his government would do in its first few months in office. Davey suggested that the theme should be "one hundred days of decision." Gordon flew to Halifax to explain the idea to Pearson, who liked it but feared that voters would relate it to the hundred days preceding Napoleon's defeat at Waterloo.[128] Gordon accepted this logic and drafted a timetable for ninety days of decision. In Gordon's proposal the new minister of finance would bring down a budget no later than 20 June 1963, within the government's first sixty days in office.[129] Instead of ninety days, Pearson changed the slogan to "sixty days of decision," an alteration that would not change Gordon's deadline for the government's first budget. Despite these efforts, the party did not win a majority. The Liberals won 129 seats, more than any other party but still 4 seats short of a majority. The Tories held 95 seats, Social Credit 24, and the New Democratic Party 17. Though his party would be in a weak position in the Commons, Pearson would become prime minister. Gordon was re-elected easily in Davenport, winning more votes than the NDP and Conservative candidates combined.

Many key figures thought that Pearson could not have become prime minister without Gordon's ability to organize and recruit. In 1970 Pearson remembered Gordon's role, calling him "the man around whom we all sort of gathered" and "the real foundation of ... our comeback." When he made these comments, the two men were no longer speaking to each other, but Pearson's remarks were still full of praise for his former friend. "He was ... wonderfully generous and effective in his support when I took the leadership. There was nothing he wouldn't do or couldn't do ... in building the organization, seeing people, getting people active and bring people into the party ... It was wonderful, unselfish work of political service on his part." Mitchell Sharp agreed: "I don't think the Liberal Party would have succeeded when it did in replacing the Diefenbaker administration if it hadn't been for Walter's contribution."[130]

Gordon's reward for his service was a position in the Cabinet. Around the time of the election Pearson asked Gordon casually if he would become the country's first minister of industry. Gordon replied that he wished to be able to see that the government implemented its election promises: "I questioned my ability to do this if I became the minister in charge of a new department." He remembered what had happened when St Laurent had asked him to join the ministry: "On that occasion he [Pearson] thought I should not accept the invitation unless I was to be Minister of Finance or even Minister of Trade and Commerce, then a much more important post than it was to be in the Pearson government."[131] Gordon's response to Pearson was simple: he would like to be minister of finance. Pearson's wife Maryon bristled at this comment, telling Gordon he should accept whatever portfolio the prime minister asked him to take.[132] But Pearson responded differently, accepting Gordon's demand. "What could I do after all Walter had done for the party?" he later asked Michael Barkway.[133] The matter appeared settled, but it raised some doubts in Gordon's mind about Pearson's commitment to him.[134]

As he took the finance portfolio, Gordon's political prestige was at its peak. He was, according to journalist Peter C. Newman, "in undisputed command of the Liberal policy apparatus. Nearly every initiative taken during the Sixty Days was inspired by the Minister of Finance."[135] During the campaign Pearson had joked, "If I had my choice, I'd go on a long holiday to Florida after we're elected, and let Walter run the country."[136] This comment further added to the perception that Gordon, in Kent's words, would "play the main executive role in government," while Pearson would serve as Cabinet chair.[137] Gordon later remembered, "My personal position had been built up to a point where people thought I was some kind of superman."[138]

There were many factors that accounted for Gordon's prestige and power. He benefited from an intimate relationship with the *Toronto Star*, a paper that used its extensive influence in Ontario and in the Liberal party to promote Gordon and his ideas. As a successful businessman, the head of the country's largest accounting firm, and a pioneering management consultant, Gordon was in many eyes an infallible expert in organization and finance. He had used his skills and personality to take over the Liberal party organization and policy apparatus, particularly in Ontario, the party's new stronghold. Many of the party's key figures felt an intense loyalty to Gordon because he had recruited them, helped them in their political careers, and provided the funds necessary for their success.

Though he had been largely responsible for the election of the Liberal government and he now held the senior ministry in the Cabinet, Gordon had not yet convinced the public, the party, the Cabinet, or even the prime minister of his views on foreign investment. During the election, party literature did not discuss the issue of foreign investment. The platform was designed to be a specific outline of what a Liberal government would do, but it did not contain any proposals for limiting foreign ownership in Canada. Similarly, in the 1962 and 1963 elections Gordon himself avoided the issue. The major issue in Canada was unemployment, which had a prominent role in Liberal campaign literature and in Gordon's speeches.[139] Gordon had been willing to discuss foreign investment in his earlier speeches and at the Kingston Conference, but during the election campaigns he seldom mentioned the issue, a choice that is hardly surprising given that the Liberals ran on a platform of better relations with the United States.[140]

Gordon's failure to understand the need to convince the public of his ideas was just one of several handicaps that he would bring to office. He also suffered from his rigid views on the issue of foreign investment and his reluctance to consider the conclusions of those conducting new research in the field. He was now in charge of perhaps the most cautious department in the federal government, but he remained notably impatient and eager to act quickly. Shortly before Gordon took office, one company president commented perceptively, "I'm worried about having Walter in Finance. He's the sort of fellow who will try something to see if it works."[141]

CHAPTER FOUR

It Was Walter Gordon's Budget 1963

When Walter Gordon took office as minister of finance, he had a level of influence that few of his predecessors had known. Gordon's prominence within the Liberal party was second only to the prime minister's. Indeed, in some sections of the party his status was greater than Pearson's, because he had recruited many members of caucus and they felt that he, not Pearson, was responsible for their success.[1] Gordon's reputation was enhanced by his close relationship with Pearson; the prime minister was indebted to his friend for having been the key figure in restructuring the party and bringing it to victory. In the new government Gordon was the chief spokesperson on economic issues, an assignment of special importance because of Pearson's poor understanding of these matters. Gordon seemed to have a free hand to do as he wished. He could have used his position to educate the public about the dangers of foreign ownership and slowly implement measures to limit its extent.

Gordon's prestige brought with it an enormous sense of anticipation. After two years without a budget, the country looked forward to a new regime and to having an efficiency expert as finance minister. "Rarely has a man entered the finance portfolio with such impressive credentials," proclaimed the ever-sympathetic *Toronto Star*.[2] Members of the caucus similarly anticipated great things from Gordon. "Walter was, we thought, invincible," said Cabinet colleague Judy LaMarsh.[3] These expectations did not seem to burden Gordon, who refused to slow the pace of the changes he wished to implement.

On 22 April, his first day as minister of finance, Gordon had a pleasant meeting with his top officials, Assistant Deputy Minister Claude Isbister commenting on how happy he was to be working with him.[4] Gordon showed a level of self-confidence that the public servants had not seen in his predecessors. At his first formal session with them Gordon told departmental officials that he wanted to know the exact financial position of the country, a request that illustrated his approach to problems.[5] His predecessors, many of them outstanding ministers, had been lawyers with little financial experience; in fact, Gordon was the first post-war minister of finance who was not a lawyer. Asking to see the country's balance sheet was a request his predecessors had not made, but to Gordon, an accountant, a natural one. Donald Macdonald, finance minister in the mid-1970s, once commented on those who followed Gordon: "I guess we all, particularly the lawyers, were inclined to take advice from the senior advisers."[6] Gordon did not share this inclination.

Gordon was unhappy with the situation in the Confederation Building, the home of the Finance Department. "I discovered," he said, "that the Department of Finance was completely demoralized and unorganized."[7] Though only sixty-three years old, Deputy Minister of Finance Ken Taylor looked and acted as though he were seventy-nine.[8] Those who had close contact with Taylor knew that he was no longer suited to be deputy minister, some believing that he was already suffering from the first symptoms of Alzheimer disease, an illness with which he would later be diagnosed.[9] Upon assuming office, Gordon told Taylor that he had asked the prime minister to appoint Robert Bryce deputy minister. Taylor's "nose was naturally out of joint," remembered Gordon.[10] The difficulty intensified when Pearson decided to delay Bryce's transfer from the Privy Council Office until after the presentation of the budget.

There were also some problems with the assistant deputy ministers. Wynne Plumptre, according to Brian Land, the minister's executive assistant, "clearly resented being passed over" for the deputy minister's job.[11] Some have speculated also that the new Liberal government distrusted Plumptre because of his close friendship with Donald Fleming, Gordon's predecessor.[12] Simon Reisman, another assistant deputy minister, created further problems for Gordon. Reisman was a difficult person at the best of times, and Gordon had fought with him when Reisman was assistant director of research for the Gordon Commission. In later years Reisman had not mellowed; indeed, his confidence may have grown. "Whatever the issue at stake," wrote social critic John Ralston Saul, "his ego strode before him ... While the old-style public servants had exercised a certain reserve, Reisman seemed to be permanently throwing tantrums and shouting at people."[13] Gordon later remembered that, in the absence of a strong deputy minister to co-ordinate the department, the assistant deputy ministers "went their own way."[14]

The biggest difference between Gordon and the bureaucrats was in their approach to problems. Gordon liked to work quickly; his practice was to identify problems, solve them, and apologize for any mistakes he had made. "My view of politics is that you do the thing first and then clean up the mess afterwards," he once said. "If you had to wait until the plan was perfect, you'd never get anything done."[15] The civil servants feared making mistakes and were reluctant to take risks, particularly after having endured public criticism from Prime Minister John Diefenbaker. One incident illustrates the contrasts between Gordon and his officials. When Gordon's private secretary, Nancy Burpee, ordered a red typewriter, a high official in the Treasury Board sent a long memorandum explaining why government-issued typewriters had to be grey.[16] Land summarized Gordon's attitude: "If you can't get a damned typewriter, how can you draft a municipal loan fund in a month?"[17] Incidents like this led Gordon to doubt whether the bureaucracy could draft a bold budget – one that would include measures to limit foreign investment – within sixty days. Despite these problems, he still wished to move swiftly to carry out his plans. After a few days in Ottawa, Gordon described the situation to Douglas LePan: "I thought I was back at the Royal Commission with everybody explaining why no new idea could work and why everything would take ten years to do. I have ordered some dynamite and hope to stir things up."[18]

On his first day as minister Gordon told Taylor that he intended to hire outside consultants to help write his first budget, which he had to deliver, according to election promises, within the sixty days of decision.[19] According to C.M. "Bud" Drury, Gordon's Cabinet colleague and brother-in-law, "Walter suffered from ... his lack of faith in his civil servants. He felt he could get better advice outside the civil service."[20] Gordon hired Rod Anderson of Clarkson Gordon; David Stanley, a financial consultant with Wood Gundy; Martin O'Connell, an investment dealer with Harris and Partners; and Geoff Conway, a doctoral student in business administration at Harvard and a former Clarkson Gordon tax specialist. Stanley, O'Connell, and Conway had worked with Peter Oliphant of Shell Canada writing Liberal policies for the 1962 and 1963 election platforms.[21] Stanley had also drafted a contributory pension plan that was the basis for the scheme that became the Canada Pension Plan, and during the 1963 election he wrote all of Pearson's speeches, replacing Tom Kent, who was running for Parliament in British Columbia.[22]

The advisers undertook separate assignments. Conway focused on taxation, including a tax on the takeover of Canadian firms by non-residents; O'Connell worked on a municipal development loan fund and a housing bonus, and Stanley concentrated his attentions on the Canada Development

Corporation.[23] Anderson, who had little contact with the other three advisers, stayed in Ottawa for two weeks gathering information on the state of the country's finances, particularly the deficit. "It seemed very hard to get figures," he recalled.[24] The work of the advisers was made public in the *Financial Post* on 18 May.[25]

The public servants were clearly irritated by the presence of the advisers. Peter C. Newman described the relations between the minister and his top officials as "cold war." For Assistant Deputy Minister Claude Isbister the situation was worse: "It was like the Department of Finance dealing with an invading army." The assistant deputy ministers found that some of the advisers were acting as a praetorian guard, trying to assume executive authority in Gordon's absence. The senior officials refused to allow the advisers to act as intermediaries, insisting on dealing directly with Gordon. Though they got along well with O'Connell, the members of the department found Conway and Stanley more difficult. Because he was confident and blunt, Stanley occasionally irritated the bureaucrats. Much more annoying was Conway, who was, according to Brian Land, "brilliant and full of ideas." Enthusiastic and intense, Conway showed little sensitivity or tact in his dealings with the civil servants. Their resentment could be seen in the ironic way they referred to the advisers, Reisman calling them "the carpet-baggers," Isbister "the three gnomes," and G.G.E. Steele "the three unwise men." Because of the advisers' presence, relations between the top officials and Gordon were, in Isbister's words, "very strained during the budget preparation." For Plumptre, two of the advisers "were so offensive and so intolerant as to make coherent communication virtually impossible."[26]

The advisers were no more pleased with the senior officials. They got along well with Isbister and Steele, but they found Reisman difficult to deal with and had little contact with Plumptre, whose competence they questioned. They also found Plumptre to be very patronizing; he often lectured others about the protocol of the relationship between the minister's office and the department. To the advisers he seemed more concerned with formalities than substance.[27]

The difficulties between the bureaucrats and the advisers could have been predicted. As a top management consultant once wrote, "when outsiders are given executive authority, directly or indirectly, they automatically run into considerable opposition from the permanent members of the organization in question."[28] Gordon should have known better; he had written these words himself in 1946 after Paul Martin had asked him to chair a committee to make recommendations on a reduction in the size of the civil service. Yet, as minister of finance he displayed his characteristic impatience and ignored his own advice.

After several days of budget preparation, departmental officials began to feel that, in Reisman's words, "we were heading into a disaster." The four assistant deputy ministers asked Taylor to tell Gordon that the officials "know what he wants, and some of it is doable and some will be doable in the future. We think we can make something of this." Within thirty-six hours they had redrafted the budget, with Plumptre doing most of the writing. Taylor liked the draft and Gordon accepted it without much comment, though Reisman had the impression that he was pleased with it. That day Reisman bumped into Tom Kent and told him that the budget would be a good one.[29]

Gordon was not happy with Plumptre's draft after all. He rejected it, according to Reisman, "on political grounds."[30] The speech was very dull, and Gordon believed that it "did not reflect all the points of view I wished to make." On the minister's request, Stanley drafted an entirely new budget speech that, in Gordon's words, "portrayed my understanding of the Liberal government's philosophy and policy."[31]

The main ideas in the budget came from Walter Gordon himself. The Department of Finance was reduced to a technical, supporting role, estimating, for example, how much proposed programs would cost. The advisers also had little influence over the content of the budget, being primarily concerned with the text of the speech. Parliamentary secretary E.J. "Ben" Benson, executive assistant Brian Land, the officials, and the advisers all agreed that Gordon determined the content of the budget himself. "It was," in Land's words, "Walter Gordon's budget."[32]

The budget included several measures to limit foreign investment in Canada. The first and most controversial was a tax on the sale of shares in Canadian companies to non-residents. Before coming to Ottawa, Conway had suggested a 10 to 15 per cent tax on these transactions, a tax that, he advised, would be "quite easy to administer." But Gordon was carried away with the enthusiasm of his budget and began, in Stanley's words, "to exaggerate everything."[33] What emerged in the budget was an inflated version of Conway's original proposal: a 30 per cent tax on foreign takeovers that Tom Kent later called a "Draconian measure."[34]

Conway had also recommended that Gordon raise the withholding tax on dividends paid to non-residents by companies that did not have a certain minimum level of Canadian ownership. Gordon accepted this suggestion in modified form; he lowered the 15 per cent tax to 10 per cent on dividends paid by firms with at least one-quarter Canadian ownership, and raised the tax to 20 per cent on dividends paid by other firms. Companies with at least 25 per cent Canadian ownership were given further preferential treatment with changes to the depreciation allowance, allowing them to write off machinery and equipment at a faster rate than other firms.

His officials at finance were troubled by Gordon's proposals. Claude Isbister thought that it was too difficult to know exactly what percentage of a company was foreign-owned, and some of the new measures could therefore not be administered. In a memorandum dated 31 May 1963 he cautioned Gordon that "the path of prudence in these circumstances is to err on the side of doing a little less rather than more during the first trial period, while still trying to make a good start in the desired direction." Isbister warned against the changes in the withholding tax, which "will involve a number of regrettable consequences," and predicted problems with the balance of payments and domestic employment, and retaliation against Canadian residents with income from foreign countries. Gordon had proposed a 10 per cent differential between the withholding tax on dividends paid by companies with at least one-quarter Canadian ownership and the dividends paid by others, achieved by increasing the rate on some companies by 5 per cent and lowering the rate on others by the same amount. Isbister proposed a simple 10 per cent reduction for companies with at least 25 per cent Canadian ownership. "We would still be offering a differential of 10 percentage points as an incentive measure of the kind desired," Isbister advised. "Furthermore, you would be able to say in your budget you are offering incentives of a substantial nature but that you are not penalizing the foreign investor."[35]

Underlying Isbister's concerns was his attitude towards foreign investment. "I was never convinced that foreign investment was a major problem for the Canadian economy," he remembered many years later. In his view all owners, Canadian or American, managed their businesses to make a profit, and there was little difference in the way they went about it. He understood that there might be some problems with the practices of foreign owners, but he preferred to create regulations to prevent any excesses. He also believed that Gordon's proposals would not solve even the minor problems he saw with foreign investment. Gordon planned to limit incoming investment but proposed no measures to deal with existing foreign ownership. In Isbister's view the problem was not with takeovers but with existing investment.[36]

Louis Rasminsky, governor of the Bank of Canada, expressed similar reservations. Rasminsky had told Gordon that the takeover tax was a mistake, worrying about the administrative difficulties and the effect on foreign investment. Gordon did not heed Rasminsky's advice: "Gordon knew exactly what he wanted – he was not given to self-doubt – and what he wanted was not advice but support." Rasminsky told Gordon that he would be surprised if Pearson agreed to the takeover tax. On Gordon's suggestion, the two men met the prime minister for lunch at the Bank of Canada. Rasminsky expressed his views strongly, criticizing Gordon's proposals to increase corporate taxes and personal income taxes. His main area of concern, however, was the proposed change to the withholding tax on dividends paid to non-residents: "In taking this action the government would be unleashing forces whose magnitude it is unable to measure." Rasminsky warned that the proposal "could result in massive attempts at liquidation of non-resident-owned investment here and precipitate a fresh exchange crisis." He supported the views Isbister had expressed to Gordon, saying that the government would be in a stronger position "if this principle is expressed at the present time in the form of carrots for Canadians rather than sticks for Americans. If the carrots and the clear statement of Government wishes do not work, the Government will be in a much better position in later budgets to bring out a few sticks. I think therefore the withholding tax should be 15-5 and not 25-15 or even 20-10." Rasminksy was concerned also about the administration of the tax: "There are too many ways by which smart lawyers and operators can avoid this." At the end of the meeting Pearson asked for the notes that Rasminsky had scribbled on the back of an envelope, leading him to believe that the prime minister had been "impressed by the arguments that I made."[37]

Rasminsky's warnings, however, had not alarmed the prime minister. Before the meeting Pearson had "expressed great delight" with the budget and told Gordon that "he felt it would put the Liberal Party on the map." After the meeting he advised Gordon not to take Rasminksy's objections seriously.[38] Pearson continued to believe that Gordon's budget was a good one; a few days before its presentation he told Maurice Lamontagne, "Oh, this will be the most original budget. I cannot tell you more, but this will be formidable."[39] Part of the problem, of course, was Pearson's weak understanding of fiscal and monetary policy. David Stanley, who travelled with the leader during the 1963 election, later described Pearson as "a complete ingenue" on questions of finance. J.W. Pickersgill agreed, saying that the prime minister "didn't fully understand the budget." This weak grasp of economic issues meant that Pearson had to depend on the counsel of others. He tended, however, not to trust the advice of bankers or economists. The prime minister, in Allan MacEachen's words, "didn't react as a worried man to many of the forebodings of the Department of Finance and the Bank of Canada." He did, however, owe a great debt to his friend Walter Gordon and was reluctant to reject advice from a man he thought had the best economic mind in the country. Pearson had, according to his executive assistant, Mary Macdonald, "given Mr. Gordon pretty well carte blanche." He did not like to interfere with the finance portfolio, leaving the finance minister to handle the details of the budget. "He didn't take much interest," said his son Geoffrey.[40]

In explaining the budget's weakness, many have noted the constraints of the sixty days of decision. Years later Tom Kent said that the takeover tax was "a somewhat hastily prepared measure, and it was not the sort of thing you should do unless you've ... taken much greater care than obviously had been taken to make sure that it will work."[41] The sixty-day deadline, however, was not unfairly imposed on Gordon. Even under his own timetable for ninety days of decision, he had wanted a budget presented in the first sixty.[42] Moreover, his instinct was to work quickly, regardless of the deadline. Shortly after taking office Gordon told Martin O'Connell, "We only have sixty days to make a mark; after that we'll be captured by the officials."[43] Years later Gordon still denied that he had rushed the preparation of the 1963 budget: "It wasn't prepared too hastily. I had been thinking for about eight months." Gordon had assumed that he would be minister of finance, and had been considering the measures he would propose: "I was quite clear about them. So I wasn't starting from scratch."[44]

Gordon's comments show that he had not understood that time was needed, not for him to contemplate his own views but for others to examine them and consider their implications. In this sense the budget's proposals on foreign investment were prepared too quickly. Accustomed to the business world, Gordon did not realize that as a politician he had to convince Canadians of the value of his ideas. In his memoirs Gordon admitted his "failure to obtain public acceptance of these various measures," saying that it was "unfortunate, to say the least."[45]

Budget day was 13 June. That morning, following tradition, Gordon presented his budget to Cabinet. Some ministers expressed reservations on the lack of a tax increase, on the application of the sales tax to building supplies, and on the possible rise in expenditures. The Cabinet minutes, however, show no record of any opposition to the takeover tax or the changes to the withholding tax on dividends.[46] "There was no point in saying anything," explained Paul Hellyer, "because there was nothing that could be done. The speech had already been translated and printed with copies sent to Bank of Canada offices across Canada for distribution when it was released in the Commons. The only course was to grin and bear it while hoping for the best."[47]

When Gordon rose in the Commons at eight o'clock that evening, there was a tremendous ovation from the Liberal side because, in Pearson's words, "if anybody was the architect of our political victory, he was."[48] The three advisers were among Gordon's many supporters in the packed gallery. Notably absent, however, were the top officials from Gordon's department. Plumptre was in Washington to explain the budget to American officials, while Isbister was in Ottawa; the other two assistant deputy ministers were out of town at a golf tournament.[49] Isbister admitted that the officials were not present, believing that their absence was Gordon's choice.[50] True, the officials had not been invited to the gallery for the speech, but one must wonder if, under normal circumstances, they would have waited for an invitation or treated their attendance at the budget speech as part of their normal duties.

Gordon's speech announced that the government's policy was "to encourage direct foreign investment in new enterprises in this country on the basis of partnership with Canadian residents." Foreign capital was welcome, but only if it established new enterprises in Canada. He deplored takeovers of existing Canadian firms, which he said "rarely confer any benefit on the Canadian economy." He stressed the importance of some Canadian participation in foreign-owned firms. "I suggest," he said, "that a 25 per cent equity interest is in most cases appropriate to ensure that a Canadian point of view is always available when company policy decisions are arrived at."[51] Gordon's proposals did not include any measures to regulate the practices of businesses operating in Canada. He did not see this as Parliament's role, depending instead on the minority Canadian owners to defend the country's interests. For Gordon, Canadian interests required firms to process Canadian raw materials in Canada, actively pursue export markets, purchase parts and supplies from Canadian sources, employ Canadian professional firms, and conduct research in Canada. Some economists later questioned whether 25 per cent Canadian ownership could achieve these goals. Melville Watkins, then a neoclassical economist, pointed out that "scarce Canadian capital will have been used up buying the shares of companies with certainty that control remains in foreign hands, thereby reducing the availability of funds to genuine Canadian enterprises."[52] Economist Edward Safarian, Canada's leading expert on foreign ownership, agreed: the proposal would result in less real control of industry by Canadians.[53] A few years later Safarian estimated that a 25 per cent share of the larger foreign companies – those with assets of $25 million or more – would cost Canadians $1 billion, a staggering sum.[54]

After the speech Gordon hosted a lavish reception in his office. Isbister was the only assistant deputy minister to attend, though he left after a few minutes. Also present was Sinc Abell, director of the department's Federal-Provincial Relations Division, who, in Benson's words, "was very outspoken" and resented the role the advisers had played in the budget preparation. After a few drinks Abell lashed out at Benson: "This is an ignorant budget prepared by ignorant people. Your victory party is premature. Just you wait till this hits the fan."[55]

The press reaction to the budget was divided. Though traditionally hostile to measures that would limit trade or capital flows, the *Winnipeg Free Press* said that there "can be little quarrel" with the proposals designed to promote Canadian ownership. The *Toronto Star*, not surprisingly, was fulsome in its praise, saying that Gordon had "broken new ground" in trying to curb American control of Canadian industry: "This is the first time that a Canadian government has enunciated as national policy its resolve to regain Canadian control of our industrial resources by means other than mere exhortation." The *Globe and Mail*, however, criticized the budget for being restrictive rather than bold and expansionist: "The stick is much in evidence but the carrot is lacking." The paper was particularly critical of Gordon's "negative and defensive approach" towards foreign investment. One of the sharpest attacks on the budget appeared in the *New York Times*, which lamented that "Canada is adopting a form of protectionism that represents a retreat to economic nationalism." The newspaper insisted that "American companies have done nothing to infringe on Canadian independence" and attributed Gordon's measures to "exaggerated Canadian fears of American domination." The most surprising reaction came from *La Presse* of Montreal, which described the measures to reduce foreign control of industry as "rather timid."[56]

On the takeover tax, opinion was also mixed. The *Globe and Mail* suggested that the government could not enforce the measure, pointing out that when "traders sell shares they do not always know if the buying agent is acting for a foreign resident or not." Requiring a company to verify who owned its shares would "impose a serious burden, particularly on very large businesses." The *Toronto Star* presented a different view, acknowledging that the takeover tax was "a harsh capital levy" but insisting that "drastic measures are justified to halt the process by which more and more once-Canadian companies are passing under foreign control."[57]

A furore erupted in the House of Commons the day after the budget speech when the Opposition asked whether anyone other than the public servants had helped to prepare the budget. Gordon reacted poorly, trying to dodge the question by saying, "I take full and sole responsibility for everything which was contained in the budget."[58] Pickersgill later remembered that the finance minister "cut a sorry figure" when replying to the question of the advisers.[59] "The so-and-sos caught me with my guard down," Gordon told a friend.[60] The budget debate had begun on a sour note.

The debate was a low point in Canadian parliamentary history. The discussion focused on the role of the advisers and not on the substantive measures in the budget, which deserved serious, well-informed consideration by the Opposition. Day after day Gordon was grilled on the relationship of the advisers to their firms, on the knowledge they had of the budget's contents, and on their role in the budget preparation. Question Period in the House of Commons had no time limit, and as a result the interrogation continued for hours, often with many opposition members yelling at the same time. Pearson could not recall any minister "having had more bitter attacks levelled at him" in the Commons.[61] During the debate Gordon remembered breaking his jaw in a boxing match at RMC, and, as he had done almost forty years earlier, he refused to give up despite being seriously injured.[62] Eventually he was vindicated on the issue of the advisers when the deputy attorney general gave his opinion that they had been properly retained as employees of the government.[63]

The most curious feature of the debate over the advisers was the reaction of the press. The *Toronto Star*, Gordon's chief promoter, criticized his actions by saying that he had "committed a serious indiscretion in permitting persons on the payrolls of two Toronto investment firms to help him draft the federal budget." Equally surprising was the reaction of the *Toronto Telegram*, one of the most Conservative papers in the country, which defended the finance minister: "Do Mr. Gordon's denigrators mean to imply that his special advisers are not honorable men and have not lived up to their oaths of office? If so, let them come out from behind their parliamentary immunity and say so, subject to the laws of libel and slander and the redress of the courts, the same as anyone else. If they do not, they have no case."[64]

The tempest over the advisers weakened Gordon's position and made it difficult to defend against some sharp attacks on the controversial sections of the budget. At 5:30 P.M. on 18 June, Gordon met with several members of the board of the Montreal Stock Exchange, including the president, Eric Kierans, who had written a highly inflammatory letter that he released to the press before presenting it to the finance minister. The opening sentences set the tone for the letter: "The financial capitals of the world have just about had enough from Canada. Last Friday, the initial reaction to the budget was one of bewilderment and dismay. Yesterday, it was anger and scorn. Today, our friends in the Western World fully realize that we don't want them or their money and that Canadians who deal with them in even modest amounts will suffer a 30% expropriation of the assets involved. And their reaction? If that is what Canadians want, let them have it!" Kierans was contemptuous of the 30 per cent takeover tax and of Gordon's statement that foreign takeovers rarely conferred any benefit on the Canadian economy: "This is complete and utter nonsense. A non-resident take-over confers great benefits on the Canadian economy ... The new owners bring the advantages of new technology, new research and development, new products and ideas which can immensely benefit the Canadian consumer and which will be denied him otherwise. The former owners receive funds which become available in new Canadian enterprises or in government undertakings which contribute to the expansion of our economy ... *All this is elementary.*"[65] The minister was, according to Kierans, "rather astonished at the violence of the attack." Gordon was particularly shocked when Kierans told the stockbrokers present at the meeting that if the government went ahead with these measures, they should sell the markets short.[66]

With stock prices beginning to drop, Gordon believed that he had little choice but to withdraw the 30 per cent takeover tax.[67] On 19 June, the day after his meeting with Kierans, Gordon announced that he was rescinding the tax. Despite a long-standing tradition that important financial decisions are announced only after the close of markets across Canada, Gordon made his statement at 2:41 P.M., while Canadian markets were still trading.[68] He later explained to the Cabinet that "he felt he should announce the decision quickly to stop a serious further decline in stock market prices," but his explanation does not ring true.[69] The markets in Toronto and Montreal, which closed at 3:00 P.M., would not likely have fallen much further in the remaining nineteen minutes of trading. Under pressure, Gordon had forgotten the importance of waiting until the stock markets closed. "That was sheer panic, of course," remembered Tom Kent. "It was a terrible error."[70] The result of the premature announcement was chaos during the final minutes of trading on the major exchanges, and further attacks on Gordon by the Opposition and the press.[71]

After Gordon's retreat on the takeover tax, the situation in the Commons grew worse. Paul Hellyer described the scene graphically: "Nothing excites wolves more than the scent of blood from a wounded deer so instead of abandoning the chase when the takeover tax was withdrawn the pack closed in with fangs bared. There was bedlam in the House with as many as a dozen opposition MPs catcalling or attempting to ask questions at the same time."[72] "I'm trying to keep my head out of the way of the sledge hammers as best I can," Gordon told a friend.[73] Seated in the gallery during many of the attacks on her husband, Liz Gordon remembered the budget debate as "absolutely ghastly."[74]

On 20 June, the sixtieth day of decision, Gordon offered his resignation. In a private meeting with the prime minister he said that he would give up his position if Pearson "would like me to do so."[75] Pearson responded by asking Gordon if he still had confidence in himself, to which Gordon replied in the affirmative, a response that apparently settled the matter. The resignation seems not to have been genuine, and was more likely designed to force Pearson to declare his support for Gordon. As Gordon later recalled of his offer to resign, "I wasn't all that keen to do it anyway."[76]

In the Cabinet meeting on 20 June, Pearson reported Gordon's willingness to resign. The minutes record that the ministers pledged to back Gordon: "The Cabinet ... agreed that the government would give full support to the Minister of Finance in the House of Commons and would treat any motion calling for the resignation of the Minister of Finance as one of non-confidence in the government." Pickersgill did not think Gordon should resign, believing it would be "a sign of weakness to sacrifice a minister who was under fire." One minister pointed out that only the prime minister, "with the authority and prestige at his command, could deal effectively with the charges that had been made against the honour of the Minister of Finance."[77]

Despite the agreement that the ministers would defend him, Gordon never felt that he had their full support. "One of the difficulties," he later recounted, "was the reluctance of most ministers to come to my defence."[78] Gordon's friends in the Cabinet agreed. Judy LaMarsh was particularly critical of her fellow ministers: "The Prime Minister didn't speak; Martin, Pickersgill, [Lionel] Chevrier, and especially Sharp, who was already eyeing the job, didn't try to stand with him. Some team!"[79] LaMarsh was wrong; Sharp did stand with Gordon, giving an outstanding speech on the use of the advisers.[80] In addition to several back-benchers, two ministers and two parliamentary secretaries spoke in support of the budget – the same number who would speak in favour of Sharp's first budget in 1966. Moreover, when Gordon's budget was discussed in the House of Commons at committee stage, Pickersgill gave what he considered "the best fighting speech I ever made in Parliament."[81] In the Commons, Gordon received the same level of support enjoyed by his successors.

The question is why Gordon did not get more help, considering the difficulties he was facing. Pearson, who intervened several times in the debate, did not give a full speech, likely because of a tradition that the prime minister does not participate in the budget debate, instead expressing his confidence in the minister by allowing him to defend himself. Pearson had told the Cabinet that he would speak, but only if Diefenbaker raised the stakes by participating himself.[82] A speech by Pearson would undoubtedly have drawn Diefenbaker into the debate, which could have further weakened Gordon's position. The leader of the Opposition had oratorical and demagogic powers that could destroy Gordon, a man who had never felt comfortable in the Commons.

Like Pearson, the Cabinet was in a difficult position. Many ministers had little or no financial expertise. Judy LaMarsh, who disparaged her colleagues' failure to defend Gordon, herself did not participate in the debate, explaining that she was "somewhat stunned and too uncertain of the financial field to offer any help by trying to stand and speak for him."[83] In a cabinet of twenty-six, with twenty lacking any ministerial experience, many would have shared LaMarsh's feeling of shock and uncertainty. Moreover, most ministers, concerned particularly with the measures to limit foreign investment, thought that Gordon had prepared a poor budget. In Hellyer's words, they did not know "how to defend the indefensible." Lionel Chevrier agreed: "It was pretty hard to come to the assistance after the fact." While Gordon did not get the level of support he wanted, he also did not express his need for help. According to Pickersgill, most ministers would have spoken on the budget had they been asked to do so, "but it was never suggested."[84] Instead, in the words of Peter C. Newman, Gordon maintained "a superhuman aloofness" and remained within "a self-protective shell of disengagement."[85]

On the morning of 4 July and the evening of 5 July, the Cabinet met at the prime minister's summer residence at Harrington Lake, where Pearson was recovering from an operation to remove a cyst from his neck. Concerned with its minority position in the Commons, the government made several changes to the budget, including an amendment to remove the 11 per cent sales tax exemption on building materials in stages rather than all at once. LaMarsh remembered that, "item by item, we backtracked from the proposals in the Budget speech and left it in shreds around Walter." LaMarsh did not defend Gordon – she was "too green" – but she was bitter at the prime minister's silence: "Pearson's standing by his most important minister would have impressed us all deeply, as we *were* impressed by his failure to do so."[86] Gordon found the whole experience depressing.[87]

The 1963 budget was the major turning-point in the political career of Walter Gordon and an enormous setback to his efforts to limit foreign ownership in Canada. Though he and Pearson seemed to remain friends, Gordon now rightly doubted the prime minister's faith in him. "After the 1963 election everything was beautiful until the first budget at which time my eyes were truly opened," Gordon recalled.[88] He was right to question Pearson's attitude. The budget, according to Paul Hellyer, "shook the Prime Minister's faith in his finance minister."[89] Indeed, Pearson, who had originally wanted Gordon to be minister of industry, now hoped that he could move him out of finance. Talking to diplomat Arnold Heeney, Pearson said frankly "that he hoped within a couple of months to have induced Walter to take another portfolio." Pearson, however, was afraid that Gordon would "insist on resigning his seat," bringing about "a serious split in the party."[90] Pearson's desire to move Gordon from finance may have been shaped by Graham Towers, a long-time friend on whom he often relied for advice. Pearson also heard the views of his wife Maryon, who was close to Towers and becoming "increasingly cool and distant" towards Gordon.[91]

The budget fiasco and Pearson's reaction to it damaged Gordon's position in the government. Afterward, as LaMarsh remembered, "Pearson leant less on Walter and more on the old-style politicians, Pickersgill and Martin." Paul Hellyer observed that, as a result of the 1963 budget, Gordon's standing in the government was "eroded considerably. The façade of invincibility had been removed." Land agreed that Gordon's "stature was never the same" after the 1963 budget.[92]

The episode also damaged Gordon's standing in the business community. Shortly after Gordon presented the budget, E.P. Taylor, president of Argus Corporation, wrote a critical letter to the prime minister, urging him to replace Gordon: "In the first place, as you may remember me telling you, I have always felt that my friend, Walter Gordon, has not the qualifications or the viewpoint to guide the finances and economy of our country, notwithstanding his undoubted talents in other directions. For the good of all concerned, I do hope that you will appoint a new Minister of Finance in the not too distant future." In the summer of 1963 Gordon entered the York Club in Toronto, where Harry Wilson, president of National Trust, asked him, "Walter, how does it feel to enter a club where everyone hates your God-damned guts?"[93]

There are many reasons why the response of businesspeople was so bitter and personal. Part of the problem was that Gordon was one of their number. As an accountant Gordon had advised companies on how to minimize taxes, but now that he was closing the loopholes, Bay Street considered him a traitor. Beland Honderich speculated that the reaction would have been less caustic had Gordon not been a member of the economic elite. Tom Kent had a different impression, however. The main problem was that the business community thought that Gordon's policies were too left-wing. Bay Street was prepared to forgive Gordon's views on social policy when they thought Gordon could restore order to government after the chaos of the Diefenbaker years. The 1963 budget, however, destroyed Gordon's image of competence and unleashed the long-standing disapproval of his ideas.[94]

Gordon's reputation among American officials dropped even more than it did in the business community. Charles Ritchie, Canada's ambassador in Washington, documented the American reaction in his diary: "The Americans are intensely irritated by our new Budget, which is being attacked in violent tones by the press." Ritchie had lunched with Bill Armstrong, "a good friend to Canada in the State Department," who had recounted the view of another American official: "What Canadians need in financial terms is a psychoanalyst's couch." Richard Holton, assistant secretary of commerce, called the budget a "dash of cold water in the face." For the most part, American officials avoided public criticism of the budget, fearing a repeat of the rupture with Canada that had occurred in the Diefenbaker years.[95] They were, however, clearly surprised and disappointed by the budget's tone.

Canadian officials recalled that Gordon himself was greatly shaken by the entire affair. "Walter had come in full of steam and initiative and had got beaten down," Isbister remembered. After the budget Gordon "played a quiet administrative role." Steele thought that he "lost heart." Reisman described the situation in his colourful way: "He was dead after that budget, but it took him a little while to lie down."[96]

The sixty days of decision were a crucial period for the Pearson government, for Walter Gordon, and for those concerned with foreign investment in Canada. In the first few days Gordon was in a unique position to spread his ideas, to educate the public, and to begin slowly implementing his agenda. By the sixtieth day Gordon's prestige was permanently damaged, and his ability to impose restrictions on foreign investment was crippled. As minister of finance he would never reintroduce his proposed measures. Nine years later journalist Christina Newman noted the budget's enduring effect on efforts to reduce foreign investment in Canada, saying that "its failure dogs the movement still."[97] Gordon's efforts to limit American ownership could recover from this setback only with the help of events that would foster widespread disenchantment with the United States and disillusionment with American society.

CHAPTER FIVE

A Lion in Winter
1963–1965

In the wake of the disastrous 1963 budget Walter Gordon ceased to be a crusader fighting to reduce foreign investment, becoming instead a defensive figure, carefully trying to rebuild his position for some future battle. By the end of his term as finance minister, two years later, Canada was no more economically independent of the United States than it had been when he took office. Gordon had fought against a United States tax that would reduce American capital in Canada, relying heavily on the same cautious officials whose advice he had rejected when drafting his first budget. He had not pushed his proposal for a national development corporation with enough vigour to see it approved by Cabinet and Parliament. Fearing American retaliation, he had angered the Canadian magazine industry by exempting two major American periodicals from legislation designed to reduce the dominance of foreign publications. Except for his rhetoric and the measures introduced in his first budget, Gordon's record as finance minister was one not of a leader trying to limit Canada's dependence on the United States but of a traditional Canadian politician trying to balance domestic and international forces.

Only days after the ordeal of his first budget, Gordon had to deal with another crisis. On 18 July 1963 American President John F. Kennedy announced his proposal for a tax to reduce the flow of American dollars abroad. For years the American government had been experiencing difficulties with the country's balance of payments. The American dollar was the principal international currency, functioning as the major reserve currency for most countries in the Western world. By the early 1960s the large number of dollars in circulation had begun to undermine international confidence in the currency, and the Organization for Economic Co-operation and Development started to press the American government to reduce the supply. As a result, the Kennedy administration introduced the interest equalization tax: a 15 per cent levy on purchases of foreign shares, and a tax on foreign bonds ranging from 2.75 to 15 per cent, depending on the term to maturity.

The tax would have a devastating effect on Canada. It would lessen the return to Americans investing in Canada, meaning that Canadian interest rates would have to rise to prevent a significant loss of capital. Louis Rasminksy, governor of the Bank of Canada, used an example to illustrate the problem: if Ontario Hydro wanted to issue a bond, it would have to increase the interest rate by roughly one point to make up for the tax.[1] With unemployment still at high levels, the process of monetary expansion and declining interest rates would be reversed. Walter Gordon recognized the threat: "I expected it would mean a run on the Canadian dollar which, if not checked, would cause a devaluation of the currency, a second devaluation within a period of fourteen months. This would mean a financial crisis of major proportions."[2] Though the tax would help to achieve Gordon's goal of limiting foreign investment in Canada, its focus was much different. It did not apply to new direct investments but rather to portfolio purchases of stock or debt securities, including federal, provincial, and municipal bonds.

Upon hearing the news from a representative of the United States Treasury, Gordon rushed to his office to prepare a statement for the Commons that afternoon. Gordon's comments were mild, seeking to calm the situation. He recognized that the tax would have "wide repercussions" and "may well have an important effect upon Canada's balance of payments and upon the Canadian economy as a whole." He was reluctant to comment further "until there has been time to give careful study and consideration to all the implications of the President's proposals."[3] Despite Gordon's remarks, the tax was greeted by heavy selling on Canadian stock exchanges, with the Toronto industrial average falling 21 points, a 3 per cent drop that was one of the largest in the market's history.[4] The day after the announcement, Canada experienced a $100-million loss of foreign exchange reserves, a higher daily loss than had occurred even at the peak of the 1962 exchange crisis.[5]

By the morning of Friday, 19 July, a gloomy mood dominated the Department of Finance. With the help of his officials Gordon had tried to push the American government to exempt Canada from the tax. The efforts had not succeeded, and discussion shifted from gaining an exemption to minimizing the impact of the tax. Gordon had resigned himself to devaluing the Canadian dollar on Monday.[6] Rasminsky, returning from salmon fishing in a small river on the Gaspé Peninsula, insisted that the Americans would not benefit by applying the tax to Canada and that they "simply must be made to see this." "This pronouncement was not received very warmly," he remembered, "as part of Thursday and all of Friday had been spent in an unsuccessful effort to do precisely that, and here was I, fresh from the salmon pools, saying what should be done."[7]

By Friday noon Gordon had agreed that a delegation of Canadian officials should go to Washington to argue for an exemption. Rasminsky, Assistant Deputy Minister of Finance Wynne Plumptre, and Edgar Ritchie of external affairs flew to the American capital, where they were joined by the Canadian ambassador, Charles Ritchie. In meetings with senior American officials Rasminsky outlined in detail Canada's balance of payments. He emphasized that the United States exported more goods and services to Canada than capital. Canada paid for American goods and services with all the capital it imported from the United States, plus money earned in other countries. Therefore, Rasminsky argued, "far from being a drain on the United States' balance of payments, Canada was in fact a source of support."[8] A tax on Canadian borrowing in the United States was in neither country's interest.

After two days of discussion and negotiation, the American officials agreed to exempt Canada from the new tax on condition that the Canadian government not increase its reserves by borrowing in the United States. The achievement was largely Rasminsky's, as Charles Ritchie noted in his diary: "I watched with silent admiration the superb and sustained diplomatic performance of Louis Rasminsky, the Governor of the Bank of Canada, in convincing the Americans, much against their previous stand, that the interests of the United States would best be served by granting us an exception from the tax."[9] Gordon greeted the news of the exemption with elation. When announcing the agreement on the evening of Sunday, 21 July, he was reported to be smiling publicly for the first time since his budget.[10]

The significance of these events is open to debate. Gordon believed that the tax illustrated the dangers of Canada's economic reliance on the United States.[11] Others, however, believed the problem was not the interdependence of the two economies but rather Gordon's attempts to separate them. Gerald Wright, who has studied the political aspects of this issue more closely than any other scholar, has concluded that Canada was not initially exempted from the tax partly because of Gordon's budget. American officials were not retaliating against Canada, but they had understood the Gordon budget to mean "that Canada wished to stand on her own feet." In their view Canada no longer wanted a privileged relationship with the United States because special exemptions "would apparently cost Canada in terms of national self-esteem."[12] The Gordon budget also made it difficult for the Canadian delegation to obtain the exemption. At the end of the negotiations American Undersecretary of State George Ball told Rasminsky, "your last budget hasn't made it easier for us to agree to do what we've just done."[13]

The legacy of Gordon's first budget extended far beyond the interest equalization tax. After his painful experience in 1963 Gordon's second budget, presented on 16 March 1964, was a bland document that avoided controversy. According to journalist Peter Stursberg, "There was nothing in it – no changes in taxes, no Canadianism, nothing which might not have been drawn up by an official in a caretaker government."[14] In 1963 Gordon had raised the withholding tax on dividends paid by foreign-owned firms to non-residents from 15 to 20 per cent, effective January 1965. In the second budget he restored the tax to its original rate. "We are now almost back where we were before the first budget," one American authority told the *Financial Post*; "the anti-American aspects have been about eliminated now."[15] According to Gordon, this action was taken at the urging of the prime minister, who "wished to meet the complaints of the u.s. State Department and some sections of the Canadian business community."[16] Gordon believed that the government had made a mistake in backing down, but after his first budget he was in no position to challenge the prime minister on this issue.

Gordon's second budget was also noteworthy for its failure to mention his proposal for a Canada Development Corporation. The idea had its origins in the Gordon Commission hearings, when Gordon Ball, president of the Bank of Montreal, had proposed the creation of a corporation to invest in new Canadian ventures or existing enterprises "that cannot obtain adequate financing from other private sources."[17] The idea was not adopted by the Gordon Commission but appeared as a policy of the CCF in the 1957 election campaign.[18] In 1960 Prime Minister John Diefenbaker and Alvin Hamilton, minister of northern affairs and national resources, considered establishing a corporation that would, in Hamilton's words, "give Canadians a chance to get at these big returns that there are in resource industries."[19] Because of the firm opposition of Finance Minister Donald Fleming, however, the government dropped the idea.[20] Gordon resurrected the proposal in 1961 in *Troubled Canada*, where he described the project tentatively: "It might be desirable ... to create a National Development Corporation to sponsor and invest in large economic undertakings that may not be expected to pay returns for a considerable period."[21] Gordon's proposal was given more form and substance in the Liberal election platform. The party's 1963 policy book promised that a Liberal government would "set up a National Development Corporation. This corporation will seek capital from the public, so that investors and the government will work together to finance new enterprises in Canada. The aim of the corporation will be to increase Canadian production and to reverse the trend towards absentee ownership of Canadian industry."[22]

After the Liberal victory in 1963 the concept – now called the Canada Development Corporation – appeared and vanished many times. The Pearson government's first Throne speech repeated the campaign promise.[23] When Gordon recruited outside advisers to help him draft the 1963 budget, one of them, David Stanley, was appointed to work on the CDC. Stanley, however, accomplished little before he was reassigned to write the budget speech.[24] On the sixtieth day of decision Gordon introduced a resolution to the House that called for the creation of a corporation with share capital of $1 billion.[25] The matter did not come up again in 1963. Gordon later explained, "We made quite a thing about this when we first took office but I was unable to push it because of budget difficulties."[26]

The budget difficulties did not last long, but they damaged Gordon's influence and prevented him from bringing forward a bill to create the CDC. Not trusting the Department of Justice, Gordon sent Alan Hockin, assistant deputy minister of finance, to Toronto to work on the project with two of Gordon's friends: Toronto lawyer Alex MacIntosh and Power Corporation president Maurice Strong. Hockin, MacIntosh, and Strong drafted the necessary legislation, but the project was not mentioned in the February 1964 Throne speech or in Gordon's second budget in March.[27] The problem, for Pearson, was the atmosphere that Gordon's first budget had created.[28] In Tom Kent's words, "action was inhibited in 1964 by the government's induced caution about anything that smacked of economic nationalism."[29] In 1965 the CDC re-emerged as a government priority, both in the Throne speech and in Gordon's third budget speech. Gordon again introduced a resolution to the Commons, this time providing more details than before, but the CDC was never debated.[30] When Parliament was dissolved on 7 September 1965, Gordon still had not taken concrete action on the issue.

One of the reasons for Gordon's failure to create the CDC was his inability to explain the details of his plan, particularly the goals of the corporation. Shortly after the 1963 election Jack McArthur, financial editor of the *Toronto Star*, outlined the problem facing Gordon: "How can the development corporation be a 'bidder of last resort' for Canadian companies threatened by foreign ownership and still expect to make money?"[31] The two goals of accumulating capital and of keeping Canadian companies out of foreign hands would clash from time to time. Which route would the corporation take in cases of conflict between these two objectives? If the corporation's aim were to maximize profit, this would limit its ability to save Canadian firms from foreign ownership, a task that would not always be lucrative. To attract investors, however, the company had to be profitable.

Because he never resolved this paradox, Gordon's proposal faced opposition from many of his Cabinet colleagues. Pearson later claimed to have supported the idea, but the record is not clear.[32] "Gordon never made a case for the corporation which was convincing to a majority of the Cabinet or even to the Prime Minister," remembered Jack Pickersgill.[33] Mitchell Sharp also recalled that Gordon was never able to explain the idea in a way that answered the basic questions about the CDC's purpose.[34]

Gordon's proposal did not win any wide-based support among the public and faced hostility from the business community. Canadians, explained David Stanley, were indifferent: "Basically, the public at large does not appear to be seriously concerned with the problem the Corporation is designed to alleviate, occasional demonstrations of nationalistic fervour notwithstanding. Therefore it is doubtful if the idea will catch any groundswell of public support." The attitude of Bay Street, Stanley thought, was hostile. The business community was "instinctively conservative" and had "too large a stake in the status quo to view such a significant addition to the financial structure of the country with anything but alarm."[35] The *Globe and Mail*, mirroring the views of Bay Street, called the CDC "the beginning of a program of nationalization of Canadian industry, cooked up by ivory-tower theoreticians of the Liberal Government in Ottawa. They might at least be frank about it, say so, and take their socialism to the voters for judgment."[36] Stanley predicted that the "most probable reaction to the CDC would be almost uniformly antagonistic."[37]

By the spring of 1964 Gordon had outlined his intentions more clearly, including his plans to win public support for his idea. He had decided that the key was in the way that he promoted the idea: "It must appeal to people's patriotism and their desire to preserve and retain Canada's national identity, i.e., the desire to share in Canada's growth potential – to 'buy back Canada.'" At the same time Gordon recognized that Canadians would be reluctant to risk their money in such a project: "It must appeal to people's cupidity, to most people's concern about investing their money safely. I suspect that safety is of more importance to the majority of people than the rate of return they earn." He discounted the opposition of Bay Street, believing that "in the last analysis, the financial community will co-operate if the Corporation is 'respectably' managed and if there is money to be made."[38] In the spring of

1965 Gordon outlined his plans for the CDC in his first meeting with economist Abraham Rotstein. Afterward, Rotstein wrote to Peter Newman: "I was impressed first by how much better a political tactician he is than I had imagined. He outlined his plans to move the country along slowly on his Canada Development Corporation. The plans are very good."[39]

In mid-1965 Gordon began a concerted effort to implement the CDC. In speeches in June, September, and October he outlined his ideas in greater detail, in what political economist Donald Forster described as "an eloquent defence of the proposal and its goals."[40] The authorized share capital would be $1 billion, of which 10 per cent would be held by the government. No other investor could own more than 3 per cent of the shares, which would be priced originally at $5 each. The government would appoint a board of directors, but once shares had been sold to the public, the shareholders would elect the directors, with the government retaining the right to appoint a small number. Gordon also tried to solve the problem of the corporation's objectives. He continued to argue that the CDC would help to save Canadian firms from foreign control, but he stressed the paramountcy of earning a high rate of return: "The purpose of the C.D.C.," he said bluntly, "will be to invest in large enterprises with the sole objective of making a profit."[41] Despite Gordon's advocacy, legislation to create a Canada Development Corporation did not get first reading until January 1971, more than five years after he left the finance portfolio.

Gordon also failed in his efforts to prevent foreigners from owning a controlling interest in Canada's chartered banks, an issue that had long concerned him. He had first become interested in the question in the 1930s, when Clarkson Gordon conducted a considerable amount of work for chartered banks.[42] His royal commission had studied the banking industry, and the *Final Report* had discussed the question of foreign ownership of banks, insisting that the government take action "to prevent any substantial measure of control of these institutions from coming into the possession of non-residents."[43]

Shortly after he had become finance minister, Gordon met with representatives of the First National City Bank of New York, commonly known as Citibank. They told him that they had concluded in principle a deal to purchase the Dutch-owned Mercantile Bank. Gordon replied that they should not complete the transaction until the government had finished its upcoming revision of the Bank Act: "I said that if he proceeded with the transaction in light of my warnings, I would not expect him to blame the Government for any action Parliament might take. Mr. Elderkin, the Inspector General of Banks, who was present at the interview, pointed out that Parliament could go so far as to refuse to renew the charter of the Mercantile Bank."[44] Citibank ignored Gordon's warnings and, in September 1963, purchased controlling interest in the Mercantile Bank.

The revision of the Bank Act proceeded slowly. On 22 September 1964 Gordon announced that he would include measures to prevent non-residents from owning more than 25 per cent of any bank and any one owner from owning more than 10 per cent.[45] He also announced that he would introduce similar amendments to the Insurance Companies Act and the Trust and Loan Companies Act, limiting foreign ownership in these sectors. In this, Gordon was successful. A bill restricting the ownership of insurance, loan, and trust companies was introduced the day after his announcement and approved by Parliament in March 1965.

Gordon's proposed amendments to the Bank Act were not presented to the Commons until May 1965. The bill's section on foreign ownership did not apply to those who already owned more than the limit on 22 September 1964, the day Gordon had made his original policy announcement. Shareholders owning more than the 10 per cent limit on that date would be exempted from this new requirement. Another section, however, said that no bank could have liabilities of more than twenty times its authorized capital stock if more than 25 per cent of its shares were owned by any one owner or group of owners.[46] This clause meant that Citibank would have to reduce its ownership of the Mercantile Bank to 25 per cent – not 10 per cent – before the bank could expand. Pearson called an election before the legislation was passed, meaning that the Bank Act revisions would have to be reintroduced in the next Parliament.

Gordon had only marginally more success in his efforts to introduce legislation to protect Canadian magazines. For decades, foreign periodicals had dominated the Canadian market. By the 1950s Canadian magazines were experiencing serious financial difficulties, while their American competitors held an 80 per cent share of the Canadian market.[47] Liberal Finance Minister Walter Harris responded in 1956 by introducing a 20 per cent tax on advertising in non-Canadian publications. In mid-1958, however, the new Conservative government repealed the Harris tax. After an outcry from the Canadian magazine industry, the Diefenbaker government appointed the Royal Commission on Publications, chaired by Grattan O'Leary, editor of the *Ottawa Journal*. The O'Leary Commission reported quickly, recommending that the government no longer allow a tax deduction for advertising in foreign periodicals and that it amend the Customs Act to prevent the entry into Canada of foreign magazines containing advertising aimed primarily at the domestic market.[48] The Diefenbaker government announced that it would carry out the O'Leary recommendations, but no action was taken by the time Parliament was dissolved in 1962. After the election the government again promised to adopt the recommendations, this time with an exemption for the Canadian versions of *Time* and *Reader's Digest*, editions consisting of mostly American content but with advertising directed at the Canadian market. Again, the government had not carried out this promise by the time Parliament was dissolved.

Almost immediately upon taking office the Pearson government was subjected to heavy pressure to implement the O'Leary recommendations. As Tom Kent remembered, "By the time we inherited the problem, it was becoming more desperate. *Maclean's* was operating at a heavy loss. There was little doubt that, if nothing was done, it and other commercial magazines would disappear before long ... There would be no Canadian publications on a national scale."[49] Cy Laurin, vice-president of Maclean-Hunter – the firm that published two of Canada's largest circulation magazines, *Maclean's* and *Chatelaine* – wrote an urgent letter to Gordon the day after the government took office. "The government dithering that has followed the O'Leary Report has been such that Canadian publishers might have suffered less if the Commission had never been appointed ... The whole Canadian magazine industry has been weakened almost to the point of no return ... May I urge that the Throne Speech contain a statement that the matter will be dealt with ... Believe me, Walter, Canadian magazines are in deep trouble."[50] Gordon, however, was more interested in foreign investment than in American control of the publishing industry. There would be no mention of the problem in the Throne speech and no measures in the 1963 budget to help shore up Canadian magazines. They would have to wait until next time; the first Gordon budget was about ownership of industry, not control of the media.

After his disastrous first budget, Gordon did not feel that he could put forward measures to limit the extent of American control of the magazine industry.[51] Gordon's officials advised him to let the matter rest. Assistant Deputy Minister Plumptre, a former associate editor of *Saturday Night*, suggested that he take no action. "The time has probably passed," Plumptre said, "when Government action in this field was worth while. I believe that a few Canadian magazines will continue to survive on a national basis without special support by a 'magazine tax' or other means, although not as many magazines as I personally would have liked to see in the field." According to Plumptre, any efforts by the government to redress the situation would damage Canada's relations with the United States and lead to charges that the government was interfering with freedom of the press, problems that greatly outweighed any advantages to government action.[52] Gordon accepted this advice. On 30 September, he presented Cabinet with a memorandum, likely drafted by Plumptre, outlining the available options. Gordon recommended that "the Prime Minister should announce that there is no solution that will satisfactorily meet the situation of the Canadian magazines and the Government therefore has decided not to recommend any action to Parliament in this field."[53]

Tom Kent disagreed strongly with Gordon's recommendation. On 2 October he wrote a memorandum for the prime minister that eloquently argued the importance of culture in preserving Canadian independence. The memorandum raised many points that Gordon had never mentioned in his speeches or his writings:

In a country of our size, the periodical press is the only national voice, apart from the CBC, which can provide "the thread which binds together the fibres of a nation." If we are serious at all about a national identity, national magazines (together with the main daily newspapers) are, above all others, the undertakings that it is important to have controlled and managed by Canadians. This is a great deal more important than minority shareholdings and directorships in most industries. No doubt we cannot refuse to recognise the possibility that Canadian magazines will die despite anything practicable we can do to help them. But to take death for granted, and do nothing, would be, in my view, a sharp failure to discharge a responsibility to the nation.

Kent recognized the difficulties in removing the tax deduction for advertising in the Canadian editions of *Time* and *Reader's Digest*, both founded in 1943, but he argued that "the roots of these two publications in Canada are too deep to be got out without a bigger explosion than we can afford."[54] He proposed that legislation exempt *Time* and *Digest*, while preventing the introduction of new Canadian editions of American magazines.

In the 1964 Throne speech the government promised legislation "to strengthen the position of periodicals published in Canada."[55] Two days later, on 20 February, Pearson outlined the policy, essentially the same as that proposed more than a year earlier by the previous government. Cabinet had accepted the O'Leary recommendations, but with squatters' rights for *Time* and *Digest*: the customs tariff would be amended to prevent split runs from entering Canada if more than 5 per cent of their advertising content was directed at Canadians, and the Income Tax Act would be amended to prohibit tax deductions for advertising in non-Canadian periodicals.

Media reaction was mostly negative. Cy Laurin of Maclean-Hunter called the government's proposals "the best practical solution," but other commentators were harshly critical. On one side, the *Halifax Chronicle-Herald* opposed the basic principles of the proposals, saying that they were "objectionable because of their narrowly nationalistic spirit." On the other, the *Toronto Star* criticized the legislation for not going far enough by exempting the two American magazines: "This is a fatal weakening of the O'Leary Report. It will do absolutely nothing to help national magazines … in their struggle for survival." The *Star* worried that the government's policy "may well be the death-knell for Canadian national magazines." The *Globe and Mail* agreed, saying that the measures did nothing to help Canadian magazines and were "close to meaningless" because they exempted *Time* and *Reader's Digest*, "the most serious rivals which Canadian magazines face in the advertising field."[56]

An impasse was reached when Gordon, not liking the exemption for *Time* and *Reader's Digest*, refused to introduce the legislation in March as part of his second budget.[57] "Walter Gordon," Tom Kent remembered, "became troubled about the proposal, and he was greatly concerned that his second budget be non-controversial." The tax resolutions were prepared, but Gordon ignored them in his budget speech. According to Kent, "There was again uncertainty as to when, if ever, anything would be done."[58] Attempting a compromise between those Liberals who supported an exemption for *Time* and *Digest* and those, like Gordon, who opposed it, Kent wrote a lengthy memorandum to the prime minister. He insisted that the government had to keep the exemption for the two American publications but ought to introduce "something else to satisfy the people who are opposed to Time and Digest." He suggested that the measures to protect Canadian magazines should apply also to newspapers, radio, and television: "I do not think there is any doubt of its political appeal. Considerably the greater part of the newspaper industry is committed to support it. And it would draw the teeth of opposition to Time and Digest." Kent also repeated a suggestion made originally by Gordon Robertson, clerk of the Privy Council, who had proposed a qualified exemption for the two American magazines: the periodicals would be exempted only if they achieved 55 per cent Canadian content within three years.[59]

Gordon was not interested in a qualified exemption. He noted in the margin of Kent's memorandum that he "would be inclined to leave this out – not practicable for Time and Reader's Digest." As Kent later recalled, "If there had to be an exemption, he preferred that it be simple and unconditional." Content with the extension of the policy to newspapers, radio, and television, Gordon now accepted the complete exemption for *Time* and *Digest*.[60]

Many of Gordon's supporters in the Liberal caucus reluctantly agreed to the exemptions, fearing retaliation by the American government. External Affairs Minister Paul Martin discussed the issue several times with American Secretary of State Dean Rusk: "This was an issue to which the American government attached great importance."[61] Gordon later remembered that "the U.S. State Department went into action." American officials urged that the Canadian government not do anything that would upset Henry Luce, owner of *Time*: "It was submitted that Mr. Luce had great power in the United States through his magazines – Time, Life and Fortune – and that if he were irritated, the results could be most damaging both to Canada and the U.S. Administration." The government concluded – and, as Gordon noted, "quite rightly in my opinion – that there was considerable validity to these assertions respecting the influence of Mr. Luce and, accordingly, the Canadian edition of Time Magazine was exempted from the legislation."[62] "Members of the caucus," recalled then-Liberal MP Pauline Jewett, "had it explained to them by members of the cabinet that, should the government go ahead and include *Time* and *Reader's Digest*, Washington ... would 'retaliate' against us."[63]

Gordon later justified his actions by saying that the matter arose when the Canadian-American automobile agreement "was under heavy attack in Congress" and that the American government had threatened to withhold approval.[64] Originally, however, the Auto Pact was not a factor. The government announced the exemption in February 1964, and Gordon had agreed to it by May.[65] The Auto Pact negotiations did not begin until July, and agreement was not reached until December. According to Pearson's memoirs, "Contrary to some reports, the exemption of *Time* and *Reader's Digest* was a decision quite unrelated to our negotiation of the Auto Pact with the United States."[66] The Auto Pact only became an issue in 1965, long after Gordon and Pearson had accepted the exemption for the two American magazines. When Gordon tried to convince the Liberal caucus to support the legislation, he mentioned the Auto Pact, but it played no role in his own decision.[67]

In April 1965 Gordon finally introduced legislation to implement the government's policy on magazines. The reaction was immediate and forceful. Grattan O'Leary dismissed the proposals as a fraud.[68] The government, he said, had accepted the principle of his commission's report "and then proceeded to make a mockery of the principle – to strangle the principle in its cradle." The publishers of *Time* and *Reader's Digest* were "in effect issued Canadian passports – given a green light to go ahead with their destruction of our Canadian periodicals."[69] O'Leary also quoted the *Globe and Mail*, which had declared that "Mr. Gordon's legislation merely locks the two biggest wolves in with the sheep."[70] Even more critical was an exaggerated article in which the *Winnipeg Free Press* traced the history of press control. The article was adorned offensively with pictures of those individuals who had interfered with freedom of the press: George III, Adolf Hitler, Benito Mussolini, Joseph Stalin, Juan Perón, Fidel Castro – and Walter Gordon.[71]

Peter Newman, the former national affairs editor of *Maclean's* who had worshipped Gordon, wrote a highly critical letter to him:

I've been such a strong admirer of all your undertakings in the past, and now feel very much let down. It seems to me that your proposals to exempt the Canadian editions of Time and Reader's Digest from the magazine law are totally indefensible. It would have been far better to do nothing – then at least there would have been the hope that some enlightened government in the future would have had the courage to act. By your action, you have given these two American magazines monopoly control over the Canadian periodical market, and now no new Canadian magazine can be launched with any hope of success. I find it difficult to believe that Time and Digest are really strong enough to bend you to their will, but I am faced with no other possible explanation, and I weep for my country.[72]

Newman later told Abraham Rotstein that Gordon had explained his actions by saying that "the pressure Time and Digest put up against any laws that would have endangered their magazine monopoly here was just fantastic. Nothing, not even if we'd sent tanks armed with nuclear warheads to Castro, could have got the Americans madder." With sadness Newman noted that "the Canadian government backed down before the power of Time Inc.!"[73] But Gordon's argument did not convince Newman, who later wrote a stinging letter to Rotstein, containing all the bitterness of a hero-worshipper whose illusions had been destroyed:

You are reading the letter of an *ex*-Walter Gordon disciple. His militant sponsorship of legislation forever garotting Canadian periodicals and awarding Time and Digest a monopoly over the Canadian magazine industry, is a step that has disillusioned me, more than I can admit (in print). Aside from the fact that magazines are my livelihood (and newspapers merely a temporary madness) surely the most important aspect of nationalism is to build up a purely Canadian cultural barrier to preserve this society against American cultural intrusion, which is the most dangerous form of imperialism. With no national newspapers (or any chance of such a venture) Gordon has now handed over to two American magazine empires the monopoly over the printed word for national distribution in Canada. I think he's inconsistent and stupid.[74]

Newman should not have been surprised by Gordon's actions. Had Newman studied the man more closely, he would have found that Gordon always stressed the economic aspects of American influence and seldom even mentioned the American cultural intrusion. Control of the media was never a major area of concern for Walter Gordon.

Gordon was also little interested in the country's symbols, such as the flag. During the election campaign Pearson had promised that his government would give Canada a distinctive flag to replace the Red Ensign. Though opposition was fierce, Pearson persisted, displaying great tenacity. Years later Gordon praised the flag as a "symbol of the New Canada" and a lasting tribute to Pearson's memory, but in 1964 he showed little interest.[75] He did not participate in the long, drawn-out flag debate, and the name of Canada's "gentle patriot" does not appear in the most authoritative book on the history of Canada's flag.[76] Gordon also opposed Pearson's plan to create the Order of Canada, perhaps believing – as did Mitchell Sharp – that the state in a democratic system should not confer distinctions on individuals.[77] For Pearson, the status nationalist, the flag and the Order of Canada were among his government's greatest achievements. But to Gordon these were merely symbols, unimportant when the country was controlled by the economic power of the United States.

Perhaps more puzzling was Gordon's strong support for the Auto Pact. Gordon had long been interested in the automotive industry. In the 1930s he had studied the industry for the Tariff Board, which had accepted his proposal for an increase in the automotive tariff. His company, Canadian Corporate Management, owned several firms that benefited from the tariff, including Walker Metal Products, one of the few large Canadian-owned auto-parts manufacturers.[78] In 1961 the Royal Commission on the Automotive Industry, chaired by Vincent Bladen, recommended changes in the tariff schedules to encourage manufacturers to use more Canadian-made parts.[79] The Liberals, then in opposition, began to discuss the approach they should take on forming a government. Gordon proposed a plan similar to Bladen's, using the tariff as a means of increasing automotive production in Canada.

As Tom Kent remembered: "I had, of course, been involved in the early stages of the development of the idea, which had begun before the government was formed, and it was very definitely basically Walter Gordon's idea."[80]

After winning the 1963 election, the new Liberal government introduced a duty-remission plan that lowered duties on a company-by-company basis depending on the amount of production each firm did in Canada. When the United States threatened a countervailing duty, Gordon lost his temper, shouting at the American Treasury secretary over the telephone.[81] The two governments eventually agreed to solve the problem by negotiating a trade agreement. Mitchell Sharp recalled the important role that Gordon played. "Those of us who were concerned at that time were surprised that Walter Gordon, who would have opposed integration of industry in this way, actually proposed it. It was worked out by his officials with American officials and proposed by him ... But it was surprising in a way that Walter Gordon, who was such a strong economic nationalist, should have embraced this plan."[82] The resulting agreement called for free trade in automobiles and parts for those manufacturers who met certain criteria. A company could qualify for tariff-free treatment if it produced in Canada the same proportion of vehicles as it sold in Canada. Gordon liked the agreement – more a case of managed trade than free trade – particularly the safeguards that guaranteed that a certain amount of production would take place in Canada. As Gordon recalled, "It is true that it accepted the rationalization of the automobile industry on a continental basis. I did not like this in principle, but as three companies dominated the industry on both sides of the border, this acceptance merely acknowledged the existing fact. It is not a pattern that should be adopted for other industries."[83] According to Reisman, Gordon didn't understand that the Auto Pact "was the slippery slope" to free trade.[84]

As Gordon's term as finance minister was coming to an end, many more Canadians were beginning to share his anxiety about American influence in Canada. An important factor in the change of public sentiment was the publication in March 1965 of George Grant's *Lament for a Nation*. Grant was the grandson of George Parkin and of George Munro Grant, and the son of W.L. "Choppy" Grant, the headmaster of Upper Canada College and an early influence on Gordon's life and ideas. Gordon, the Grants, and the Parkins were all part of the same intellectual tradition, believing that the greatest threat to Canada's future was the economic, political, or cultural influence of the United States. George Grant, who was harshly critical of the Liberal

Party, considered Gordon the party's only reputable spokesperson. For him Gordon, more than any other individual, "maintained the honour of Canada."[85] Poet Robin Mathews described Grant and Gordon as the "two lions" in the 1960s struggle against American influence in Canada.[86]

Lament for a Nation presented a straightforward argument: "Canada cannot survive as a sovereign nation." The book, written in anger after the defeat of the Diefenbaker government, mourned "the end of Canada as a sovereign state," arguing that Canada had become "a branch plant of American capitalism." In Grant's view the major culprit was the Liberal party: "For twenty years before its defeat in 1957, the Liberal party had been pursuing policies that led inexorably to the disappearance of Canada." As a result of these policies, an independent capitalist Canada had become an impossibility. Canadian capitalists were no longer interested in the country's independence; they could make "more money by being the representatives of American capitalism and setting up the branch plants." In Grant's view, "No class in Canada more welcomed the American managers than the established wealthy of Montreal and Toronto, who had once seen themselves as the pillars of Canada. Nor should this be surprising. Capitalism is, after all, a way of life based on the principle that the most important activity is profit-making. This activity led the wealthy in the direction of continentalism." In short, the wealthy of Toronto and Montreal no longer cared about Canada.[87]

For Grant, there were two routes open to preserve Canada: conservatism and socialism. Socialism would bring greater state control of the economy, which could be used to resist American domination: "Only nationalism could provide the political incentive for planning; only planning could restrain the victory of continentalism." But socialism could not save Canada, because the socialists were co-operating with the Liberal party in betraying their country, particularly in helping to defeat the Diefenbaker government: Canadian socialists "generally acted as if they were 'left-wing' allies of the Liberal party." Conservatism, which would preserve traditional values of justice and freedom, was Canada's other option. But in Grant's view, conservatism was impotent in the face of all-pervasive liberalism: "The impossibility of conservatism in our era is the impossibility of Canada."[88] Though he enjoyed reading *Lament for a Nation*, Gordon did not yet share Grant's pessimism, particularly the prediction that Canada was at an end: "Nothing, I suggest to you, could be a more erroneous or pernicious view of our country. Far from being an old, used-up state sliding down some historical kitchen sink into oblivion, we should look at ourselves as a young, dynamic nation just launched on the road of nation-building."[89]

Grant's book had an enormous impact in English Canada. Though written by a professor of philosophy and religion, it was easily accessible. The book sold 7,000 copies in its first six months and more than 50,000 over the next twenty-five years. Most daily newspapers published lengthy reviews of the book, and Grant began promoting his ideas on radio and on university campuses. Canadian writers are usually too cautious to use the word "masterpiece," particularly in reference to a Canadian book, but to many *Lament for a Nation* deserved this description.[90]

The book's greatest influence was on young Canadians, many of whom were becoming radicalized. At a meeting of the country's student leaders James Laxer, president of the Canadian University Press, told his colleagues that they should all read the book. "It's the most important book I ever read in my life," Laxer later remembered. "Here was a crazy old philosopher of religion at McMaster and he woke up half our generation. He was saying Canada is dead, and by saying it he was creating a country. The book's an epic poem to Canada, a magnificent statement written with incredible energy and anger." Charles Taylor, then thirty years old, had similar memories of Grant's impact. "Grant had indeed woken us up. Soon I became aware that his book had become a Bible for younger nationalists, whether we called ourselves conservatives, socialists or even liberals. Somehow he had shaken us out of our lethargy and made us determined to prove him wrong."[91] Among younger people, Grant had helped to forge a sense of nationalism. All of this, however, did not take place immediately. Several months – perhaps years – would pass before the full impact of Grant's ideas could be felt.

Another significant book on Canadian-American relations was the so-called Heeney-Merchant Report. In January 1964 Pearson and American President Lyndon Johnson agreed to create a working group to study "the practicability and desirability of working out acceptable principles which would make it easier to avoid divergencies [between Canada and the United States] in economic and other policies of interest."[92] The working group was headed by Arnold Heeney, two-time Canadian ambassador to Washington, and Livingston Merchant, two-time American ambassador to Ottawa. Their report, formally titled *Canada and the United States: Principles for Partnership*, was published in July 1965. The two officials studied several cases in Canadian-American relations, including many of particular concern to Gordon: the American interest-equalization tax, the Canadian withholding tax, the extraterritorial implications of American domestic legislation, and the position of American magazines in Canada. They concluded that both countries could best resolve disputes and protect their interests by conducting careful diplomacy behind closed doors rather than by railing at each other in public. The most controversial section of the report stated this view clearly: "It is in the abiding interest of both countries that, whenever possible, divergent views between the two governments should be expressed and if possible resolved in private, through diplomatic channels."[93] Members of the Canadian government, particularly those with diplomatic experience, accepted the report's conclusions. Paul Martin agreed with the report, and Pearson, while insisting that Canada retained its right to speak out against its neighbour, also endorsed the recommendations.[94]

The general response to the report showed how much Canadian opinion was changing. Tory MP Alvin Hamilton said the report would make Canada "a lap dog" to the United States and would be "a complete surrender of our sovereignty." Journalist Charles Lynch agreed: "If the Heeney-Merchant doctrine catches on, it seems certain to confirm our lackey status." Heeney was surprised at the vehemence of the reaction: "I expect to be hanged for all this ... Probably on Parliament Hill and in public." Much of the criticism was based on a misunderstanding of the report. The idea that differences should be settled behind closed doors was a basic principle of diplomacy, not an attempt to subject Canada to American control. As diplomat and scholar John Holmes argued, the so-called "quiet diplomacy" was merely "a simple restatement of the practice of almost all governments."[95]

Lacking both experience in foreign affairs and a diplomatic temperament, Gordon shared the views of the critics, though he did not speak out publicly against the report because of his close friendship with Arnold Heeney. "I felt, privately," Gordon said in his memoirs, "that if its recommendations were put into practice Canada would be tied more tightly than ever to the United States and that it would become increasingly difficult for us to take an independent stand on policy. We are more likely to get attention in Washington – and eventually to be more respected there – if we state our position on important policy issues clearly and publicly."[96] Confrontation, in Gordon's mind, would better serve Canadian interests than conciliation. The line between Gordon and those with experience in external affairs – like Pearson and Heeney – was clearly drawn.

By the fall of 1964 Gordon was frustrated with his accomplishments as finance minister. Under his inspiration the government had made tremendous advances in social policy, particularly in the creation of a national contributory pension plan and the implementation of a proposal for national health insurance. For Gordon, however, this was not enough. "I felt disenchanted with the way things were going ... I could see little point in continuing as a

Member of Parliament if I was unlikely to accomplish the things we had all set out to do. High on my list were steps to regain a greater measure of control over Canadian resources and Canadian business enterprises."[97] Pearson was now in a difficult position. He did not want to lose Gordon, the catalyst for many of the government's policy initiatives and the man with the organizational skills that he lacked. But Gordon, he knew, would not run the next election campaign unless he could stay in the finance portfolio. When asked to run the campaign, Gordon agreed, but with one stipulation – that "there would be no more suggestions that I should change my portfolio until I felt the job I had set out to do in finance had been completed."[98] Pearson knew that meant a continuing source of conflict between the government and the business community. But Pearson acquiesced.

As the head of the Liberal campaign committee Gordon began to push Pearson to call an election. Never having felt comfortable in the House of Commons, Gordon was particularly concerned with the Liberal party's minority position, and believed that the government was weary and needed a new mandate.[99] Paul Hellyer believed that Gordon pursued the election to enhance his own position; Gordon's reputation had been at its peak in the days following the 1963 election, and he thought, in Hellyer's view, that another election victory would restore his standing, eroded ever since by his first budget.[100]

After months of delay Pearson announced the dissolution of Parliament on 7 September 1965, starting an election campaign that showed the weakness of Gordon's position. In the early days of the campaign Pearson announced that he had recruited Bob Winters to stand as a Liberal candidate. Winters, a minister in the St Laurent government and a protégé of C.D. Howe, was known to oppose Gordon's views on foreign investment. The press highlighted the differences between Gordon and his adversaries on the foreign investment issue, Winters and Trade Minister Mitchell Sharp.[101] The press noted Sharp's blunt reply to the suggestion that Canada should limit foreign economic and cultural influence: "Anyone who looks objectively at that prescription for national survival is bound to reject it. It could only weaken our economic structure and increase the temptation to join the United States."[102]

The prime minister seemed to confirm his commitment to Gordon in a 26 October speech in Wallaceburg, Ontario, but instead raised several questions about his promises to Winters. Pearson told his audience that Gordon would be continuing as minister of finance.[103] The next day Winters called on Pearson, and the two had an angry exchange over Gordon's role in the next government. Pearson later told Gordon that, in trying to convince Winters to run, he had promised him the trade and commerce portfolio.[104] Winters likely assumed that this meant that Sharp would be moved from trade and commerce to finance. When Pearson announced that Gordon was staying in finance, Winters felt he had been tricked. Exactly what Pearson was thinking is unclear. Gordon had long said that he would leave politics when Pearson did, and by late 1965 Pearson had decided to leave within a year. Knowing that Gordon would likely soon retire from political life, Pearson may have felt justified in telling Winters and the leaders of the business community that Gordon would soon be gone.[105]

On election day, 8 November, the Liberal party won 131 seats, only two more than before, and two short of a majority. The next day Gordon told the press that he intended to return to the finance portfolio, "where there is lots of hard work to do."[106] Though he had vowed to quit if the government did not win a majority, he did not believe that the prime minister should accept his resignation, especially since Pearson had pledged that Gordon would remain in the finance portfolio and had himself promised to resign if he did not win a majority. Even so, Gordon had promised to resign, and his sense of honour would never have allowed him not to go through with this undertaking: "I had said I would submit my resignation if we did not win an over-all majority and I would never have felt comfortable if I had failed to do so."[107] On the night of the election Gordon called Pearson and "reminded him of my promise to resign if we did not get an overall majority." Dejected, Pearson responded that he would be resigning himself. Gordon said that he would call on the prime minister as soon as he arrived in Ottawa. In the meantime he drafted a letter of resignation. At the Cabinet meeting two days later "everyone urged Mike to stay on, which he agreed to do." Pearson said he would meet Gordon that afternoon, "but when the time came [he] put me off" until the next day.

When Gordon and Pearson finally met at the prime minister's residence three days after the election, the mood was tense. Pearson told Gordon "that there would have to be some major shifts in the Cabinet." Pearson intended to ask Gordon if he would accept another portfolio, but he did not intend to force the issue. Gordon assumed that he was about to be moved to another portfolio "despite what had been said before and during the campaign." He handed Pearson his resignation, reminding his friend that he had "undertaken to resign if we did not get a comfortable majority." Relieved that Gordon was leaving the finance portfolio, Pearson accepted the resignation. Gordon perceived this as an act of betrayal, and at that moment the long friendship between the two men ended, though Pearson did not realize it at the time. In

Gordon's view, "Mike was taking advantage of my offer to resign if the election went against us in order to make a change at Finance – despite his promises to me privately and his public statement during the campaign to the contrary. We both knew this."[108] Tom Kent, close to both Pearson and Gordon, outlined the situation clearly: "I think Walter was entitled to expect that while it was the right thing for him to do to offer it, it was equally the right thing that it not be accepted."[109] Despite the tremendous sense of being let down Gordon continued to conduct himself with dignity. At a dinner shortly after resigning Gordon, according to Keith Davey, "sang the praises of us all – and especially of Prime Minister Pearson."[110] Dave Ferguson of Woods Gordon remembered that Gordon did not criticize Pearson after resigning: he "made no fuss over this incident."[111] But his diary notes show clearly his level of bitterness and his sense that he had been betrayed.[112]

Gordon had served a strange term as minister of finance. He had assumed the portfolio with two main goals: to improve Canada's social safety net and to limit foreign investment in Canada. On one front he had had tremendous success. Many of the important achievements of the Pearson government – the Canada Pension Plan, Medicare, increased funding for universities – were inspired by Gordon, implemented by his followers, and facilitated by that unusual creature, a finance minister who said yes to proposals for new spending. In the words of Tom Kent, "the social programs of the Pearson period ... were very much the policies of Walter Gordon ... Without him, there could not have been the major transformation of Canadian society achieved through Medicare, the Canada Pension Plan (integrated with the reform of Old Age Security), extended family allowance, student loans, the Canada Assistance Plan, and other measures."[113] On the other front, however, Gordon was a failure. His initiative to reduce foreign investment was thoroughly defeated, and for the remainder of his term he seemed to accept the closer integration of Canada and the United States. He worked to ensure that the United States interest-equalization tax would not reduce the flow of American capital to Canada. He withdrew his proposal to raise the withholding tax to 20 per cent, one of the few measures remaining from his original budget. When his colleagues rejected his recommendation that the government take no action to stem the growth of foreign magazines in Canada, Gordon convinced the Liberal caucus to support an exemption for the two biggest American periodicals. He advanced the Auto Pact, which linked, perhaps inextricably, the Canadian and American automobile industries. He displayed little interest in the proposal to give Canada a new flag, and opposed a distinctive honours system. Gordon continued to talk about reducing American influence in Canada, and he still promoted his idea for a Canada Development Corporation, but not with enough vigour to see that Cabinet approved a specific proposal. He never reintroduced the 30 per cent takeover tax that he had been forced to withdraw from his original budget. Other than the measures to prevent foreign control of insurance, trust, and loan companies, he implemented no policies to promote Canadian independence, a goal he had been pursuing for almost a decade.

In his last months in the finance portfolio, as Gordon's failure to achieve his goals became more and more apparent, something unusual happened. There appeared the first signs that his ideas could catch the public imagination, at least in English-speaking Canada, and that some of his proposals to limit foreign control of Canadian industry could become law. The reaction to Grant's *Lament* and to the Heeney-Merchant Report revealed a growing dissatisfaction with the United States; many Canadians now wanted their country to be more independent of its neighbour. In two and a half years in office Gordon had failed, largely because he had misjudged the public mood and the need to convince Canadians of his policies. In subsequent years, events would help to persuade Canadians that Gordon's ideas had value, and Gordon would be there to shape a growing movement.

CHAPTER SIX

The Dilemma of Canadian Affluence 1966–1968

In the three years following his resignation from the finance portfolio, Walter Gordon's views on foreign investment had little impact on the policies of the Liberal government. Hoping to influence his former Cabinet colleagues, Gordon wrote a second book on public policy, published in May 1966. *A Choice for Canada* again stressed the importance of reducing Canada's dependence on outside capital, an idea Gordon tried to promote during a speaking tour that spring and fall. Despite his efforts, Gordon's proposals were firmly defeated at the Liberal policy conference in October. Eventually, Pearson succumbed to pressure from Gordon's supporters and brought him back into the Cabinet, though neither Pearson nor Gordon's caucus allies fully shared the former finance minister's ideas on foreign investment. But despite Gordon's failure to convince his colleagues, his ideas became widely embraced by the Canadian public, particularly intellectuals, writers, and students.

Changing demographics played an important role in the rising popularity of Gordon's views. The rising birthrate after 1945 had given power and influence to the large number of young Canadians who were coming of age in the late 1960s. And in any society, a large number of young people means greater social, cultural, and political change.[1] Growing up in prosperous times, members of the new generation faced few financial worries and felt detached from their parents, who had been raised during the Great Depression of the 1930s.[2] This generation gap was widened by the fear of nuclear war, which led to a "live for today" attitude, as countless young Canadians believed their world was on the eve of destruction. Intent on taking control of their own destiny, many young people began to question authority in all its forms. As the *Globe and Mail* noted in August 1966, there was a "curious mood of rebellion, of resentment, not perhaps clearly recognized but nevertheless expressed [in ways that show] Canadians are doubting all former stable things."[3] This mood created favourable conditions for what came to be called the "new nationalism" in Canada.

The new nationalism also benefited from the celebration of Canada's centennial in 1967, an event that raised the level of visible patriotism across the country. In the words of historian Michael Bliss, "All of 1967 was a year to buy books about Canada, see Canadian plays, celebrate being a Canadian."[4] Montreal hosted the world's fair, and communities across Canada engaged in centennial projects, from creating new parks to building new libraries, schools, or arenas.[5] The standard designs on Canada's coinage were changed to commemorate the event, and most Canadians became familiar with "CA-NA-DA," a song that captured the euphoric spirit of a country celebrating its hundredth birthday. "With money and attention lavished on national festivities as never before, we became aware of Canada as never before," remembered art historian Susan Crean. The centennial celebrations, in Crean's words, "raised hard questions about the future of our country."[6]

More important in shaping public opinion were events outside the country. For many Canadians, racial strife in the United States and that country's involvement in the Vietnam War called American values into question. "We cannot at present discuss our relations with the United States in a cool, rational frame of mind," wrote historian Frank Underhill in 1966.[7] Canada's neighbour seemed violent and self-destructive, especially to people living near Detroit and Rochester, cities that experienced race riots and urban guerrilla warfare. Several prominent Americans were assassinated in the years between 1963 and 1968: President John Kennedy, black leaders Malcolm X and Martin Luther King Jr, and presidential candidate Robert Kennedy. Canadians also witnessed the violence of the battle over civil rights in the American south. In March 1965 the radical Student Union for Peace Action (SUPA), one of many Canadian protest groups that appeared in the 1960s, organized a demonstration in Toronto in support of the thousands marching from Selma to Montgomery, Alabama, in defence of black voting rights. SUPA organizers were taken by surprise when a crowd of at least a thousand, on hearing that the American marchers had twice been turned back by state police using nightsticks and tear-gas, gathered for a sit-in protest outside the U.S. consulate.[8] In 1967 John W. Warnock, an American citizen and professor of political science at the University of Saskatchewan, noted that "the mood of Canadians has changed considerably." Why the change? According to Warnock, "Many Canadians have been disturbed by U.S. policy and tactics in

Vietnam, and by the inability of the United States to offer a solution to poverty and racism in the United States. Such policies reveal significant flaws in the U.S. political and economic system."[9]

Significant numbers of Canadians first began questioning the war in early 1965, with the start of the American bombing of North Vietnam. Between June 1965 and June 1966, the number of Canadians who thought the United States should continue its part in the war dropped from 66 per cent to 45 per cent.[10] By 1967 a growing number of individuals, many of them leaders in their field, began to challenge American involvement. This opposition was particularly strong in the academic community and was fostered by the large number of American expatriates, many of them draft evaders, who had found refuge in Canadian universities. In his extensive study of anti-Americanism, Paul Hollander argues that the Americans in Canadian universities helped to confirm and perhaps deepen the "apprehensions about the United States ... infusing [them] with especially vehement critical sentiments toward American society."[11] Opposition also grew among the general population, fuelled in part by the media's vivid depiction of the war. In April 1967, for instance, the *Star Weekly* magazine devoted eleven pages to the impact of the war on Vietnamese children. The cover showed a Vietnamese girl with a patch over one eye and a long gash under the other. The headline was set in red type: "HOW CANADA TURNED ITS BACK ON VIET NAM'S MAIMED CHILDREN." The issue included ten photographs, seven in colour, many of them depicting maimed and disfigured youngsters.[12] The portrayal of the war was even more gruesome on television, a medium that transformed the conflict into the "living-room war," a phrase coined by American journalist Michael J. Arlen.[13]

In the academic community, many of those who fervently condemned the Vietnam War would later embrace Gordon's ideas. One example was Abraham Rotstein, a young professor at the University of Toronto. In 1964 Gordon had written to praise Rotstein's review of Harry Johnson's book *The Canadian Quandary*, saying, "I am delighted that someone has had the courage to take on Harry Johnson and debunk him."[14] First meeting Gordon in May 1965, Rotstein was impressed that they had similar views on Vietnam.[15] As managing editor of the *Canadian Forum* after 1967, Rotstein had considerable influence in Canadian intellectual circles.[16] Also condemning the Vietnam War was Melville Watkins, another intellectual who would later become closely associated with Gordon. In a letter to the editor of the *Globe and Mail* in 1965, Rotstein, Watkins, and several other professors denounced the United States for the torture of prisoners in Vietnam: "We earnestly hope that Canada will leave no doubt in Washington and in the United Nations concerning her condemnation of these uncivilized practices wherever they occur."[17] Watkins, a professor of political economy at the University of Toronto, later remembered, "I was radicalized by Vietnam. The anti-war movement in Canada developed into anti-imperialism and for me that translated into nationalism."[18] The same was true for many others.

Rotstein and Watkins were instrumental in organizing a teach-in at the University of Toronto in October 1965. Teach-ins had begun in the United States as a way of protesting American policy towards Vietnam. According to Rotstein, the goal of the Toronto teach-in was "to bring both government representatives and university people from both sides of the iron curtain to discuss the theme of the present response to revolution in underdeveloped areas." The discussion would focus on the situations in Vietnam and the Dominican Republic. Gordon was good friends with the teach-in's honourary chairman, University of Toronto President Claude Bissell, and two other members of the honourary board, Escott Reid and Tuzo Wilson. He encouraged the organizers and helped them in their efforts to obtain the necessary legal status to give tax receipts to donors.[19]

Held in Varsity Arena, the teach-in drew six thousand students, 120 journalists, and, by radio, one million listeners. Rotstein and Watkins described the receptive audience: "They applauded, booed, gave standing ovations and asked questions with a quick intelligence and flair that had never been dreamt of in the lecture hall." One of the speakers was George Grant, who told listeners, "Our greatest obligation as Canadian citizens is to work for a country which is not simply a satellite of any empire." For many young intellectuals – such as Ed Broadbent and Mel Watkins – the teach-in was an overwhelming experience. Other young Canadians would have similar experiences at universities across the country.[20]

Reaction to the war and to American domestic problems was particularly sharp in the literary community. The 1960s saw the unprecedented growth of Canadian literature and the creation of several small, nationalistic publishing houses. One of the best examples was the House of Anansi Press, founded in 1967 by two young professors of English, Dennis Lee and Dave Godfrey. Anansi's best-selling book was the *Manual for Draft-Age Immigrants to Canada*, which sold 45,000 copies in less than two years.[21] Early Anansi authors included Lee, Godfrey, Margaret Atwood, Al Purdy, George Grant, and American poet Allen Ginsberg. They came from different backgrounds, but, recalled Douglas Fetherling, Anansi's first employee, they had one thing in common: "They were all, at some fundamental level, against more or less the same thing: Americanism, with its republican brutality and hatred of culture."[22] Despite the relatively limited circulation of most of Anansi's books, the press had an important impact on the Canadian literary community.

In the late 1960s the works of Canadian writers, including several Anansi authors, expressed a highly negative view of American politics and society. To many the United States was a violent place, an opinion graphically illustrated in a poem by Margaret Atwood:

> Your righteous eyes, your laconic
> trigger-fingers
> people the streets with villains:
> as you move, the air in front of you
> blossoms with targets[23]

In a similar vein C.J. Newman began a poem with these jarring lines:

> America you bastard
> murderer of dreams[24]

For Raymond Souster, the problem was American foreign and domestic policy both:

> America
> how do you turn quiet home-loving men in five short years into hate-
>   fired Black Muslim avengers who write and scream out to their
>   brothers: break doors, smash windows at night or any time, bust
>   in every store window, drag all you can carry, set fire, kill or
>   maim whitey, pump holes into every dirty cop or get him good
>   with a brick or your own two hands ...
> America
> the world has watched you in Vietnam and even its hardened stomach
>   has been turned, you have all but buried yourself in your own
>   Coca-Cola beer can litter, your bar-to-bar Saigon filth so well
>   aped by the small men you came to save but instead have cor-
>   rupted forever; after your crazy "weed killer" squadrons have
>   bared all the trees, after your Incinderjell has roasted all available
>   corpses, then perhaps we'll see at last every barbed wire death
>   camp, count every tin can house left standing, see how much rice
>   still grows ...[25]

Writers were critical also of American influence in Canada. In a parable by Lionel Kearns, Americans were portrayed as wolves who "exported vast quantities of shit, creating a demand for it by TV advertising, phoney sweepstakes and outright force of arms."[26] In Al Purdy's "Homo Canadensis" an American lectured Canadians on their unwillingness to oppose American influence, referring to previous incidents that had aroused a sense of indignation in Canada: "Anybody know about the Alaska Panhandle deal, or remember the Herbert Norman case, by any chance? Well, I'm telling you, this country is being taken like a glass of beer. It's a matter of economics. And none of you guys really give a damn, just slop your beer and want to be taken by some big bellied American in Washington."[27] Barry Lord offered a solution that sounded like an extreme version of Gordonism:

Let us advise the profiteers that the plunder called development is at an end. I say to people like George Grant, Farley Mowat, Alvin Hamilton, Walter Gordon, Tommy Douglas, James Minifie – whoever will stand for a genuinely free Canada – that we must all join in such a struggle, a Canadian independence movement ... We must take Canada back, by whatever means our owner makes necessary, and then give the resources and industries of this land to its own people. Let us organize a new Canada in which people, not American-controlled corporations, come first.[28]

Gordon expressed his concern over the Vietnam War and American influence in Canada in his second book, published in May 1966. *A Choice for Canada: Independence or Colonial Status* was written "to stimulate serious discussion of issues I see as important and to have these considered prior to the Liberal policy convention in the fall."[29] The book disappointed many of those who expected revelations about Gordon's struggle inside the Pearson Cabinet and found instead, in the words of one writer, "a rather dull restatement of Gordonism."[30] The book was written in Gordon's usual pedestrian style, which Peter C. Newman described as "the dry style of a manual on bee keeping."[31] Still, the book had a considerable impact on the Canadian public, selling 12,000 copies within six months.[32] During the week the book appeared the *Globe and Mail* published four articles on Gordon in a single day; the *Toronto Star* ran four stories over two days, while the *Star Weekly* gave Gordon a five-page spread.[33] In the words of political scientist John McLeod, "Never before in Canadian history has a political manifesto been the subject of such ballyhoo."[34] Eric Kierans, who more than anyone else had destroyed Gordon's first budget, first realized the book's popularity while on a speaking tour in the spring of 1966. After speaking, Kierans found the audience "invariably mentioned" Gordon's book and George Grant's *Lament for a Nation*. According to Kierans, "the sharp discussions that followed gave me an insight into the deep hold over young people that these two spirited Canadians exercise."[35]

In *A Choice for Canada* Gordon became the first prominent Liberal to argue publicly that Canada should oppose American escalation of the war in Vietnam. The Canadian government should do everything possible "to help the Americans extricate themselves from their present predicament before it is too late." At the same time Canadians "should do everything we can to mobilize world opinion and world influence to stop the so-called escalation of the war." Quiet diplomacy was out of the question: "This is one of the occasions when Canada should be prepared to risk the displeasure of the United States by speaking out, if there is any chance that our speaking out would do some good."[36]

Gordon's main concern, however, was not Vietnam but foreign investment in Canada. In his new book he again suggested that the tax laws be changed to favour firms with at least 25 per cent Canadian ownership. He also proposed the introduction of a tax on foreign takeovers of Canadian businesses, similar to the one he had been forced to withdraw in 1963. He again pushed for the creation of a Canada Development Corporation that could purchase existing companies, "including companies which otherwise might have been sold to foreigners."[37]

Gordon implied, as he had often done before, that foreign ownership in Canada was increasing: "Some may think it is unnecessary to continue stressing the need for Canada to retain her independence. But considering the rate at which it is being lost, I believe we should keep on pointing out what is happening." Though the proportion of foreign ownership had not changed significantly since the publication of the Gordon Report, he gave a different impression, devoting four pages of his new book to listing the many foreign takeovers that had occurred since 1959. He lamented International Paper's dominance over the forest-products industry in eastern Canada but, not surprisingly, did not mention his own role in helping that company to strengthen its position. His list of foreign takeovers did not include Canadian Corporate Management's sale of six businesses to the American-owned company in the late 1950s.[38]

In his new book Gordon criticized the extraterritorial application of American laws, which showed "how foreign ownership can influence the day-to-day operations of the Canadian economy."[39] As minister of finance, however, Gordon had not sought a legal or diplomatic solution to the problem of extraterritoriality. Indeed, he had not even raised the issue in intergovernmental negotiations because he did not consider it sufficiently important.[40] Nevertheless, he cited the threat of extraterritoriality as a reason for reducing the level of foreign investment in Canada.

Gordon repeated his view that foreign-owned firms prevented their Canadian subsidiaries from seeking export markets that might compete with the parent company. This conclusion, however, was based not on any research but on anecdotal evidence: "Subsidiaries of American corporations in Canada have been told on occasion not to promote sales of their products in particular export markets where the parent company or another of its subsidiaries has an established interest."[41] Gordon was aware that recent studies contradicted him. At the annual meeting of the American Economic Association in 1963, A.E. Safarian had presented the results of his research on the exports of American-owned companies in Canada.[42] He determined that the parent firm restricted the export policy of only one-tenth of the American-owned enterprises he studied. Most subsidiaries found that foreign ownership helped their exports, including those to the United States. Safarian's research, which Gordon had encouraged, suggested that economic considerations – particularly the inability to compete – were to blame for any cases where companies failed to export.[43] These economic factors had the same effect on both Canadian and foreign-owned firms. Safarian's research seemed to confirm the conclusions of a report that Gordon had commissioned in the late 1950s as head of the Canadian-American Committee's subcommittee on investment.[44] That study, written by John Lindeman and Donald Armstrong, found that there was no significant difference between the export performance of foreign-owned and Canadian firms.[45] Edward English, a former researcher on the Gordon Commission, came to similar conclusions after studying the chemical, machinery and equipment, and consumer-durables industries. English found that foreign-owned firms in these industries were willing to export when the tariff enabled and encouraged exports.[46] Most subsequent studies supported Safarian's conclusion that foreign-owned firms were no less likely to export than their Canadian counterparts.[47] Gordon, however, was unconvinced by this academic research.

Gordon also attacked the performance of foreign-owned firms in other areas. He asserted that they tended to import parts and components from outside Canada, conducted less research in Canada, and were less likely to have Canadian officers and employ Canadian professional firms.[48] On many of these points, research suggested that Gordon's fears were unfounded. Scholarly studies supported some of Gordon's conclusions, but even those economists who backed his views argued that economic factors, not the nationality of the owners, caused the difference between the performance of Canadian and foreign-owned firms.[49] Companies tried to increase profits, not to conduct government policy. As Safarian suggested, "Where behaviour that has been defined as undesirable by public authorities does appear, it can often be related more closely to aspects of the economic environment of the subsidiary and only distantly, if at all, to the fact of foreign ownership."[50]

Gordon's views on the significance of nationality were unclear. In a speech in 1965 he asserted "that factors of production such as capital *do* have a nationality."[51] Yet in 1967, when discussing his own business experience, Gordon suggested a different interpretation: "If there's an important decision which is affecting export policy or pricing policy or something important, then I fancy I would expect the decision to be made by the owners and made in the interests of maximizing the profit of the total corporation ... I was a businessman for a good many years; I think I understand the motivations of businessmen. Certainly, if you are running a parent corporation with subsidiaries any place, you are thinking of the total corporation and its interests rather than the particular interests of any subsidiary."[52] Gordon argued that the problem was not so much the nationality of the owners but their desire to maximize profit for the parent company. In the case of Canadian-owned firms Gordon judged that profit-making was in the country's best interest, the perspective not of a worker, a farmer, or a public servant but of a Canadian capitalist. Gordon wanted to deal with the perceived poor performance of American firms not by passing laws encouraging them to buy parts in Canada, hire Canadians, or conduct more research but by giving more control to Canadian entrepreneurs. The country's interests were best protected by Canadian owners, not by Parliament. Gordon knew many of the more selfish and cynical elements of the business community, and must have realized that Canadian entrepreneurs would not always work in what he believed was the country's best interest. He was himself a great philanthropist and likely disapproved of those members of the business community who seemed not to have a conscience. His desire to put more power in the hands of the Canadian business community was not, therefore, merely a reflection of Gordon's position as a capitalist. It also reflected a more deep-seated suspicion of American economic power.

In *A Choice for Canada* Gordon changed his sales technique. In the early 1960s he had asserted that there was an economic cost to regaining control of the economy and that Canadians should be prepared to make the sacrifice.[53] He now insisted that his policies would help to raise the standard of living: "The greater production of goods and services in Canada, which would result from the proposals for improving our balance of payments and the lower costs of servicing foreign capital, would increase our living standards."[54] Gordon clung to this argument for the rest of his life, despite its rejection by most academic economists.[55] He had, according to Harry Johnson, ignored a basic law of economics: "The law is simply that, if the economy is operating at or near full employment as the Canadian economy has been and as governmental policy should ensure it will, foreign investment can be cut only if the economy cuts back on its investment and its growth rate, or cuts back on its consumption to increase its domestic saving and finance its growth itself."[56] A reduction in investment had to carry with it a cost to the Canadian economy.

Though it was slowly narrowing, the chasm between Gordon and the professional economists was particularly wide on the issue of trade. As head of the Royal Commission on Canada's Economic Prospects, Gordon had tried to suppress a study on the economic cost of the tariff and in 1960 had argued that "some moderate protection will be needed if Canadian secondary industry is to prosper and to provide employment for a substantial proportion of the total working force." For Gordon this was "one of the facts of Canadian economic life that there is just no escaping."[57] In *A Choice for Canada*, however, Gordon's views on the tariff appeared to have shifted. He now maintained that he was "very much against tariffs that protect high cost and inefficient industries," and after the book was published, he indignantly denied suggestions that he was a protectionist.[58] In the atmosphere of the mid-1960s it had become more and more difficult to defend protectionist policies. John Dales' book *The Protective Tariff in Canada's Development* had outlined the ways the tariff had decreased Canada's standard of living, an argument that had a significant impact on the Canadian intellectual community. Moreover, Canada had been largely successful in the Kennedy Round of tariff negotiations under the General Agreement on Tariffs and Trade, and the United Nations Conference on Trade and Development had condemned protectionism as damaging to less-developed countries. Though he had toned down his support for the tariff, however, Gordon never abandoned his view that Canadian industry required some substantial measure of protection.[59] Nor did he acknowledge that one of the effects of the tariff was extensive foreign ownership and the branch-plant mentality that he so despised. As economist Mel Watkins wrote, "One wishes he would pay ... more attention to the economists when they demonstrate ... the extent to which foreign control has been increased by the very existence of the tariff."[60]

A Choice for Canada received a mixed reception from politicians. John Turner told a press conference in Regina that the book did not "represent the main stream of Liberal thinking."[61] Eric Kierans criticized Gordon's ideas, saying that the proposed measures were "neither feasible nor worthy of us. These measures look no better now than they did in '63."[62] But Kierans' views had begun to change. He had been outraged when, in December 1965, the United States government had issued guidelines to American subsidiaries abroad, asking them to help the country's balance-of-payments position by remitting more profits to their head offices.[63] In early 1966, after giving a speech critical of the United States, Kierans said to Gordon, "Walter, we're getting closer all the time."[64] His review of Gordon's book reflected this change in attitude: "The former Minister of Finance's well-known hostility toward foreign, particularly American, investment seemed finally justified when the United States government applied their famous guidelines to Canada." Kierans did not accept all of Gordon's ideas, but he was becoming more sympathetic to the former finance minister: "If Mr. Gordon were reappointed to the present Cabinet, it would be strengthened. We cannot accept his economic nationalism but his spirit and his concern for Canada are sorely needed."[65]

The day before the book appeared, Mitchell Sharp gave a speech in Toronto that suggested that his views were not very different from Gordon's. Sharp recognized the problems with foreign investment, saying that Canada could not "go on indefinitely being such an important consumer of scarce capital from abroad." But for Sharp the solution was to encourage Canadian ownership, not to discriminate against foreign owners, a policy that he considered "shortsighted." Sharp stressed that his priority was to deal with unemployment, not foreign investment: "I don't think that Canadian independence can be very meaningful or attractive to the unemployed or under-employed."[66] *A Choice for Canada* had been distributed to many journalists before its official release, and Gordon thought that Sharp had plagiarized the section on the Canada Development Corporation: "Obviously Sharp has seen the proofs of this book before his Toronto speech as several sentences in the speech seem to be taken word for word from the book."[67] A close comparison of Sharp's speech and Gordon's book suggests nothing of the sort. The two men had similar ideas on many areas of government policy, but Sharp did not use Gordon's words. Gordon's unreasonable suspicions instead reveal a growing tension between him and Sharp.

Writing in the *Tamarack Review*, Abraham Rotstein was one of the few professional economists to praise the book: "Beneath Walter Gordon's standoffish style and his clouded political career, there still remains at an intuitive

level, I believe, the soundest political instinct of any of our public figures."
Gordon was "the one public figure to have come closest to the dilemma of
Canadian affluence" because he understood that the new technology in Canada "has become available only through American ownership of our industrial enterprises." Rotstein commended him for not having adopted George
Grant's "posture of despair" in the face of the technological society and for
offering "a clear direction in mobilizing Canadian capital and taking measures against the further increase of American control of our economy."[68]
Rotstein's comments are noteworthy because he was the only economist to
review the book and not examine Gordon's understanding of the economics
of foreign investment.

By contrast, the reaction of other academic economists was negative, even
hostile, focusing on Gordon's weak grasp of economic theory. David Slater,
a former researcher for the Gordon Commission and editor of the *Canadian
Banker*, called the book "very biased and distorted." Slater was troubled
by "the rather extreme, autarchical, complicated discriminatory nature of
Mr. Gordon's recommendations." He praised the chapter on social policy,
where Gordon was "at his liberal best." On foreign investment, however,
Slater was harshly critical, particularly of Gordon's failure to produce substantial evidence to prove his case:

In discussing Foreign Investment, Mr. Gordon introduces us to the myriad ways in
which foreign-owned and controlled companies May limit Canadian exports, May be
biased toward importing materials and capital goods from abroad, May be biased
toward importing business services, May this, May that, May something else. In a
cockeyed world, anything is possible; but what is the world really like? What are the
fair rules of evidence in "establishing the facts" in an exercise of advocacy? If you
can find one or two examples to support your contention, can you reasonably argue
that your case is proved?[69]

As economist Bernard Bonin pointed out, the attacks on Gordon focused on
one point: "the almost total lack of proof for the views he advances."[70] On
the one hand, the economists were unreasonable in expecting a political manifesto to provide a detailed empirical study of Canadian industry, but on the
other, Canadians had a hard time accepting policies designed to solve a problem that Gordon could not prove existed.

In Quebec the reaction to Gordon's book was cold. *A Choice for Canada*
was Gordon's only book to be translated into French, but despite extensive
efforts to promote the book, sales were poor.[71] Quebeckers, including the

province's new leaders, showed little interest in Gordon's ideas on foreign ownership, preoccupied as they were with Quebec's relationship with the rest of Canada. Years later, René Lévesque, Pierre Trudeau, and Gérard Pelletier showed their indifference to Gordon's views on foreign ownership by failing even to mention the issue in their memoirs.[72]

After the book's release Gordon embarked on a campaign to spread his views. He tried to convince prominent academics and businessmen to speak publicly in support of his ideas, and sought to stimulate debate in the pages of the *Financial Post*, *Canadian Forum*, *Saturday Night*, and the *Toronto Star*.[73] He gave a series of speeches in seven Canadian cities between May and October.[74] Gordon's tone had become strikingly more urgent: "time is running out" for Canadian independence, he insisted. He proposed two-thirds Canadian ownership by the year 2000, a significant change from his earlier assertion that 25 per cent was enough to ensure that firms respected Canada's interests.[75] In Calgary, Gordon faced a hostile audience. "No doubt this was due in part to the considerable American presence in Calgary," he explained.[76] In Edmonton, Winnipeg, Port Arthur, and Sudbury, however, his reception was much better than he expected.[77]

As the Liberal party policy conference of October 1966 approached, the battle-lines were sharply drawn. Led by Manitoba leader Gildas Molgat, the four provincial Liberal associations in western Canada jointly submitted resolutions, the first of which was antagonistic to Gordon's views: "Be it resolved that the Government of Canada make every effort to attract international capital for the development of industry in Canada, while at the same time actively encouraging Canadians to participate in the development of their own nation."[78] Gordon's own proposals were moderate in tone, as he sought to win broad-based support. His primary objective continued to be the reduction of foreign ownership and control, though he noted the need for foreign capital: "We should continue to welcome inflows of foreign capital, particularly if it is invested in bonds and other fixed term securities ... We will need continued inflows of capital that is invested in equity (ownership) securities. However, we must ensure that more of this type of foreign investment is associated in partnership with Canadian capital." Gordon did not specifically recommend discriminatory measures to achieve his goals, instead proposing "incentives to Canadians to invest in business enterprises and resources in this country." But he did urge that the government promote policies, "including tax policies," to "reduce foreign ownership and control of Canadian industry and resources to not more than one-third in the next twenty-five years." This objective could not likely be achieved without some discriminatory measures.[79]

Delegates arriving at the conference received a series of background papers commissioned by the organizing committee. David Slater wrote the paper for the workshop on economic growth and development, and, not surprisingly, he opposed Gordon's views: "While the country has incurred both economic costs and gains from the size and form of her foreign investment relations, on balance Canada has been a substantial net economic beneficiary, in my belief." The ill effects of foreign investment had been, in Slater's opinion, "grossly exaggerated." He pointed to the work of his fellow economists, concluding "that Canada has been a substantial net economic beneficiary from the size and structure of her foreign investment relations."[80]

The policy conference took place in the ballroom of the Chateau Laurier Hotel in Ottawa. On Monday, 10 October, the delegates approved a resolution that instructed the government to begin negotiating a free trade agreement with the United States. "The Gordon group was not happy with that resolution," wrote journalist Victor Mackie. "But they were so busily engaged in organizing their forces to stand off the Western attack on Mr. Gordon's economic nationalism that they let it pass almost by default."[81] That day Gordon's followers held two large meetings to mobilize support for his policies.[82] Perhaps realizing that his side was outnumbered, Donald Macdonald, a Toronto member of Parliament and strong supporter of Gordon, approached Mitchell Sharp. He asked the minister of finance to support Gordon's resolutions, indicating that Gordon was willing to consider any changes Sharp might suggest. Sharp thought the proposals had "a strongly nationalistic flavour," which he did not share. "I told Macdonald I did not wish to be associated with the resolutions."[83]

On Tuesday, in a policy workshop on "Economic Growth and Development," Sharp spoke against Gordon's proposals. He tried to strike a moderate tone, accepting Gordon's concerns while rejecting his solutions. "We have reason to be concerned about our continued reliance upon massive imports of capital," Sharp asserted. In his view, however, "The best way to weaken Canadian independence is to follow narrowly nationalistic policies." Sharp proposed that the party adopt "positive policies, not negative policies," vaguely suggesting that the government "encourage Canadian industries."[84] Gordon, too, tried to portray himself as a moderate. He began by stressing his agreement with Sharp: "We agree on objectives and there is little difference between us on measures to achieve them." He described his own proposals as "a middle course," and insisted that by adopting them the party would "receive a tremendous public response from all parts of the country, particularly from young people." Despite his appeal, Gordon's proposals were shelved by an overwhelming vote of 650 to 100.[85]

Shortly after this defeat Gordon's representatives arranged a meeting in a small back room with Sharp, Molgat, and other senior delegates from western Canada. In the name of party unity the group hammered out a compromise statement that was adopted unanimously in the plenary session later that day. According to the new resolution, "the government should take steps to encourage greater Canadian ownership of the economy, without discouraging foreign investment." The delegates also endorsed the CDC, already a long-standing government policy, using verbatim Gordon's draft resolution.[86] The party rejected, however, the key part of Gordon's proposals, the section that recommended the reduction of "foreign ownership and control of Canadian industry and resources to not more than one-third in the next twenty-five years."[87] On the issue he judged most important, Gordon was clearly defeated.

Gordon tried to appear positive about the conference outcome, telling the press, "I got 95% of what I wanted."[88] As he explained in a private letter, "The resolutions on foreign ownership of the Canadian economy were so conflicting that our side thought it had won – or at least it did so until the Press informed us the following day that those who shared my views had been thoroughly discomfited."[89] To others, however, Gordon admitted that he had lost. He wrote to Lawrence Pennell, a close ally in Cabinet, and explained his reaction: "I was disappointed in the Convention and particularly in the fact that a good majority of the delegates made it quite clear they are not interested in doing anything about the increasing foreign control of our economy."[90] Gordon blamed his defeat on a lack of organization: "We were out-smarted and out-manoeuvred at the Convention."[91]

Gordon, it now appeared, had no constituency in the Liberal party, only friends. Peter Newman noted the change in Gordon's stature from 1963 to 1966: "In those brave early days, he was the Leader's confidante, the moulder of great victories, the maker of political miracles, but now he is dispossessed and the umbrella of Liberalism is no longer broad enough to cover this man and his passionate ideas."[92] According to Bruce Hutchison, the conference "was the final destruction of Walter Gordon."[93] Gordon recognized his growing powerlessness: "Quite frankly, I am not at all sure that I can accomplish very much in the position I am in at present."[94]

After his defeat at the policy conference Gordon decided to retire from political life. On 29 October he told Pearson of his intention to resign from Parliament. "I said I could not put in another year like the last one and intended to resign my seat ... during the Xmas recess. I added that I would be honest in giving my reasons – that I am not in sympathy with the Party's present policy direction."[95] In the summer of 1966 Pearson had planned to bring Gordon back into the Cabinet, even offering him the transport portfolio, but after the confrontation at the policy conference he thought that Gordon's return had become impossible.[96] Gordon's only options were to resign or to stay in Parliament as a back-bencher, a job that he never enjoyed.

When they heard of his intention to quit, several of Gordon's caucus colleagues intervened. On 9 November members of the Ontario caucus held a dinner in Gordon's honour, intending to show Pearson their support for Gordon.[97] Roughly thirty MPs and senators attended, including Pearson and Sharp, with several paying tribute to Gordon. "Strong men wept," remembered Jimmy Walker, who had organized the dinner. "It was a most emotional evening. We said, 'Walter, stay. You're the heart and soul of the spirit of Liberalism in this party.' "[98] On 12 December Maurice Lamontagne wrote a memorandum to Pearson recommending that Gordon prepare a new platform and take charge of the federal organization in Ontario. "Mr. Pearson should insist until he gets an affirmative answer," he wrote. "Walter Gordon is the best qualified Liberal to carry out these two important jobs effectively and our party simply cannot afford to lose his services."[99] The next week Treasury Board President E.J. "Ben" Benson suggested that Gordon be appointed minister without portfolio with responsibility for organizing the work of the Cabinet.[100] Under considerable pressure, the prime minister finally relented and urged Gordon to meet with him before resigning. In Pearson's view, "It was better to have him in the Cabinet with the collective responsibilities of membership than have him attacking our financial and economic policies from without."[101]

On 29 December Pearson and Gordon met to discuss his return to Cabinet. The prime minister asked Gordon to take responsibility for organizing the work of Cabinet and the business of the party. Gordon was intrigued by these suggestions, but as he had indicated to Benson, he did not like the title of minister without portfolio. Instead, Gordon suggested that he should be deputy prime minister or possibly president of the Privy Council. Gordon was also reluctant to rejoin the Cabinet given the policy differences between him and the other members of the government. He told Pearson that he would only return if he and Sharp could settle their disagreements. The matter was not resolved, but Gordon agreed to delay his resignation. Pearson would outline in writing what he wanted Gordon to do in Cabinet, and they would meet with Sharp on 3 January.[102]

In the meantime Gordon proposed the measures he expected the Cabinet to take upon his return. He suggested that within two months the government should prepare a policy paper on foreign investment that would be referred to the Standing Committee on Finance, Trade and Economic Affairs, with appropriate legislation to be introduced in the fall. The paper would outline the creation of a commission to enforce guidelines for foreign-controlled companies on matters such as exports and purchasing policy. Moreover, all companies with a net worth of more than $25 million – foreign-owned or not – would be required to make shares gradually available to the public by listing them on the stock exchanges. After twenty-five or thirty years, at least two-thirds of the shares of any major corporation would be held publicly: "The objective would be to break the present parent-subsidiary structure in the case of all 'large' companies. This would be accomplished by the proposed diffusion of ownership which would not be discriminatory against u.s. or other foreign corporations because it would apply as well to Canadian controlled companies."[103] Gordon did not discuss fully the implications of this policy, which would have radically restructured Canadian industry.

In a meeting with Pearson and Gordon on 3 January, Sharp rejected Gordon's proposals. Instead, the three agreed to establish a Cabinet committee to supervise the work of a task force of experts charged with examining the problem of foreign investment. The committee would then outline the government's policy in a white paper, which would be studied by Parliament. As Pearson recalled, "We agreed – Sharp only with great reluctance and against his better judgment – that Mr. Gordon would be Chairman of this Cabinet group, the other members of which would be picked by me." The three also discussed government policy towards the Mercantile Bank, which was wholly owned by Citibank of New York. In the meeting, remembered Pearson, "Walter was bitter and uncompromising on the Mercantile Bank." According to government policy, Citibank would have to reduce its level of ownership to 25 per cent. Sharp and Pearson agreed that no concessions would be made to Citibank, though the exact nature of the agreement was unclear. In Pearson's mind, "Sharp and I felt we had agreed only to no change of policy but that we were not precluded from giving an extension of time, to remove allegations of unfair discrimination, if the Bank agreed to become 75% Canadian." Gordon understood simply "that there would be no compromising on the subject of the Mercantile Bank."[104]

With the policy differences seemingly settled and the promise of a senior position, Gordon was prepared to return to the Cabinet. On 4 January he received a letter from Pearson inviting him back, but he found it completely unacceptable because it did not include any reference to the committee on foreign ownership or his supervision of the Cabinet. In a highly unusual move, Gordon redrafted the letter and sent it back to Pearson. In Gordon's draft the prime minister would ask him to supervise the work of the Cabinet, screen matters being brought before Cabinet, ensure that Cabinet decisions were implemented, participate in a small ministerial committee that would plan and organize legislative and government business, chair a committee that would write a white paper on foreign investment, plan and organize political tactics, chair a group to plan party policy, and liaise between Cabinet and caucus, and between Cabinet and the National Liberal Federation. These wide-ranging powers would have made Gordon de facto co-prime minister. Pearson approved the draft and agreed to send a letter along those lines. He also agreed orally that Gordon would initially be appointed minister without portfolio but would assume the title of president of the Privy Council after Guy Favreau's appointment to the bench. At a press conference later that day Pearson announced Gordon's return to Cabinet, though he refused to answer questions about Gordon's specific responsibilities.[105]

Pearson's second letter asking Gordon to return to Cabinet, sent the next day, was considerably more vague than Gordon's draft, which he had approved. It discussed most of the issues raised in the draft, but rather than assigning Gordon responsibility for supervising the work of Cabinet, it said that he would "collaborate with me in the organizing of Cabinet business and in facilitating and expediting the decisions which are made."[106] Later, regretting the misunderstandings between him and Gordon, Pearson wrote: "It would have been better ... if we could have been clearer in all our understandings, indeed have reduced them to writing."[107] But Gordon had pushed to have the prime minister's commitments made clear, explicit, and in writing, all to no avail. Pearson preferred to be vague and avoid conflict, perhaps because he could not accept Gordon's demands.

The Cabinet response to Gordon's return was mixed. Those who had worked as intermediaries in bringing him back, including Benson, Pennell, and Allan MacEachen, were naturally pleased. Judy LaMarsh, a strong Gordon partisan, was also happy to see his return.[108] For political reasons both Mitchell Sharp and Paul Martin welcomed Gordon's reinstatement.[109] Many other ministers, however, were troubled by his return. Robert Winters and John Connolly did not want Gordon in the Cabinet, and neither did Paul Hellyer and Jack Pickersgill, who feared that he would become a further source of division in an already divided Cabinet.[110] "Walter is a loner who must be top dog or he won't play," Hellyer recorded in his diary. In his view, Gordon's return was due to "the power of the *Toronto Star*, Peter Newman, good press relations."[111]

After Gordon's appointment as minister without portfolio, he discovered opposition to the creation of the Cabinet committee on foreign investment. On 17 January he met with Pearson, Sharp, and Winters to discuss the matter, and was annoyed when Sharp suggested that Pearson head the committee instead of Gordon. In Gordon's view, "There is no doubt that (a) Sharp & especially Winters are strongly opposed to doing anything (Sharp would go along with a whitewash approach) (b) that Mike will renege if he can (perhaps I am being unfair) (c) that nobody really gives a damn."[112] Nevertheless, on Gordon's insistence Pearson agreed to appoint him committee chair. On 23 January the prime minister announced the creation of the committee of ministers to "examine the structure of Canadian industry, with special reference to foreign ownership and control." The studies for the committee would be conducted by the Task Force on the Structure of Canadian Industry in consultation with a committee of senior public servants.[113]

Gordon began to wonder when he would be made responsible for co-ordinating the work of the Cabinet. On 9 February, Pearson promised that, after Gordon's appointment as Privy Council president, "the rest would follow."[114] On 4 April, Gordon was sworn in as president of the Privy Council, and over the next few days he had several brief conversations with Pearson about assuming control of the Privy Council Office, which functioned as the prime minister's government department. When Gordon Robertson, clerk of the Privy Council and secretary to the Cabinet, heard of the promise to Gordon, he explained that the changes would mean that Pearson "would have no department serving him as prime minister." According to Robertson, Pearson only recognized the problem at that point. "I think he hadn't thought it through," Robertson remembered. "Pearson hadn't realized that the secretary to the cabinet spoke to him as deputy minister to minister."[115] Pearson told Gordon that "he had not dreamed of all the problems" with the appointment until he had talked to Gordon Robertson. Gordon was upset and angry, and felt betrayed, telling Pearson that he wished he had not returned to Cabinet.[116] On Pearson's suggestion, the two met with Robertson on 26 April. Robertson insisted that the Privy Council Office staff "was really an extension of the P.M.'s staff and that any change in set up would not work out." Gordon replied that he had been promised control of the Privy Council Office when he had returned to Cabinet, and that if this promise was not kept, he would resign as soon as the task force had completed its work.[117] The next day Gordon sent a blunt letter to Pearson: "After thinking the matter over since our conversation yesterday, I feel I should ask you now, without further delays, to implement the various proposals and undertakings you made to me last January or, alternatively, to explain to me why you are not prepared to do so."[118] Pearson took almost three weeks to reply, but in the meantime Gordon realized that he would not hold the position he had been promised. "Inevitably Walter Gordon became quite depressed," remembered Keith Davey. "He felt detached. He found himself in a minority position in the Cabinet, no longer the leader of the team."[119]

The Mercantile Bank issue was another source of tension between Gordon and Pearson. In July 1966, Sharp introduced his version of the Bank Act amendments, essentially unchanged from Gordon's proposals, though he did remove the 6 per cent ceiling on interest rates charged by chartered banks. The provisions on foreign ownership were the same, but the limitation on the growth of foreign-owned banks would only come into effect on 15 December 1967. Mercantile's size would then be frozen until Citibank reduced its ownership to 25 per cent.[120] Gordon's memoirs record that on 9 February 1967 he heard that Sharp wanted to give Mercantile three years to expand, on the understanding that during this period it would sell 75 per cent of its stock to Canadians. "I was astonished," Gordon remembered.[121] Gordon's astonishment is odd; Sharp had indicated to Cabinet on at least two earlier occasions that he wished to arrange a compromise with Mercantile.[122] Nevertheless, Gordon told Pearson that he wanted the whole matter settled and that he now believed that Citibank should reduce its level of ownership to 10 per cent, not 25 per cent as specified in both his and Sharp's version of the bill.[123] To the prime minister it appeared that Gordon wanted to make conditions so difficult that Citibank would leave Canada, while Sharp and Pearson merely "wanted to get them to comply with the law, sell 75% of their stock to Canadians and become a Canadian bank."[124] Sharp agreed: "What Gordon wanted, I had to conclude, was to keep Citibank out of Canada."[125]

On 20 February, the day before he was to leave for a speaking tour in western Canada, Gordon asked the prime minister what Sharp planned to do with the Bank Act. "Mike replied that Sharp had decided not to do anything at all – certainly at this time. He might bring the matter up again later on but there will be no changes proposed in the present Bank Act revision. I repeated my concern about the matter and said I was pleased nothing was going to be done."[126] With Pearson's reassurance, Gordon left for Calgary. Two days later, he was called out of a meeting with eight hundred students at United College in Winnipeg to take an urgent call from Industry Minister Charles "Bud" Drury, his brother-in-law. "Bud said Sharp had spoken to him about a proposed deal with Mercantile to be dealt with by the Committee on

Finance, Trade & Economic Affairs that afternoon ... I told Bud the score ... & said I would resign if anything was done in my absence and without my approval."[127] Gordon said that he tried calling the finance minister, but Sharp would not take his calls; he left a message, but Sharp did not return it. Later in the day the minister appeared before the Finance Committee. At the beginning of the meeting he read two messages from the Mercantile Bank, asking for "a period of time" to make shares available to Canadians. "I think it is in that light that we should consider whether or not the Committee is disposed to be sympathetic to the request of the Mercantile Bank," Sharp announced. Responding to questions from Liberal MP Bryce Mackasey and other committee members, Sharp made it clear that he supported an extension: "I do not believe that an extension of the date is contrary to the spirit of the act, and it is possible that it would advance the cause of converting the Mercantile Bank into a predominantly Canadian-owned institution, which I believe is the best outcome."[128] Mackasey moved an amendment to the legislation that would give Mercantile five years to expand before being obliged to cut down to 25 per cent ownership. The amendment passed unanimously. Gordon thought, no doubt accurately, that Mackasey acted "with the knowledge and approval of the Minister of Finance."[129] Gordon called Pearson at about 11 P.M.: "I said I felt I had been *double-crossed*." Either Sharp would have to abide by the earlier agreement, "or I would have to resign."[130]

Gordon cancelled the rest of his speaking engagements and returned to Ottawa to confront Sharp. Before the Cabinet meeting on 23 February he met with Pearson and Sharp and reiterated his position that if concessions were to be made to Mercantile, the bank should be forced to comply with the requirements governing other banks, namely that no individual should be permitted to hold more than 10 per cent of the shares. "Sharp was completely adamant that he would make no concessions to me whatever and I said that in these circumstances he or I would have to go." In the Cabinet meeting later that day Sharp denied having initiated the amendment and insisted that it was developed by the committee, a rather dubious contention given that the committee minutes show his clear support for the amendment. In Gordon's view, "These assertions did not seem to be well received by members of the Cabinet who pointed out that the responsible minister must control the Committee dealing with his own legislation."[131]

Cabinet agreed that the problem should be resolved by the prime minister and a group of six ministers, including Gordon and Sharp. The next day, they met in the prime minister's office and, with Benson acting as mediator, reached a compromise. If Citibank would agree to sell 75 per cent of its shares to Canadians over a five-year period, the government would consider allowing Mercantile to grow, provided that its liabilities were limited to no more than twenty times its capitalization. If Citibank agreed to reduce its holdings to 10 per cent, it would not be subject to this restriction.[132] In essence, Citibank could reduce its ownership to 10 per cent by selling additional shares, thus expanding the bank's equity. Later that evening Gordon, Sharp, and Benson met to discuss ways of implementing the agreement. According to Gordon, "Sharp was very difficult. He argued the matter all over again & repudiated this morning's understandings … After about an hour he banged out of the office, angry and in a bad temper."[133] That evening Benson mediated a new agreement by telephone.[134] In Cabinet he would propose two amendments to the legislation, one saying that the five-year extension would not be automatic but would require Cabinet approval, and the other preventing any shareholder from acquiring more shares if he already possessed more than 10 per cent. Both Gordon and Sharp accepted these terms. Benson also planned to put forward two Cabinet resolutions that would express the government's position on any application for an extension. First, no extension on the ownership provisions would be given unless Citibank had given substantial evidence that it intended to sell 75 per cent of its shares to Canadians. Second, Mercantile's capital would not be increased until Citibank's share was reduced to 10 per cent. The resolutions, if Cabinet agreed, would be communicated to Citibank officials, but not made public. Sharp opposed the resolutions but agreed to abide by the Cabinet's decision. With the matter apparently settled, Gordon left for a two-week vacation in Jamaica.[135] On 28 February, Cabinet accepted the two amendments but postponed consideration of the controversial resolutions until Gordon's return.[136]

The next day, the compromise collapsed when its details were leaked to the press.[137] Sharp could no longer support the amendments because it would look as though he was backing down to Gordon. On 2 March, Gordon received a telephone call in Jamaica from Pennell, who advised him to return to Ottawa for the next Cabinet meeting. Sharp had announced that he wanted to have the issue settled as soon as possible.[138] In a press interview in Toronto on 4 March, Sharp repudiated the amendments that he had previously approved: "I've heard no suggestion of any change and I'm the minister of finance."[139]

There was, in Gordon's words, "a flaming row in cabinet" on 7 March.[140] Afterward, Pearson again met with several ministers to settle the matter. This time, no agreement was reached. Benson, who had negotiated the previous compromise, said that he would resign if Gordon did, believing that most of the Cabinet was on their side.[141] After still further negotiation the talented Benson convinced both sides to return to the agreement approved at the 28 February Cabinet meeting, though the amendments now would be introduced to the Commons by Liberal back-benchers. There would be no Cabinet resolution on the increase in Mercantile's capital, an issue that would be left open until the bank made a specific request. This compromise ended the byzantine struggle over the Bank Act, which the House of Commons finally passed on 21 March 1967.

The case of the Mercantile Bank provides an interesting contrast with Gordon's approach to foreign magazines. As auditor of many of the major Canadian banks, Gordon's accounting firm had a vested interest in their future. He knew that foreign companies were less likely to hire Canadian professional firms and more likely to employ the firm serving the parent company. Gordon, however, had no similar community of interests with Canadian magazines. He could see and understand the power and influence of banks in the business community, the world he knew best. He did not, in contrast, fully comprehend the power of magazines over Canadian cultural life, an area that was more esoteric and difficult to identify. As a result, Gordon was willing to give "squatters' rights" to *Time* and *Reader's Digest*, but not to the Mercantile Bank. In his opinion, "If we allowed Citibank to come here in a big way, sooner or later we would have to allow others in as well."[142] But he never advanced the same argument to limit the growth of the two American magazines or to force an end to their Canadian editions. The key to the puzzle, in Gordon's view, was money, not culture or ideas.

After the bank issue was settled, Gordon took a controversial step. On 13 May, a few days after it had become clear that he would not control the Cabinet agenda, Gordon spoke in Toronto on the Vietnam War. He had criticized the war in *A Choice for Canada*, and afterward had become "increasingly concerned about the devastation and the terrible cruelties inflicted on the inhabitants of that country who had been involved in almost continuous war for several generations." Gordon felt "an urge to express my own horror and revulsion about the escalation of the war." He was at odds with government policy on Vietnam, disagreeing with "Paul Martin's statements on the subject, which, while sometimes hard to interpret, seemed on the whole to support the policies and actions of the United States."[143] In his speech Gordon quoted extensively from American critics of the bombing, including Senators George McGovern and Robert Kennedy. For Gordon, the conflict was a local issue: "The U.S., for its part, has become enmeshed in a bloody civil war in Vietnam which cannot be justified on either moral or strategic grounds."[144] Gordon saw the war as a great moral issue, and, when preparing his speech, he remembered the criticism of those Germans who had remained silent while Hitler persecuted the Jews.[145] He may also have been motivated by a general distaste for the actions of the American government. Peter Newman summarized this sentiment in exaggerated terms: "Whether they were sending their hunter-killer teams into Vietnamese rice paddies or into Canadian boardrooms, Gordon saw most Americans as pushy imperialists who must be kept at bay."[146] Gordon gave the speech "in the knowledge that it would anger many people," and, according to executive assistant David Smith, he "might even have taken some secret pleasure from that."[147]

Writers have attempted to trace the origins of Gordon's views on the war, but with little success. Richard Gwyn thought that Abraham Rotstein "was the principal author" of the speech. Douglas Ross, in his outstanding history of Canadian policy towards the Vietnam War, asserted that "Gordon's views had been strongly shaped" by Rotstein and James Steele, a professor of English at Carleton University.[148] Rotstein, however, remembered that Gordon had developed his ideas on Vietnam himself and that they already had similar opinions of the war when they first met.[149] Steele never knew Gordon personally and could not say if he had influenced his ideas.[150] More likely, Gordon's views were merely an extension of his long-standing opposition to American policy in Asia, a position he expressed publicly as early as 1954.[151]

Although Gordon's speech was mild, it outraged several Cabinet members, including the prime minister. In private Pearson had voiced views similar to Gordon's, but he had not expected Gordon to express them publicly.[152] On 17 May, Pearson chaired a special Cabinet meeting to discuss Gordon's speech. No officials were present at the meeting, so the Cabinet secretary had to write the minutes from an account given to him orally by the prime minister.[153] Gordon's biggest critic was External Affairs Minister Paul Martin, who felt rightly that Gordon was interfering with his portfolio.[154] Martin later denied Gordon's accusation that he wanted his colleague fired, though his comments were ambiguous: "All I wanted him to do was follow the precepts of cabinet government. He had a right to speak out publicly on a matter he felt keenly about, but not as a member of the government that was instituting policy."[155] Martin might not have wanted Gordon fired, but he clearly believed that Gordon should have resigned, which amounted to the same thing. Winters, Sharp, Arthur Laing, and especially Hellyer were also critical of Gordon. Jean Marchand was a lone voice in defending Gordon, saying that he had read the speech and agreed with it. "It was a stormy meeting," Gordon remembered, "in the course of which I said I made no apologies – that I meant what I said – and would do it again. I had no intention of resigning but the p.m. could of course dismiss me if he wished to."[156]

During the meeting Pearson, always at his best in times of crisis, read a prepared statement outlining the government's policy on Vietnam. Pearson took issue with Gordon's argument that the United States was to blame for continuing the conflict: "The important thing is to end the war. It is not important now to establish blame or responsibility for the war; or who has the major responsibility for prolonging it; or who is most guilty of atrocities or cruelties. No single country bears sole responsibility in these matters. To concentrate condemnation and criticism for any of them on the u.s.a. – and to make public pronouncements to that effect – is wrong and unnecessary." Even so, Pearson made it clear later in the statement that Gordon was correct in calling on the United States to take the first steps to end the war: "We hope that the u.s.a., as the strongest of the warring parties, will take the initiative by bringing the bombing to an end and demanding that talks begin at once for an armistice and a settlement." The prime minister's declaration ended with a firmness that he seldom displayed: "Every member of this Government agrees with this policy and will make no statement or adopt no attitude that will make its pursuit more difficult." Because of the paragraph stressing the importance of an American initiative to restore the peace, Gordon said that he "could accept the statement despite its criticisms of myself." In the end, Cabinet accepted Pearson's policy statement and agreed that only the prime minister would speak about the matter to the press and the Liberal caucus. This meant that Gordon could not defend himself when Pearson criticized him more harshly to the press and the Liberal caucus than he had in the Cabinet room.[157]

The response to Gordon's speech showed that he had struck a chord with the Canadian public. Gordon received 1,081 letters, of which only 19 were unfavourable. The most common word used to describe the speech was "courageous."[158] The speech also motivated other prominent Canadians to speak out, including retired diplomat Escott Reid, the principal of York University's Glendon College. As he wrote in his memoirs, "If Walter Gordon, a cabinet minister, could risk his political career by urging that the United States stop its bombing, surely I could risk criticism from the board of governors of York University."[159] A month after Gordon's speech, Reid, University College Principal Douglas LePan, and Scarborough College Principal Wynne Plumptre, all former public servants, issued a public letter to Pearson, urging the government to call for a halt to the American bombing of North Vietnam.[160]

After being publicly rebuked by the prime minister, Gordon avoided controversy, intending to wait for the task force report before resigning. Gordon had asked Abraham Rotstein, one of the few economists who shared his views, to head the task force.[161] Rotstein declined, but suggested Mel Watkins, a recommendation seconded by Liberal MP Pauline Jewett.[162] In the early 1960s Watkins had been a neo-classical economist critical of Gordon's ideas, calling the 1963 budget not just pre-Keynesian but pre-Cambrian.[163] The Vietnam War had radicalized Watkins, and by 1967 his ideas had begun to change. In one of their early meetings he told Gordon that he was a New Democrat. "He said not to worry," Watkins remembers, "that many of his strongest supporters were similarly misguided and he couldn't afford to be choosy." While preparing the task force report, Watkins met weekly with Gordon, who had "a considerable influence" on his ideas. "Working for Walter Gordon certainly made me more of a nationalist," he recalls.[164]

All the task force members were academic economists. The key participants were Watkins, Rotstein, Safarian of the University of Toronto, and Stephen Hymer of Yale. The other members were Bernard Bonin of the University of Montreal, Claude Masson of Laval, Gideon Rosenbluth of the University of British Columbia, and William Woodfine of St Francis Xavier University. At the Massachusetts Institute of Technology, Watkins and Hymer had been students of Charles Kindleberger, a great innovator in trade theory and the study of the international movement of capital. Watkins, like Rotstein, was also a disciple of Harold Innis, whom Watkins describes as "an anti-Imperialist ... profoundly suspicious of great aggregations of power. And he was very opposed, as an intellectual, to American imperialism."[165] Watkins, Rotstein, and Hymer had all been strong opponents of American involvement in Vietnam.[166]

As economist and historian Ian Drummond noted, "Rotstein aside, the general character of the task force might be called mainstream reformist. All the anglophone members were products of prominent American postgraduate schools." The members were young: at the time of their appointment one was in his twenties; five were in their thirties; and the other two were in their forties. The oldest, Gideon Rosenbluth, was only forty-six. The task force members represented a wide range of opinions, and there were, in Bonin's words, "some lively debates." Safarian and Rotstein, for example, differed on the performance of foreign-owned firms, with Rotstein tending to be more critical of negative performance. On the issue of extraterritoriality the key members agreed.[167]

The appointment of Safarian, Canada's foremost expert on foreign investment and the only economist to publish an empirical study of foreign-owned firms in Canada, had come at the insistence of Mitchell Sharp.[168] Safarian had written several books and articles that were critical of Gordon's ideas. He agreed with Gordon on the dangers of extraterritoriality, but they differed over whether the government should encourage Canadians to buy American-owned firms. Safarian also disagreed with Gordon's view that foreign-owned firms tended to perform worse than their Canadian counterparts; Safarian believed that it was a more complex issue, concluding, for example, that foreign-owned firms hired fewer Canadians but were more likely to export. What mattered was not ownership but the economic setting. He preferred that the government offer tax incentives to conduct research and development or to encourage Canadian entrepreneurial talent, and did not see any point in encouraging foreign-owned firms to sell shares to Canadians.[169] The *Toronto Telegram* noted the conflict between the ideas of Gordon and Safarian, predicting that Safarian would issue a minority report.[170]

Because of his political agenda, Gordon wanted the task force to complete its work quickly, perhaps in as little as three months.[171] This was a characteristic that Gordon displayed throughout his life: the desire to assess a situation quickly, propose solutions, and then correct any mistakes. As a result of Gordon's short time-line, the task force did not have time for public consultations, though members did confer with experts in Japan, Britain, France, and the United States. Most members of the task force had teaching commitments and could only work full time for one summer.[172]

Senior civil servants treated the task force with derision.[173] Officials at the Bank of Canada, the Department of Finance, and the Department of Trade and Commerce were unsympathetic. According to Gerald Stoner, who chaired the committee of officials that worked with the task force, senior public servants had a "fear of excessive nationalism" and were worried about what the task force might do. Stoner was particularly concerned about Watkins, who "was wild" and "harum-scarum."[174] For Simon Reisman, the exercise "was a bloody nuisance." He encouraged Watkins to take his time with the task force: "Do this right, my boy, and you'll have a great future."[175] At an early meeting with Watkins and Safarian, Reisman said that he believed "that the Task force could not carry out its work in a reasonable way in less than 12 to 15 months."[176] The prediction later proved correct, but Watkins was probably right in thinking that Reisman and the other officials were trying to delay his work.[177]

Completed in late December 1967, the task force report was submitted to the committee of ministers in January. Originally, Gordon had intended to issue a statement of government policy in the form of a white paper, but neither the officials nor the ministers had any intention of letting the economists write such a document.[178] Instead, the Cabinet committee recommended that the report be tabled in the Commons and referred to the Finance Committee without any government endorsement.[179] Before the Cabinet had decided whether to release the report publicly, Gordon, responding to a question from T.C. Douglas, told the Commons that it would be tabled as soon as the French translation became available.[180] After having presented Cabinet with this *fait accompli*, Gordon proceeded to argue for an announcement that, "subject to certain specific reservations, the government agreed in principle with the substance of the report."[181] Privately, Pearson said that he agreed with this approach.[182]

A financial crisis delayed the tabling of the report. In January 1968 Canada experienced a $350-million loss in its holdings of gold and U.S. dollars. Stoner, secretary to the Cabinet and acting clerk of the Privy Council, anticipated a run on the Canadian dollar, which would lead to a devaluation and "heavily restrictive domestic policies." On 9 February he gave Pearson a memorandum outlining the financial crisis and making several recommendations on how to deal with it. He proposed that Pearson announce that the Watkins Report "has not in any sense been endorsed by the government" and that the prime minister impose "a firm embargo on any substantive comment on the Report by any member of the government, until the government has reached a decision on it."[183] In Cabinet on 13 February, Sharp opposed publication of the report because of the financial crisis, the same position taken by Winters in a letter to the prime minister.[184] Officials told Watkins that the report could not be tabled at that time because of Canada's economic predicament.[185]

By this time neither Gordon nor Watkins was interested in playing by the rules of bureaucratic Ottawa. Faced with the possibility of the report's not being released, Gordon threatened to resign and to explain his reasons publicly.[186] When Stoner called to say that the tabling of the report would have to be delayed, Brian Land, Gordon's former executive assistant, went to the Queen's Printer in Hull and took a couple of boxes of the report, as a way of preventing it from being suppressed.[187] At the same time Watkins leaked the report to the *Toronto Star* and told the senior government officials that the newspaper would publish it if they tried to prevent its distribution.[188] The government was left with no option, and on 16 February the report was released with a statement that the government had not endorsed its contents.

Entitled *Foreign Ownership and the Structure of Canadian Industry: Report of the Task Force on the Structure of Canadian Industry*, the report was remarkable in its moderate tone, which showed that the concerns of the officials were unfounded. It concluded that Canada would continue to need foreign capital for the foreseeable future, though there were some problems with the performance of foreign-owned companies in Canada. Foreign firms, for example, had fewer Canadians on boards and in senior management positions than did domestic firms, a conclusion that vindicated Gordon's earlier arguments. In some other areas, however, the report rejected Gordon's assumptions. The economists found that foreign companies conducted more domestic research and development than their Canadian-owned counterparts, contrary to Gordon's belief. The task force concluded that, over all, foreign-owned subsidiaries performed at roughly the same level as Canadian-owned firms but distinctly worse than their foreign parents. The members believed that the economic environment was much more important than the nationality of the owners.

The task force made several suggestions for maximizing the benefits from foreign investment while reducing the costs. The report recommended a new government agency to co-ordinate policies on foreign investment and monitor the activities of foreign-owned enterprises in Canada. Foreign-owned firms would be required to provide more information to the government for "public disclosure, economic analysis, and government surveillance of firms." The report recommended that the government take several steps to foster competition to increase the efficiency of Canadian industry. Anti-combines policy should "be revised and applied more vigorously without respect to the nationality of ownership of firms." The Department of Industry should "provide leadership and planning in rationalizing Canadian industries, as through the encouragement of mergers of existing sub-optimal firms." Canadian tariff policy, "which presently facilitates imperfections of competition," should also be revised to promote competition. Specifically, "the government should continue to promote multilateral tariff reduction."[189]

The biggest danger of foreign ownership was the extraterritorial application of foreign laws, which had a political and an economic price: "The intrusion of American law and policy into Canada by the medium of the Canadian subsidiary erodes Canadian sovereignty and diminishes Canadian independence." Moreover, there were "direct economic costs" when Canada had to forego exports because of "American restrictions on trade with Communist countries and directives to subsidiaries to help the American balance of payments." The task force recommended special steps to block the intrusion of American law. A new government export agency would ensure that purchase orders from communist countries were filled by American-owned subsidiaries by buying products from the subsidiaries and exporting them itself. It would be a criminal offence for subsidiaries to refuse to sell to the agency. Legislation should also be introduced "to prohibit Canadian compliance with foreign anti-trust orders, decrees or judgements."[190]

The task force made several recommendations to encourage greater Canadian participation in domestic industry. It urged that the government establish the Canada Development Corporation, though the specific proposal resembled Sharp's suggestions more than Gordon's. Tentatively, the report suggested that the government provide stronger incentives for large corporations to sell shares to Canadians, though it recognized "costs as well as benefits to this recommendation." On balance, the task force thought "the use of Canadian capital for purely Canadian private ventures or for the Canada Development Corporation is preferable to its use for buying minority holdings in foreign-controlled subsidiaries." The report specifically rejected any drastic approach, saying that "any wholesale substitution of domestic for foreign capital over any short period of time is neither feasible nor desirable."[191] According to Watkins, it was "not terribly realistic" for Canadians to try to buy back control of foreign-owned industry in Canada.[192] The task force further showed its moderation in refusing to suggest that the government stop or even discourage takeovers of Canadian companies by foreign firms.

There was some favourable press for the recommendations of the task force. On the day its report was released, the *Toronto Star*, benefiting from an advance view, published a special eight-page supplement. According to Peter Newman, the report set out "a bold, new national policy for Canada which would alter the country's economic setting and gradually return to domestic hands control over the nation's destiny." Though critical of the special agency to trade with communist countries, the *Financial Times*, now published and edited by Michael Barkway, was also favourable: "In short, it provides reasonable answers to one of our biggest political and economic problems."[193]

In Quebec, though the report received much less attention than it had in the rest of the country, the reaction was generally favourable. *La Presse* of Montreal said that the report expressed a "Gordon-style economic nationalism" but was more conciliatory in the sense that it tried to avoid confrontation. As a result, the report was "filled with positive solutions that address the problem with a totally new rigour." *Le Soleil* of Quebec City agreed. The report recommended measures that would help to deal with the foreign investment problem without discriminating against foreign investors.[194]

Many of the report's critics clearly had not read or understood the report, basing their reviews on *a priori* judgments. The *Winnipeg Free Press*, for example, criticized the "plans for discrimination against foreign investment," saying that they were "calculated to inflict terrible damage on the national economy, to increase the downward pressure on Canada's currency and to drive a wedge through the Liberal party at its April convention." In truth, the Watkins Report was remarkable for not recommending policies that would discriminate against foreign investment. The *Free Press* editorial did not comment on the proposal for tariff reduction, a policy the paper had advocated for years, further suggesting that the editors had not read the report. Maurice Western of the *Free Press* criticized one of the most innocuous proposals, the requirement for increased disclosure, which he saw as a "nursemaid approach to business." He also attacked the effort to prevent extraterritoriality, arguing that the proposals would harm Canadian-American relations. In a similar vein, the *Toronto Telegram* was harshly critical of the report, saying "the times are dangerous for any future restrictive policy on the foreign multi-national corporation."[195] The editorial never specified which proposals it considered restrictive.

Perhaps the most interesting aspect of the media's coverage of the report was the context in which the report and these opinions were presented. The *Globe and Mail*, for example, published half a page of excerpts, while overleaf was a photograph and a story about state troopers in Georgia who, during a peaceful protest over school conditions, had dragged forty blacks to a bus and charged them. Next to the picture were several reports on the war in Vietnam, including a story about an American B-52 bomber that missed its target and dropped fifty tons of explosives on innocent civilians, killing forty, including several women and children.[196]

Outside of Ontario the response to the report was frosty. In a letter to Pearson the premiers of the prairie provinces argued that the report could "seriously hamper the orderly development of the primary resources of western Canada. It is evident that our region must depend, to a very large extent, on foreign capital for the development of both our resources and our manufacturing industries." The three premiers criticized the decision to publish the report "at a time when American foreign investment policy is restrictive." The recommendations "can only have an adverse effect on future foreign investment in Canada."[197] In contrast, the report was virtually ignored in

Quebec. According to Bonin, "u.s. direct investment was not seen as much of a threat; on the contrary, it was seen as a way of reducing the dominance of English Canada."[198]

In Gordon's view, most federal politicians were afraid of commenting on the Watkins Report.[199] Pearson had announced his retirement in December and had little interest in the task force. Gordon tried with some success to force the Liberal leadership candidates to declare publicly whether they supported the report.[200] Eric Kierans was the first to comment, calling it "a superb report" and saying that he would have signed it himself. Allan MacEachen said blandly that he "wouldn't mind" making the report a basis for government policy on foreign investment, and described the general reasoning of the report as "pretty sound." Dramatically declaring himself "a Canadian nationalist," John Turner said that he supported the objectives of the Watkins Report, but he disagreed with the establishment of a Crown agency to deal with extraterritoriality, favouring instead a form of statutory compulsion. Turner endorsed the idea of the Canada Development Corporation, "to organize public and private consortiums to promote large development enterprise – not to buy back Canadian industry." He also wished to expand information on corporate behaviour on a non-discriminatory basis. The other leadership candidates refused to comment.[201]

The reaction from Canadian economists was largely negative. Many said that the report had not established the reasons for concern over foreign investment clearly enough, and they could not understand the danger of extraterritoriality. H.E. English noted that the report did not criticize the performance of foreign firms, focusing instead on the problem of extraterritoriality: "One is tempted to suggest that those who are preoccupied with the foreign ownership issue have been moved from a battlefield where Safarian's evidence has dealt them a defeat to another field where there is still sufficient shortage of evidence to enable them to make a stand."[202] Harry Johnson called the report "mutated Gordonism," missing the significant differences between the views of Gordon and those of the task force members. Johnson said he hoped that the report would be "the final contribution of the Honourable Walter L. Gordon to the propagation of his well-known views on the dangers to Canada of foreign, specifically American, direct investment in this country." Johnson was particularly disparaging of the report's "superficial" discussion of the multinational corporation, "weak" examination of Canada's balance of payments, and "even weaker" chapter on the capital market. He was not wholly negative, however. He considered the export trade organization to combat extraterritoriality "an ingenious proposal," and he praised the recommendations for further disclosure by private firms, saying that "the *Report*'s criticism is convincing and its proposed avenues of report ingenious." In general, Johnson was pleased with the report's moderate tone: "It has the virtue of putting the emphasis on improvements in the Canadian policies that set the environment within which international corporate competition operates, rather than on actions directed at hampering and hectoring the subsidiaries of foreign corporations operating in Canada."[203]

In all, the report was a success. It became well-known around the world and was translated quickly into Japanese.[204] Safarian found that economists in Sweden, Japan, Australia, and France knew of the report. Several of the major proposals were enacted by subsequent governments, including those pertaining to disclosure, the creation of the Canada Development Corporation, and the establishment of an agency to monitor foreign firms. "Almost everything was done at some point," noted Safarian with satisfaction.[205] The only major recommendations not to be adopted were those related to extraterritoriality, one area where the report had little impact. The report was also significant for having made foreign investment a more respectable topic for debate among economists. Harry Johnson's review, for example, showed more serious consideration and less disdain than he had previously expressed in discussing the issue of foreign investment.

Another important legacy of the task force was its effect on Mel Watkins. Watkins had been radicalized by the war in Vietnam, and working on the task force report, in his words, "made me into an economic nationalist." In later years he began to favour more drastic solutions, including the nationalization of foreign firms. After the report was presented, Watkins found that the NDP embraced him "like a long lost brother." In the 1968 election, party officials asked Watkins to tour with leader T.C. Douglas, but Gordon reminded him that he had promised to stay out of politics for one year following the report's release. Watkins, out of deference to Gordon, declined the invitation.[206] Later, Watkins would become one of the leaders of the new nationalism.

With the tabling of the report Gordon had to decide if he should continue his political career. He had strongly considered seeking his party's leadership in the spring of 1966, and discussed the issue with Pearson several times.[207] In one of these conversations Pearson said that he would help Gordon win the leadership, showing, in the words of John English, Pearson's tendency "to tell people all too often only what they wanted to hear."[208] At one point Gordon met with several of his close followers, including Gordon Edick, Keith Davey, and David Anderson, at the Park Plaza Hotel in Toronto. He asked for their honest opinion on whether he should seek the leadership. One by one they hesitantly discussed the idea. Edick, speaking last, said that he would walk on hot coals if it would help Gordon, but he did not think that he should run. Gordon was too old; he wasn't a good speaker, and he was not prepared to compromise his principles to get elected. "You're right and I know that," Gordon responded. He thanked Edick for his honesty and announced that he would not be a candidate. It was "the saddest time of my life," remembered Edick, a tough construction contractor who cried when recounting the story to his wife.[209]

In January 1968 Gordon announced publicly that he would support Jean Marchand for leader, and when Marchand refused to run, Gordon reluctantly endorsed Pierre Trudeau, a man he saw as "inexperienced, [and] somewhat tactless" but "progressive in his social thinking" and "extremely attractive personally."[210] Trudeau had told Gordon that, after a quick review, he agreed in principle with the main recommendations of the Watkins Report.[211] On 19 February, Gordon submitted his letter of resignation, which he agreed to delay because of the Liberal defeat on a vote in the House of Commons.[212] The resignation became effective 11 March 1968, and ended Walter Gordon's remarkable political career.

The great irony of Gordon's life in politics was that he began to win converts on the issue closest to his heart at the precise moment when his political influence was ebbing away. In the late 1950s an upsurge in anti-American sentiment grew out of McCarthyism, the suicide of Herbert Norman, and the publicity generated by Walter Gordon, Michael Barkway, and James Coyne. The pattern was repeated a decade later, when concern about American influence in Canada was rekindled by the war in Vietnam, social problems in the United States, and the public statements and writings of Gordon and George Grant. In both decades Gordon's presence ensured that much of the anti-American sentiment was channelled into a concern over economic matters, particularly opposition to foreign ownership of Canadian industry. Prominent Canadians expressed concerns over American cultural and political power, but the main focus was always on the economic side.

Gordon's role was crucial because he created a generation of leaders to promote the new nationalism. Before their work on the task force report Abraham Rotstein and Mel Watkins were largely unknown to most Canadians. Gordon's insistence on creating the task force brought these two, particularly Watkins, to public prominence, a position they would use to great effect in subsequent years. Walter Gordon had become the bridge between the imperialism of his youth and the new nationalism of the late 1960s and early 1970s.

CHAPTER SEVEN

The New Nationalism
1968–1987

In the years after Walter Gordon retired from politics, many Canadians came to regard him as a respected elder statesman who had understood the country's problems long before most of his colleagues. "Gordon appears to be having the last laugh," said the 1972 edition of a popular introductory text on Canadian politics.[1] He was no longer an eccentric with strange economic ideas but was instead the prophet of the "new nationalism."[2] More than anyone, Walter Gordon was the father of this movement, and it reflected his concerns and priorities.

The term "new nationalism" was first used in the late 1960s to describe the growing feeling of distress over American influence in Canada.[3] The concern took many forms and was not confined to economic affairs. Some commentators discussed Canada's defence policy, arguing that NATO was "an instrument for great-power control and influence over smaller powers" and that Canada should push for an end to all military alliances.[4] Beginning in late 1968, James Steele and Robin Mathews, professors of English at Carleton University, campaigned for an increase in the number of Canadian-born professors in the country's universities.[5] John Warnock complained that Canadian newspapers were "barely distinguishable from those of the United States" and suggested that Canadian-content regulations should be extended to cover not only broadcasting but "other areas of the mass media."[6] Some lamented the Americanization and commercialization of hockey.[7]

Despite the broad scope of their concerns, the new nationalists focused their attention on Canada's economic reliance on the United States. "Canada today is witnessing a surge of nationalism which has taken the specific form of the desire to be free of American economic domination," wrote economist

W.H. Pope in 1971.[8] The foreign investment question was central, even appearing in books and articles examining Canada's cultural and intellectual relationship with the United States. Ian Lumsden, in an article on the American influence over the Canadian academic community, asserted that the main problem was economic: "The Americanization of Canada is first and foremost a function of the penetration of the Canadian economy by American monopoly capitalism."[9] In her 1976 examination of Canadian culture Susan Crean pointed to the new nationalists' focus on economic questions: "The warnings of economic nationalists concerning American control of the Canadian economy are well known. But in the cultural sphere we are only beginning to make the connection between U.S. domination of the media and the suppression of Canadian culture and independence."[10]

The priorities of the new nationalism reflected Gordon's own objectives. He had emphasized economic matters, and had used his position to propel sympathetic economists like Mel Watkins and Abraham Rotstein into the public eye. Cultural nationalists had no similar friend at court to put their concerns before Cabinet, to ensure that their ideas made the front page of the country's largest-circulation newspaper, and to give prominent positions to their spokespersons. They had no Walter Gordon to ensure that the survival of Canadian culture was a matter of continuous national debate.

The new nationalists accepted Gordon's argument that foreign investment posed a threat to Canada's survival, but could not adopt his attitude towards the tariff, which contradicted his views on investment. Many of the new nationalists argued that tariff reduction – even free trade – was necessary to reduce the level of foreign investment in Canada. The Watkins Report had suggested that "the government should continue to promote multilateral tariff reduction" and criticized Canadian trade policy, "which presently facilitates imperfections of competition."[11] This view was adopted by most of the new nationalists in the early 1970s. In *Silent Surrender*, a book that Rotstein called "perhaps the classic statement of the case against the multinational corporation in Canada," Kari Levitt argued that "policies directed towards the protection of Canadian enterprise against penetration by U.S. direct investment will have to be complemented by a lowering of Canadian tariffs on commodity imports from all sources."[12] W.H. Pope supported Levitt's position, insisting that lower tariffs would increase efficiency, reduce prices for the Canadian consumer, and decrease the profits of foreign subsidiaries in Canada. In his view "the tariff should be abolished on any class of goods manufactured in Canada preponderantly by American-owned firms."[13] A zealous convert to the new nationalism, Eric Kierans argued that free trade would help to solve some of Canada's "most pressing problems," including the dilemma of foreign control.[14] Gordon, however, continued to oppose any significant reduction in the tariff, though the issue was much less prominent in his speeches, articles, and books than it had been in the late 1950s and early 1960s, likely reflecting the influence of his new allies.

Gordon's friends also seemed to influence his ideas on Quebec's place in Canada. In general, the new nationalists were sympathetic to the goals of Quebec nationalists. Outlining the views of the extreme left of the New Democratic Party, the Waffle Manifesto declared that "there is no denying the existence of two nations within Canada, each with its own language, culture and aspiration."[15] Denis Smith, Gordon's biographer, also showed considerable sympathy for Quebec nationalists: "Quebecers' desire to protect their language and collective existence ... has now been transmuted into a confident and open determination to make their own destiny as free men. This is not an ignoble ambition. If any community can be said to deserve the opportunity for political independence, Quebec today is that community."[16] A minority of new nationalists openly supported the separation of Quebec from the rest of Canada, including Kari Levitt, Mel Watkins, and poet Dennis Lee.[17]

Gordon was concerned about the situation in Quebec, though he did not share the views of those Canadians who supported Quebec's independence. He could not recognize Quebec as a nation because he never saw nationality as an expression of language or culture, always defining it in economic or political terms.[18] In the early 1960s he had shown little interest in events in Quebec and had only a limited understanding of the aspirations of the province's new leadership. As late as 1964 he thought that fear of Quebec separatism was "greatly exaggerated."[19] Here he departed from the Liberal tradition, which had always thought the main challenge to Canada's survival was internal. On this question Gordon showed affinity with the Conservatives, believing that the major threat to Canada's existence came from the United States.

Gordon's growing concern over Quebec likely reflected a realization that events in the province posed a serious threat to Canada's independence from the United States. In 1969 he said, "If Quebec should separate ... then it is not likely that the rest of Canada would survive absorption by the United States ... We must try to find a formula which will keep Quebec within Confederation."[20] In an article in *Canadian Forum* in 1971 Gordon argued that English Canadians should support substantive changes to the Constitution to satisfy Quebeckers: "But any suggestion that any group should have the right

to separate and, in the process, to destroy the country would be a very different thing indeed."[21] In October 1972 he criticized the prime minister's
unwillingness to cede federal powers to Quebec, saying that he was "as concerned about the way Trudeau is going about things in Quebec" as he was
about "the great sell-out to the Americans."[22] He began to support the transfer of important powers to Quebec, suggesting that Quebec, and any other
province that wanted the responsibility, be given full control over all social
programs – except unemployment insurance – with no requirement that the
province maintain a national standard.[23] Five years later, in an article that irritated Trudeau, Gordon supported special status for Quebec: "I can see no reason why Quebec, subject to minority rights and interests, should not have
complete control over cultural matters and education; over health and welfare
and other social security matters (with the exception of unemployment insurance); and a veto over immigration from abroad (although not from other
provinces). There may be other fields that should be allocated specifically to
Quebec including responsibility for communications."[24] Even so, Gordon
believed that the federal government must not cede any of the powers necessary to combat foreign economic control, which remained, for him, the most
important issue facing Canada. Gordon's sympathy towards Quebec in the
1970s resulted from his desire to preserve Canada and not from a belief that a
transfer of powers to the provinces would improve the federal system, and
he continued to pay less attention to the Quebec question than to his major
concern, American investment.

To preserve Canada from American economic domination Gordon and
other prominent new nationalists agreed that the state would have to play an
important role in the economy. Gordon had long believed in significant state
intervention. As he said in 1960 in a speech at the University of British
Columbia, "I am afraid that, in the age in which we live, governments – provincial as well as federal – must be prepared to take the initiative and give a
lead upon occasion if Canada is to remain free and independent and if we are
to have a high level of employment throughout the country."[25] The new
nationalists agreed, advocating policies that called for government intervention in many areas of the economy, including the surveillance of industry and
the screening of foreign investment.

State activity was central to the new nationalism, and it was on this point
that the movement split. In September 1969 a press conference announced
the creation of the Waffle group within the NDP. The group's manifesto, co-
authored by Mel Watkins, history doctoral student James Laxer, and several
others, focused on American ownership in Canada: "The major threat to

Canadian survival today is American control of the Canadian economy."[26] The "barbarous war in Vietnam" and the struggle over civil rights were a cause of the group's disenchantment with the United States: "The American empire is the central reality for Canadians. It is an empire characterized by militarism abroad and racism at home." The manifesto diverged from Gordon's views with an attack on the capitalist system: "An independence movement based on substituting Canadian capitalists for American capitalists, or on public policy to make foreign corporations behave as if they were Canadian corporations, cannot be our final objective. There is not now an independent Canadian capitalism and any lingering pretensions on the part of Canadian businessmen to independence lacks credibility." The only solution to Canada's problems was socialism: "Capitalism must be replaced by socialism, by national planning of investment and by the public ownership of the means of production in the interests of the Canadian people as a whole ... to pursue independence seriously is to make visible the necessity of socialism in Canada."[27] Watkins – "the group's Mohammed," in the words of one journalist – was developing into a traditional Marxist.[28] At the NDP convention in Winnipeg in October 1969, the Waffle Manifesto was defeated by a vote of 499 to 268, but this did not kill the movement.[29] Encouraged by having won the support of more than a third of the delegates, Watkins and his colleagues continued their fight to put the foreign investment issue at the centre of the NDP platform.

Gordon and Rotstein rejected Watkins' view that socialism was necessary to limit the extent of foreign ownership. In Gordon's view, "It is not necessary to change our whole economic and social structure in order to retain our independence."[30] He was noticeably frustrated with Watkins, his former protégé: "It would be the height of folly to accept the thesis that if Canadians wish to retain their economic freedom and independence we must adopt the policies of the radical left. Anyone who thinks a wealthy, affluent country like Canada will choose socialism should have his head read."[31] Abraham Rotstein, Watkins' long-time friend and ally, was another harsh critic of the Waffle's insistence on socialism. The first priority, in Rotstein's view, was to limit foreign ownership: "What political strength we have for this battle should be deployed in the most effective way. Fervency in the pursuit of the classical socialist objective of nationalization runs the risk of compounding our failure in achieving an independent Canada ... Those who add needless risks to this task assume a grave responsibility." Though Rotstein himself was a socialist, he realized that most Canadians would not support the Waffle Manifesto: "The struggle for Canadian independence must come first because we will lose it forever if we wait until a majority of Canadians are prepared to nationalize I.B.M. and Inco." The nationalist movement in Canada was weak, and it needed the support of "all classes and segments of society in order to be successful."[32]

Rotstein reacted to the Waffle position by advocating "functional socialism," a term coined by Swedish economist Gunnar Adler-Karlsson. Functional socialism placed the emphasis not on ownership but on the functions of ownership, including "the right to set wages, hours, and conditions of work ... to set prices of components and final products, to determine the timing and extent of economic expansion, to invest or take over other companies, to distribute profits and dividends, to send sums abroad, and even to pollute the environment." "The primary emphasis then," in Rotstein's view, "is not on titles to property but on putting an increasing number of the functions of ownership under national control." This meant increased regulation of industry: "The main thrust of Canadian policy, in my view, should centre on regulation of the multinational corporation ... the aim should be to restore national control over a much wider range of functions, from research and development policy through to assuring the presence of Canadian personnel at the operating and management levels. The objective of this regulation should be to restore Canadian priorities on a broad front."[33] Rotstein seemed to agree with Harry Johnson, who had said, "What matters for the efficiency and well-being of an economy is not who owns the property, but how efficiently and progressively it is managed."[34]

In downplaying the importance of ownership, Rotstein differed from Watkins and Gordon. He rejected both the nationalization of industry and efforts to return foreign-owned firms to private Canadian ownership. Noting that foreign investment in Canada amounted to roughly $40 billion, he concluded that " 'Buying back,' whether with public funds, private funds, or a combination of both, seems a hopeless task."[35] Regulation was the only option, a position rejected by a now cynical Watkins: "We have something of a track record in this regard in this country – in whose interest have we regulated the CPR and Bell Canada?"[36]

Despite this breach in the leadership of the new nationalism, the movement continued to gain support. A Gallup Poll in 1972 showed that 67 per cent of Canadians thought that Canada had enough capital from the United States, up from 46 per cent in 1964. The opposition to further foreign investment was strongest in Ontario, where 73 per cent thought that there was now enough American capital in Canada, and weakest in Quebec, where 58 per cent held this point of view.[37] This changing mood was further reflected in Gordon's continued presence in public debate after leaving Cabinet. According to biographer Denis Smith, "Nothing else can explain his prominent role in Canadian public life since 1968: not character, not rhetorical power, not fascination for the martyr."[38]

The rising concern over the American connection could be seen also in the large number of books published in the late 1960s and the 1970s on aspects of Canadian-American relations. In 1973 the best-selling novel in Canada was Richard Rohmer's *Ultimatum*, a book that portrayed the annexation of Canada after the federal government refused an ultimatum to give the United States unrestricted access to Canadian natural gas. Five years later Donald Creighton wrote a novel entitled *Takeover*, a story of the purchase of a Canadian distillery by an American from Kentucky. Many collections of articles examined the Canadian-American relationship from a critical point of view. Often using dramatic titles to define their contents, these works included Al Purdy's *The New Romans*, Ian Lumsden's *Close the 49th Parallel Etc*, Robert Laxer's *(Canada) Ltd.*, Rotstein's *The Precarious Homestead*, and Rotstein and Gary Lax's two books, *Independence: The Canadian Challenge* and *Getting it Back*. Economists and political scientists also contributed several monographs with equally striking titles, the best-known being Warnock's *Partner to Behemoth*, Levitt's *Silent Surrender*, and Pope's *The Elephant and the Mouse*. Levitt's book alone sold 25,000 copies in less than two years; Purdy's sold 35,000. This body of literature not only reflected the growing support for the new nationalism but also helped to promote the movement.[39]

The nationalists also profited from the active support of the *Toronto Star*. From 1970 to 1979 Walter Gordon served as a director of the paper. In 1971, as a member of the board of Torstar, the *Star*'s parent company, Gordon engineered the purchase of the *Toronto Telegram*'s circulation lists for $10 million, provided that publisher John Bassett would fold the paper. In the view of others in the media, the circulation list was worth only a few thousand dollars; the purchase of the list, after all, did not mean that *Telegram* subscribers would be bound to read the *Star*. Gordon's deal led easily to accusations that the *Star* had paid a competitor to go out of business.[40] The agreement demonstrated the extent of the relationship between Gordon and the *Star*, a relationship that had editorial, political, and financial aspects. The *Star*, Canada's largest-circulation and wealthiest paper, had enormous power over public opinion. "Its influence and its consequences have been staggering for national politics and policies," wrote journalist Douglas Fisher.[41] The *Star*'s editors considered foreign investment one of the most important problems facing the country. According to Alan Heisey, a businessman and media commentator, the *Star* gave the new nationalism more coverage than any other single issue: "No other element of national or international life, no English-French relationship, no Viet Nam, no gap between the rich and the poor has claimed the share of attention that the new nationalism has."[42]

The inability of the United States to come to terms with its problems at home and abroad played a significant role in forcing Canadians to re-evaluate the American role in Canadian economic, political, and cultural life. In the introduction to the 1970 edition of *Lament for a Nation* George Grant captured the mood as he had in 1965:

The years of the Vietnam war have been an exposition (a veritable Expo) of the American empire. It does not take much intelligence or patriotism to be glad that one's children are not drafted for that war. The mainland of that empire no longer seems so rewarding a place to live. Even the Canadian bourgeoisie can see the perhaps unresolvable racial conflict, the expansion and decay of its cities, the increase of military influence on its constitutional life, the breakdown between the generations, the effects of environmental spoliation, etc. etc. ... Such events make possible a nationalist appeal to many voters.[43]

Many Canadians had been distressed over the Vietnam War, and in the late 1960s and early 1970s they were graphically reminded of it with the massacre of more than five hundred Vietnamese civilians at My Lai and the shooting of four anti-war demonstrators at Kent State University. Gordon also thought that Canadian attitudes towards the United States hardened after the Nixon government's 1971 decision to impose a 10 per cent import surcharge, a move that seriously limited Canada's exports to its largest trading partner.[44] These events were followed by the Watergate scandal, which discredited not only American policies but also the integrity of the country's leaders.

Like the other leaders of the new nationalism, Gordon continued to be distressed by the policies of the American government. In a 1970 speech he called the war in Vietnam "a humiliating disgrace, not only to the people of the United States, but to all of us who live in the Western world." In his view, "There can be no acceptable justification for American support of a corrupt and dictatorial government in Saigon which entails the killing and the maiming of hundreds of thousands of civilians, the defoliation of the countryside, and the acts of barbarism with which we have been made all too familiar on our television screens." Gordon also became openly critical of the social problems in the United States. He deplored "the race problem and the violence which has occurred and may be expected to occur again in the principal cities across the line." The United States had become a "sick society" that did not tolerate dissent and a country where it was unsafe to walk the streets at night.[45] These factors stimulated his already strong distrust of the United States.

After he left politics, Gordon's increasing unease with the United States led him to focus on one issue – American control – straying from his moderation in the early 1960s.[46] When foreign ownership did not appear on the agenda of the 1969 Liberal party meeting at Harrison Hot Springs, Gordon refused to attend. The next year he began to speak of the "last chance for Canada." During the 1970s Gordon argued for a majority Canadian share of all major businesses, a considerable change from the early 1960s, when he thought that 25 per cent domestic ownership of Canadian companies would be sufficient to protect the country's interests. In 1970 he suggested that Canada adopt the "Mexican formula" of 51 per cent domestic ownership of major corporations, with mostly Canadians as senior executives and as directors.[47]

Gordon's ideas had a strong impact on the 1970 recommendations of the Commons Standing Committee on External Affairs and National Defence, chaired by Liberal MP Ian Wahn. The committee report, commonly known as the Wahn Report, was released in August and repeated many of the proposals put forward by the Watkins task force. The report advocated multilateral tariff reduction, the creation of the Canada Development Corporation, and the establishment of a government bureau to compile information and co-ordinate government policy on foreign investment. The report, however, moved one step beyond the Watkins task force with a recommendation that the bureau also be responsible for combating the extraterritorial application of foreign law and for screening foreign takeovers of Canadian companies. The report urged the government to prevent takeovers of Canadian companies in "key sectors" of the economy and to terminate the special income tax exemptions for advertisers in *Time* and *Reader's Digest*. The committee members also adopted Gordon's proposal for a policy of at least 51 per cent Canadian ownership of large companies, arguing that "the Committee recognizes that as a general rule it is desirable that Canadians should control Canadian companies by owning at least 51% of their voting shares, particularly in the important sectors of the economy where American control is now most highly concentrated, and that we should move toward this goal as rapidly as capital requirements and other relevant circumstances permit."[48] According to Wahn, this idea came directly from Walter Gordon's speeches and articles.[49]

The mood in Cabinet had not changed much since Gordon had fought to release the Watkins Report. Mitchell Sharp took strong exception to the 51 per cent recommendation, and some individuals who shared his views made a determined effort to prevent the committee from approving the report: according to Wahn, one of Sharp's colleagues recommended that Liberal members not attend the committee meeting, and a Liberal official told him that, if he did not drop the 51 per cent suggestion, his committee would not have quorum and could not approve the report. In the face of this effort to block his work, Wahn succeeded in recruiting other Liberal MPs to replace the absentees. Through all this, Wahn had no indication of the prime minister's views.[50]

The press reacted strongly against the report, particularly the committee's decision to adopt Gordon's proposal for majority Canadian ownership of major firms. The *Toronto Telegram* said the committee was "totally unreal in its demand for 51 percent Canadian ownership of all companies presently operating in Canada ... The effect of the Wahn report, as published this week in the press, if ever implemented, would be to turn off the tap of capital investment in this country." The reaction of the *Montreal Star* was similar, saying that "the recommendation defies credulity" and was "hard to take seriously." The *Globe and Mail* said the proposal "isn't very practical" and attacked the plan for a control bureau, arguing that it "would be just about the biggest bureaucracy this country has yet conceived, with all a bureaucracy's ability to strangle initiative, impede progress and take arbitrary action." The *Toronto Star*'s editorial page did not discuss the report's main proposals, its silence likely implying disapproval, while columnist Jack McArthur directly attacked the recommendation for majority Canadian ownership, focusing on the committee's failure to answer key questions about its proposal: "Can we really do it; if not, why; if so, how; where's the money coming from; are there better alternatives; what kind of timetable; what would it do to patterns of growth, savings and investment."[51]

During this period Gordon and his allies had become increasingly concerned about the attention the media was paying to Watkins' conversion to socialism and to the debate in the NDP over foreign investment. In Rotstein's view Watkins had "emerged out of the vacuum left by the departure of Gordon from the political scene."[52] Gordon's supporters worried that Watkins and Laxer had snatched the foreign investment issue for the NDP.[53] "The NDP is likely to steal a good portion of the vote if the Liberals fail to bring in a strong policy to deal with the economic independence issue," Gordon warned.[54]

In February 1970 Rotstein and Peter C. Newman invited Gordon to lunch at the Victoria Room of the American-owned King Edward Hotel. The three agreed to form the Committee for an Independent Canada (CIC), an organization that would circulate a petition asking the government for measures to foster greater participation by Canadians in the country's economy. In September 1970 the CIC was officially launched at a press conference in Toronto, though the October Crisis in Quebec forced the group to postpone the petition drive until the new year.[55]

The CIC was designed to be a reasonable alternative to the Waffle movement. In the words of journalist Christina Newman, Gordon and Rotstein were dismayed that "the Waffle was the only organized independentist movement in the country ... because they believed it would isolate nationalistic ideas in a fringe movement so remote from the Canadian political mainstream that they could never be realized."[56] For Rotstein, it was clear "that many people in Canada were not going to move in the direction of socialism as a precondition for independence. In our view we needed a more broadly based movement."[57]

It is unclear how many members the CIC had at its peak. The *Toronto Star* declared that there were 35,000 at one time, and Gordon claimed the organization had 12,000 in 1971.[58] There is reason to believe these figures were inflated. At the annual meeting in March 1973 the organization told the press that membership stood between 7,000 and 8,000, but Chairman Mel Hurtig discovered that membership was in fact at less than 4,000.[59]

The early membership of the CIC included a large number of writers and academics. Among the members of the steering committee were political figures (Eddie Goodman, Alvin Hamilton, Harry Hays, Maurice Lamontagne, Keith Davey, Judy LaMarsh, and Pauline Jewett), writers (Robin Mathews, Al Purdy, Farley Mowat, Hugh MacLennan, Christina Newman, Pierre Berton), publishers (Jack McClelland and Mel Hurtig), journalists (Claude Ryan, Beland Honderich, and Adrienne Clarkson), and scholars (George Grant, W.L. Morton, Douglas LePan, Lloyd Axworthy, Kenneth McNaught, and Denis Smith). Flora MacDonald agreed to serve as executive director. McClelland and Ryan were the organization's first co-chairs, while Gordon, as father of the movement, held the position of honorary chair. The membership included very few large capitalists and virtually no prominent Quebeckers.[60] Indeed, the CIC never functioned as a truly bilingual organization, and at its first convention only one of the two hundred delegates was from Quebec.[61]

The CIC was, in the words of *Last Post* magazine, "the strongest threat to the Waffle's tenuous leadership of 'the nationalist movement.' "[62] Prominent members of the Waffle, such as Watkins, Laxer, and Cy Gonick, were conspicuous in their absence from the list of CIC sponsors. Mel Hurtig remembered that the Waffle leaders "were immediately antagonistic towards us."[63] And, he might have added, the CIC was antagonistic towards the Waffle. Eddie Goodman, who served as CIC chairman and succeeded Gordon as honorary chair, bitterly attacked Waffle members in a letter to Hurtig: "They are purveyors of hate; they mislead the public and constantly trifle with the truth. It is my opinion that they cause irreparable harm to the nationalist movement in Canada ... I think they regard us as their enemies and so they should."[64]

Unlike the Waffle Manifesto, the CIC's "Statement of Purpose" was intentionally vague, in an attempt to win as many members as possible. The main goal was to encourage the government to "adopt legislative policies that will significantly diminish the influence ... exerted by outside powers – their citizens, their corporations and their institutions – on Canadian life." The statement reflected Gordon's priorities, with the first proposal addressing the issue of foreign ownership. The CIC urged the government to reduce the level of foreign investment by establishing an agency to "supervise the conduct of foreign-controlled operations in Canada, and in particular any new takeovers," by creating a Canada Development Corporation and by adopting a policy on the sale of Canada's energy resources. The other six recommendations were clearly designed to elicit broad-based support. The CIC wanted a "greater allocation of resources ... to the less well developed regions of the country," autonomy for trade unions in Canada, policies to limit pollution, more Canadian content in the curriculum at educational institutions, a foreign policy "designed to ensure Canadian independence," and more Canadian content in newspapers, magazines, radio, and television.[65] These proposals were, however, secondary to the concern over foreign investment. When describing the group in his memoirs, Goodman stressed the primary goal: "The CIC was a politically disparate group concerned about the effect on all aspects of national life of the ever-growing control of the Canadian economy by foreign, particularly American, corporations ... The original purpose of the committee was very simple. It was to collect a quarter of a million signatures on a petition requesting the government to take steps to limit foreign ownership of Canada's economy and resources."[66] Goodman's memoirs do not even mention the CIC's six other proposals. Hurtig agreed with Goodman's view: the CIC "was essentially an organization of economic nationalism."[67] When the government ended the special tax breaks for *Time* and *Reader's Digest*, Hurtig commented that on a priority list of forty-five items, the CIC would rank this action forty-third.[68] Cultural problems were subordinate to the goal of limiting American investment in Canada.

In the few months following the creation of the organization, CIC members worked hard to publicize their cause and to collect signatures for the petition urging the government to take action to regain control of the Canadian economy. Gordon made fifty speeches from November 1970 to May 1971.[69] In June 1971 eight members of the CIC met with Trudeau and National Revenue Minister Herb Gray, with Gordon doing most of the talking. They presented the petition with 170,000 signatures and asked the government to increase the proportion of Canadian ownership, establish a Canada Development Corporation, safeguard Canadian content in textbooks and the media, and create an agency to supervise the conduct of foreign firms and review proposals for any new takeovers.[70] Gordon thought that "Trudeau seemed most receptive," but Goodman had a different impression, believing that the prime minister was not prepared for the meeting and that his response "amounted to little more than the conventional platitudes."[71] Regardless of the government's reaction, committee members began to feel optimistic. In December 1971 Mel Hurtig told Denis Smith, "There is no question any more in my own mind that we're now beginning to win Walter's battle and that Walter's image throughout the country has changed significantly."[72]

The CIC published two books, held several conventions, and collected the petition of 170,000 signatures, but eventually began to fade from public view. Attention shifted from the CIC towards organizations with more limited, specific goals. Hurtig began to pay more attention to the Association of Canadian Publishers. John Trent, the CIC's policy co-ordinator, became more involved with the Social Science Federation of Canada. Others tried to promote Canadian content in elementary schools through the Canada Studies Foundation. Walter Gordon himself had interests in the Canada Studies Foundation and began to devote much of his time and financial resources to the Canadian Institute for Economic Policy, which he had helped to found.[73] Other organizations that pursued specific policies to limit foreign influence in Canada included the Canadian Council of Film Makers, the Canadian Federation of Independent Business, the Canadian Arctic Resources Committee, the Association of Canadian Television and Radio Actors, and the Public Petroleum Association of Canada. Some of these groups were founded long before the birth of the new nationalism, but in the 1970s they all advocated policies to limit foreign influence in Canada.

The Committee for an Independent Canada folded in 1981. According to political scientists Bruce Doern and Brian Tomlin, it "had been too elitist in its membership structure, with very little of its money coming from ordinary individual members," and had been "intellectually dominated by one man, the former Liberal finance minister Walter Gordon, the godfather of contemporary Canadian nationalism."[74] This is a fair assessment of the CIC's weaknesses. The committee was well funded by Gordon and his friends – of the first $12,000 donated to the committee, $5,000 came from Gordon and Canadian Corporate Management – but it never had broad-based financial support.[75] "Our expenses were financed by contributions from a relatively few individuals and business enterprises," Gordon admitted. He was not troubled by the organization's demise, saying that he had only intended it to function for "two to four years at which time it was certainly my thought that the C.I.C. would be wound up."[76]

Gordon and the CIC were successful in raising awareness of the issues of foreign investment in the 1970s and forcing the government to take tentative steps to deal with the problem. By 1970 Trudeau recognized that the mood in Canada had shifted: "I think the times have changed a bit and that in four years Canadians have become a lot more nationalist economically than they were before."[77] The government created the Canada Development Corporation in 1971. Though Gordon had not succeeded in implementing the proposal while he held the finance portfolio, many still considered him the father of the CDC because he had brought the idea to the public's attention and had campaigned tirelessly for it.[78] Also in 1971, the Canadian Radio-Television Commission imposed stringent Canadian-content regulations for broadcasters.

In March 1970 Trudeau had asked Herb Gray, then a minister without portfolio, to write a Cabinet paper proposing a policy to deal with foreign investment. Originally, the report was intended to be an internal policy document, not a public report, unlike the Watkins and Wahn reports.[79] To help write the report, Gray created a working group that included lawyer and consultant Joel Bell and public servants Harvey Lazar and Roberto Gualtieri.[80] The report was completed and submitted to Cabinet in May 1971, but the government refused to comment on its contents or release it to the public. In November 1971 *Canadian Forum*, under Rotstein's direction, published a leaked version of the report. The government officially released the report, entitled *Foreign Direct Investment in Canada*, in May 1972.

At 523 pages the Gray Report was so long that economist Ian Drummond found it "hard to believe that even Herb Gray read every word."[81] The report rejected Gordon's recommendation that every major firm have at least 51 per cent Canadian ownership, saying that the proposal could be "very costly to the economy." Furthermore, the working group questioned whether Canadian capitalists were the best defenders of the country's interests, saying that

"Canadian control of a business is not in itself a guarantee of sound performance and is not, therefore, a satisfactory means for achieving Canada's broad national objectives." To maximize the benefits and reduce the costs of foreign ownership, the Gray Report proposed a screening agency, along the lines of the Canadian Ownership and Control Bureau recommended in the Wahn Report. The agency would oversee all "existing foreign controlled companies" and any new investment by foreigners. The report also suggested that the government consider policies to require Canadian ownership in "key sectors" of the economy, such as banking and communications.[82]

Most of the media support for the report came from Ontario. Jack McArthur of the *Torono Star* praised it as "a mild document." It was, he wrote, "a moderate, natural expression of concern." The proposal for a screening agency was a "spectacularly simple and sensible idea ... Basically, the Gray Report appears to favor a commonsense approach." The *Star*'s editors vigorously supported the proposed screening agency, saying that unless the government adopted the recommendation, "it will have betrayed the dream of an independent Canada." The *Kitchener-Waterloo Record* agreed, commending the report for rejecting "superficial solutions like a 51-per-cent Canadian shareholder guarantee" and for advocating "a difficult but flexible screening agency which seems best fitted to meet Canada's needs."[83]

In western Canada and in the Atlantic provinces, areas hungry for new investment to stimulate development, the reaction was largely negative. The *Halifax Chronicle-Herald* asked a key question for many Canadians living on the periphery: "In light of high unemployment in the country, particularly in slow-growth areas, would Ottawa be morally right to bar the door to new job opportunities – in the Atlantic provinces for instance?" The *Edmonton Journal* agreed, saying that the report's recommendations were "wrought with serious inherent dangers" and that "the country's economic development could suffer serious setbacks." The *Regina Leader-Post* worried about the bureaucracy needed to run the screening agency: "Giving a gaggle of guardian bureaucrats such decisive power over the regulation of foreign capital inflow, policing of investment aims, and the realization or otherwise of the Canadian economic dream, is almost reminiscent of Mussolini's corporate state."[84]

In Quebec, Claude Ryan, one of the few francophones among the founding members of the Committee for an Independent Canada, attacked the report for ignoring "the existence in Canada of two distinct societies." Writing in *Le Devoir*, Ryan insisted that the problem of foreign investment existed at two levels in Quebec. Economic activity in Quebec was strongly influenced not only by decision-makers located abroad but also by English Canadian decision-makers whose culture was foreign to most Quebeckers.[85] Ryan's comments explained why Gordon's ideas never gained a foothold in Quebec: to most francophone Quebeckers, American capital was no more foreign than capital from English-speaking Canada.

Gordon's ideas remained most popular in Ontario, where the provincial government responded to the leaked version of the Gray Report by issuing the *Report of the Interdepartmental Task Force on Foreign Investment*, a document prepared by six civil servants. Released in December 1971, the so-called Honey Report was named for Peter Honey, the Treasury official who was its principal author. Noting that foreign investment threatened "this country's continued economic independence and its cultural distinctiveness," the report argued for a policy of "moderate nationalism" to limit foreign investment. The report suggested that "radical measures aimed at Canadian-izing industries at a fast pace be avoided as self-defeating, primarily because they would engender fear and uncertainty and perhaps precipitate an invest-ment crisis." Committee members discussed various options but made no specific recommendations, remarking that the task force was designed to have a "diagnostic" function and would not issue a "blueprint for action."[86]

Days after the release of the Honey Report, the Ontario legislature reacted to the growing concern over foreign influence in Canada by referring the report to the newly created Select Committee on Economic and Cultural Nationalism, chaired by Russell Rowe. The committee's preliminary report, issued in March 1972, argued that the Ontario government should not wait for Ottawa to announce its policy on foreign investment. Instead, the provin-cial government should stop foreign-owned firms in Ontario from receiving funds from provincial incentive programs, force them to make "a portion" of their stock available to Canadian investors, and require them to have at least 20 per cent Canadian directors.[87]

The federal government's response to the Gray Report finally appeared in 1972 with a bill to create the Foreign Investment Review Agency (FIRA). The agency would not, as the Gray Report had proposed, have authority to super-vise new enterprises established from outside Canada, licensing and franchise agreements, or new investments by existing foreign-owned subsidiaries. It would deal only with the takeover of Canadian firms by foreign interests. The response of the CIC was immediately hostile. Rotstein called the bill "a travesty of a policy ... that will block further progress for the lifetime of this government." He was particularly critical of Mitchell Sharp, who had tried to block the release of the Watkins Report years earlier: "The Governor-

General's award for spineless accommodation must go, by virtue of seniority, to Mitchell Sharp ... The multinational corporations could not have asked for a better policy than the one the Government provided. Mitchell Sharp must be drawing some satisfaction from his double role as Minister of External Affairs both for the multinational corporations and for this country." Gordon's response was similar: "This legislation is just a disgrace. It represents no steps of any consequence, and the committee [CIC] must oppose it or the public will think the problem has been dealt with." He insisted that the government had repudiated the Gray Report, a decision that "may turn out to be the beginning of the end for Canada."[88]

At the committee hearings on the bill, Goodman presented the view of the CIC. Committee Chairman Robert Kaplan tried to prevent Gordon from speaking, but acquiesced when Goodman threatened to tell the press that the Liberal party had muzzled Walter Gordon.[89] Gordon announced clearly his opposition to the government's proposals: "I suggest that this bill may confuse some members of the Canadian public into believing that members of Parliament are really and seriously concerned about the Canadian independence issue and are doing something important about it." He believed that the bill would do little to stem the growth of foreign investment. The real issue, in Gordon's mind, was not new capital from abroad, but the growth of foreign investment "through the expansion of existing Canadian subsidiaries of foreign parent corporations."[90] The government eventually won the CIC's support for the bill by amending the proposal to allow FIRA to screen not only the takeovers of Canadian firms but also the expansion of foreign-owned companies and the establishment of new foreign-owned enterprises. Gordon, however, was not satisfied. In his view FIRA was "a joke ... designed to deal with the fringes and not with the substance" of foreign ownership.[91] Watkins expressed his agreement with Gordon: FIRA was "like having a referee at a rape."[92]

Another reaction to the growth in nationalist sentiment appeared in the autumn of 1972, when Secretary of State for External Affairs Mitchell Sharp published a paper examining Canada's relations with its southern neighbour. Sharp argued that Canadians had three options: "(a) we can seek to maintain more or less our present relationship with the United States with a minimum of policy adjustments; (b) we can move deliberately toward closer integration with the United States; (c) we can pursue a comprehensive, long-term strategy to develop and strengthen the Canadian economy and other aspects of our national life and in the process reduce the present Canadian vulnerability."[93] Sharp preferred the third option, which he saw as a moderate and gradual effort to reduce Canadian dependence on the United States, without the need for "the more extreme kinds of nationalistic measures that were being advocated in some quarters at the time."[94] Noting that the options paper was issued a few days before a general election, Trudeau's biographers, Christina McCall and Stephen Clarkson, have suggested that it was more a response to public pressure than a program the government actually intended to implement.[95]

Throughout the 1970s Gordon's views on foreign ownership became more extreme. He began to argue that the government should gradually force the largest foreign firms to sell most of their shares to Canadians. He first suggested the idea in March 1970, when he recommended that the government introduce legislation requiring large foreign-owned companies to sell a majority of shares within five years.[96] Over the next several years he honed the details of the proposal. In 1972 he recommended that Parliament pass "a formal resolution ... to the effect that within five years' time no foreign corporation together with its associated affiliates may own more than, say, 10% or 20% of the voting shares of any Canadian company over a certain size."[97] In a 1974 speech in Washington, Gordon suggested that the resolution should deal only with the five hundred largest foreign-controlled companies in Canada.[98] The idea was presented in final form in an October 1974 article in the *Financial Post* and then in Gordon's third book, *Storm Signals*, published in October 1975. He proposed that Parliament direct the owners of the thirty-two largest foreign-owned companies to sell a majority of shares to Canadians over ten years. The large oil companies would be sold first, over a period of one to three years; other large resource firms would be sold within five years, and the largest manufacturing and commercial companies in seven years. In ten years Canadians would own at least 75 per cent of all companies in Canada with more than $250 million in assets.[99]

Storm Signals demonstrated Gordon's intensified distrust of American economic power. He spoke of the nefarious reach of American corporations around the world: "The alleged activities of I.T.&T.'s subsidiaries in Chile aimed at the overthrow of the late President Allende are a case in point ... Canadians would be naive to believe that the top executives of multinational corporations with subsidiaries in Canada would refrain, or in the past have refrained, from exerting influence on the policies of this country."[100] But Gordon seemed naïve in implying that only foreign-owned companies tried to shape government policy. Canadian corporations also worked hard to influence the government, but in Gordon's mind Canadian owners were simply defending the country's interests. He never seemed to accept the idea that

Canada's interests did not necessarily coincide with those of the country's corporate elite.

Gordon's criticism of multinational corporations was particularly sharp when he discussed the large oil companies. In 1974 he proposed that the government purchase Imperial, Gulf, or Shell Oil.[101] The next year his view of the industry was more extreme: "The government should take over the foreign-controlled oil companies in Canada lock stock and barrel and then turn them over to a crown corporation to be operated in the interests of the people of this country."[102] Gordon provided little justification for his plan to nationalize the oil industry, a proposal that was less a well-considered solution to the problem than an emotional reaction to the tensions in Canadian-American relations caused by the energy shortages of the mid-1970s and the criticism by several prominent Americans of Canada's oil export controls. As he admitted in a 1976 speech, he did not "trust the motives or the policies of the international oil cartel or their representatives in this country."[103]

Gordon and his followers continued to have limited success throughout the 1970s. In 1975 the government created Petro-Canada, a national oil company with a broad mandate to help formulate a national energy policy and to increase the Canadian presence in the petroleum industry by participating in all aspects of development and sale. "Walter Gordon was in many ways the spiritual father of Petrocan," wrote Peter Foster in his study of the corporation.[104] The next year, the government withdrew the exemptions that Gordon had given to *Time* and *Reader's Digest*, meaning that the two magazines would have to increase their Canadian content to 75 per cent or lose the tax break for their advertisers. On 1 March 1976 *Time* published its last Canadian edition. "The political atmosphere in Canada appears to be growing perceptibly more nationalistic," commented Alan Rugman of the University of Winnipeg.[105]

Gordon published his memoirs in 1977. He had written the manuscript in 1968 and revised it in 1969, but decided not to publish at that time. Liz Gordon was appalled at the negative reaction to Judy LaMarsh's memoirs, which were highly critical of Lester Pearson, and feared a similar response to her husband's book.[106] According to Gordon, he was urged not to publish the memoirs by family members, "who were reluctant to have past controversies reopened." In addition, he "was reluctant to publish while Pearson was still alive" and was not convinced "that publication would help the independence cause."[107] In the late 1970s, however, after the memories of the LaMarsh controversy had subsided, Gordon decided that his political cause could be helped by the publication of his memoirs. Pearson had since passed away, and public opinion on the foreign investment issue had changed considerably.

A lack of introspection was evident in *A Political Memoir*'s shallow discussion of Gordon's years in public life and its failure to discuss the development of his ideas on foreign control. In the early 1960s Gordon had proposed tax incentives to encourage 25 per cent Canadian ownership; in the mid-1970s he supported the nationalization of all major foreign-owned oil companies and encouraged Parliament to pass a resolution instructing their foreign owners to sell a majority of shares to Canadians. In his memoirs, however, Gordon made no effort to explain why his ideas had developed in this direction. He never tried to explain his motives, and certainly never questioned them.

Gordon's memoirs were similar to his other books. Here – as in *Troubled Canada*, *A Choice for Canada*, *Storm Signals*, and *What Is Happening to Canada* – Gordon failed to prove adequately or even to lay out his case for a policy to limit foreign investment.[108] His arguments failed to convince the reader that foreign ownership threatened the country's interests. The book, and indeed Gordon's public life, rested on an assumption that extensive foreign investment was damaging for Canada, but he never established just why or how.

There was some further success for Gordon's cause in the early 1980s. In the Trudeau government's 1980 budget, Finance Minister Allan MacEachen introduced the National Energy Program, which imposed export controls and attempted to increase Canadian ownership by offering subsidies for exploration and development by Canadian firms. According to Sylvia Bashevkin, the policy "dated back to the Gordon, Watkins and Gray reports as well as to the writings of activists in the Waffle and the Committee for an Independent Canada."[109] The announcement of the National Energy Program was followed in 1981 by Petro-Canada's purchase of Petrofina Canada, and in 1982 of BP Canada, deals that increased the company's presence in the retail market. Historian Michael Bliss later called these purchases "an orgy of Walter Gordonism."[110]

Gordon's last major intervention in public life came in 1986, with a public letter to Liberal leader John Turner, published in the *Toronto Star*. Gordon proposed policies to deal with unemployment, the deficit, social security, and taxation. He devoted much attention to the ongoing free trade negotiations between Canada and the United States, saying that the price of free trade "would be unacceptably high and would carry with it the serious danger down the road of making Canada a dependency of our southern neighbor."

He urged Turner to "make it quite clear that you have no sympathy for these negotiations." While free trade was a hot issue in Canada, foreign investment was not. Gordon mentioned the issue only briefly, saying he hoped that when Turner became prime minister he would take steps to see "that Canadians, as a whole, control a much bigger stake in their own country than they do at the present time."[111]

By this time Gordon's concern over foreign economic influence in Canada seemed unimportant to most Canadians. The Vietnam War, the Watergate scandal, the assassinations and riots were all yesterday's news. The Canadian economy was no longer growing at a rapid pace, and most Canadians now welcomed American capital. In 1984 the new Conservative government of Brian Mulroney announced it was selling its interests in the Canada Development Corporation. In 1985 the government dismantled the National Energy Program and replaced FIRA with Investment Canada, an agency designed to encourage foreign investment. Two years later the government negotiated a free trade agreement with the United States. Watkins and Rotstein slowly slipped from public prominence, with few major newspapers or magazines, other than *Canadian Forum*, paying much attention to them. The crusade to limit investment had ended. "There has never been a cause that has been more firmly defeated than this one," remarked Gordon's friend and former Cabinet colleague Allan MacEachen.[112]

Gordon died of a heart attack on 21 March 1987, nine months before Canada signed the Free Trade Agreement and two years before both Clarkson Gordon and Woods Gordon adopted the name of Ernst & Young, the American firm with which they were affiliated. Yet his influence remains. The Canada Pension Plan, Medicare, the Canada Student Loans program, and Canada's extensive university system were all inspired in part by Gordon and were implemented largely by individuals he had recruited and by a government he had helped to elect. These programs remain today, in much the same form as in the 1960s, and are his most important and enduring legacy. Gordon also left behind a large number of prominent Canadians who remain committed to him and to many of his beliefs. According to James Coutts, "He left several hundred if not several thousand people in public life who were imbued with his ideas."[113] In the early 1990s three of his followers organized a public-policy discussion group in his honour. David Smith, David Zimmer, and David Ellis formed the Walter Gordon Circle at the University Club in Toronto. Roughly fifty individuals attend each of the quarterly dinner meetings, which usually feature a guest speaker, though occasionally the group hosts a debate or a roast.[114] In a February 1993 article entitled "Why Jean Chrétien will never be P.M.," Peter Newman showed the hold that Gordon still had over his followers, years after his death. "What the Liberal party needs," wrote Newman, "is a young Walter Gordon, a revolutionary proponent of change and reform, not afraid to stub his toes on genuinely fresh ideas."[115] For many of his devotees, Gordon was still the man for all seasons.

On the issue of foreign investment, however, he haunts us no more. Gordon had a clear influence over government policies in the 1970s, but this came to an abrupt end in the 1980s. He had created, in the words of journalist Barry Conn Hughes, Canada's "first major nationalist movement of this century."[116] There had been a time when it was, according to Peter Newman, "a kind of a goofy thing to be a nationalist. You were a character, like a butterfly collector." By the mid-1970s, however, many Canadians felt that they "have to excuse themselves if they're *not* for an independent Canada."[117] "Walter Gordon has won," declared Ian Drummond in 1976.[118] But by the 1990s Canadian political life showed that Gordon most surely had lost.

CHAPTER EIGHT

Conclusion

Walter Gordon espoused a very personal form of nationalism. His concerns reflected his experience as an accountant and management consultant, as the owner of several manufacturing companies, as an investor with extensive shareholdings, and as a civil servant in a government that was actively regulating the economy. Though he genuinely sympathized with those in difficulty, Gordon never fully understood the perspective of the farmer, the labourer, or the millions of other Canadians with interests different from his. Because of his limited economic expertise and a restricted outlook, his solutions were often contradictory or unclear, and were usually supported with inadequate argumentation and evidence.

Central to Gordon's views was his belief in government intervention in the economy. During the Depression he had been touched by the plight of homeless men sleeping in the ravine near his family's mansion, and had helped the Royal Commission on Price Spreads examine the flaws of a *laissez-faire* economy. He served as a senior public servant during the Second World War, a period when the government was controlling most aspects of Canada's economic life. These were formative experiences that convinced Gordon that the state could and should play an active role in managing the economy – to provide social programs, to regulate key industries, to determine the nationality of those who owned Canadian companies, and to control the flow of investment and trade.

Though he once said that if he were younger he would smack anyone who called him a protectionist, Gordon was just that.[1] As royal commission chair he circulated a memorandum opposing any move towards substantial tariff reduction, fearing that it would tempt manufacturing plants to move south of the border. Later he tried to suppress a study that argued the advantages of free trade. In his speeches in the 1960s he rejected even the most gradual move towards free trade, saying that it would lead to disruptions, unemployment, and the end of Canada's political independence. These views likely arose from his experience as an owner of several manufacturing enterprises. One of these companies, Canadian Cottons, had failed because of its inability to compete in the international marketplace. Gordon had seen the loss of jobs that resulted from the company's collapse, and the destruction of the small communities where mills had been located. He also saw the profits for his companies that manufactured auto parts, firms that thrived because of the automotive tariff that Gordon had been instrumental in creating in the 1930s. The experiences of these companies shaped Gordon's perspective and made it difficult for him to abandon his protectionist leanings, even when they contradicted his other views. Though his main priority was to reduce the level of foreign investment, Gordon supported the tariff, which had the opposite effect – a contradiction he never addressed. He lacked any formal training in economics, and could not see trade issues from any other perspective. He had witnessed the benefits of the tariff, and that was all that mattered.

Underlying Gordon's economic ideas was a strong sense of the differences between Canada and the United States. American neutrality in the early years of the First World War had a profound impact on the Gordon family. Later, in his twenties, Gordon had tried to live and work in New York but rejected American society and returned to Canada. In 1970, he publicly expressed his distaste for the United States, saying that Canada's neighbour was "a sick society."[2]

As a businessman, Gordon believed that Canadian and American firms had fundamentally different interests. A friend of many business leaders on both sides of the border, he was sensitive to the slight distinctions between the corporate culture in the two countries. He had faith in the Bay Street elite, a private club of which he and many of his closest friends were members. Gordon's outlook was different from that of most Canadians, and as a result he placed much more importance on the nationality of those who owned the companies operating in Canada.

Though critical of foreign-owned companies, Gordon worried little about their practices. He criticized their performance on several occasions, but these comments were designed to legitimize his program to limit outside investment. Certainly he never proposed legislation to encourage firms to seek export markets, to hire more Canadians, or to import fewer parts and components. These issues did not even appear in his speeches of 1960, which are key to understanding Gordon because, as he later said, his ideas did not change substantially afterward.

On those occasions when he raised questions about performance, Gordon concentrated on areas where he had first-hand experience. He noted that foreign-owned firms employed fewer Canadians in managerial and professional positions than did Canadian-owned firms, an insight he gained as head of two of the country's top professional firms. Reflecting his position as owner of several companies that produced automotive parts, he complained that American firms were less likely to purchase components, equipment, and supplies in Canada. But Gordon paid little attention to many other important aspects of performance. Though he occasionally mentioned the extraterritorial application of foreign laws, he was not particularly concerned with the problem and never pursued measures to deal with it. In a similar vein, he was not troubled that raw materials were being exported for processing abroad, a subject forcefully raised by organized labour at the royal commission hearings. Not having witnessed these problems himself, he could not appreciate the concerns that others expressed.

Gordon thought the best solution to the dilemma of American investment was to convince or compel foreign-owned firms to sell shares to Canadians. Beginning with his royal commission's *Preliminary Report*, he suggested changes to the tax laws to favour companies with at least 25 per cent domestic ownership. He never acknowledged that these measures would strengthen – rather than limit – American control by dispersing limited Canadian capital. Later in life he pursued this objective more strongly, proposing that foreign-owned firms sell most of their stock to Canadians. As his critics pointed out, this policy would have primarily benefited individuals who, like Walter Gordon, had the funds and the inclination to invest in the stock market.

Concentrating on issues of trade and investment, Gordon seldom spoke of Canadian culture. Born to a family of accountants and business people, and educated in engineering, he never appreciated the subtle and indefinable importance of culture in a country's self-definition. Claiming that Citibank's presence endangered Canada's financial sector, Gordon tried to force the company out of the country; but he made no effort to get rid of the Canadian editions of *Time* and *Reader's Digest*, which posed a similar threat to the Canadian periodical industry.

If there be any doubt about Gordon's priorities, consider what he did when Pearson gave him *carte blanche* to write his first budget in 1963. Gordon introduced incentives for foreign-owned firms to sell 25 per cent of their shares to Canadians, and a tax to discourage Canadians from selling their companies to foreigners. But his budget included nothing to encourage foreign firms to hire Canadian managers and professionals or to increase their use of local parts and components. He offered, at that time, no measures to protect Canadian magazines, and recommended that the Cabinet take no action in the future.

The paradox of Walter Gordon is that his views, so narrow in their origins and nature, had such widespread appeal. Gordon first had an impact in the mid-1950s, when his royal commission helped to provoke discussion of the level of American ownership in Canada. The McCarthy hearings and Herbert Norman's suicide played an important part in generating opposition to American influence in Canada and support for Gordon's program. This pattern was repeated more than a decade later. In the late 1960s Canadians became increasingly distrustful of the United States. Domestic conflict, including race riots and assassinations (and later the Watergate scandal), combined with the horrors of the Vietnam War to create an image of a violent, brutal, and corrupt country. Once again Gordon was on the public stage to spark a discussion on the foreign investment issue.

Though the circumstances of the time were crucial to Gordon's success, one cannot ignore the importance of his own abilities, personal relationships, and wealth in the rise of the new nationalism. Because of his background and charm, he had close friendships with many members of the political and financial establishment. He had extraordinary organizational skills, which helped him to secure key positions in the private sector and with government departments, boards, and commissions. Through these assignments Gordon gained an intimate understanding of power, the corporate world, and the workings of government.

Using his knowledge of government and business, Gordon helped to prevent the *Toronto Star* from being sold on the open market. He forged a solid bond with the editors and owners of the *Star* by arranging for them to purchase the paper, a transaction that made them wealthy. In subsequent years the newspaper gave front-page coverage to all of Gordon's important pronouncements and to many of his not so important ones. The *Star*'s reports and editorials further disseminated his views in the city and province most likely to accept them.

As an organizer and friend of Lester Pearson, Gordon gained a key position in the Liberal party. He first met Pearson when the two worked for the Royal Commission on Price Spreads, a post Gordon obtained through his success in serving earlier public inquiries. When Pearson needed help revitalizing the party, Gordon lent his considerable strength, restructuring the organization, recruiting candidates and campaign workers, and raising funds. Gordon's success in this endeavour led Pearson to appoint him minister of finance.

The positions that Gordon held as a result of his organizational talents and personal friendships – royal commission chair, minister of finance, and president of the Privy Council – afforded him a place from which to spread his ideas on foreign investment. By chairing the Royal Commission on Canada's Economic Prospects, Gordon became a public figure, a position that he maintained, with the help of the *Star*, for three decades. As a senior member of the Pearson government, he continued to draw attention to himself and his views.

More than any other Canadian, Walter Gordon made foreign investment a subject of national public debate. He created the first two public inquiries to examine the issue, the Gordon royal commission and the Watkins task force, both of which laid the groundwork for subsequent investigations. He gave prominent positions to Mel Watkins and Abraham Rotstein, economists who added further fuel to the public debate. After his retirement from politics Gordon continued the fight by inspiring the creation of the Committee for an Independent Canada, making hundreds of speeches, writing three books, and funding nationalist groups and individuals. In short, Gordon channelled a growing disenchantment with the United States into a movement to limit American investment. He was the father of the new nationalism.

Notes

ABBREVIATIONS

AO   Archives of Ontario
ARP   Abraham Rotstein Papers
CGP   Clarkson Gordon Papers
GWPP   Gerald Wright Personal Papers
LBPP   Lester B. Pearson Papers
NA   National Archives of Canada
NFTSA   National Film, Television, and Sound Archives
POR   Premier's Office Records (Ontario)
PSP   Peter Stursberg Papers
RDF   Records of the Department of Finance
RDND   Records of the Department of National Defence
RPCO   Records of the Privy Council Office
RRCCEP   Records of the Royal Commission on Canada's Economic Prospects
RRCPS   Records of the Royal Commission on Price Spreads
RTB   Records of the Tariff Board
TKP   Tom Kent Papers
WGP   Woods Gordon Papers
WLGP   Walter L. Gordon Papers

PREFACE

1   In constant 1986 dollars, the Gross Domestic Product per capita increased from
$4,994 in 1939 to $17,232 in 1979. These figures are derived from Statistics
Canada, *Canadian Economic Observer*, 7, 27.

CHAPTER ONE

1 Gordon, *Political Memoir*, 13.
2 Ernst & Young Archives, WGP, vol. 4, Walter Gordon file, Susan Padmos and Al Steiner interview with Walter Gordon, 5 Jan. 1982.
3 McCall-Newman, *Grits*, 25–6.
4 Ernst & Young Archives, CGP, unpublished memoirs of H.D.L. Gordon, 48–9; NA, Records of Statistics Canada, RG31, reel T-6498, district 117, sub-district 15, sub-division 11, pp 13–14.
5 The information on Gordon's deal with the Canada Land and Emigration Company comes from Dobrzensky, *Fragments of a Dream*, 252; Reynolds, *In Quest of Yesterday*, 130; Cummings, *Early Days in Haliburton*, 170–1. Some of Lockhart Gordon's correspondence on behalf of the company can be found in NA, Mossom Boyd & Company Papers, MG28 III I, vols. 148–9.
6 AO, Records of the Ministry of the Attorney General, RG22, MS584, reel 157, file 62874, estate file of William Henry Lockhart Gordon. The author's estimate of the present value of the estate is based on the Consumer Price Index. See Canada, Statistics Canada, *The Consumer Price Index, May 1993*, 50; *The Consumer Price Index, December 1994*, 23.
7 The court is now named the Federal Court of Canada, and the presiding judge is called the chief justice.
8 CGP, unpublished memoirs of H.D.L. Gordon, 74–7.
9 Little, *Story of the Firm*, 19–25; MacKenzie, *Clarkson Gordon Story*, 21–4; CGP, unpublished memoirs of H.D.L. Gordon, 31.
10 H.D. Lockhart Gordon, "Fifty Years Ago," 97.
11 Walter Gordon's thoughts on the building are found in Gordon, foreword to *Toronto: No Mean City*, vii. The building was recently torn down. Its façade was disassembled, stone by stone, and restored within BCE Place at the corner of Bay and Front, just south of its original location.
12 CGP, unpublished memoirs of H.D.L. Gordon, 20–1, 24, 41; Kathleen Griffin interview; NA, WLGP, MG32 B44, vol. 32, file 15, Gordon, "Reflections on Canada and Its Future," intro., second draft, 23 Feb. 1981; "The Graduating Class 1926," *R.M.C. Review*, June 1926, 80.
13 Bennett, *The 4th Canadian Mounted Rifles*, 19–21, 159; Young, *War Book of Upper Canada College*, 165. See also Waite, *Lord of Point Grey*, 18.
14 NA, RDND, military personnel file of H.D.L. Gordon, Brigadier-General Chas. A. Smart, "Annual Confidential Report for 1917."
15 McCall-Newman, *Grits*, 25. Both Walter and his father disliked the superior, condescending attitude of many of the English. Jane Glassco interview; CGP, unpublished memoirs of H.D.L. Gordon.

16 See Stacey, *Canada and the Age of Conflict*, 1:228.

17 Griffin interview.

18 CGP, unpublished memoirs of H.D.L. Gordon, 24.

19 Griffin interview.

20 Interviews with Glassco and Kyra Montagu; Newman, "What Really Happened," *Maclean's*, 19 Oct. 1963, 76; Newman, *Distemper of Our Times*, 215.

21 NA, RDND, military personnel file of H.D.L. Gordon, Gordon to Adjutant-General, 10 June 1918.

22 CGP, unpublished memoirs of H.D.L. Gordon, 37.

23 H.D. Lockhart Gordon, "Fifty Years Ago," 98.

24 Richardson, "Canada's Accounting Elite," 1–21, espec. 14.

25 Griffin interview.

26 The Synod Journals can be found at the Archives of the Anglican Diocese of Toronto.

27 Archives of the Anglican Diocese of Toronto, St James Cathedral file, "A Guide to the Cathedral Church of St. James, Toronto," 1932, 48.

28 Historians have not adequately explored the subject of imperialist sentiment within the Anglican church. Carl Berger touched on the sense of divine mission shared by many imperialists, but had little to say about the Church of England. Berger, *Sense of Power*, 217–32.

29 "Free Speech," *Canadian Churchman*, 11 May 1905, 297.

30 "Daughters of the Empire," *Canadian Churchman*, 16 Feb. 1905, 100.

31 The comment on Gordon's being an atheist is derived from interviews with Griffin and John Gordon.

32 John Kenneth Galbraith, "Robertson Davies," *New York Times*, 14 Feb. 1982. Reprinted in Galbraith, *View from the Stands*.

33 Gordon enrolled at the UCC preparatory school in the fall of 1915, but withdrew shortly thereafter when he moved with his mother to England. Young, *Roll of Pupils*, 268.

34 Charity Grant interview; obituary for G.T. Denison, *College Times*, Summer 1925, 63.

35 Grant, "Current Events," 171. For Grant's views on the empire, see Grant, "Truncated Imperialism," 250–1.

36 NA, Grant Papers, MG30, D59, vol. 4, W.L. Grant to Arthur Glazebrook, 17 Dec. 1910. See also Bissell, *Young Vincent Massey*, 163–4.

37 WLGP, MG32 B44, vol. 32, file 15, draft introduction to "Reflections on Canada and Its Future," 23 Feb. 1981.

38 A.F.W. Plumptre, editorial, *College Times*, Summer 1923, 4. Years later, Plumptre displayed some of the imperialist's distrust of the United States, an attitude that may have been a product of his UCC education. See Plumptre,

"Special Trade Deal with U.S.A.," 18–19. Later Plumptre became a leading Canadian internationalist, playing a key role as Canadian executive director at the International Monetary Fund and the World Bank. See Plumptre, *Three Decades of Decision*.

39 W.H. Bilborough, "How Are We To Keep Canadians in Canada," *College Times*, Christmas 1924, 53.

40 L.M. Gelber, editorial, *College Times*, summer 1924, 4.

41 Knox, "Canadian Capital Movements," 299.

42 *Crazy Twenties*, 8; Vipond, *Mass Media in Canada*, 37–43.

43 *Crazy Twenties*, 8.

44 Vipond, "Canadian Nationalism," 44; Vipond, *Mass Media*, 24.

45 *Crazy Twenties*, 43.

46 Ibid.

47 Vipond, *Mass Media*, 30–7; Morris, *Embattled Shadows*, 238–40; Magder, *Canada's Hollywood*, 19–48.

48 These views differed markedly from another brand of Canadian nationalism that was becoming more popular in the 1920s. A large number of Canadian nationalists, particularly those under the age of forty, were concerned less with resisting the United States than with developing political and cultural autonomy from Britain. Vipond, "National Consciousness," 521–36.

49 Grant, *Robertson Davies*, 122; Grant interview.

50 NA, Davies Papers, MG30 D362, vol. 30, file 16, "Some Reminiscences of W.L. Grant," 3 Apr. 1969.

51 Interviews with Griffin, Grant, and Elizabeth Gordon; McCall-Newman, *Grits*, 25. Gordon remembered Alison Ignatieff in his will. Ontario Court (General Division), Toronto, estate file of Walter Gordon, file 3547/87.

52 Davies Papers, MG30 D362, vol. 20, file 16, "Some Reminiscences of W.L. Grant," 3 Apr. 1969, 4.

53 Kilbourn, *Toronto Remembered*, 172. Robertson Davies' biographer has described UCC as "a place where an unconventional boy like Davies could find a niche." Grant, *Robertson Davies*, 110.

54 Kilbourn, *Toronto Remembered*, 173; Grant, *Robertson Davies*, 122.

55 Leacock, "The Struggle To Make Us Gentlemen," 28. Similarly, Clarkson Gordon aimed to turn its accounting students into gentlemen. See Moon, "Finishing School," 6–8, 23.

56 FitzGerald, *Old Boys*; Howard, *Upper Canada College*. For an engaging account of one student who was unyielding in the face of UCC discipline, see Black, *Life in Progress*, 10–16.

57 Griffin interview.

58 George Monk interview.

59 Interviews with Hartland Molson and Monk; Vokes, *Vokes: My Story*, 16–17, 21; Smith, *As You Were!* 1:291–3; Preston, *Canada's RMC*, 247; Brock, *"Fight the Good Fight,"* 6.

60 For the Arnold Case, see Graham, *The Price of Command*, 21–3; Preston, *Canada's RMC*, 238–43.

61 Department of National Defence, Directorate of History, Records of the Department of National Defence, file 171.013 (D3), "Advisory Board of the Royal Military College, Report of the Sub-Committee on Administration of Discipline," 3 Apr. 1924.

62 Griffin interview.

63 Gordon had written a junior matriculation at UCC; most of his classmates at RMC had completed a senior matriculation.

64 Monk interview.

65 Interviews with Guy Smith, Edwin Beament, and C.C.I. Merritt.

66 Interviews with Monk, Molson, and Guy Smith; Smith, *As You Were!* 2:375; "The Graduating Class 1926," *R.M.C. Review*, June 1926, 80; "Field Sports," *R.M.C. Review*, Nov. 1924, 54.

67 John Gordon interview.

68 Smith, *As You Were!* 1:280. Robert Bennett and T.L. Brock also remembered being urged to "show guts." Smith, *As You Were!* 1:291; Brock, *"Fight the Good Fight,"* 5.

69 Panet, "Royal Military College," 448.

70 Interviews with B.B. Osler and H.C. Thomas MacDougall. Gordon obliquely referred to this incident in his memoirs. Gordon, *Political Memoir*, 151.

71 Griffin interview.

72 Canada, Royal Military College, *Regulations and Instructions*, 19.

73 Osler interview; Smith, *As You Were!* 1:280.

74 Quoted in Smith, *As You Were!* 1:292. The memoirs of Maj.-Gen. Chris Vokes are an example, perhaps extreme, of the inability of the RMC graduate to express himself. Two paragraphs, each two sentences long, illustrate Vokes's choppy, childlike way of expressing himself:

I had an allowance of $5 a month at R.M.C. That was the regulation allowance. I spent it on chocolate bars and pots of honey. Chocolate bars were five cents each. (*Vokes: My Story*, 18)

75 Quoted in Smith, *As You Were!* 1:323.

76 "Second Class," *R.M.C. Review*, Nov. 1924, 33; Richard M. Alway interview with Walter Gordon, *Canadian Public Figures on Tape*, tape 4; Tom Axworthy interview with Gordon, 26 Sept. 1969, cited in Axworthy, "Innovation and the Party System," 108.

77 Skinner, "Research Contributions," 198; interviews with Jack Biddell, Marcel Caron, Michael Mackenzie, and Ross Skinner.

78 Information on the character traits of the Gordons, father and son, came from the following interviews: Mackenzie, Molson, Osler, Skinner, Alex Adamson, Royce Frith, Griffin, and William Kilbourn.

79 Confidential sources.

80 Interviews with Mackenzie and Donald Scott. See also MacKenzie, *Clarkson Gordon Story*, 70.

81 Skinner interview.

82 Gordon, *Political Memoir*, 14.

83 NA, RDND, military personnel file of H.D.L. Gordon, Gordon to Adjutant-General, 10 June 1918; Oliver, *G. Howard Ferguson*, 220; Oliver, *Public and Private Persons*, 230–1.

84 Gordon, *Political Memoir*, 15.

85 Ibid., 16.

86 Osler interview.

87 Montagu interview. In a general discussion of Gordon's character, his former Cabinet colleague Allan MacEachen commented, "The brash New Yorker would not go over well with Walter Gordon." Allan MacEachen interview.

88 Jane Glassco remembers her grandmother as a formidable and terrifying woman; Glassco interview. Walter Gordon's marital connections did not end there. His sister Isabelle was married to James Wright, vice-president of Canadian Pacific Railway. Another sister, Kathleen, was married to Anthony Griffin, chair of Triarch Corporation, president of Meridian Technologies, and director of Consumers' Gas and Victoria & Grey Trust; Griffin was grandson of Sir William Mackenzie, the president of Canadian Northern Railway and the founder of Brazilian Traction, Light and Power. Mackenzie is the subject of a recent biography: Fleming, *Railway King*. Gordon's sister-in-law Jane Counsell was married to C.M. "Bud" Drury, a long-time public servant and Liberal Cabinet minister. He was the son of Victor Drury, chair of Provincial Transport and president of International Holdings, and bother of Chipman Drury, who served as president of Quebec Industries and as mayor of Westmount.

89 Thomas H. Ferns, "John Leith Counsell," 39–40; Glassco interview.

90 Petryshyn, "A.E. Smith," iv, 103; Smith, *All My Life*, 84; Angus, *Canadian Bolsheviks*, 219; Rodney, *Soldiers of the International*, 31–2, 71–2, 122; Canada, Department of Labour, *Labour Organization*, 208–9.

91 Griffin interview.

92 Tom Axworthy interview with Walter Gordon, cited in Axworthy, "Innovation and the Party System," 136.

93 Gordon was a part owner of *Canadian Forum* from the spring of 1934 to the spring of 1935, when it was owned by a group of left-leaning Liberals. In 1935 Gordon's group sold the periodical to the League for Social Reconstruction, and the new editor became Graham Spry, Gordon's close friend. NA, ARP, MG31 D73, vol. 4, file 61, Gordon to Rotstein, 30 July 1964; *Canadian Forum*, May 1934, 282; Prang, "Some Opinions of Political Radicalism," 8–9.

94 McCall-Newman, *Grits*, 22. Gordon was particularly close to Graham Spry. When pregnant, Spry's wife Irene stayed with the Gordons until her first child was born. Irene Spry interview; Potvin, *Passion and Conviction*, 134, 137.

95 Molson interview.

96 Interviews with Keith Davey, Ferguson and Glassco; Davey, *Rainmaker*, 39, 82; NA, Judy LaMarsh Papers, MG32 B8, vol. 7, first draft of memoirs, chap. 4, p 13.

97 See NA, RRCPS, RG33/18, vol. 11, "Evidence of W.L. Gordon on the T. Eaton Co. Limited"; various documents in vols. 72, 73, 74; vol. 92, file 403; Canada, House of Commons, Special Committee on Price Spreads and Mass Buying, *Proceedings and Evidence*, 3:3051–222, 3413–84; Wilbur, *H.H. Stevens*, 127–8.

98 RRCPS, RG33/18, vol. 139, Norman Sommerville to H.D. Lockhart Gordon, 29 June 1934.

99 Richard Wilbur interview with Walter Gordon, 24 Feb. 1960, cited in Wilbur, *H.H. Stevens*, 127.

100 Most writers believe that the two first met while working on the commission. See, for example, Bothwell, *Pearson*, 25; Smith, *Gentle Patriot*, 19. Neither Gordon nor Pearson, however, says this in his memoirs. Gordon refers to Pearson's work on the commission without saying when they first met. Pearson's memoirs do not even mention Gordon when discussing his work for the royal commission. Gordon, *Political Memoir*, 18; Pearson, *Mike*, 1:76–7. The only strong evidence that the two first met on the commission can be found in Library of Parliament, Peter Stursberg interview with Walter Gordon, 2 June 1977.

Liz Gordon said that she had known Pearson before her marriage, and added that Walter met him through her "long before" the Price Spreads Commission. Although already acquainted, Pearson and Gordon only became friends during the commission. Gordon interview. See also Michel Brunet, review of *A Political Memoir*, 85.

101 Pearson, *Mike*, 1:76–8; English, *Worldly Years*, 168–71.

102 Gordon worked full-time for the board for about a year, and then again occasionally every year until 1939.

103 NA, RTB, RG79, vol. 366, file 91, part 7, Clarkson, Gordon, Dilworth & Nash to the Tariff Board, 14 Dec. 1935, 65–6.

104 RTB, RG79, vol. 31, file 91–9, part 2, WLG [Walter Lockhart Gordon], "The Tariff Board – Canada: Confidential Memorandum," Apr. or May 1936.

105 WLGP, MG32 B44, vol. 34, file 12, "Ups and Downs: Political Memoirs of Walter L. Gordon," chap. 1, p 18. This passage was removed from the manuscript before publication.

106 Gordon, *Political Memoir*, 19.

107 Canadian Corporate Management owned Dominion Forge, Western Tire & Auto Supply, and Walker Metal Products, which the *Financial Post* described as "one of the few large Canadian-owned auto-parts manufacturers in Canada." "Walker Metal Products bought by Chrysler Canada," *Financial Post*, 18 Jan. 1964, 5.

108 After graduating from RMC, Gordon was obliged to serve five years in the nonpermanent militia. From 1927 to 1933 he was a lieutenant in the 48th Highlanders of Canada, and for one night a week, and a camp once a year, he participated in the activities of the regiment. Molson interview; Smith, *As You Were!* 2:375; Beattie, *48th Highlanders*, 430; NA, RDND, military personnel file of Lieutenant Walter Lockhart Gordon.

109 Interviews with Griffin and Molson. Robert Bryce remembered that the gout even made Gordon's bureaucratic work difficult. NA, NFTSA, Institute for Research on Public Policy Collection, Ian Stewart interview with Robert Bryce, 18 July 1990, 97 minutes, acc. no. 1990-0334.

110 The creation of the Foreign Exchange Control Board is discussed briefly but effectively in Fullerton, *Graham Towers*, 118–20.

111 MacKenzie, *Clarkson Gordon Story*, 34.

112 NA, RDF, RG19, vol. 656, file 184-B, "Plan of Organization," 25 Sept. 1939; vol. 3998, file 184L, press release, 4 Oct. 1939; vol. 3426, "Summary Directory," 6 Oct. 1939; vol. 656, file 184-C, "Directory of Foreign Exchange Control Board," 18 Jan. 1940; vol. 2678, file F-07, "Foreign Exchange Control Board," organizational chart, 23 Jan. 1940; vol. 3426, "Office Memorandum," 24 Jan. 1940; Bank of Canada, Foreign Exchange Control Board Records, box 33, file 42-1, "Inter-Company Transactions," 29 Sept. 1939; W.L. Gordon and M.W. Mackenzie memo, 10 Oct. 1939.

113 MacKenzie, *Clarkson Gordon Story*, 36–7.

114 The information on the history of J.D. Woods Co. is based on CGP, D.B. Watson, "The History of Woods, Gordon & Co.," Apr. 1976; Ernst & Young Archives, WGP, vol. 1, minutes of directors meetings; vol. 4, Susan Padmos and Al Steiner interview with Walter Gordon, 5 Jan. 1982; Woods Gordon Video Collection, "Woods Gordon 50th Anniversary," 1982, sd. col. videocassette, 33 minutes; "Interview – Walter and Duncan Gordon with Len Delicaet," probably 1981 or 1982, sd. col. videocassette, 30 minutes; Mellett, *From Stopwatch to Strategy*, 4.

115 David MacKenzie dates the agreement to 1939. Minutes of directors' meetings and an interview with Walter Gordon both show that the two firms joined forces in 1940. See MacKenzie, *Clarkson Gordon Story*, 57; WGP, vol. 1, minutes of directors' meeting, 6 Nov. 1940; vol. 4, Susan Padmos and Al Steiner interview with Walter Gordon, 5 Jan. 1982.

116 Gordon, *Political Memoir*, 33.

117 Ibid. In a 1969 interview Gordon recalled Clark as "the greatest guy I've ever met." Cited in Axworthy, "Innovation and the Party System," 112.

118 For more on this trend, see Owram, *Government Generation*. See also Bryce, "William Clifford Clark," 413–23.

119 Pickersgill, *My Years with Louis St Laurent*, 180.

120 "Figure Wizard," *Financial Post*, 24 Jan. 1942, 6. For Gordon's original proposal, see RDF, RG19, vol. 2697, file 100-23, WLG, "Advisability of Some Declaration of Policy Respecting Dominion and Provincial Fields of Taxation Etc," 2 Mar. 1941.

121 Burns, *Acceptable Mean*, 29.

122 For a history of the Wartime Prices and Trade Board, see Jewett, "Wartime Prices and Trade Board." Gordon's role in reorganizing the board is described well in Waddell, "Wartime Prices and Trade Board." Gordon's memoranda on this issue can be found in RDF, RG19, vol. 3992, file W-2-2. Gordon was appointed to the board weeks after his work to reorganize it, likely as recognition of his contribution. See RDF, RG19, vol. 394, file 101-102S, PC8838, 13 Nov. 1941.

123 Gibson and Robertson, *Ottawa at War*, 204–5.

124 Institute for Research on Public Policy Collection, Ian Stewart interview with Robert Bryce, 18 July 1990, 97 minutes, acc. no. 1990-0334.

125 Gordon, *Political Memoir*, 36.

126 Ibid., 43. Gordon's explanation for leaving Finance is supported by a frank interview with Robert Bryce. Institute for Public Policy Collection, Ian Stewart interview with Robert Bryce, 18 July 1990, 97 minutes, acc. no. 1990-0334.

Gordon said that he stayed with the Department of Finance until the spring of 1942, but he probably left in February. His resignation from the Wartime Prices and Trade Board and the Commodity Prices Stabilization Corporation was dated 23 Feb., and his $600 monthly allowance ended on 28 Feb. RDF, RG19, vol. 394, file 101-102S, Gordon to Ilsley, 23 Feb. 1942; "Press Release," 18 Mar. 1942; NA, Records of the Civil Service Commission, RG32, series C-2, vol. 817, V.M. Johnson to K.W. Taylor, 18 June 1963.

127 WLGP, MG32, B44, vol. 34, file 12, "Ups and Downs: Political Memoirs of Walter L. Gordon," chap. 1, p 23. This comment was deleted from the manuscript before it was published.

128 WGP, vol. 1, 1940–44 minutes file, Walter Gordon to Donald Gordon, 27 Feb. 1942.

129 The firm prepared studies on dairy distribution, bakeries, small flour mills, gasoline distribution, leather footwear, and textiles. Queen's University Archives, Gordon Papers, vol. 10, file 110, David Sim to Donald Gordon, 6 Nov. 1942.

130 WGP, vol. 1, 1940–44 minutes file, Donald Gordon to Walter Gordon, 6 Jan. 1943.

131 Canada, Royal Commission on Administrative Classifications in the Public Service, *Report*. For a discussion of the report, see Hodgetts et al., *Biography of an Institution*, 209–17; Wilson, *Canadian Public Policy*, 399.

132 Gordon, *Political Memoir*, 45.

133 Cole, *Canadian Bureaucracy*, 55.

134 Hodgetts et al., *Biography of an Institution*, 214.

135 Ibid., 213. See also "The Royal Commission Report," 110.

136 Cited in Hodgetts et al., *Biography of an Institution*, 212.

137 NA, Records of Parliament, RG14, vol. 512, reel T-3531, sessional paper no. 106a, 20th Parliament, 3rd Session, 17 Feb. 1947; Canada, House of Commons, *Debates*, 10 Feb. 1947, 242–3.

138 Woods Gordon Video Collection, "Woods Gordon 50th Anniversary," 1982, sd. col. videocassette, 33 minutes; WGP, vol. 4, Susan Padmos and Al Steiner interview with Walter Gordon, 5 Jan. 1982; "Experts Study Ontario Hydro in All Phases," *Financial Post*, 15 Feb. 1947, 5.

139 NA, Claxton Papers, MG32 B5, vol. 32, W.L. Gordon file, Claxton to Gordon, 17 Sept. 1948; Gordon, *Political Memoir*, 51–4.

140 Litt, *Massey Commission*, 133.

141 WGP, vol. 4, Susan Padmos and Al Steiner interview with Walter Gordon, 5 Jan. 1982; AO, POR, Frost Administration, General Correspondence Files, RG3-23, file 126-G, Woods Gordon, "Department of Highways, Ontario, Organization and Administrative Practices," 14 May 1954.

142 WGP, vol. 4, Susan Padmos and Al Steiner interview with Walter Gordon, 5 Jan. 1982.

143 Claxton Papers, MG32 B5, vol. 32, W.L. Gordon file, Gordon to Brooke Claxton, 9 Feb. 1954.

144 McLeod, "Moses with a Maple-Leaf," 22.

145 Gordon, *Political Memoir*, 25–6. The current value of this figure was derived from the exchange rate and the Consumer Price Index. Canada, Statistics Canada, *Canada's International Investment Position*, 257; *Consumer Price Index, May 1993*, 50; *Consumer Price Index, December 1994*, 23.

146 Booth, "Agglomerator Inc.," 42.

147 Gordon, *Political Memoir*, 26.

148 Ibid., 25.

149 Alexander Bruchovsky, "This Conglomerate Still Buys," *Financial Post*, 28 Mar. 1970, 19.

150 Interview with Robert Douglas Stuart, Jr.; "u.s. Envoy Belittles Peril of Control of Resources," *Globe and Mail*, 17 Apr. 1956, 1, 10; "Triangle at Ottawa," *Saturday Night*, 12 May 1956, 5.

151 Canadian Corporate Management, *Annual Report*, 1985, 32. CanCorp owned Easy Heat, Inc., of New Carlisle, Ind., and Electro-Therm, Inc., of Laurel, Md.

152 Russell Gormley interview; Eric Richter, "Canadian Cottons Sells Off Assets," *Financial Post*, 1 Aug. 1959, 1; Booth, "Agglomerator Inc.," 42; "Who's Who in Foreign Business," *Fortune*, Mar. 1962, 62.

153 Austin, "Life Cycles," 539; Canada, Tariff Board, *Report*, 1:81, 85.

154 Mahon, *Politics of Industrial Restructuring*, 52.

155 NA, Records of the Department of Industry, Trade and Commerce, RG20, vol. 766, file 23-100-C49, Canadian Cottons, Limited, "Annual Report for the Year ended March 31, 1959."

156 Henry N.R. Jackman, letter to author, 24 Oct. 1995.

157 WLGP, MG32 B44, vol. 20, file 1, Gordon to Jack Davis, 15 Aug. 1966.

158 Interviews with Benson and Glassco; Library of Parliament, Peter Stursberg interview with Tom Kent, 30 Mar. 1977; Tom Earl interview with Mitchell Sharp, 19 Jan. 1984; Sharp, *Which Reminds Me*, 89.

159 Library of Parliament, Peter Stursberg interview with Jean Marchand, 10 Aug. 1976.

160 Library of Parliament, Peter Stursberg interview with James Coutts, 22 Apr. 1977.

161 Pearson interview. Walter Gordon was aware, at least after the friendship was over, that he and Pearson had viewed their relationship differently. "I doubt if he thought I was his closest friend ... I looked upon him as as close a friend as I had." Library of Parliament, Peter Stursberg interview with Walter Gordon, 2 June 1977.

162 NA, Heeney Papers, MG32 E144, vol. 2, Heeney diary, 24–25 Sept. 1955.

163 Tom Kent, letter to author, 8 Aug. 1995. Journalist Bruce Hutchison had a similar impression: "Like all his friends, I sensed behind his frank speech and intimate manner a deep gulf of reticence. Outside of his family, I doubt that anyone else ever crossed that gulf." Hutchison, *Far Side of the Street*, 249.

164 Tom Kent, letter to author, 8 Aug. 1995.

165 Gordon remembered this figure in 1965. See WLGP, MG32 B44, vol. 16, file 11, Gordon memorandum, 5 Dec. 1965. Today, this amount would be worth about $750,000.

166 Walter and Liz Gordon's philanthropy was an important part of their life. It would have been out of character for Walter to ask a friend for money for a cause that he was not fully supporting himself. Ferguson interview; Tom Kent, letter to author, 8 Aug. 1995. In 1965 Gordon remembered, "Naturally, I contributed substantially myself, despite the fact I was not well off in those days!" WLGP, MG32 B44, vol. 16, file 11, Gordon memo, 5 Dec. 1965.

167 NA, LBPP, MG26 N5, vol. 46, file 136-141, Bernard Ostry interview with Lester Pearson, transcript of roll 138, p 1.

168 Gordon, *Political Memoir*, 50.

169 Interviews with Glassco and Frith.

170 Interviews with Glassco and Montagu.

171 Denis Smith Personal Papers, Smith interview with Gordon, 22 Nov. 1971.

172 Copeman, *Short History of the Gout*, 116–17. Without this treatment, Gordon would not have been able to run for Parliament or serve as minister of finance. In a letter to Pearson in 1960, Gordon wrote that he would like to serve as minister of finance. He acknowledged the importance of the new medicine to this decision: "At long last, I seem to have got my gout under control with the result that I feel better than I have for many years." LBPP, MG26 N6, vol. 12, Walter Gordon 1960–61 file, Gordon to Pearson, 9 Mar. 1960.

173 W.A. Wilson, "A Humanitarian without Gush," *Winnipeg Free Press*, 28 Mar. 1987, 6.

174 John Gordon interview.

175 In 1966 his political colleagues hosted a dinner in his honour. After several emotional tributes, many of those present were in tears. Gordon stood to respond to the tributes, saying blandly, "I'm very moved by this demonstration." Denis Smith interview with Keith Davey, 25 Nov. 1971, cited in Smith, *Gentle Patriot*, 295.

   Equally emotional was his seventieth birthday party, attended by over nine hundred friends and colleagues. Gordon responded to their tributes by saying, "I don't know what to say. If I could cry, I would cry." Pat McNenly, "Walter Gordon at 70 Gets Happy Birthday from 900 at Party," *Toronto Star*, 28 Jan. 1976.

176 Newman, *Distemper of Our Times*, 217.

177 Coutts interview.

178 Mel Hurtig interview; Newman, "What Really Happened," 22, 76; Newman, *Distemper of Our Times*, 215.

179 Axworthy interview with Gordon, Axworthy, "Innovation and the Party System," 128.

180 Newman, *Distemper of Our Times*, 217.

181 Smith, *Gentle Patriot*, 355. Similarly, J.W. Pickersgill, who was not sympathetic to Gordon's ideas, remembered that Gordon became very impatient with John Connolly and George McIlraith when they asked basic questions about his policies. J.W. Pickersgill interview. See also Tom Kent in Stursberg, *Lester Pearson and the Dream of Unity*, 136.

182 WLGP, MG32 B44, vol. 37, file 8, "The Need to Streamline Our Parliamentary Procedures," Gordon speech to Osgoode Hall Legal and Literary Society, 20 Mar. 1967.

183 Jane Finlayson, "Remembering Past Politics," *Ottawa Citizen*, 17 Dec. 1973.

184 Mackenzie interview.

185 Interviews with Coutts, MacEachen, and Peter C. Newman; Jutras, "Cancorp," 70.

186 Little, *Story of the Firm*, 43, 49; Edick interview.

187 Interviews with Coutts, Ferguson, and Skinner.

188 Mitchell Sharp interview.

189 LBPP, MG26 N3, vol. 72, A.J.E. Child to Pearson, 8 July 1963.

190 WLGP, MG32 B44, vol. 37, file 1, speech to the Canadian Club of Toronto, 6 Dec. 1954.

191 Gordon, *Political Memoir*, 22.

192 The Gray Report showed that of the $72 million spent on foreign consultants in 1964, 90 per cent came from firms with a majority foreign ownership. Canada, *Foreign Direct Investment*, 204.

193 Benson interview.

194 Interviews with Glassco and Montagu.

CHAPTER TWO

1 A poll taken in 1946 showed that 50 per cent of Canadians thought the Soviet Union wanted to dominate the world, while a mere 25 per cent of Americans showed the same distrust of the Stalinist government. "Quarter's Polls," 114.

2 Pearson, *Words and Occasions*, 71.

3 NA, Howe Papers, MG27 III B20, vol. 153, file 89-2 (31), Howe speech to the American Society of Tool Engineers, Montreal, 29 Oct. 1949.

4 Wolfe, "Economic Growth and Foreign Investment," 16.

5 Leacy, *Historical Statistics*, series G190.

6 Urquhart and Buckley, *Historical Statistics*, 183.

7 Leacy, *Historical Statistics*. This figure was derived by dividing the Gross National Expenditure in constant (1971) dollars (series F55) by the estimated population (series A1).

8 Before the rise of McCarthyism in the United States, there were very few Canadian public figures who openly questioned American foreign policy or Canada's alliance with the United States. Historian Arthur Lower, economist Harold Innis, and journalist André Laurendeau were the exceptions that prove the rule.

In 1952 Lower wrote that the Canadian business community was "completely imbued with the branch plant colonial mentality. As a result, Canada does not enjoy all her own wealth. She is an exploited area in a more intense sense than India ever was." Lower, *Canada: Nation and Neighbour*, 39–40.

In a lecture at the University of Nottingham in 1948, Innis parodied the title of Lower's most famous work, *Colony to Nation*: "Paradoxically, the stoutest defenders of the Canadian tariff against the United States were the representatives of American capital investors. Canadian nationalism was systematically encouraged and exploited by American capital. Canada moved from colony to nation to colony." Innis, "Great Britain, the United States and Canada," 121.

In 1949 Laurendeau opposed Canada's entry into the North Atlantic Treaty Organization. Horton, *André Laurendeau*, 151.

9 Gordon, *Storm Signals*, 11.

10 Canada, House of Commons, *Debates*, 23 Nov. 1953, 237.

11 Ibid., 3 Dec. 1953, 596.

12 "McCarthy: Curiosity in Politics," *Ottawa Journal*, 26 Nov. 1953; *Canadian Forum*, Oct. 1954, 149.

13 Keirstead, *Canada in World Affairs*, 36. Member of Parliament Colin Cameron wrote, "The latest accomplishment of the McCarthyites has been to turn the last firm, disinterested friend the United States had in the world into a hostile and suspicious neighbor." Cameron, "Canada's Revolt," 460.

14 Creighton, "Canada and the Cold War," 244–5.

15 William McGuffin, "Canada Must Abandon U.S. Diplomacy Ideas Says Prof. Creighton," *Toronto Star*, 14 Aug. 1954, 17; Taylor, *Radical Tories*, 35.

16 NA, WLGP, MG32 B44, vol. 37, file 1, "China and the Far East," speech in Toronto, 6 Dec. 1954, 7. The *Globe and Mail* cited Gordon's speech in an editorial criticizing American policy towards China. "Mao is No Transient," *Globe and Mail*, 7 Dec. 1954.

17 Tinker, "I'm Leaving Canada," 21, 48; "U.S. Students Are Surprised by Antagonism," *Globe and Mail*, 16 Apr. 1956, 3; Aronson, "The Northern Frontier"; Resnick, *Land of Cain*.

18 Barkway, "The Fifties," 29. In 1955 journalist Grant Dexter recorded that Pearson knew "from his contact with the Old Man [St Laurent] that he continues to be irritable, unhappy and tired." Queen's University Archives, Dexter Papers, vol. 1, memo, 3 Apr. 1955. The diplomat Arnold Heeney had a similar impression of St Laurent in 1956: "My own judgement is that he is bone tired & worried deeply

about the present and the future. It is almost a pathetic spectacle. In long intervals he says nothing & is completely withdrawn ... It seems to me we are approaching a crisis." NA, Heeney Papers, MG30 E144, vol. 2, Heeney Diary, 28 Mar. 1956.

19 Gordon, *Political Memoir*, 59.

20 Queen's University Archives, Taylor Papers, collection 5139, box 1, file 19, Walter L. Gordon, "Canada's Future – A Proposed Survey," Mar. 1955.

21 Gordon, *Political Memoir*, 60.

22 Tom Kent, "Mr. Howe Hot, Civil Servants Cold," *Winnipeg Free Press*, 21 Apr. 1958. See also Bird, "Prophet in Ottawa," 1–2.

23 Gordon, *Political Memoir*, 64; *Storm Signals*, 12. Scholars have accepted Gordon's version. See Smith, *Gentle Patriot*, 33; Bothwell and Kilbourn, *C.D. Howe*, 302; Creighton, *Forked Road*, 258.

24 The commission was announced in the budget speech on 5 Apr. 1955. Several records show that Howe was in Ottawa that week. Howe Papers, MG27 III B20, vol. 183, file 53, Howe to W.J. Henderson, 4 Apr. 1955; NA, RPCO, RG2, vol. 2657, Cabinet Conclusions, 4, 6 Apr. 1955; Canada, House of Commons, *Debates*, 4 Apr. 1955, 2656; 5 Apr. 1955, 2704, 2706, 2723.

Howe left Ottawa for Vancouver on 7 April, departing the next day for Honolulu, Fiji, and Sydney, Australia. See NA, Records of the Department of Trade and Commerce, RG25, vol. 4314, file 11563-8-40, part 1, "Canadian Minister Embarks on Australian Tour," *Grey River Argus*, 6 Apr. 1955; "Canadian Trade Mission," *New Zealand Herald*, 11 Apr. 1955; press release, 9 Apr. 1955; Secretary of State for External Affairs to High Commissioner for Canada, Canberra, 2 Mar. 1955.

In a letter to Tom Kent, journalist Grant Dexter wrote that "when Harris brought the [royal commission] proposal before cabinet, Howe took it as an expression of no confidence ... He lost his temper and there was quite a quarrel ... The decision was not made until Tuesday, the day of the budget, and went against Howe." Dexter Papers, collection 3621.3, vol. 1, Dexter to Tom [Kent], 29 Apr. 1955. See also Walter Harris interview; University of Toronto Archives, Bothwell Papers, B84-0024, box 14, Bothwell interview with Walter Harris, 31 Aug. 1978.

25 Bothwell Papers, B84-0024, box 14, Bothwell interview with Walter Harris, 31 Aug. 1978; Dexter Papers, vol. 1, Dexter to Tom [Kent], 29 Apr. 1955.

Word that the Cabinet had considered Towers made it to the press. The *Ottawa Citizen* reported that the government had offered Towers the appointment but he had declined. J.A. Hume, "Former Bank Governor May Head CBC Probe," *Ottawa Citizen*, 15 Aug. 1955.

Geoffrey Pearson confirmed that his father would have liked Towers to chair the commission. Geoffrey Pearson interview.

26 Andrew MacKay interview; Gordon, *Political Memoir*, 60.

27 LePan, *Net and the Sword.*

28 David Slater interview. LePan did not respond well to the pressure of his work for the commission. In December 1956 he was bed-ridden with pneumonia, and refused Gordon's advice to take a holiday. In July 1957 he was hospitalized for exhaustion. This time he spent four weeks in hospital before moving to a convalescing home. He returned to the commission in September. See various letters in NA, RRCCEP, RG33/35, vol. 20, file 1-5; vol. 21, file 1-6-1, part 2; University of Alberta Archives, Stewart Papers, file 68-1-1478.

LePan told Barry Anderson that he had suffered a heart attack a few months before the completion of the final report. John Claxton, the commission's legal counsel, also remembered that LePan had a heart attack. Anderson, "Royal Commissions," 183; John Claxton interview.

29 Interviews with H. Edward English, Douglas Fullerton, Anthony Hampson, and Slater; Fullerton, *Dangerous Delusion*, 30. Fullerton remembered that the rumours of Gordon's views on trade and investment caused some problems with recruitment. Hampson and Slater confirmed that Gordon's leanings caused some concern but did not think it affected recruiting. The quality of the research staff would seem to confirm their view.

30 NA, Sauvé Papers, MG32 B4, vol. 109, file 10, [Walter Gordon], "The Purpose of the Enquiry and the Questions to which it should suggest answers," 15 June 1955; "Outline of the Studies to be Undertaken for the Royal Commission on Canada's Economic Prospects," 14 June 1955.

31 "Gordon Commission Starts on Big Fact-Finding Tour," *Financial Post*, 20 Aug. 1955, 1.

32 University of Toronto, Thomas Fisher Rare Book Library, LePan Papers, collection 104, vol. 53, LePan to Denis Smith, 14 Mar. 1972.

33 Sauvé Papers, MG32 B4, vol. 109, file 10, [Walter Gordon], "The Purpose of the Enquiry and the Questions to which it should suggest answers," 15 June 1955.

34 WLGP, MG32 B44, vol. 37, file 1, "The Royal Commission on Canada's Economic Prospects," speech in Edmonton, 29 Aug. 1955. Published as "What Will Canada's World Position Be At Century's Three Quarter Mile Post?" *Montreal Star*, 9 Sept. 1955. The speech was paraphrased in Fraser, "Will Ottawa Open The Cashbox?" 9, 95. See also "Gordon Commission Starts on Big Fact-Finding Tour," *Financial Post*, 20 Aug. 1955, 1, 3.

Gordon raised the issue again publicly after the hearings had begun. In February 1956 he gave a speech in which he noted, "The question is being asked what the implications may be of a continuation of American and foreign investment in the country at the same rate at which it has been going on during the recent past." The Canadian Press report of this speech was published in several newspapers. "Canadians Can Be Independent," *Winnipeg Tribune*, 25 Feb. 1956.

35 RRCCEP, RG33/35, vol. 49, file 3-11, part 1, L.F. Grant to Gordon, 1 Sept. 1955.

36 Heeney Papers, MG30 E144, vol. 2, Heeney Diary, 7 July 1955.

37 Claxton interview.

38 MacKay interview.

39 RRCCEP, RG33/35, vol. 25, file 2-8-3, part 1, Walter Gordon, "Some Implications of Canada's Economic Development," speech in Quebec City, 23 May 1957.

40 RRCCEP, RG33/35, reels C-1533 to C-1545.

41 See, for example, Jim Senter, "Striking Employees Charge Mall Is Anti-Canadian," *Globe and Mail*, 19 Mar. 1956. During a labour dispute at the Mall Tool Company in Etobicoke, Ontario, the workers argued that the American owner was motivated by anti-Canadian sentiment and not by the desire to accumulate capital.

42 RRCCEP, RG33/35, reel C-1539, Canadian Pulp and Paper Association, "Submission to Royal Commission on Canada's Economic Prospects," Jan. 1956, 69.

43 Stewart Papers, file 68-1-1478, John L. Hayward to Gordon, 3 Feb. 1956.

44 RRCCEP, RG33/35, reel C-1540, "Appendix to the Report of the Association of Professional Engineers on Ontario to the Royal Commission on Canada's Economic Prospects," Feb. 1956, 1.

45 The *Vancouver Province* said that the increase in concern over foreign investment in early 1956 was "the result of the catalytic action of the Gordon Economic Commission": "A Dollar's Nationality Does Matter," 24 Mar. 1956.

46 Barber, *Good Fences*, 119.

47 Michael Barkway, "Memo to the Gordon Commission: How Far Are We From the Wood-Hewing Age?" *Financial Post*, 7 Jan. 1956, 19.

48 "Who Owns Canada?" *Hamilton Spectator*, 13 Feb. 1956. This increasing concern was also noted in "Satellite Status in Financing," *Windsor Star*, 28 Feb. 1956.

49 "Unless U.S. Economic Ties Shattered Canada's Future Lost, Drew Warns," *Hamilton Spectator*, 20 Mar. 1956, 7.

50 Gerald Waring, "Reporting," *Brandon Sun*, 22 Mar. 1956.

51 NA, LBPP, MG26 N9, vol. 11, Mar.-Sept. 1956 file, "Some Aspects of Canadian-American Relations," speech to the Canadian Club, Montreal, 27 Mar. 1956.

52 Canada, Dominion Bureau of Statistics, *Canada's International Investment Position, 1926–1954*.

53 Ibid., *Canada's International Investment Position, Selected Years 1926 to 1949*.

54 Newman, "Who *Really* Owns Canada?" 11. The report was reprinted in 1958. Canada, Dominion Bureau of Statistics, *Historical Catalogue*, 148. A year and a half after being published, the report was referred to as "the now classical D.B.S. study." Bird, "Canadianizing the U.S. Subsidiaries," 6.

55 "Is the Pace of Expansion Worth the Price We Pay?" *Financial Post*, 7 Apr. 1956, 36.

56 Editor's introduction to Michael Barkway, "The Great American Flood," *Financial Post*, 14 Apr. 1956.

57 Canada, Dominion Bureau of Statistics, *International Investment Position 1926–1954*, 34.

58 T.M. Eberlee, "Growth of U.S. Influence Worrying Canadian M.P.'s," *Toronto Star*, 7 Apr. 1956, 3.

59 Quoted in Newman, "Who *Really* Owns Canada?" 11. Newman called this an "off-the-cuff statement." It does not appear in Diefenbaker's speech notes. Diefenbaker Centre Archives, Diefenbaker Papers, MG01/XXI, vol. 15, file 551, speech to the Alberta Progressive Conservative Association, Edmonton, 7 Apr. [1956].

60 Canada, House of Commons, *Debates*, 11 Apr. 1956, 2825–6.

61 Ibid., 17 Apr. 1956, 2995.

62 "Serious Thinking Is Needed Here," *Financial Post*, 14 Apr. 1956, 1.

63 Canada, House of Commons, *Debates*, 9 July 1956, 5801; "U.S. Money Welcome – On Our Terms," *Financial Post*, 13 Oct. 1956, 1; WLGP, MG32 B44, vol. 14, file 3, Michael Barkway, "How Independent Can We Be?" speech to the Study Conference on National Problems [Kingston Conference], Sept. 1960.

64 "U.S. Envoy Belittles Peril of Control of Resources," *Globe and Mail*, 17 Apr. 1956, 1, 10. (This was the *Globe*'s lead story.) See also "Triangle at Ottawa," *Saturday Night*, 12 May 1956, 5.

65 House of Commons, Standing Committee on External Affairs, Minutes, 17 Apr. 1956, 36.

66 Ibid., 20 Apr. 1956, 65.

67 Canada, House of Commons, *Debates*, 17 Apr. 1956, 2995, 3004.

68 Howe Papers, MG27 III B20, vol. 164, file 89-2 (70), "Public Policy and Economic Expansion," speech to Hamilton Chamber of Commerce, 23 Apr. 1956.

69 Canada, House of Commons, *Debates*, 15 May 1956, 3935.

70 Schwartz, "Canadian National Identity," 117. Less detail is provided in Schwartz, *Public Opinion and Canadian Identity*.

71 Memorial University of Newfoundland, Centre for Newfoundland Studies, Gushue Papers, collection 30, box 8, file 3-11, Gordon to Grauer, Lussier, Gushue, Stewart and LePan, 22 May 1956; WLG [Walter L. Gordon], "Foreign Control of Canadian Industry," 26 Apr. 1956.

72 Ibid.

73 Denis Smith Personal Papers, Gordon to Smith, 24 Feb. 1972.

74 LePan Papers, vol. 53, LePan to Denis Smith, 14 Mar. 1972; MacKay interview; Queen's University Archives, Deutsch Papers, collection 1022a, box 2, file 15, R.B. Bryce to Deutsch, 15 Jan. 1957.

75 RRCCEP, RG33/35, vol. 20, file 1-6-1, Gordon to R. Gushue, 20 Sept. 1956;
Gushue to Gordon, 5 Oct. 1956; Gordon to Gushue, 9 Oct. 1956; Stewart Papers,
file 68-1-1479, Gordon to A.E. Grauer, 20 Sept. 1956; press release, 1 Oct. 1956.

76 Michael Barkway, "Our Share in Growth at Lowest Since '14," *Financial Post*,
13 Oct. 1956, 25.

77 Bothwell Papers, B79-0055, box 2, Bothwell interview with Mitchell Sharp,
26 May 1977.

78 Frank Clarke interview with Mitchell Sharp, 22 Feb. 1992. The author is greatly
indebted to Frank Clarke, who generously shared the results of his research.

79 WLGP, MG32 B44, vol. 17, file 13, C.D. Howe, "American Investments in Canada," speech in Chicago, 15 Oct. 1956. See also RRCCEP, RG33/35, vol. 50,
file 3-11, part 1.

80 English, *Worldly Years*, 134–5.

81 Canada, Royal Commission on Canada's Economic Prospects, *Preliminary
Report* (Ottawa 1956). The report is dated December 1956, when it was presented
to the government. It did not receive public release, however, until after it was
tabled in the House of Commons, 10 Jan. 1957.

   The quotation is from Denis Smith interview with Douglas LePan, 19 Nov.
1971, cited in Smith, *Gentle Patriot*, 366, note 16. LePan, who politely declined
an interview with the author, made similar comments to Frank Clarke. Frank
Clarke interview with Douglas LePan, 20 Feb. 1992. Douglas LePan, letter to
author, 8 Feb. 1994.

   John Claxton and Jack Davis also believed that Gordon had dominated the
commission. Claxton interview; NA, PSP, MG31 D78, vol. 30, Stursberg interview
with Jack Davis, 10 Dec. 1980.

82 Canada, Royal Commission on Canada's Economic Prospects, *Preliminary
Report*, 22. The commission forecast 4.5 per cent economic growth per year from
1955 to 1980. The real figure was 4.8 per cent. Daub, *Canadian Economic Forecasting*, 213.

83 Canada, Royal Commission on Canada's Economic Prospects, *Preliminary
Report*, 73–4.

84 Ibid., 86, 89–90.

85 Ibid., 90–3.

86 Queen's University Archives, TKP, vol. 1, file 1957 (1), Deutsch to Kent, 16 Jan.
1957. Deutsch's views are also outlined in Deutsch Papers, collection 1022a,
box 2, file 15, Deutsch to Mitchell Sharp, 28 Feb. 1957; Deutsch to R.B. Bryce,
22 Jan. 1957.

   Tom Kent also called the report "half baked," and Bruce Hutchison wrote that
many experts had applied that label to the commission's work. "Half-Baked,"

Winnipeg Free Press, 14 Jan. 1957, 17; Bruce Hutchison, "The Commission Laid an Egg," *Victoria Times*, 7 Feb. 1957. Stefan Stykolt and Harry Eastman called the report "woolly." Stykolt and Eastman, "Disturbing Prospects," 247.

87 Johnson, "Canada's Economic Prospects," 104; repr. in Johnson, *Canadian Quandary* (1963), 3–10.

88 Johnson, "Canada's Economic Prospects," 107; Stykolt and Eastman, "Disturbing Prospects," 246–7; Viner, "Gordon Commission Report," 321; Tom Kent, "The Case for Liberal Tariff Policy," *Winnipeg Free Press*, 2 May 1958.

89 Stykolt and Eastman, "Disturbing Prospects," 247; Johnson, "Canada's Economic Prospects," 108.

90 "An Encouraging Blueprint," *Regina Leader-Post*, 12 Jan. 1957, 13; "The Gordon Commission's Report," *Vancouver Province*, 11 Jan. 1957; "Not the Law and the Prophets," *Montreal Gazette*, 15 Jan. 1957; "The Gordon Report," *Montreal Star*, 14 Jan. 1957; Albert Turner, "Keep Policies Flexible to Assure Our Future Is Challenge to Gov't," *Toronto Telegram*, 14 Jan. 1957; "Ce que sera le prochain quart de siècle pour le Canada," *La Presse*, 11 Jan. 1957.

91 "The Gordon Report," *Winnipeg Tribune*, 16 Jan. 1957; "Half-Baked," *Winnipeg Free Press*, 14 Jan. 1957, 17; "The Gordon Report: A Second Look," *Vancouver Province*, 22 Jan. 1957.

92 Grant Dexter, "Protectionism in the Gordon Report," *Winnipeg Free Press*, 26 Jan. 1957; Bruce Hutchison, "The Commission Laid an Egg," *Victoria Times*, 7 Feb. 1957.

93 "The Danger Is Very, Very Real," *Calgary Herald*, 14 Jan. 1957; "Foreign Investment in Canadian Industry," *Montreal Star*, 15 Jan. 1957; "Ce que sera le prochain quart de siècle pour le Canada," *La Presse*, 11 Jan. 1957; "Bay Street at Large," *Winnipeg Free Press*, 15 Jan. 1957; "Foreigners to Control Canada's Destiny?" *Toronto Star*, 26 Jan. 1957; "Who Will Own Canada?" *Star Weekly Magazine*, 16 Feb. 1957, 47.

94 Canada, House of Commons, *Debates*, 11 Jan. 1957, 119.

95 Bothwell and Kilbourn, *C.D. Howe*, 320; "Gordon Proposals Opposed by Howe," *Vancouver Herald*, 4 Feb. 1957. Howe was also reported to be angry about the commission's recommendations on the export of energy. Bruce MacDonald, "Howe Anger Roused by Gordon's Report on Export of Energy," *Toronto Star*, 11 Jan. 1957; "Howe 'Hits Roof' on Economic Report," *Vancouver Sun*, 10 Jan. 1957.

96 Grant Dexter, "A Highly Controversial Report," *Winnipeg Free Press*, 11 Jan. 1957; "Canada Needs Her Power: Sinclair," *Vancouver Sun*, 12 Jan. 1957; "Recommendation Is Against Policy," *Moncton Daily Times*, 14 Jan. 1957.

97 "Winters States Report Useful to Area," *Fredericton Gleaner*, 18 Jan. 1957.

98 Peter Dempson, "Socreds, CCF Differ on Reports," *Toronto Telegram*, 14 Jan. 1957.

99 "Thoroughly Bad for Agriculture," *Toronto Star*, 11 Jan. 1957.

100 Canada, House of Commons, *Debates*, 11 Jan. 1957, 142. Nowlan's calculations were grossly inaccurate. The report had seven pages on the Atlantic provinces, containing several recommendations to help the region's economy. Canada, Royal Commission on Canada's Economic Prospects, *Preliminary Report*, 98–104.

101 Canada, House of Commons, *Debates*, 17 Jan. 1957, 344.

102 "Griesinger Likes Report," *Windsor Star*, 12 Jan. 1957.

103 William French, "Walter Gordon: He's Changing Your Way of Life," *Globe Magazine*, 11 May 1957, 12–13; " 'Report missed boat' – Bennett," *Vancouver Province*, 11 Jan. 1957; "Bennett Attacks Wheat Curb Plan," *Victoria Times*, 11 Jan. 1957.

104 "Constructive Report," *Halifax Chronicle-Herald*, 18 Jan. 1957.

105 "Premier Attacks 'Exodus' Plan in Gordon Report," *Fredericton Gleaner*, 28 Jan. 1957, 1–2.

106 "Gordon Report Under Review," *Fredericton Gleaner*, 21 Jan. 1957, 1–2; Alex Nickerson, "Maritimes Simmer Down After Gordon Report," *Windsor Star*, 31 Jan. 1957; "Gordon Report," *Halifax Chronicle-Herald*, 19 Jan. 1957.

107 Deutsch Papers, box 2, file 15, R.B. Bryce to Deutsch, 15 Jan. 1957; Mitchell Sharp to Deutsch, 2 Feb. 1957.

108 Slater interview.

109 PSP, MG31 D78, vol. 30, Stursberg interview with Jack Davis, 10 Dec. 1980.

110 Tom Kent, "Mr. Howe Hot, Civil Servants Cold," *Winnipeg Free Press*, 21 Apr. 1958.

111 Eayrs, *Canada in World Affairs*, 154; " 'Murder by Slander' MP States of Norman; Pearson Raps Tactics," *Toronto Star*, 4 Apr. 1957, 1.

112 Canada, House of Commons, *Debates*, 4 Apr. 1957, 3059.

113 "That Precious Friendship," *Globe and Mail*, 11 Apr. 1957, 6.

114 Bowen, *Innocence Is not Enough*, 325.

115 Heeney Papers, MG30 E144, vol. 2, Heeney Diary, 16 Apr. 1957. See also Heeney, *Things That Are Caesar's*, 144.

116 William Kinmond, "Hands Off Canadians, Diefenbaker Tells U.S. As Vote Drive Opened," *Globe and Mail*, 8 Apr. 1957, 1–2.

117 See, for example, "Diefenbaker Keeps Drawing Big Crowd," *Vancouver Sun*, 23 May 1957, 22; David Ghent, " 'Pipeline Profits to Gov't Puppets' PC Chief Charges," *Toronto Telegram*, 8 Apr. 1957, 3. The author is greatly indebted to Steven Schumann for bringing these items to his attention.

118 LBPP, MG26 N6, vol. 12, Walter Gordon file, Walter Gordon, "Notes for Mike,"
    18 Apr. 1958.

119 Interviews with Hampson, William Hood, MacKay, Edward Safarian, and Slater.

120 Claxton interview.

121 Brecher and Reisman, *Canada-United States Economic Relations*, 153.

122 Ibid., 158–9.

123 Simon Reisman interview; LePan Papers, vol. 2, "Note for File," 4 July 1955.

124 Slater interview. Mackintosh, *Economic Background*. Mackintosh's work was
    the first serious study on the effect of the tariff on Canada's regions.

125 Young, *Canadian Commercial Policy*, 73; Slater interview. Since the publication
    of Young's study, economists have concluded that he greatly underestimated the
    cost of the tariff. Johnson, "Canadian-American Economic Integration," 34.

126 Fraser, "Sharp/Gordon Debate," 36; reprinted in Fraser, *"Blair Fraser
    Reports,"* 81–6.

127 Reisman interview.

128 Gushue Papers, box 8, file 3-18, WLG [Walter L. Gordon], "The Tariff and
    Secondary Manufacturing Industry," 16 May 1956.

129 Gushue Papers, box 8, file 3-18, AEG [A.E. Grauer], "Tariffs and External
    Trade," 4 June 1956.

130 RRCCEP, RG33/35, vol. 55, file 3-18, part 2, Gordon to Reisman, 10 Jan. 1957.

131 LePan Papers, vol. 9, Gordon to LePan, 23 Apr. 1957.

132 Reisman interview. In the preface to *Canadian Commercial Policy*, Young wrote,
    "Mr. Reisman, under whose direction the work was done, has been in effect joint
    author. If the other calls upon his time had been less heavy, we would have di-
    vided the drafting chores and published the study over both our names. As things
    turned out, the words are usually mine but the ideas are ours."

133 RRCCEP, RG33/35, vol. 55, file 3-18, part 2, Gordon to Lamontagne, 25 Sept.
    1957.

134 Sauvé Papers, MG32 B4, vol. 109, file 10, [Walter Gordon], "Outline of the Stud-
    ies to be Undertaken for the Royal Commission on Canada's Economic Pros-
    pects," 14 June 1955.

135 RRCCEP, RG33/35, vol. 55, file 3-18, part 2, Gordon to Lamontagne, 25 Sept.
    1957.

136 PSP, MG31 D78, vol. 33, Stursberg interview with Maurice Lamontagne, 24 Aug.
    1976.

137 See, for example, Brecher and Reisman, *Canada–United States Economic Rela-
    tions*, title page.

138 Reisman interview; Young, *Canadian Commercial Policy*, title-page. Originally,
    Gushue and Grauer had thought that the report should have the same disclaimer
    as the others. At a meeting on 30 October the commissioners approved the

longer note. The commission's papers contain no minutes of this meeting that would indicate whether Gushue and Grauer changed their minds. RRCCEP, RG33/35, vol. 55, file 3-18, part 2, Gushue to Gordon, 3 Oct. 1957; vol. 22, file 1-6-2, part 5, Gordon to M. Erb, 31 Oct. 1957.

139 RRCCEP, RG33/35, vol. 22, file 1-6-2, part 5, Gordon to M. Erb, 31 Oct. 1957.

140 Canada, Royal Commission on Canada's Economic Prospects, *Final Report*, 439–40, 442.

141 Compare ibid., *Preliminary Report*, 90–3, and *Final Report*, 393–7.

142 Canada, House of Commons, *Debates*, index to the first session of the twenty-fourth Parliament. The only reference to the Royal Commission was a question to the minister of finance on the availability of the report and the studies.

143 Tom Kent, "The Case for Liberal Tariff Policy," *Winnipeg Free Press*, 2 May 1958. Kent's articles on the final report were reprinted in Kent, *Inside the Gordon Report*.

144 Tom Kent, "The Virtues of Being Only a Bit Nasty," *Winnipeg Free Press*, 14 May 1958; Tom Kent, "How Liberalism Didn't Become Conservative," *Winnipeg Free Press*, 15 May 1958.

145 On the roots of anti-American sentiment, see Wise, "Origins of Anti-Americanism in Canada," 297–306.

CHAPTER THREE

1 Ernst & Young Archives, Woods Gordon Video Collection, "Woods Gordon 50th Anniversary," video, sound, colour, 33 minutes, 1982; Little, *Story of the Firm*, 44–5, 61; Ernst & Young Archives, CGP, "Woods Gordon Turns 50 With Flair," *Keeping Posted*, Summer 1982, 1; MacKay, *People's Railway*, 215.

2 "Canadian International Paper May Buy Six Specialty Firms," *Financial Post*, 13 Dec. 1958, 1; "Canadian International Paper Confirms Specialty Purchase," *Financial Post*, 2 May 1959; Financial Post, *1959 Survey of Industrials* (Montreal 1959), 281; Alastair Gillespie interview; "Gordon 'Chameleon' Says Iannuzzi," *Toronto Telegram*, 3 Nov. 1965.

3 NA, PSP, MG31 D78, vol. 31, Stursberg interview with Robert Fowler, 17 Dec. 1976.

4 Interviews with John Brunton and S.J. Sinclair. Sinclair, who ran Western Tire and Supply, a CanCorp company, recalled that the issue of foreign ownership never came up during his involvement.

5 Jutras, "Cancorp," 68.

6 Canadian Corporate Management, *Annual Report 1968* (Toronto 1969); Canada, Dominion Bureau of Statistics, *Inter-Corporate Ownership 1965*, 252; ibid., *Inter-Corporate Ownership 1969*, 400, 785; Gillespie interview.

7 The share value would continue to grow. In 1967 a common share was worth roughly $53. Canadian Corporate Management Company Limited, *Annual Report 1968*. The author is indebted to David Azzi for locating a copy of this report at the W.A.C. Bennett Library, Simon Fraser University.

8 Gillespie interview.

9 Harkness, *J.E. Atkinson*, 86; Fetherling, "Lion in Winter," 52; Richard Doyle interview.

10 Archives of Ontario, POR, Frost Administration, Premier's Correspondence, RG3-24, box 2, Cabinet – Charitable Gifts Act – Star file, "The Toronto Star Reports to the Public." The *Star* was also a client of Woods Gordon. Marcel Caron interview.

11 Harkness, *J.E. Atkinson*, 354.

12 Fetherling, "Lion in Winter," 53.

13 Ibid.; "H.C. Hindmarsh Dies, Toronto Star President," *Editor & Publisher*, 29 Dec. 1956, 50; "The Last Showdown," *Time*, 31 Dec. 1956, 57; Rohmer, *E.P. Taylor*, 217–18.

14 Beland Honderich interview. See also POR, Frost Administration, Premier's Correspondence, RG3-24, box 2, Cabinet – Charitable Gifts Act – Star file, Walter Gordon to Leslie Frost, 5 Feb. 1958.

   In May 1993 David Macdonald, author of the official history of the *Toronto Star*, submitted the manuscript to Beland Honderich. The manuscript details Gordon's role in the sale of the *Star* to the Atkinson Foundation trustees. The *Star* has yet to publish the book, and Honderich has declined this author's request for access to the manuscript. Conversation with David MacDonald; Beland Honderich, letter to author, 21 Mar. 1995.

   John Bassett, publisher of the *Telegram* after 1952, was involved in the discussions. He confirmed that Gordon "played a role" in the sale of the paper, but refused to reveal precisely what that role was. John Bassett interview.

15 Harkness, *J.E. Atkinson*, 384; "Star Sold: Trustees' Bid Taken," *Montreal Gazette*, 27 Mar. 1958.

16 Fetherling, "Lion in Winter," 54; "The First," *Last Post*, May 1972, 29. Gordon helped Honderich find sources of cash and may also have been a major source himself. Many of Gordon's friends mentioned confidentially that Gordon had offered them financial assistance with their business ventures. It would have been in character for Gordon to offer the same help to Honderich.

17 "The First," *Last Post*, May 1972, 27; Fetherling, "Lion in Winter," 58; Templeton, *Anecdotal Memoir*, 172; interviews with George Bain, Bassett, Honderich, Hartland Molson, and Robert Nielsen; John Miller, "Bee Knew What He *Didn't* Like," *Content for Canadian Journalists*, Nov.–Dec. 1988, 30–1; "Dubs Gordon Star's Robot," *Toronto Telegram*, 30 Apr. 1962.

18 *Toronto Star*, 3–6, 8–13 June 1959.
19 Ibid., 11, 13 Oct. 1975, 17–20 Oct. 1977.
20 Nielsen interview.
21 Interviews with Doyle and Douglas Fisher.
22 Douglas Fisher, "Responsibilities of a Publisher," *Toronto Telegram*, 29 Oct. 1971.
23 Fisher interview.
24 Peter C. Newman interview.
25 Gillespie interview.
26 NA, LBPP, MG26 N1, vol. 5, Walter Gordon file, Gordon to Pearson, 21 Jan. 1949.
27 LBPP, MG26 N1, vol. 5, Walter Gordon file, Gordon to Pearson, 12 Oct. [1955].
28 Gordon, *Political Memoir*, 72. See also NA, WLGP, MG32 B44, vol. 16, file 11, memo, 5 Dec. 1965.
29 WLGP, MG32 B44, vol. 16, file 11, memo, 5 Dec. 1965. Gordon recalled in his memoirs that a few days before the convention Pearson had no money, no staff, and no campaign headquarters. Gordon said that he booked a suite at the Chateau Laurier for Pearson. Though he was the sole donor to the campaign and acted as campaign manager, Gordon exaggerated his role and the candidate's lack of preparation. Pearson's campaign may have been low-key, but it was well under way when Gordon appeared. By the time Gordon offered his assistance, Pearson had already sent a hand-signed letter to the delegates and had booked a suite at the Chateau Laurier. When Paul Martin, the other leadership candidate, arrived at the train station in Ottawa, he found that Pearson was already there greeting delegates and distributing "I Like Mike" tags. Gordon, *Political Memoir*, 72–3; Maurice Lamontagne, cited in Stursberg, *Lester Pearson and the Dream of Unity*, 48; Tom Axworthy interview with Walter Gordon, 26 Sept. 1969, cited in Axworthy, "Innovation and the Party System," 173; NA, Howe Papers, MG27 III B20, vol. 109, Pearson to Howe, 4 Jan. 1958; NA, Kidd Papers, MG32 G9, vol. 6, file 2, Gordon to Kidd, 4 Jan. 1958; Martin, *Very Public Life*, 2:315.
30 Gordon, *Political Memoir*, 76. See also LBPP, MG26 N6, vol. 12, Walter Gordon file, Gordon to Pearson, 4 Feb. 1958; Gordon to Pearson, 5 Mar. 1958; Gordon to Pearson, 10 Mar. 1958.
31 Howe Papers, MG27 III B20, vol. 109, file 75(8), Howe to Walter Harris, 5 Apr. 1958.
32 Gordon, *Political Memoir*, 70.
33 William Bragg, "Ont. Boards Probers Get Wide Power," *Toronto Telegram*, 28 May 1958.
34 Ontario, Committee on the Organization of Government in Ontario, *Report*.
35 WLGP, MG32 B44, vol. 16, file 11, memo, 5 Dec. 1965. Years later Gordon remembered that the primary reason he entered politics was his belief that

Diefenbaker was mismanaging the country. His friendship with Pearson was secondary. Richard M. Alway interview with Walter Gordon, *Canadian Public Figures*, tape 4.

36 LBPP, MG26 N5, vol. 46, file 113-118, Chris Young interview with Pearson, transcript to roll 114.

37 Tom Ardies, "Biggest Load of '60 Days' Carried Easily by Gordon," *Vancouver Sun*, 1 June 1963.

38 University of Toronto, Thomas Fisher Rare Book Library, LePan Papers, collection 104, vol. 50, Gordon to LePan, 30 Apr. 1963.

39 LBPP, MG26 N6, vol. 12, Walter Gordon 1957–59 file, Gordon to Pearson, 5 Nov. 1959.

40 WLGP, MG32 B44, vol. 16, file 11, memo, 5 Dec. 1965; Kidd Papers, MG32 G9, vol. 3, file 6, draft letter, Kidd to Duncan MacTavish, 21 Apr. 1960; Kidd to Duncan MacTavish, 22 Apr. 1960.

41 Gordon Edick interview.

42 LBPP, MG26 N6, vol. 12, Walter Gordon file, Gordon to Pearson, 9 Mar. 1960.

43 Ibid.

44 Gordon spoke in February to the Ontario Federation of Labour in Hamilton, in May to the International Municipal Conference in Chicago, in June to the Canadian Manufacturers' Association at its annual meeting in Toronto, and in August in Vancouver to the National Federation of Canadian University Students.

45 Gordon, *Political Memoir*, 85.

46 WLGP, MG32 B44, vol. 37, file 2, "Our Changing Economy," speech to the Ontario Federation of Labour, 13 Feb. 1960; WLGP, MG32 B44, vol. 37, file 2, "The Challenge of Change," speech to the Canadian Manufacturers' Association, 6 June 1960; Walter Gordon, "Some facts we must face for the long term progress of Canada," *Financial Post*, 27 Feb. 1960, 9.

47 On the relationship between foreign investment and the tariff, see English, "Are These Jeremiahs Really Necessary?" 361; Bliss, "Canadianizing American Business," 24–42; Brecher and Reisman, *Canadian–United States Economic Relations*, 117; Watkins, "Canadian Economic Policy," 70; Johnson, *Canadian Quandary* (1963), xi.

48 WLGP, MG32 B44, vol. 37, file 2, "Our Changing Economy," speech to the Ontario Federation of Labour, 13 Feb. 1960; WLGP, MG32 B44, vol. 37, file 2, "Whither Canada – Satellite or Independent Nation?" speech to the National Federation of Canadian University Students, 29 Aug. 1960.

49 Ibid.

50 Denis Smith Personal Papers, Gordon to Smith, 24 Feb. 1972.

51 LBPP, MG26 N2, vol. 96, Walter Gordon Speeches file, Gordon to Pearson, 12 July 1960.

52 Gordon, *Political Memoir*, 81. The author was unable to find this document in the Gordon papers. Denis Smith, however, did see the note. Smith, *Gentle Patriot*, 369, nn 40–1.

53 Gordon, *Political Memoir*, 81, 85.

54 LBPP, MG26 N2, vol. 108, Study Conference (3) file, Gordon to Pearson, 22 Apr. 1960.

55 Library of Parliament, "Study Conference on National Problems," (transcripts of speeches and commentaries).

56 WLGP, MG32 B44, vol. 14, file 3, Michael Barkway, "How Independent Can We Be?"

57 Ibid., Walter Gordon, "How Independent Can We Be?"

58 LBPP, MG26 N2, vol. 108, Study Conference (3) file, "Study Conference on National Problems" (summary of the discussions); Library of Parliament, "Study Conference on National Problems"; NA, ARP, MG31 D73, vol. 4, file 54, G.V. Ferguson to Rotstein, 6 Mar. 1967.

59 Interviews with Bernard Bonin, H. Edward English, William Hood, William Kilbourn, and David Slater; Lipsey, "Harry Johnson's Contributions," S35; Prest, "Harry Johnson," 121; Grubel, *Citation Counts*; Vandercamp, "Harry G. Johnson," 267; Johnson, *Canadian Quandary* (1977), xv; Kindleberger, *Life of an Economist*, 151; Watkins, "The Economics of Nationalism," S103.

60 WLGP, MG32 B44, vol. 14, file 3, Harry G. Johnson, "External Economic Relations," speech to the Study Conference on National Problems, Kingston, 6–10 Sept. 1960; LBPP, MG26 N2, vol. 108, Study Conference (3) file, "Study Conference on National Problems" (summary of the discussions); Library of Parliament, "Study Conference on National Problems."

61 LBPP, MG26 N2, vol. 108, Study Conference (3) file, "Study Conference on National Problems" (summary of the discussions); Library of Parliament, "Study Conference on National Problems."

62 Drummond, "Nationalists and Economists," 193.

63 Library of Parliament, "Study Conference on National Problems."

64 "Not Liberal," *Winnipeg Free Press*, 20 Oct. 1960. See also Harold Greer, "The Conference at Kingston Leaves Mr. Pearson as Darling Only of the Eggheads," *Globe and Mail*, 14 Sept. 1960.

65 Library of Parliament, "Study Conference on National Problems." See also Sharp, *Which Reminds Me*, 91.

66 George Brimwell, "A Scarcity of New Political Ideas," *Toronto Telegram*, 14 Sept. 1960.

67 WLGP, MG32 B44, vol. 14, file 3, T.W. Kent, "Towards a Philosophy of Social Security," July 1960. The paper was published as Kent, *Social Policy for Canada*.

68 Kilbourn interview.

69 Howe Papers, MG27 III B20, vol. 187, file 90(67), Howe to Mitchell Sharp, 20 Sept. 1960.

70 Howe Papers, MG27 III B20, vol. 109, file 75(9), Howe to William Henderson, 23 Nov. 1960.

71 According to Tom Kent, the idea came from Connolly, though Gordon credited Pearson. Kent, *Public Purpose*, 77; Gordon, *Political Memoir*, 86.

72 Tom Kent interview.

73 Kent, *Public Purpose*, 88.

74 Queen's University Archives, TKP, vol. 1, Sept.–Dec. 1960 file, Kent to Gordon, 6 Oct. 1960.

75 Kent interview.

76 LePan Papers, vol. 50, Gordon to LePan, 4 Oct. 1960.

77 NA, Pickersgill Papers, MG32 B34, vol. 104, Liberal Policies 1959–62 file, "Policy Statements," 17 Jan. 1961.

78 NA, Sauvé Papers, MG32 B4, vol. 68, Gordon file, Sauvé to Gordon, 19 Jan. 1961. Technically, the Liberal party elected its president, though in reality the individual was appointed by the leader.

79 Axworthy, "Innovation and the Party System," 203.

80 Paul Hellyer Personal Papers, draft memoirs. The author is grateful to Paul Hellyer, who provided copies of several important pages from an early draft of his memoirs.

81 PSP, MG31 D78, vol. 32, Stursberg interview with Paul Hellyer, 13 Aug. 1976.

82 Martin, *Very Public Life*, 2:343, 368.

83 Wearing, *L-Shaped Party*, 31.

84 Hellyer Personal Papers, draft memoirs.

85 David Ferguson interview.

86 See various royalty statements in WLGP, MG32 B44, vol. 11, file 5.

87 Gordon, *Troubled Canada*, 88.

88 Ibid., 88.

89 Trudeau, "A propos de 'domination économique,' " 7; Leyton-Brown, "Extraterritoriality," 189; Brewster, *Law and United States Business*. See also John Diefenbaker's account of a meeting with President Dwight Eisenhower. Canada, House of Commons, *Debates*, 11 July 1958, 2142.

90 Gordon, *Troubled Canada*, 89–90.

91 Ibid., 90, 94, 97; see also WLGP, vol. 37, file 3, Gordon speech to the Advertising & Sales Club, Montreal, 5 Dec. 1962.

92 Pizer and Cutler, *u.s. Business Investments*, 12, 110, 120, 122; Urquhart and Buckley, *Historical Statistics*, 183; Canada, Dominion Bureau of Statistics, *Trade of Canada, 1957*, 20; Canada, Statistics Canada, *Canada's International Investment Position*, 232.

93 Drummond, review of *Troubled Canada*, 284.

94 Reuber, review of *Troubled Canada*, 472.

95 Johnson, "Problems of Canadian Nationalism," 239, 241–2, 246.

96 Gordon, *Choice for Canada*, 96–7.

97 Ibid., *Storm Signals*, 114.

98 See, for example, WLGP, vol. 37, file 5, speech to the Sixth Annual Industrial and Municipal Relations Conference, Peterborough, Ont., 28 Oct. 1964.

99 Hugh MacLennan, "We Have a Fine Thing in Canada ... But Problem Is How Do We Keep It?" *Financial Post*, 31 Mar. 1962, 25; repr. as MacLennan, "Can We Stay Canadian?"

100 Robert McKeown, "John Kenneth Galbraith Says Yes," 30, 32.

101 "Elizabeth Marjorie Leith Gordon," 15; Wallace, *Producing Marginality*, 67–70; Benson and Conolly, *English-Canadian Theatre*, 89; Robertson Davies, letter to author, 25 Jan. 1994; NA, Bobak Papers, MG30 D378, vol. 5, file 11; interviews with Dorothy Gill, Kyra Montagu, and Helen Venables.

102 WLGP, MG32 B44, vol. 11, file 5, J.G. McClelland to Gordon, 20 Dec. 1961.

103 NA, Lamontagne Papers, MG32 B32, vol. 11, file 10, "The American Economic Impact on Quebec," 4 July 1958.

104 LBPP, MG26 N6, vol. 6, Canadian-American Relations file, ML [Maurice Lamontagne], "Memorandum for Mr. Pearson, Re: Notes on Canada–u.s. Economic Relations," 25 Nov. 1958.

105 Interviews with Mitchell Sharp and J.W. Pickersgill.

106 PSP, MG31 D78, vol. 33, Stursberg interview with Tom Kent, 30 Mar. 1977.

107 LBPP, MG26 N6, vol. 38, Liberal Caucus file, Office of the Leader of the Opposition, "Memorandum to the Members of the Liberal Caucus," 15 Oct. 1962.

108 Christina McCall-Newman interview with J.W. Pickersgill, 13 Nov. 1981, cited in McCall-Newman, *Grits*, 45.

109 PSP, MG31 D78, vol. 36, Stursberg interview with Geoffrey Pearson, 30 May 1978.

110 Interview with Geoffrey Pearson.

111 PSP, MG31 D78, vol. 33, Stursberg interview with Tom Kent, 30 Mar. 1977.

112 Schwartz, "Canadian National Identity," 117; Bashevkin, "Does Public Opinion Matter?" 401; Fletcher and Drummond, *Canadian Attitude Trends*, 38.

113 WLGP, MG32 B44, vol. 19, file 12, Penetration Research Ltd., "A Survey of the Political Climate of Ontario and Quebec," Jan. 1963, 32, 36. Similarly, in the

late 1950s and early 1960s the Gallup Poll asked people what were the main issues facing Canada. Foreign investment was not listed. See Schwartz, "Canadian
National Identity," 444–5.

114 WLGP, MG32 B44, vol. 19, file 13, Penetration Research Limited, "A Survey of
the Political Climate of Ontario and Quebec – Wave III," 22 Mar. 1963, 15, 45.

115 Newman, "James Coyne and the Great Debate," 42; Stevenson, "J.E. Coyne,"
14; Barkway, "Why Coyne Was Asked To Resign," 18–20; Granatstein, *Canada
1957–1967*, 64.

116 Coyne, "U.S. Trade," 37.

117 Walter L. Gordon, "How To Be Good Friends," *Financial Post*, 15 Oct. 1960, 6;
Bank of Canada Archives, Records of the Bank of Canada, SP/G.2.60-10, James
Coyne, "Living within Our Means," speech to the Canadian Club of Winnipeg,
18 Jan. 1960. Coyne's speech was reprinted as *Living within Our Means* and
"Living within Our Means."

118 WLGP, MG32 B44, vol. 37, file 2, "Our Changing Economy," speech to the
Ontario Federation of Labour, 13 Feb. 1960; Records of the Bank of Canada,
SP/G.2.60-12, James Coyne, "Inflation and Unemployment," speech to the
Ontario Chamber of Commerce, Hamilton, 12 May 1960. See also NA, Coyne
Papers, MG31 E20, vol. 1, file 1.

119 "Foreign Domination Seen By Coyne," *Calgary Herald*, 5 Oct. 1960; James E.
Coyne, "We Are Now at Perhaps the Most Critical Crossroad of All," *Financial
Post*, 8 Oct. 1960, 25–7.

120 WLGP, MG32 B44, vol. 14, file 3, "How Independent Can We Be?" comments at
the Study Conference on National Problems, Kingston, 6–10 Sept. 1960.

121 NA, RDF, RG19, vol. 4099, file B-30-1961, A.F.W. Plumptre to K.W. Taylor,
14 Oct. 1960.

122 Eastman, "Why the Economists Dislike Coyne," 24; Smith and Slater,
"Economic Policy Proposals," 119.

123 "Text of 'Fire Coyne' Letter to Dief by 17 Professors," *Toronto Star*, 8 Dec.
1960; H. Scott Gordon, *Economists versus the Bank of Canada*, v–vi. In total,
twenty-nine economists signed the letter, several after it was reported in the press.

124 H. Scott Gordon, *Economists versus the Bank of Canada*, 42–3, 46.

125 Tom Ardies, "Biggest Load of '60 Days' Carried Easily by Gordon," *Vancouver
Sun*, 1 June 1963.

126 Gordon, *Political Memoir*, 114, 116; Kent, *Public Purpose*, 192.

127 English, *Worldly Years*, 250; PSP, MG31 D78, vol. 29, Stursberg interview with
Keith Davey, 27 Jan. 1977; Denis Smith Personal Papers, Smith interview with
Pearson, 30 June 1972.

128 Pearson's memoirs record his saying "that I, as a historian, had reminded myself of Napoleon's 'hundred days.' " Gordon also remembered that Pearson raised the objection to the hundred days. Keith Davey, however, attributes the objection to Maryon Pearson, a version of events accepted by Pearson's biographer, John English. Gordon, *Political Memoir*, 126; Pearson, *Mike*, 3:83; Davey, *Rainmaker*, 75; English, *Worldly Years*, 263.

129 NA, Liberal Party of Canada Papers, MG28 IV 3, vol. 694, Election 1963 Correspondence and Reports file, Gordon to Pearson, 20 Mar. 1963. Later, Gordon insisted that he had rejected Pearson's argument that one hundred days would be associated with Napoleon and the Battle of Waterloo. Quoted in Stursberg, *Lester Pearson and the Dream of Unity*, 90.

130 PSP, MG31 D78, vol. 29, Stursberg interview with James Coutts, 22 Apr. 1977; vol. 28, Stursberg interview with Lionel Chevrier, 17 Aug. 1976; English, *Worldly Years*, 266; Davey, *Rainmaker*, 114; LaMarsh, *Bird in a Gilded Cage*, 63; LBPP, MG26 N5, vol. 46, file 113–118, Chris Young interview with Pearson, transcripts for rolls 114, 115; Library of Parliament, Tom Earle interview with Mitchell Sharp, 2 Feb. 1984. See also PSP, MG31 D78, vol. 29, file 13, Peter Stursberg interview with John Connolly, 20 June 1979; WLGP, MG32 B44, vol. 3, file 8, Keith Davey to Gordon, 31 Jan. 1966; Library of Parliament, Tom Earle interview with Richard Stanbury, May and June 1986; Tom Earle interview with Daniel Lang, 30 Sept. and 7 Oct. 1987; LBPP, MG26 N5, vol. 46, file 142-147, Bernard Ostry interview with Pearson, transcript for roll 144.

131 In a 1965 memorandum Gordon remembered that Pearson had offered him the Department of Industry before the election. In his memoirs Gordon wrote that this conversation took place after the election. WLGP, MG32 B44, vol. 16, file 11, Gordon memo, 5 Dec. 1965. Gordon, *Political Memoir*, 130.

132 WLGP, MG32 B44, vol. 16, file 11, memo, 5 Dec. 1965.

133 University of Toronto Archives, Bothwell Papers, B88-0074, box 2, William Kilbourn interview with Michael Barkway, 14 Dec. [1968].

134 Gordon, *Political Memoir*, 130.

135 Newman, *Distemper of Our Times*, 12.

136 Quoted in ibid., 12–13.

137 Kent, *Public Purpose*, 110.

138 WLGP, MG32 B44, vol. 16, file 11, memo, 5 Dec. 1965.

139 See for example, Gordon's 12 Dec. 1961 speech in Charlottetown, where he said that "the first and primary objective of the federal government" should be curing unemployment. LBPP, MG26 N2, vol. 96, Walter Gordon Speeches file, Walter L. Gordon, "The Liberal Program for Recovery," speech to the Queens Liberal

riding association. See also Gordon's comments in his maiden speech in the House of Commons. Canada, House of Commons, *Debates*, 3 Oct. 1962, 170.

140 See WLGP, MG32 B44, vol. 37, files 3–4.

141 Quoted in Fraser, *Search for Identity*, 211.

CHAPTER FOUR

1 Brian Land interview.

2 "The New Pearson Team," *Toronto Star*, 23 Apr. 1963.

3 LaMarsh, *Bird in a Gilded Cage*, 63. According to journalist Blair Fraser, "Walter Gordon had been regarded in Liberal ranks as omniscient and infallible, and even the opposition viewed him with something approaching awe." Fraser, "How Walter Gordon Has Recovered," 2.

4 Claude Isbister interview.

5 G.G.E. Steele interview.

6 Jamie Swift interview with Donald Macdonald, 26 June 1986, cited in Swift, *Odd Man Out*, 83.

7 PSP, MG31 D78, vol. 31, Stursberg interview with Walter Gordon, 2 June 1977.

8 Land interview.

9 Interviews with Douglas Fullerton, Tom Kent, Land, David Stanley, and Steele; NA, PSP, MG31 D78, vol. 31, Stursberg interview with Gordon, 2 June 1977; Library of Parliament, Tom Earle interview with Robert Bryce, 4–8 July 1983.

10 PSP, MG31 D78, vol. 31, Stursberg interview with Gordon, 2 June 1977.

11 Land interview.

12 In 1957 Plumptre had allowed Fleming to live in his house until he could find a more permanent place to live. Simon Reisman interview; Fleming, *So Very Near*, 1:352.

13 Saul, *Voltaire's Bastards*, 103.

14 PSP, MG31 D78, vol. 31, Stursberg interview with Gordon, 2 June 1977.

15 Quoted in Godfrey, review of *A Political Memoir*, 14.

16 Land interview; Newman, *Distemper of Our Times*, 15. Land believed that Ernest Steele was the official who wrote the memorandum.

17 Land interview.

18 University of Toronto, Thomas Fisher Rare Book Library, Douglas LePan Papers, collection 104, vol. 50, Gordon to LePan, 30 Apr. 1963.

19 NA, LBPP, MG26 N3, vol. 51, 251-1963 Special Advisers file, K.W. Taylor to E.A. Driedger, 28 June 1963.

20 Library of Parliament, Tom Earle interview with C.M. Drury, 15, 22, 29 Jan. 1988. Gordon had worked as a consultant on the 1941 budget, and when chairing his royal commissions had employed many outsiders. Canada, House of Commons, *Debates*, 14 June 1963, 1200.

21 Martin O'Connell interview.

22 Stanley interview; Edwin Mahoney, "Financial Analyst Helps Pearson," *Toronto Telegram*, 13 Mar. 1963, 39; David Stanley Personal Papers, Gordon to Stanley, 20 Sept. 1984. I am grateful to Mr Stanley for giving me copies of several documents from his personal papers.

23 O'Connell interview; LBPP, MG26 N3, vol. 51, 251-1963 Special Advisers file, K.W. Taylor to E.A. Driedger, 28 June 1963.

24 Rod Anderson interview.

25 Clive Baxter, "New Breed of '$1-a-Year Men' Helping Liberals Make Plans," *Financial Post*, 8 May 1963.

26 Newman, *Distemper of Our Times*, 17; interviews with Isbister, Land, Reisman, and Steele; Denis Smith Personal Papers, Smith's notes of letter from Plumptre to Gordon, 25 June 1969.

27 Interviews with Land and Stanley.

28 NA, King Papers, MG26 J1, vol. 404, reel C-9170, pp 365070-3, Gordon to Paul Martin, 17 Oct. 1946.

29 Interviews with Isbister, Kent, and Reisman.

30 Reisman interview.

31 Gordon, *Political Memoir*, 139; Stanley interview.

32 Interviews with E.J. Benson, Land, Stanley, and Reisman; PSP, MG31 D78, vol. 28, Stursberg interview with Edgar J. Benson, 30 Aug. 1976.

33 Donald Macdonald, a Liberal MP and a strong supporter of Gordon, believed that Gordon got "carried away with the enthusiasm" of the 1963 budget. According to Stanley, whatever the suggestion, Gordon would double or triple it. If someone proposed a 5 per cent tax, Gordon said, "make it 15." Interviews with Donald S. Macdonald and Stanley.

34 NA, WLGP, MG32 B44, vol. 8, file 10, Geoff Conway to Gordon, 13 Apr. 1963; Kent, *Public Purpose*, 233.

35 Bank of Canada Archives, Rasminsky Papers, LR76-541, Claude Isbister, "Non-Resident Taxes," memo for the minister, 31 May 1963.

36 Isbister interview.

37 Louis Rasminsky interview; NA, NFTSA, Institute for Research on Public Policy Collection, Michael Hicks interview with Louis Rasminsky, 28 Aug. 1989, 90 minutes, acc. no. 1989-0485; Rasminsky Papers, LR76-549, Rasminsky, "Some

Comments on the Budget," 31 May 1963; Rasminsky to Ken Taylor, 31 May 1963.

38 Gordon, *Political Memoir*, 139–40.

39 PSP, MG31 D78, vol. 33, Stursberg interview with Maurice Lamontagne, 24 Aug. 1976.

40 Interviews with J.W. Pickersgill and Stanley; PSP, MG31 D78, vol. 35, Stursberg interview with Allan MacEachen, 20 Apr. 1977; vol. 36, Stursberg interview with Geoffrey Pearson, 22 and 30 May 1978; Hutchison, *Far Side of the Street*, 251; Library of Parliament, Tom Earle interview with Mary Macdonald, 14 Apr. 1984. George McIlraith later commented, "The Prime Minister really had given, if you like, all his confidence to this one minister." Cited in Stursberg, *Lester Pearson and the Dream of Unity*, 139–40.

41 PSP, MG31 D78, vol. 33, Stursberg interview with Tom Kent, 30 Mar. 1977.

42 NA, Liberal Party of Canada Papers, MG28 IV 3, vol. 694, Election 1963 Correspondence and Reports file, Gordon to Pearson, 20 Mar. 1963.

43 O'Connell interview. Tom Kent remembered that, in a similar vein, Gordon "felt that his power to make his views prevail was greatest if he moved fast, while the government was new and Mike was in an enthusiastic mood." Kent, *Public Purpose*, 236–7.

44 PSP, MG31 D78, vol. 31, Stursberg interview with Gordon, 2 June 1977.

45 Gordon, *Political Memoir*, 146.

46 NA, RPCO, RG2, vol. 6253, file 2, Cabinet minutes, 13 June 1963.

47 Hellyer Personal Papers, draft memoirs.

48 LBPP, MG26 N5, vol. 46, file 142-147, transcript to roll 144, Bernard Ostry interview with Pearson, 3 Nov. 1970. In a similar vein, Paul Hellyer described the "tumultuous applause" as a "fitting tribute" to "one of the principal architects of the Liberal victory." Hellyer Personal Papers, draft memoirs, chap. 11, p 22.

49 O'Connell interview.

50 Isbister interview.

51 Canada, House of Commons, *Debates*, 13 June 1963, 1001, 1006.

52 Watkins, "Canadian Economic Policy," 77. See also Watkins, review of *Canadian Quandary*, 79–80.

53 Safarian, "Foreign Ownership and Control," 237.

54 University of Toronto Archives, Safarian Papers, B89-0032, box 3, A.E.S. [A.E. Safarian], "Estimate of the Cost of Getting a 25% Stock Issue," 8 Sept. 1967.

55 Interviews with Benson and Isbister; Newman, *Distemper of Our Times*, 19.

56 "The Budget," *Winnipeg Free Press*, 14 June 1963; "Deliberate Moves To Three Goals," *Toronto Star*, 14 June 1963; "Promise and Performance," *Globe and*

Mail, 15 June 1963, 6; "Canada Waves the Flag," *New York Times*, 18 June 1963, 36; "Un budget timide," *La Presse*, 14 June 1963.

57 "A Make-Work Program?" *Globe and Mail*, 18 June 1963; "A Budget for Independence," *Toronto Star*, 15 June 1963.

58 Canada, House of Commons, *Debates*, 14 June 1963, 1169.

59 Pickersgill, *Road Back*, 201.

60 WLGP, MG32 B44, vol. 3, file 1, Gordon to W.A.G. Kelley, 26 June 1963.

61 LBPP, MG26 N3, vol. 51, 251-63 pers. & conf. file, Pearson to Clifford Curtis, 15 July 1963.

62 Gordon, *Political Memoir*, 151. "To show guts" was the highest praise at RMC, and Gordon refused to give up during the boxing match. Interestingly, former Conservative Finance Minister George Nowlan used similar language to describe Gordon's reaction to the budget debate: "What I admire in Walter Gordon is guts. I don't think many men could have done what he did, take what he took … and still be able to stand there day after day with a calm face and a steady voice and at least a pretence of a smile. When a man shows that kind of courage you can't help admiring him." Fraser, "How Walter Gordon Has Recovered," 2.

63 LBPP, MG26 N3, vol. 51, 251-1963 Special Advisers file, E.A. Driedger to R.B. Bryce, 8 July 1963.

64 "Mr. Gordon's Indiscretion," *Toronto Star*, 15 June 1963, 6; "Who Shall Serve?" *Toronto Telegram*, 18 June 1963.

65 LBPP, MG26 N3, vol. 51, Kierans to Gordon, 18 June 1963.

66 Stursberg, *Lester Pearson and the Dream of Unity*, 130–1.

67 Newman, *Distemper of Our Times*, 20. Before Gordon's decision to withdraw the takeover tax, the Toronto average of twenty industrial stocks dropped ten points, the biggest decline in twelve months. "Lift Tax; Stocks Rebound," *Toronto Star*, 19 June 1963; "Complex Task," *Edmonton Journal*, 20 June 1963.

68 Newman, *Distemper of Our Times*, 21.

69 RPCO, RG2, vol. 6253, file 2, Cabinet minutes, 20 June 1963.

70 PSP, MG31 D78, vol. 33, Stursberg interview with Tom Kent, 30 Mar. 1977.

71 "Graham Scolds Gordon," *Ottawa Journal*, 20 June 1963. Trans-Canada Pipe Lines Ltd., for example, dropped 11 per cent by 2:30 P.M., and then rose 10 per cent over the next half-hour. "Sixty-Day Blues," 20.

72 Paul Hellyer Personal Papers, draft memoirs.

73 WLGP, MG32 B44, vol. 3, file 1, Gordon to Hugh Faulkner, 26 June 1963.

74 Elizabeth Gordon interview.

75 Gordon's memoirs imply that he offered to resign on 19 June, a date repeated in Kent's memoirs. Peter Newman and Denis Smith say that the resignation was tendered on the morning of 20 June. Cabinet minutes support Newman and Smith;

Gordon's offer to resign is not mentioned in the 19 June meeting, first appearing in the minutes for 20 June. Gordon, *Political Memoir*, 149; Smith, *Gentle Patriot*, 165; Newman, *Distemper of Our Times*, 22; Kent, *Public Purpose*, 233; RPCO, RG2, vol. 6253, file 2, Cabinet minutes, 19 and 20 June 1963.

76 Stursberg, *Lester Pearson and the Dream of Unity*, 132.

77 RPCO, RG2, vol. 6253, file 2, Cabinet minutes, 20 June 1963; Pickersgill, *Road Back*, 203.

78 WLGP, vol. 34, file 13, "Ups and Downs: Political memoirs of Walter L. Gordon," 4 Mar. 1977, chap. 8, p 29.

79 LaMarsh, *Bird in a Gilded Cage*, 65.

80 Canada, House of Commons, *Debates*, 24 June 1963, 1515–18.

81 Ibid., 2 July 1963, 1758–64; PSP, MG31 D78, vol. 33, Stursberg interview with J.W. Pickersgill, 14 Oct. 1976.

82 RPCO, RG2, vol. 6253, file 2, Cabinet minutes, 21 June 1963.

83 LaMarsh, *Bird in a Gilded Cage*, 65.

84 Paul Hellyer interview; Hellyer Personal Papers, draft memoir; PSP, MG31 D78, vol. 28, Stursberg interview with Lionel Chevrier, 17 Aug. 1976; vol. 36, Stursberg interview with J.W. Pickersgill, 14 Oct. 1976.

85 Newman, "What Really Happened," 76.

86 LaMarsh, *Bird in a Gilded Cage*, 65.

87 Benson interview.

88 WLGP, MG32 B44, vol. 16, file 11, memo, 5 Dec. 1965.

89 Hellyer, *Damn the Torpedoes*, 31. See also Library of Parliament, Peter Stursberg interview with Paul Martin, 30 Sept. 1976.

90 NA, Heeney Papers, MG30 E144, vol. 2, Memoir Chapter 19 file, Heeney Diary, 23 Aug. 1963. Queen's University Archives, Crerar Papers, vol. 131, Pearson to Crerar, 9 July 1963.

Sharp and Lamontagne also recall that the prime minister seriously considered replacing Gordon. Mitchell Sharp interview; PSP, MG31 D78, vol. 33, Stursberg interview with Maurice Lamontagne, 24 Aug. 1976; vol. 37, Stursberg interview with Mitchell Sharp, 26 July 1976; Sharp, *Which Reminds Me*, 116.

91 Fullerton, *Graham Towers*, 289; English, *Worldly Years*, 272; Fullerton interview; WLGP, MG32 B44, vol. 16, file 11, memo, 5 Dec. 1965.

92 LaMarsh, *Bird in a Gilded Cage*, 66; PSP, MG31 D78, vol. 32, Stursberg interview with Paul Hellyer, 13 Aug. 1976; Land interview.

93 LBPP, MG26 N3, vol. 57, E.P. Taylor to Pearson, 12 July 1963; Keith Davey interview.

94 Interviews with Beland Honderich, Kent, and Michael Mackenzie.

95 Ritchie, *Storm Signals*, 52; "Pearson-U.S. romance cooling off?" *Ottawa Citizen*, 25 June 1963; Harold Morrison, " 'Discriminatory Aspects' Feeling of U.S. Treasury," *Ottawa Journal*, 15 June 1963, 17.
96 Interviews with Isbister, Reisman, and G.G.E. Steele.
97 Newman, "Growing Up Reluctantly," 56; repr. as Newman, "Short Life and Premature Death," 79–94.

CHAPTER FIVE

1 NA, PSP, MG31 D78, vol. 37, Stursberg interview with Louis Rasminksy, 1 and 15 June 1978.
2 Gordon, *Political Memoir*, 158.
3 Canada, House of Commons, *Debates*, 18 July 1963, 2329.
4 Wright, "Cooperation and Independence," 143; Grady, "Canadian Exemption," 94.
5 Canadian-American Committee, *Recent Canadian and U.S. Government Actions*, 12; NA, RDF, RG19, vol. 3930, file 5085-04-2, pt 3, Louis Rasminsky, "U.S. Interest Equalization Tax," memo for Arnold Heeney, 14 Aug. 1964.
6 Grady, "Canadian Exemption," 97; GWPP, Wright interview with Walter Gordon, 20 Oct. 1971. Dr Wright kindly shared his interview notes with me.
7 Rasminksy interview.
8 Ibid. See also Plumptre, *Three Decades of Decision*.
9 Ritchie, *Storm Signals*, 72.
10 Rasminsky interview.
11 Gordon, *Political Memoir*, 159.
12 Wright, "Persuasive Influence," 142; Wright, "Cooperation and Independence," 141; GWPP, Wright interview with Merlyn Trued, 5 Apr. 1972.
13 PSP, MG31 D78, vol. 37, Stursberg interview with Louis Rasminksy, 1 and 15 June 1978; RDF, RG19, vol. 3930, file 5085-04-2, part 3, Louis Rasminsky, "U.S. Interest Equalization Tax," memo for Arnold Heeney, 14 Aug. 1964.
    Denis Smith noted, "The annoyance caused in Congress by the Canadian budget made it difficult to offer Canada an exemption in the original announcement of the interest equalization tax." Smith, *Gentle Patriot*, 177.
14 Stursberg, "Ottawa Letter," Sept. 1964, 9.
15 C. Knowlton Nash, "Gordon's 'Downhill Stroll' Makes U.S. Much Happier," *Financial Post*, 21 Mar. 1964, 18.
16 Gordon, *Political Memoir*, 179.
17 NA, RRCCEP, RG33/35, reel C-1541, Gordon R. Ball, statement before the royal commission, 21 Feb. 1956, 7, 13.

18 In discussing the CDC, Gordon told a reporter, "It was first mentioned to my knowledge in the report of the royal commission on Canada's economic prospects. I remember writing the section." Jack Cahill, "Gordon's Budget: 'It's Not Socialism, It's Just Common Sense,'" *Vancouver Sun*, 4 May 1965.

The author has been unable to locate any reference to the proposal in either the *Preliminary Report* or the *Final Report* of the Gordon Commission. The *Preliminary Report*, however, does contain the following vague reference: "If ... Canadians are to invest in new large-scale ventures, it may be necessary to devise new mechanisms for concentrating available venture capital" (83). On the CCF policy, see Douglas Fisher, "The Development of the CDC," *Toronto Telegram*, 5 Feb. 1971, 20.

19 Stursberg, *Diefenbaker: Leadership Gained*, 112; NA, WLGP, MG32 B44, vol. 4, file 1, Peter Newman to Gordon, 5 Apr. 1964.

20 In 1965 Fleming described the proposal graphically: "this monster first reared its ugly head seriously in the summer of 1960. I fought it off while I held the portfolio of Finance." NA, Fleming Papers, MG32 B39, vol. 156, file 5, "Business and Government," speech to the Trust Companies Association of Canada, Toronto, 29 Apr. 1965. See also Fleming, *So Very Near*, 2:225, 653.

21 WLGP, MG32 B44, vol. 4, file 1, Peter C. Newman to Gordon, 5 Apr. 1964; Gordon, *Troubled Canada*, 127. In the early 1960s the idea was also being promoted by the other prominent Canadian who was criticizing American economic influence in Canada, James Coyne. See Newman, *Renegade in Power*, 305–6.

22 NA, Chevrier Papers, MG32 B12, vol. 9, file 6, "The Policies of the Liberal Party," 1963, 8.

23 Canada, House of Commons, *Debates*, 16 May 1963, 7.

24 David Stanley interview.

25 Canada, House of Commons, *Debates*, 20 June 1963, 1371.

26 Ernst & Young Archives, CGP, G.G. Richardson re WLG file, Gordon to George Richardson, 6 Mar. 1964.

27 Alan Hockin interview; Dimma, "Canada Development Corporation," 303.

28 NA, LBPP, MG26 N5, vol. 46, file 148-154, transcript of roll 148, Bernard Ostry interview with Pearson, 9 Nov. 1970.

29 Kent, *Public Purpose*, 346.

30 Canada, House of Commons, *Debates*, 5 Apr. 1965, 3; 26 Apr. 1965, 434–5; 28 Apr. 1965, 677.

31 Jack McArthur, "Meet Mr. Gordon Money Magician," *Toronto Star*, 24 May 1963.

32 LBPP, MG26 N5, vol. 46, file 148-154, transcript of roll 148, Bernard Ostry interview with Pearson, 9 Nov. 1970.

33 J.W. Pickersgill, "At Times the Tory Political Propaganda Appears Undistorted by Facts," review of *Gentle Patriot*, by Denis Smith, *Globe and Mail*, 1 Dec. 1973.

34 PSP, MG31 D78, vol. 37, Stursberg interview with Mitchell Sharp, 26 July 1976.

35 CGP, G.G. Richardson re WLG file, David Stanley, "Canada Development Corporation," memo, 22 Nov. 1963.

36 "Back Door Socialism," *Globe and Mail*, 28 Apr. 1965, 6. See also "The Wrong Approach," *Globe and Mail*, 27 June 1963, 6.

37 CGP, G.G. Richardson re WLG file, David Stanley, "Canada Development Corporation," memo, 22 Nov. 1963.

38 CGP, G.G. Richardson re WLG file, Gordon to George Richardson, 7 May 1964.

39 NA, ARP, MG31 D73, vol. 4, file 78, Rotstein to Peter Newman, 26 May 1965.

40 WLGP, MG32 B44, vol. 37, file 6, "Canada Development Corporation," speech to the Canadian Textiles Institute, Ste Adèle, Que., 3 June 1965; "The Canada Development Corporation," speech to the Canadian Institute of Actuaries, Ottawa, 20 Sept. 1965; "Polymer – and the Canada Development Corporation," speech to the Canadian Club, Sarnia, 7 Oct. 1965. Forster's comments are found in Donald Forster, "The Economy," in *Canadian Annual Review for 1965*, ed. John Saywell (Toronto 1966), 342–3.

41 WLGP, MG32 B44, vol. 37, file 6, "Canada Development Corporation," speech to the Canadian Textiles Institute, Ste Adèle, Que., 3 June 1965; "Gordon Says CDC Bill Ready in Fall," *Montreal Star*, 4 June 1965.

42 Little, *Story of the Firm*, 36.

43 Canada, Royal Commission on Canada's Economic Prospects, *Final Report*, 397.

44 WLGP, MG32 B44, vol. 16, file 10, Gordon to Pearson, 5 Nov. 1963.

45 Canada, House of Commons, *Debates*, 22 Sept. 1964, 8316.

46 House of Commons, Bill C-120: An Act respecting Banks and Banking, first reading, 6 May 1965, sec. 53, 75.

47 Litvak and Maule, *Cultural Sovereignty*, 30.

48 Canada, Royal Commission on Publications, *Report*, 74.

49 Kent, *Public Purpose*, 317.

50 WLGP, MG32 B44, vol. 10, file 14, C.J. Laurin to Gordon, 23 Apr. 1963.

51 Tom Kent, letter to author, 22 Jan. 1996.

52 WLGP, MG32 B44, vol. 10, file 14, A.F.W. Plumptre to Gordon, 25 Apr. 1963.

53 LBPP, MG26 N6, vol. 12, Walter Gordon 1963–64 file, Gordon to Cabinet, 30 Sept. 1963. The editors of Pearson's memoirs incorrectly used much of the text of this memo as though Pearson had written it. Pearson, *Mike*, 3:133.

54 Queen's University Archives, TKP, vol. 3, Oct. 1963 file, Kent to Pearson, 2 Oct. 1963.

55 Canada, House of Commons, *Debates*, 18 Feb. 1964, 2.

56 "Pearson's Plan for Canadian Magazines," *Toronto Star*, 21 Feb. 1964, 2; "Once Again," *Halifax Chronicle-Herald*, 22 Feb. 1964, 4; "Death Knell of Canadian Magazines?" *Toronto Star*, 24 Feb. 1964, 6; "Dangerous and Impractical," *Globe and Mail*, 24 Feb. 1964, 6. The *Ottawa Citizen* also considered the legislation unsatisfactory because it exempted the two American periodicals. "The Pending Magazine Legislation," *Ottawa Citizen*, 22 Feb. 1964, 6.

57 Tom Kent, letter to author, 22 Jan. 1996.

58 Kent, *Public Purpose*, 319.

59 TKP, vol. 3, May 1964 file, Kent to Pearson, 11 May 1964.

60 Ibid., Kent to Gordon, 24 May 1964; Kent, *Public Purpose*, 321; Tom Kent, letter to author, 22 Jan. 1996; GWPP, Wright interview with Gordon, 20 Oct. 1971.

61 Quoted in Stursberg, *Lester Pearson and the American Dilemma*, 232. See also Pearson, *Mike*, 3:133–4. American Treasury Secretary Douglas Dillon all but threatened retaliation, saying that the legislation violated the General Agreement on Tariffs and Trade and that the United States might demand compensation. Bruce Macdonald, "Canada, U.S. Still Split But in a Friendlier Way," *Globe and Mail*, 1 May 1964, B1.

62 WLGP, MG32 B44, vol. 37, file 9, speech at West Humber Collegiate, Etobicoke, Ont., 21 May 1969. See also vol. 16, file 11, memo, 5 Dec. 1965.

63 Jewett, "The Menace is the Message," 52.

64 Gordon, *Political Memoir*, 205–6; Gordon, *Choice for Canada*, 97; WLGP, MG32 B44, vol. 2, file 1, Gordon to Belle MacMillan, 5 Aug. 1966; PSP, MG31 D78, vol. 31, Stursberg interview with Gordon, 2 June 1977.

65 TKP, vol. 3, May 1964 file, Kent to Gordon, 24 May 1964.

66 Pearson, *Mike,* 3:134. Tom Kent, Paul Martin, and Edgar Ritchie also agreed that in 1964 the exemption was unrelated to the Auto Pact. Tom Kent, letter to author, 22 Jan. 1996; GWPP, Wright interview with Paul Martin, 23 Apr. 1971; Wright interview with Edgar Ritchie, 22 June 1971.

67 GWPP, Wright interview with Gordon, 20 Oct. 1971; Gordon, *Choice for Canada*, 97.

68 "U.S., Canadian Publishers Plan Battle Against Budget," *Toronto Star*, 27 Apr. 1965, 1.

69 Canada, Senate, *Debates*, 28 June 1965, 282.

70 "To Serve his Obsession," *Globe and Mail*, 24 June 1965, 6.

71 "Press Control Has a Long History," *Winnipeg Free Press*, 19 June 1965.

72 WLGP, MG32 B44, vol. 10, file 14, Peter C. Newman to Gordon, 29 Apr. 1965.

73 ARP, MG31 D73, vol. 4, file 78, Peter Newman to Rotstein, 18 May 1965.

74 Ibid., 7 July 1965.

75 Gordon, *Political Memoir*, 218.

76 Matheson, *Canada's Flag*.

77 Sharp, *Which Reminds Me*, 154–5; Sharp speech at the Pearson Centennial Symposium, Ottawa, 22 Apr. 1997.

78 "Walker Metal Products bought by Chrysler Canada," *Financial Post*, 18 Jan. 1964. Canadian Corporate Management's holdings also included Dominion Forge and Western Tire & Auto Supply. Industry Canada, Annual Return of Corporations for Canadian Corporate Management Co. Limited, sec. A, 31 Dec. 1962; Canadian Corporate Management, *Annual Report 1965*. Copies of many of Canadian Corporate Management's *Annual Reports* may be found at the W.A.C. Bennett Library, Simon Fraser University.

79 Canada, Royal Commission on the Automotive Industry, *Report*.

80 PSP, MG31 D78, vol. 33, Stursberg interview with Kent, 30 Mar. 1977. See also Kent, *Public Purpose*, 311.

81 Bothwell, *Canada and the United States*, 93.

82 PSP, MG31 D78, vol. 37, Stursberg interview with Mitchell Sharp, 26 July 1976.

83 Gordon, *Political Memoir*, 169.

84 Simon Reisman interview.

85 Charity Grant interview; WLGP, MG32 B44, vol. 23, file 4, George Grant to Gordon, 16 May 1967.

86 NA, Mathews Papers, MG31 D190, vol. 18, file 7, Mathews to Mel [Hurtig], 6 Nov. 1968.

87 Grant, *Lament for a Nation* (1965), 2, 4, 9, 47, 69, 86.

88 Ibid., 15, 68, 75. See also Cayley, *George Grant in Conversation*, 97.

89 WLGP, MG32 B44, vol. 23, file 4, Gordon to George Grant, 19 May 1967; vol. 37, file 6, speech to Junior Board of Trade, Toronto, 19 Oct. 1965.

90 Christian, *George Grant*, 244, 279; Fulford, "The Angry Loser," 6; Emberley, foreword to *Lament for a Nation* (1995), 16.

91 Christian, *George Grant*, 254; Steed, *Ed Broadbent*, 73; Taylor, *Radical Tories*, 148. Gordon's biographer, Denis Smith, had a similar reaction to the book. Denis Smith interview.

92 Heeney and Merchant, *Canada and the United States*, annex A.

93 Ibid., 49.

94 Martin, *Very Public Life*, 2:398; Heeney, *Things That Are Caesar's*, 197.

95 "Can't They Read?" *Ottawa Journal*, 16 July 1965; Charles Lynch, "Conspiracy of Silence," *Ottawa Citizen*, 14 July 1965, 7; Terence Robertson, " 'Talk Softly' Heeney Explains Himself," *Toronto Star*, 23 July 1965; Holmes, "Merchant-Heeney Revisited," 199.

96 Gordon, *Political Memoir*, 174.

97 Ibid., 219–20. See also PSP, MG31 D78, vol. 31, Stursberg interview with Gordon, 2 June 1977; WLGP, MG32 B44, vol. 16, file 11, memo, 5 Dec. 1965.

98 WLGP, MG32 B44, vol. 35, file 1, "Ups and Downs: Political Memoirs of Walter L. Gordon," chap. 12, pp 2–3; vol. 16, file 11, memo, 5 Dec. 1965; Gordon, *Political Memoir*, 220; PSP, MG31 D78, vol. 31, Stursberg interview with Gordon, 2 June 1977.

99 Gordon, *Political Memoir*, 223.

100 Hellyer, *Damn the Torpedoes*, 134. See also PSP, MG31 D78, vol. 32, Stursberg interview with Hellyer, 13 Aug. 1976.

101 "Will the Real Liberal Please Stand Up?" *Globe and Mail*, 30 Sept. 1965, 6; "An Issue Mr. Winters Cannot Dodge," *Toronto Star*, 14 Oct. 1965; "Where Do They Stand on Foreign Ownership?" *Toronto Star*, 20 Oct. 1965; "Gordon to Keep Finance," *Montreal Star*, 27 Oct. 1965; Arthur Blakely, "Gordon Fends Off Challenge by Winters Comeback Bid," *Montreal Gazette*, 29 Oct. 1965; NA, Dornan Papers, MG32 G1, vol. 12, election 1965 file, "1965 Election: Chronological Highlights," summary for 26 Oct.

102 "Will the Real Liberal Please Stand Up?" *Globe and Mail*, 30 Sept. 1965, 6. See also Bruce Hutchison, "Canadian Shift in Attitude Due," *Christian Science Monitor*, 3 Dec. 1965, 25.

103 Gordon, *Political Memoir*, 230; "Gordon to Keep Finance," *Montreal Star*, 27 Oct. 1965; Arthur Blakely, "Gordon Fends Off Challenge By Winters Comeback Bid," *Montreal Gazette*, 29 Oct. 1965.

104 WLGP, MG32 B44, vol. 16, file 11, memo, 15 Jan. 1966.

105 Much of Gordon's memorandum of 15 Jan. 1966 supports this interpretation. WLGP, MG32 B44, vol. 16, file 11, memo, 15 Jan. 1966.

106 "I Hope to Stay in Finance, Gordon says," *Toronto Star*, 9 Nov. 1965.

107 Gordon, *Political Memoir*, 232–3. This section of the memoirs is based on a memorandum Gordon wrote shortly after the election. WLGP, MG32 B44, vol. 16, file 11, memo, 5 Dec. 1965. The letter of resignation, dated 9 November, was delivered to Pearson on 11 November. WLGP, MG32 B44, vol. 16, file 11, Gordon to Pearson, 9 Nov. 1965.

108 WLGP, MG32 B44, vol. 16, file 11, memo, 5 Dec. 1965; Denis Smith Personal Papers, Smith interview with Pearson, 30 June 1972; LBPP, MG26 N5, vol. 45, memoirs 3-8 file, [Lester Pearson], "Election Analysis," 10 Dec. 1965.

109 PSP, MG31 D78, vol. 33, Stursberg interview with Tom Kent, 30 Mar. 1977.

110 Davey, *Rainmaker*, 107.

111 David Ferguson interview.

112 Various diary notes in WLGP, MG32 B44, vol. 16, file 11.

113 TKP, 5123, box 1, file 21, Kent to John Saywell, 3 July 1991.

CHAPTER SIX

1　Moller, "Youth as a Force," 254.

2　For a discussion of this generation gap, see Kettle, *Big Generation*, 28–32, 44–5; Westhues, "Inter-generational Conflict," 387–408.

3　Cited in Edmonds, *Years of Protest*, 10.

4　Bliss, *Years of Change*, 9.

5　The author is an alumnus of Centennial School, Coquitlam, BC.

6　Crean, *Who's Afraid of Canadian Culture?* 7.

7　Underhill, foreword to *Nationalism in Canada*, xix.

8　Kostash, *Long Way from Home*, 9–10.

9　Warnock, "Why I Am Anti-American," 11.

10　Ross, *In the Interests of Peace*, 303, 446 n 91.

11　Hollander, *Anti-Americanism*, 416.

12　*Star Weekly*, 1 Apr. 1967.

13　Arlen, *Living-Room War*.

14　NA, ARP, MG31 B73, vol. 4, file 61, Gordon to Rotstein, 30 July 1964; Rotstein, review of *The Canadian Quandary* by Harry Johnson, 80–3.

15　Abraham Rotstein interview.

16　Dobbs, "Uniquely Cool Nationalism," 26; Drummond, *Canadian Debate*, 17.

17　Alexander Wittenberg et al., "Vietnam Torture," letter to the editor, *Globe and Mail*, 31 July 1965, 6.

18　Steed, *Ed Broadbent*, 73. See also Jamie Swift interview with Watkins, 7 Aug. 1985, cited in Swift, *Odd Man Out*, 193–4.

19　ARP, MG31 D73, vol. 4, file 31, Rotstein to E.J. Benson, 4 Aug. 1965; file 61, Gordon to Rotstein, 28 July 1965.

20　Fox, "Teach-In," 172; Rotstein and Watkins, "Communication Is a New Key," 174; Kostash, *Long Way from Home*, 46; Grant, "Protest and Technology," 128; Steed, *Ed Broadbent*, 73; Watkins, "Learning To Move Left," 72; Ross, *In the Interests of Peace*, 305.

　　At a 1966 teach-in at the University of Alberta, for example, students heard George Grant describe the Vietnam War as "genocide." Don Moren, "Canada Needs Own Identity," *The Gateway* (University of Alberta), 23 Feb. 1966, 1.

21　Satin, *Manual for Draft-Age Immigrants*. The title-page of the fourth revised edition (Toronto 1969) shows the number of copies published.

22　Fetherling, *Travels by Night*, 113.

23　Atwood, "Backdrop Addresses Cowboy," 10.

24　Newman, "1966," 72.

25　Souster, "Death Chant," 67–8. See also Lee, "Third Elegy," in *Civil Elegies*.

26 Kearns, "Parable of the Seventh Seal," 100.

27 Purdy, *Cariboo Horses*, 95.

28 Lord, "'mericans," 150–1.

29 McLeod, "Moses with a Maple Leaf," 22.

30 "Once Again, Here's Walter," 46.

31 Peter C. Newman, "Gordon's Ideological Showdown," *Montreal Star*, 6 May 1966.

32 NA, WLGP, MG32 B44, vol. 1, file 10, McClelland and Stewart, Royalty Statement, 1 Nov. 1966.

33 *Globe and Mail*, 6 May 1966, 1, 6, B1, B5; *Toronto Star*, 6 May 1966, 1, 6, 55; *Toronto Star*, 7 May 1966, 1; *Star Weekly*, 14 May 1966, 2–4, 6–7.

34 McLeod, "Moses with a Maple Leaf," 21.

35 Kierans, *Challenge of Confidence*, 9.

36 Gordon, *Choice for Canada*, 10.

37 Ibid., 114–17, 119.

38 Ibid., viii, 82–7.

39 Ibid., 91.

40 GWPP, Wright interview with Gordon, 20 Oct. 1971. I am grateful to Dr Wright, who generously shared his interview notes with me.

41 Gordon, *Choice for Canada*, 88–89.

42 Safarian, "Exports of American-Owned Enterprises," 449–58. See also Safarian, *Foreign Ownership of Canadian Industry* and *Performance of Foreign-Owned Firms*.

43 Edward Safarian interview, and *Foreign Ownership of Canadian Industry*, vi. Gordon lent Safarian a secretary and a car, and helped him to arrange interviews with corporate executives.

44 Arthur Smith interview.

45 Lindeman and Armstrong, *Policies and Practices*, 52.

46 English, *Industrial Structure*.

47 On the specific issue of exports by foreign-owned firms, see Wilkinson, *Canada's International Trade*, 130; McFetridge and Weatherby, *Notes on the Economics of Large Firm Size*, 81; Vernon, *Sovereignty at Bay*, 158–62; Vernon, *Storm over the Multinationals*, 114. The only notable study to argue that Canadian firms were more likely to export than their foreign-controlled counterparts is Hanel and Palda, *Innovation and Export Performance*, iv.

48 Gordon, *Choice for Canada*, 88–9, 100.

49 The best summary of the research into foreign ownership in Canada is Safarian, *Foreign Direct Investment*.

50 Safarian, *Performance of Foreign-Owned Firms*, 5.

51 WLGP, MG32 B44, vol. 37, file 6, speech to the Albion College Regional Meeting of the American Assembly, 14 May 1965.

52 Pat Carney, "Mr. Gordon: 'I Went Away and Wrote a Book,' " *Vancouver Sun*, 1 Apr. 1967.

53 For example, see WLGP, MG32 B44, vol. 37, file 2, speech to National Federation of Canadian University Students, University of British Columbia, 29 Aug. 1960; file 5, speech to the Economic Club of New York, 20 Apr. 1964; speech to the Sixth Annual Industrial and Municipal Relations Conference, Peterborough, Ont., 28 Oct. 1964.

54 Gordon, *Choice for Canada*, 124–5.

55 For example, see Gordon, *Storm Signals*, 95.

56 WLGP, MG32 B44, vol. 13, file 12, Harry G. Johnson, "What Choice for Canada?" speech to the Canadian Club of Montreal, 26 Sept. 1966.

57 Ibid., vol. 37, file 2, speech to the National Federation of Canadian University Students, University of British Columbia, 29 Aug. 1960.

58 Gordon, *Choice for Canada*, 108; Fraser, "Sharp/Gordon Debate," 36. Once, when Gordon was called a protectionist, he replied, "If anybody calls me a protectionist again – well, if I was a little younger, I'd smack him right in the eye." " 'I'm Not a Protectionist,' Gordon Says Expansively," *Vancouver Sun*, 27 Sept. 1966.

59 A year before his death Gordon issued an open letter to Brian Mulroney opposing free trade. Walter Gordon and Abraham Rotstein, "An Open Letter to the Prime Minister, Re: Free Trade with the United States," *Toronto Star*, 23 Jan. 1986, A20.

60 Watkins, "Is Gordon's Game Worth the Candle?" 77–8.

61 Quoted in Cahill, *John Turner*, 111.

62 Eric Kierans, "Where is Canada Going?" review of *A Choice for Canada* by Walter L. Gordon, *Montreal Star*, 14 May 1966.

63 On Kierans' reaction to the guidelines, see Swift, *Odd Man Out*, 135–47; McDougall, *Politics and Economics*, 84–93.

64 Vincent Egan, "Gordon Ends His Silence, Comes Out Swinging in Defence of 1963 Budget," *Globe and Mail*, 6 May 1966.

65 Kierans, "Where is Canada Going?" *Montreal Star*, 14 May 1966.

66 NA, Blair Papers, MG32 C11, vol. 23, Mitchell Sharp, "Strengthening Canada's Independence," speech to the Association of Canadian Advertisers, Toronto, 4 May 1966; Mitchell Sharp, "Sharp's Plan for Canadian Independence," *Financial Post*, 7 May 1967, 17.

67 WLGP, MG32 B44, vol. 17, file 1, Gordon to Blair Fraser, 16 May 1966. See also vol. 32, file 13, Gordon to Denis Smith, 23 Mar. 1973.

68 Rotstein, "Canadian Affluence," 90–1.

69 Slater, "Gordon's New Book," 49–51. Repr. as "Gordon Misconstrues Choices for Canada," *Vancouver Sun*, 24 June 1966.

70 Bonin, "M. Walter Gordon," 345–6.

71 Gordon, *Le Canada à l'heure du choix*; WLGP, MG32 B44, vol. 1, file 10, Claude Hurtubise to Jack McClelland, 18 Oct. 1966.

72 Lévesque, *Memoirs*; Trudeau, *Memoirs*; Pelletier, *Years of Impatience* and *Years of Choice*.

73 WLGP, MG32 B44, vol. 9, file 5, G.R. Conway to Gordon, 9 June 1966; Gordon to Conway, 6 July 1966.

74 The speeches may be found in WLGP, MG32 B44, vol. 37, file 7.

75 Ibid., speech to students of Simon Fraser University and the University of British Columbia, 25 Sept. 1966.

76 Ibid., vol. 35, file 1, "Ups and Downs: Political Memoirs of Walter L. Gordon," draft ms, chap. 13, p 20.

77 Ibid., vol. 9, file 12, Gordon to Lamontagne, 19 Sept. 1966.

78 NA, LBPP, MG26 N6, vol. 38, "Resolutions to be submitted by the Liberal Associations of the Provinces of Manitoba, Saskatchewan, Alberta and British Columbia" [summer 1966]. See also NA, Liberal Party of Canada Papers, MG28 IV 3, vol. 1054, "Schedule 'A' – Highest Priority Resolutions submitted by the British Columbia Policy Committee" [summer 1966].

79 WLGP, MG32 B44, vol. 9, file 12, "The Role of Foreign Capital in Canadian Economic Development" [Sept. 1966].

80 LBPP, MG26 N6, vol. 38, David W. Slater, "Economic Growth and Development" [1966].

81 Victor Mackie, "Molgat Captains West in Smashing Gordon's Myth," *Winnipeg Free Press*, 12 Oct. 1966, 1, 16.

82 Anthony Westell, "Liberals Reject Gordon's Nationalism," *Globe and Mail*, 12 Oct. 1966, 1, 4; NA, PSP, MG31 D78, vol. 37, Stursberg interview with Mitchell Sharp, 26 July 1976; University of Toronto Archives, Bothwell Papers, B79–0055, box 2, Robert Bothwell interview with Mitchell Sharp, 26 May 1977.

83 Mitchell Sharp interview; Sharp, *Which Reminds Me*, 145.

84 Sharp, *Which Reminds Me*, 146.

85 Anthony Westell, "Liberals Reject Gordon's Nationalism," *Globe and Mail*, 12 Oct. 1966, 1, 4.

86 Interview with Gildas Molgat; LBPP, MG26 N4, vol. 159, file 391, part 3, "Plenary Sessions Decisions," Oct. 1966; WLGP, MG32 B44, vol. 9, file 12, "The Role of Foreign Capital in Canadian Economic Development" [Sept. 1966].

87 WLGP, MG32 B44, vol. 9, file 12, "The Role of Foreign Capital in Canadian Economic Development" [Sept. 1966].

88 Ibid., vol. 13, file 12, Tom Axworthy, "Mr. Gordon, the Press and the Convention," Manitoba Young Liberal Association, *Keynote*, 31 Oct. 1966. See also John Walker, "Sharp Forces Win the Day," *Ottawa Citizen*, 12 Oct. 1966, 1.

89 WLGP, MG32 B44, vol. 10, file 3, Gordon to John R. Laing, 18 Oct. 1966.

90 Ibid., vol. 11, file 15, Gordon to L.T. Pennell, 26 Oct. 1966.

91 Ibid., vol. 14, file 6, Gordon to Earl H. Orser, 26 Oct. 1966.

92 Newman, *Home Country*, 114.

93 Quoted in Newman, *Distemper of Our Times*, 416.

94 WLGP, MG32 B44, vol. 14, file 6, Gordon to Earl H. Orser, 26 Oct. 1966.

95 Ibid., vol. 16, file 11, memo, 29 Oct. [1966].

96 NA, Lamontagne Papers, MG32 B32, vol. 10, file 9, Lamontagne to Pearson, 21 Feb. 1967; WLGP, MG32 B44, vol. 16, file 11, "Lunch with L.B.P.," 9 June 1966; memo, 30 Nov. 1966.

97 Keith Davey interview.

98 Quoted in Stursberg, *Lester Pearson and the Dream of Unity*, 278. See also Davey, *Rainmaker*, 112.

99 WLGP, MG32 B44, vol. 16, file 11, Maurice Lamontagne, "The Federal Liberal Party," 12 Dec. 1966.

100 Ibid., memo, 20 Dec. 1966.

101 LBPP, MG26 N6, vol. 12, Pearson, "The Return of Walter Gordon," 9 Mar. 1967.

102 WLGP, MG32 B44, vol. 16, file 11, memo, 20 Dec. 1966; memo, 29 Dec. 1966.

103 Ibid., memo to Pearson, "The Foreign Control issue," 29 Dec. 1966.

104 LBPP, MG26 N6, vol. 12, "The Return of Walter Gordon," 9 Mar. 1967; WLGP, MG32 B44, vol. 16, file 12, memo, 4 Jan. 1967.

105 WLGP, MG32 B44, vol. 16, file 12, memo, 4 Jan. 1967; Gordon draft of letter from Pearson to Gordon, 3 Jan. 1967; "The Prime Minister's Press Conference," 4 Jan. 1967; LBPP, MG26 N6, vol. 12, Pearson to Gordon, 31 Dec. 1966; "The Return of Walter Gordon," 9 Mar. 1967.

106 WLGP, MG32 B44, vol. 16, file 12, Pearson to Gordon, 5 Jan. 1967.

107 LBPP, MG26 N6, vol. 12, "The Return of Walter Gordon," 9 Mar. 1967.

108 Ibid.

109 Ibid.; PSP, MG31 D78, vol. 34, Stursberg interview with Paul Martin, 30 Sept. 1976; vol. 37, Stursberg interview with Sharp, 26 July 1976.

110 Interviews with Paul Hellyer and J.W. Pickersgill; Hellyer, *Damn the Torpedoes*, 199; PSP, MG31 D78, vol. 34, Stursberg interview with Martin, 30 Sept. 1976; LBPP, MG26 N6, vol. 12, "The Return of Walter Gordon," 9 Mar. 1967.

111   Hellyer, *Damn the Torpedoes*, 200.

112   WLGP, MG32 B44, vol. 16, file 12, memo, 18 Jan. 1967.

113   LBPP, MG26 N11, series C-2, vol. 190, file 236-A, "Statement by the Prime Minister," 23 Jan. 1967.

114   WLGP, MG32 B44, vol. 16, file 12, "Conversation with LBP," 9 Feb. 1967.

115   Gordon Robertson interview.

116   WLGP, MG32 B44, vol. 16, file 12, memo, 17 Mar. [should read Apr.] 1967.

117   Ibid., memo, 26 Apr. [1967].

118   Ibid., Gordon to Pearson, 27 Apr. 1967.

119   Davey, *Rainmaker*, 112.

120   House of Commons, Bill C-222: An Act respecting Banks and Banking, first reading, 7 July 1966.

121   Gordon, *Political Memoir*, 269.

122   Privy Council Office, Cabinet minutes, 24 and 31 Jan. 1967.

123   WLGP, MG32 B44, vol. 16, file 12, "Conversation with L.B.P.," 9 Feb. 1967; Gordon to Pearson, 15 Feb. 1967.

124   LBPP, MG26 N6, vol. 12, "The Return of Walter Gordon," 9 Mar. 1967.

125   Sharp, *Which Reminds Me*, 144.

126   WLGP, MG32 B44, vol. 16, file 12, memo, 20 Feb. 1967.

127   Ibid., memo, 23 Feb. 1967.

128   Canada, House of Commons, *Proceedings of the Standing Committee on Finance, Trade and Economic Affairs: Decennial Revision of the Bank Acts* (Ottawa 1967), 2:2075–7, 2080.

129   Gordon, *Political Memoir*, 270.

130   WLGP, MG32 B44, vol. 16, file 12, memo, 23 Feb. 1967.

131   Ibid., vol. 16, file 12, "Notes of my remarks to Cabinet yesterday," 24 Feb. 1967.

132   Ibid., Robert Winters, "Aide Memoire Re: Mercantile," 24 Feb. 1967; Gordon, "Memorandum of discussion in the Prime Minister's office," 24 Feb. 1967.

133   Ibid., Gordon, second memo, 24 Feb. 1967; NA, Winters Papers, MG32 B24, vol. 87, file 2, Robert Winters, aide memoire, 24 Feb. 1967.

134   Smith, *Gentle Patriot*, 317.

135   WLGP, MG32 B44, vol. 10, file 3, Gordon to A.R.M. Lower, 25 Feb. 1967; Fayerweather, *Mercantile Bank Affair*, 122.

136   Smith, *Gentle Patriot*, 317.

137   Tom Hazlitt, "Tougher on Citibank: Gordon Wins Cabinet Fight," *Toronto Star*, 1 Mar. 1967, 1.

138   WLGP, MG32 B44, vol. 16, file 12, memo, 3 Mar. [1967].

139   "No yielding on Mercantile says Sharp, but Gordon Silent," *Toronto Star*, 6 Mar. 1967.

140 Gordon, *Political Memoir*, 272.

141 WLGP, MG32 B44, vol. 16, file 12, memo, 9 Mar. 1967.

142 Gordon, *Political Memoir*, 270.

143 Ibid., 280.

144 WLGP, MG32 B44, vol. 37, file 8, "The War in Vietnam," speech to the Arts of Management Conference, 13 May 1967.

145 Ibid., vol. 32, file 13, Gordon to Denis Smith, 23 Mar. 1973.

146 Newman, "Gordon's Bold Quest," 36; Newman, *Sometimes a Great Nation*, 237.

147 WLGP, MG32 B44, vol. 22, file 11, Gordon to J. Bilak, 23 May 1967; David Smith interview.

148 Gwyn, *49th Paradox*, 71. Ross cites Gordon's memoirs and Denis Smith's biography, though neither supports his contention that "Gordon's views had been strongly shaped by" Steele and Rotstein. Smith merely notes that Steele and Rotstein had provided Gordon with background material. Gordon does not mention Rotstein, noting only that he had spoken to Steele, "who held strong views of the Vietnam situation." Ross, *In the Interests of Peace*, 309; Smith, *Gentle Patriot*, 401, n 75; Gordon, *Political Memoir*, 281.

149 Rotstein interview.

150 Gordon spoke to Steele four days before his speech. In March, Steele had made a speech at the University of Toronto in which he was highly critical of Canadian policy towards the war. Gordon thought Steele too critical of Pearson, but was influenced by his views. He obtained a copy of Steele's speech and sent one to Pearson. WLGP, MG32 B44, vol. 16, file 12, Gordon to Pearson, 10 May 1967; James Steele interview.

151 WLGP, MG32 B44, vol. 37, file 1, "China and the Far East," speech in Toronto, 6 Dec. 1954.

152 Ibid., vol. 16, file 12, draft of letter from Gordon to Pearson, 19 May 1967; Geoffrey Pearson interview.

153 Privy Council Office, Cabinet minutes, 17 May 1967. After the meeting Pearson recounted the discussion to Gordon Robertson, who wrote the minutes.

154 Gerald Stoner interview; WLGP, MG32 B44, vol. 24, file 7, Gordon to Rotstein, 31 May 1967.

155 Martin, *Very Public Life*, 498.

156 WLGP, MG32 B44, vol. 16, file 12, memo, 23 May 1967. See also memo, 17 May 1967.

157 Ibid., Pearson memo, 17 May 1967; Gordon memo, 23 May 1967. See also Gordon memo, 17 May 1967.

158 WLGP, MG32 B44, vol. 24, file 1, Muriel [Mersey] to Gordon, [May or June 1967]. The letters may be found in vols. 22–4.

159 Reid, *Radical Mandarin*, 372.

160 "Three World Specialists Urge PM to Seek End of U.S. Bombing," *Toronto Star*, 27 June 1967, 1, 4. This story did not appear in all editions of the paper.

161 Rotstein interview.

162 Interviews with Rotstein and Mel Watkins; Godfrey and Watkins, *Gordon to Watkins to You*, 22.

163 Bothwell, Drummond, and English, *Canada since 1945*, 303; Drummond, *Canadian Debate*, 12; Watkins interview. A similar phrase was used by the NDP's director of research, economist Russell Irvine: "In some ways it is an even more backward budget than those of Mr. Nowlan and Mr. Fleming. They were merely pre-Keynesian. Mr. Gordon is almost pre-Cambrian" ("Ottawa: the First Session," 75).

164 Watkins, "Learning to Move Left," 68–92; Watkins, *Madness and Ruin*, 26; Watkins interview.

165 Watkins, "Learning to Move Left," 69.

166 Bernard Bonin interview.

167 Drummond, *Canadian Debate*, 13; interviews with Bonin, Safarian, and Watkins.

168 Interviews with Rotstein and Safarian.

169 Safarian interview.

170 "A Prediction," *Toronto Telegram*, 16 Mar. 1967.

171 Watkins interview.

172 Bonin interview.

173 Ibid.

174 Stoner interview.

175 Interviews with Stoner and Simon Reisman; Watkins, "Foreign Ownership '94," 31.

176 NA, RPCO, RG2, vol. 2698, Industry Dept file, Watkins, "Memorandum on meeting with Simon Reisman," 22 Feb. 1967.

177 PSP, MG31 D78, Stursberg interview with Mel Watkins, 29 June 1978.

178 Watkins interview.

179 WLGP, MG32 B44, vol. 8, file 9, minutes of the Ministerial Committee on the Structure of Canadian Industry, 22 Jan. 1968; vol. 20, file 4, M.A. Crowe, "Memorandum to Cabinet: Report of the Task Force on the Structure of Canadian Industry," 24 Jan. 1968.

180 Canada, House of Commons, *Debates*, 25 Jan. 1968, 5940. Privy Council Office, Cabinet minutes, 25 Jan. 1968; Victor J. Mackie, "Cabinet Strain over Gordon's Latest Move," *Ottawa Journal*, 30 Jan. 1968.

181 WLGP, MG32 B44, vol. 8, file 9, Cabinet minutes, 1 Feb. 1968.

182 Ibid., vol. 16, file 14, memo, 31 Jan. 1968.

183 O.G. Stoner Personal Papers, "Memorandum for the Prime Minister," 9 Feb. 1968.

184 WLGP, MG32 B44, vol. 8, file 9, excerpt from Cabinet minutes, 13 Feb. 1968.

185 Stursberg, *Lester Pearson and the American Dilemma*, 249; Watkins, "Learning to Move Left," 74.

186 Stoner interview.

187 Brian Land interview.

188 Watkins interview.

189 Canada, Privy Council Office, *Foreign Ownership and the Structure of Canadian Industry*, 395, 398, 401–2, 404, 406.

190 Ibid., 360–1, 407–9.

191 Ibid., 91, 362, 412–3. Watkins indicated to the government that the task force gave the highest priority to the proposals on extraterritoriality and the lowest to the proposals on minority holdings in foreign-owned companies. NA, RDF, RG19, vol. 4669, file 8580-05-01, part 4, Watkins, "Task Force on the Structure of Canadian Industry," 8 Sept. 1967.

192 "Watkins on Watkins: Tone Was Un-Gordonian," *Financial Times*, 18 Mar. 1968.

193 *Toronto Star*, 16 Feb. 1968, 23–30; Peter Newman, "Watkins Report Sees Bold, New Canada," *Ottawa Journal*, 16 Feb. 1968; "The Choice to be Made," *Financial Times*, 19 Feb. 1968.

194 Roger Champoux, "Le pays des jamais contents," *La Presse*, 17 Feb. 1968, 4; "La propriété étrangère," *Le Soleil*, 17 Feb. 1968, 20.

195 "Anti-Americanism," *Winnipeg Free Press*, 19 Feb. 1968; Maurice Western, "A Brief for Economic Nationalism," *Winnipeg Free Press*, 16 Feb. 1968; "Gordon's Policy Redefined," *Toronto Telegram*, 16 Feb. 1968.

196 "Georgia Troopers Drag Off Negro Students," *Globe and Mail*, 16 Feb. 1968; "U.S. Bombs Off Target Kill 42 Near Saigon," *Globe and Mail*, 16 Feb. 1968.

197 WLGP, MG32 B44, vol. 24, file 14, E.C. Manning, W. Ross Thatcher, and Walter Weir to Pearson, 20 Feb. 1968.

198 Bonin interview.

199 WLGP, MG32 B44, vol. 24, file 14, Gordon to R[obin] D. Mathews, 11 Mar. 1968.

200 "Gordon Makes Watkins Report a Leadership Issue," *Toronto Star*, 16 Feb. 1968; Peter Thompson, "… and Gordon asks Liberals to Speak Up," *Toronto Telegram*, 16 Feb. 1968; "Gordon Says Watkins Good," *Montreal Star*, 27 Mar. 1968.

201 "Liberals Will Stay in Power – Kierans," *Toronto Star*, 22 Feb. 1968, 3; Stan Fischler, "Kierans Calls Watkins Report on Foreign Owners 'Superb,'" *Toronto*

Star, 19 Feb. 1968, 1–2; "Foreign Control: Why the Great Silence?" *Toronto Star*, 26 Feb. 1968; WLGP, MG32 B44, vol. 24, file 14, John Turner press release, 16 Mar. 1968; "Sharp Says Watkins Report Not Leadership Race Topic," *Toronto Star*, 19 Feb. 1968, 42; "Where the Candidates Stand on Foreign Investment," *Toronto Star*, 2 Apr. 1968.

202 English, "Larger Issues," 18.

203 Johnson, "Watkins Report," 615, 617, 619–22.

204 Canada, Privy Council Office, *Gaikoku shihon to kokumin keizai*.

205 Safarian interview.

206 Watkins, "Learning to Move Left," 82; Watkins interview; Godfrey and Watkins, *Gordon to Watkins to You*, 22.

207 WLGP, MG32 B44, vol. 16, file 11, memo, 15 Mar. 1966; "Lunch with L.B.P.," 30 Mar. 1966; "Lunch with L.B.P.," 9 June 1966; memo, 14 June 1966.

208 Ibid., memo, 15 Mar. 1966; English, *Worldly Years*, 389.

209 Interviews with Davey, Gordon Edick, and David Smith.

210 Harold Greer, "Marchand Is Wooed by Gordon," *Montreal Star*, 3 Jan. 1968; WLGP, MG32 B44, vol. 13, file 14, Gordon to Claude H. Vipond, 8 Mar. 1968; Gordon, *Political Memoir*, 299–300; McCall-Newman, *Grits*, 113; "Gordon Supports Trudeau," *Toronto Star*, 26 Mar. 1968.

211 WLGP, MG32 B44, vol. 32, file 13, Gordon to Denis Smith, 23 Mar. 1973.

212 Ibid., vol. 16, file 15, Gordon to Pearson, 19 Feb. 1968.

CHAPTER SEVEN

1 White et al., *Introduction to Canadian Politics*, 186, n 3.

2 Alexander Ross, "Walter Gordon, Prophet, Becoming Honored at Last," *Financial Post*, 21 Mar. 1970, 7; Jane Finlayson, "Remembering Past Politics," *Ottawa Citizen*, 17 Dec. 1973.

3 The first use of the term "new nationalism" may have been in Anthony Westell, "New Nationalism 'Broader, Deeper,'" *Toronto Star*, 29 Nov. 1969.

4 Warnock, *Partner to Behemoth*, 315. See also Clarkson, *Independent Foreign Policy* (espec. the sections by Charles Hanly and Kenneth McNaught); Hertzman, Warnock, and Hockin, *Alliances and Illusions*; Resnick, "Canadian Defence Policy," 93–115; Eayrs, "Road from Ogdensburg," 364–6.

5 Mathews and Steele, *Struggle for Canadian Universities*; Steele and Mathews, "Universities," 169–78. See also Cottam, *Canadian Universities*.

6 Warnock, "All the News," 126, 130.

7 Kidd, "Canada's 'National' Sport," 257–74.

8 Pope, *Elephant and the Mouse*, vii.

9   Ian Lumsden, "American Imperialism and Canadian Intellectuals," in *Close the 49th Parallel*, 322.

10 Crean, *Who's Afraid of Canadian Culture?* 5.

11 Canada, Privy Council Office, *Foreign Ownership and the Structure of Canadian Industry*, 402, 406.

12 Rotstein, "Foreign Control of the Economy," 89; Levitt, *Silent Surrender*, 33.

13 Pope, *Elephant and the Mouse*, 81–2, 103.

14 Kierans "Towards a New National Policy," 53.

15 Godfrey and Watkins, *Gordon to Watkins to You*, 105.

16 Smith, *Bleeding Hearts*, 141–2.

17 Don Murray, "Ownership Policy 'Obviously Being Watered Down,' " *Montreal Gazette*, 25 Mar. 1972, 37; Levitt, *Silent Surrender*, 152; Bashevkin, *True Patriot Love*, 161; Dennis Lee, cited in Resnick, *Land of Cain*, 192.

18 For Gordon, Canadian nationalism was the desire to preserve and promote the Canadian state and to limit the influence in Canada of other states. Walter L. Gordon, "Survival for Canada?" *Financial Post*, 2 May 1964, 6.

19 NA, WLGP, MG32 B44, vol. 37, file 5, speech to Langstaff High School, Richmond Hill, Ontario, 23 Oct. 1964.

20 Ibid., file 9, speech to the Canadian Union of Students, Sudbury, Ontario, 13 May 1969.

21 Gordon, "The Right to Self-Determination," 28.

22 NA, Bobak Papers, MG30 D378, vol. 5, file 11, Walter [Gordon] to Molly [Bobak], 2 Oct. [1972].

23 Walter Gordon, "Walter Gordon on Giving Quebec Its Due," 77.

24 Gordon, "There Is a Way," 9. See also Walter Gordon, "Special Status Should Be Acceptable: Gordon," *Montreal Gazette*, 2 Nov. 1977; Gordon, *What Is Happening*, 27–8.

Gordon's attitude towards Quebec in the 1970s marked a break with Pierre Trudeau, whom Gordon had backed for the leadership in 1968. Trudeau, according to Keith Davey, "greatly resented" Gordon's 1977 *Maclean's* article, which supported special status for Quebec. Davey, *Rainmaker*, 173.

By this time Gordon no longer held the same respect for Trudeau that he had in 1968, a change evident in a 1977 letter to Paul Martin: "I think Trudeau is wrong in his rigid attitude about Quebec ... I do wonder sometimes what would have happened if Marchand and I had decided in the fall of 1967 to get behind you for the leadership and stay on in your government. I am sure you would have been much more conciliatory with Quebec's understandable aspirations." NA, WLGP, MG32 B44, vol. 32, file 17, Gordon to Paul Martin, 23 Nov. 1977.

According to Tom Kent, Gordon's acceptance of special status came late in life and may have been influenced by his dislike of Trudeau. In his first two years as prime minister, Trudeau saw Gordon only two or three times, and only when Gordon asked for an interview. McCall-Newman, *Grits*, 127.

25 WLGP, vol. 37, file 2, speech to the National Federation of Canadian University Students, University of British Columbia, 29 Aug. 1960.

26 Godfrey and Watkins, *Gordon to Watkins to You*, 103. On the history of the Waffle, see, "Whither Waffle?" 24–5; Bullen, "Ontario Waffle"; Watkins, "Once Upon a Time," 28–30.

27 Godfrey and Watkins, *Gordon to Watkins to You*, 104–5.

28 McQueen, "Waffle Lives On," 15. See Watkins' statement that, "in a capitalist society, there are two basic classes – the capitalists and the workers. They are defined in terms of their respective relationship to production, that is, ownership vs. non-ownership of the means of production." Mel Watkins, "Trade Union Movement," 179.

29 Godfrey and Watkins, *Gordon to Watkins to You*, 118.

30 "Socialism Not Needed Gordon Declares," *Toronto Star*, 16 Apr. 1970.

31 Peter Thomson, "What Will Mr. Trudeau Do about the Yanks?" *Toronto Telegram*, 14 Mar. 1970.

32 Rotstein, intro. to *Reclaiming the Canadian Economy*, xv, xvii, xx.

33 Ibid., xii, and "Political Economy of the Multinational Corporation," in *Precarious Homestead*, 23. Rotstein first advanced this view in "Search for Independence," 146–8.

34 Harry G. Johnson, "Nationalism Irrelevant, but It May Help Rethink Future," *Financial Post*, 15 May 1971.

35 Rotstein, intro. to *Reclaiming the Canadian Economy*, xi.

36 Watkins, "Trade Union Movement," 259.

37 "U.S. Investment Not Needed," *Ottawa Citizen*, 12 Feb. 1972.

38 Smith, *Gentle Patriot*, 356.

39 Rohmer, *Ultimatum*; Fulford, "Care and Feeding of Canadian Paranoia," 7; Creighton, *Takeover*; Purdy, *New Romans*; Lumsden, *Close the 49th Parallel*; Laxer, *(Canada) Ltd.*; Rotstein, *Precarious Homestead*; Rotstein and Lax, *Independence* and *Getting it Back*; Warnock, *Partner to Behemoth*; Levitt, *Silent Surrender*; Pope, *Elephant and the Mouse*; Don Murray, "Ownership Policy 'Obviously Being Watered Down,'" *Montreal Gazette*, 25 Mar. 1972, 37; Hurtig, *At Twilight in the Country*, 154.

40 Fetherling, "Lion in Winter," 56; Wilfred List, "Tely Writer Claims Star Deal Ends Search for New Owners," *Globe and Mail*, 21 Sept. 1971; Douglas Fisher, "Autopsy on a Newspaper," *Toronto Telegram*, 28 Oct. 1971; "Text of Star Letter

Yesterday to Publisher of Telegram," *Toronto Star*, 2 Oct. 1971; interviews with John Bassett, Richard Doyle, Douglas Fisher, and Beland Honderich.

41 Douglas Fisher, "Belling Beland," *Toronto Sun*, 14 Oct. 1987.

42 Heisey, *Great Canadian Stampede*, 23.

43 George Grant, intro. to *Lament for a Nation* (1970), vii.

44 "Gordon Says More Canadians Aware of U.S. Threat," *Toronto Star*, 30 Oct. 1971.

45 WLGP, MG32 B44, vol. 38, file 1, speech to the University of Toronto Teach-In on the Americanization of Canada, 6 Mar. 1970.

46 WLGP, MG32 B44, vol. 37, file 4, budget speech to the House of Commons, 13 June 1963.

47 Smith, *Gentle Patriot*, 351; Gordon, "Last Chance for Canada," 38; "Three Businessmen," 5; Alexander Ross, "Walter Gordon, Prophet, Becoming Honored at Last," *Financial Post*, 21 Mar. 1970, 7; "Gordon Wants Business 51% Canadian-owned," *Toronto Star*, 17 Mar. 1970. NA, WLGP, vol. 38, file 1, speech to the School of Advanced International Studies, Johns Hopkins University, Washington, DC, 23 Apr. 1970; vol. 38, file 2, speech to the Canadian Club of Montreal, 12 Apr. 1971.

Almost twenty years later, in a book dedicated to Gordon, Mel Hurtig wrote of the "Last Chance for Canada." Hurtig, *Betrayal of Canada*, 169, 288.

48 Canada, House of Commons, Standing Committee on External Affairs and National Defence, *Eleventh Report*, 71–2.

49 Ian Wahn interview.

50 Ibid.

51 "It's the Road to Chaos," *Toronto Telegram*, 19 Aug. 1970; "Woolly Guidelines on U.S. Control," *Montreal Star*, 19 Aug. 1970; "Not a Helpful Exercise," *Globe and Mail*, 19 Aug. 1970, 6; Jack McArthur, "Foreign Ownership Report Leaves Us Exactly Nowhere," *Toronto Star*, 30 July 1970, 14.

52 Abraham Rotstein, "Sixties Myopia: The Great Canadian Sellout," review of *Gordon to Watkins to You*, ed. Dave Godfrey and Mel Watkins, *Globe Magazine*, 13 June 1970, 15.

53 Donald S. Macdonald interview.

54 Godfrey and Watkins, *Gordon to Watkins to You*, 23.

55 Hughes, "Progress Report," 2, 4.

56 Newman, "Growing Up Reluctantly," 58.

57 Quoted in Bashevkin, *True Patriot Love*, 23.

58 Elaine Carey, "Independent Canada Trio Enjoys Final Lunch," *Toronto Star*, 18 Dec. 1981; "Students Line Up to Join Gordon after Talk on Independent Canada," *Toronto Star*, 14 Jan. 1971.

59 WLGP, MG32 B44, vol. 30, file 2, Mel Hurtig to Eddie Goodman, 16 Oct. 1973.

60 The list of steering committee members can be found in Resnick, *Land of Cain*, 226–8.

61 Raoul Engel, "Sense of Purpose, No Battle Plan," *Financial Post*, 18 Dec. 1971.

62 "Waffle: A Gentle Tip," 6.

63 Mel Hurtig interview.

64 WLGP, MG32 B44, vol. 30, file 1, E.A. Goodman to Mel Hurtig, 22 June 1973.

65 Ibid., vol. 31, file 5, Committee for an Independent Canada, "Statement of Purpose."

66 Goodman, *Life of the Party*, 294–5.

67 Hurtig interview.

68 WLGP, MG32 B44, vol. 38, file 7, Roger Rickwood and Mark Sandilands, "The Fading of the Committee for an Independent Canada: An Examination of Organizational Rise and Decline," paper presented to the Canadian Political Science Association, Halifax, 29 May 1981.

69 Gordon, *Political Memoir*, 316.

70 WLGP, MG32 B44, vol. 31, file 9, Gordon to Rotstein, 21 July 1971; Committee for an Independent Canada, "Brief to the Prime Minister of Canada and Members of the Cabinet," June 1971.

71 Ibid., Gordon to Rotstein, 21 July 1971; Goodman, *Life of the Party*, 296.

72 WLGP, MG32 B44, vol. 32, file 13, M.G. Hurtig to Denis Smith, 16 Dec. 1971.

73 Gordon was a key figure in the Canada Studies Foundation. Of the $1,241,600 received or pledged in the first year, $25,000 came from Canadian Corporate Management, $37,500 from the Walter L. and Duncan L. Gordon Foundation, $10,000 from the *Toronto Star*, of which Gordon was a director, plus $330,000 from anonymous sources, one of whom was likely Gordon. WLGP, MG32 B44, vol. 25, file 6, "The Canada Studies Foundation: Contributions Received or Pledged" [May 1971].

According to the organization's director, Bernie Hodgetts, "There simply would not be a Canada Studies Foundation without Walter Gordon ... [He] put this whole thing together, secured the key personnel, the finances and provided the inspiration and incentives for the rest of us." Ibid., file 3, Bernie Hodgetts to Gordon, 3 June 1972.

74 Doern and Tomlin, *Faith & Fear*, 209.

75 WLGP, MG32 B44, vol. 30, file 12, Committee for an Independent Canada, "List of Donations," Oct. 1970.

76 Ibid., vol. 38, file 7, "The Committee for an Independent Canada," comments to session of the Canadian Political Science Association, Halifax, 29 May 1981.

77 Cited in Resnick, *Land of Cain*, 147.
78 Graham, *Canada Development Corporation*, 5; Dimma, "Canada Development Corporation," 294.
79 Herb Gray interview.
80 Interviews with Gray and Harvey Lazar; Stanley McDowell, "Joel Bell – The Real Author," *Globe and Mail*, 13 Nov. 1971, B6; Ross, "Joel Bell," 19.
81 Drummond, *Canadian Debate*, 21. Drummond is probably incorrect in his speculation. Gray, who closely supervised the working group, had a reputation for being excessively meticulous and likely read the entire report several times. Lazar interview.
82 Canada, *Foreign Direct Investment*, 437, 462, 493–501.
83 Jack McArthur, "Just Who's Being Paranoiac Now Mr. Trudeau?" *Toronto Star*, 13 Nov. 1971, 50; "The Policies Exist for Independence," *Toronto Star*, 12 Apr. 1972; "The Price of Foreign Investment," *Toronto Star*, 13 Nov. 1971; "Vital Blueprint for Canada," *Kitchener-Waterloo Record*, 15 Nov. 1971.
84 "A Disturbing Document," *Halifax Chronicle-Herald*, 17 Nov. 1971; "Gray Report," *Edmonton Journal*, 16 Nov. 1971; "The Grey Areas in Gray Report," *Regina Leader-Post*, 9 Nov. 1971.
85 Claude Ryan, "Le Rapport Gray et le Québec," *Le Devoir*, 16 Nov. 1971.
86 Ontario, *Report of the Interdepartmental Task Force*, 38, 51–2.
87 Ontario, Legislative Assembly, *Preliminary Report*. See also ibid., *Final Report on Economic Nationalism*, and *Final Report on Cultural Nationalism*.
88 Abraham Rotstein, "Déjà Vu," *Canadian Forum*, May 1972, 2; Goodman, *Life of the Party*, 296; Gordon, "Last Chance for Canada," 38.
89 Goodman, *Life of the Party*, 296–7.
90 Canada, House of Commons, Standing Committee on Finance, Trade and Economic Affairs, *Minutes of Proceedings and Evidence*, 13 June 1972, 36–7.
91 Irvin Lutsky, "Foreign Review Agency a Joke Walter Gordon Says," *Toronto Star*, 21 Jan. 1976. See also NA, Joubin Papers, MG31 J36, vol. 3, Walter Gordon file, Gordon to Joubin, 8 Mar. 1976.
92 "For Absent Friends," *Independencer*, Nov.–Dec. 1977, 5.
93 Sharp, "Canada–U.S. Relations," 13.
94 Sharp, *Which Reminds Me*, 186.
95 McCall and Clarkson, *Trudeau and Our Times*, 2:107, 203.
96 Peter Thomson, "What Will Mr. Trudeau Do about the Yanks?" *Toronto Telegram*, 14 Mar. 1970, 8; "Gordon Wants Business 51% Canadian-owned," *Toronto Star*, 17 Mar. 1970.
97 WLGP, MG32 B44, vol. 38, file 3, "Some Policy Proposals for the Trudeau Minority Government," 6 Nov. 1972.

98 Ibid., file 5, "A Proposal for Rectifying the Present Situation," speech to the American Society for International Law, Washington, DC, 25 Apr. 1974; "500 Foreign Firms should be Canadian Gordon Says in U.S.," *Toronto Star*, 25 Apr. 1974; Gordon, "Proposal for Rectifying the Present Situation," 17–20.

99 Walter L. Gordon, "If There's a Will, Gordon Says This is the Way," *Financial Post*, 5 Oct. 1974, 7; Gordon, *Storm Signals*, 106–8.

100 Gordon, *Storm Signals*, 25.

101 WLGP, MG32 B44, vol. 38, file 5, "Notes for Discussion Meeting," 26 Jan. 1974; vol. 38, file 5, speech to Glendon College, 31 Jan. 1974. In the first speech Gordon suggested that the government buy either Imperial or Gulf; in the second he proposed the purchase of Imperial, Gulf, or Shell.

102 "Nationalize Oil Firms, Gordon Says," *Toronto Star*, 3 May 1975. See also Walker, "Angry Economic Nationalist," 37; NA, NFTSA, Canadian Broadcasting Corporation Collection, *The Fifth Estate*, 3 Oct. 1978, sd. col videocassette, 60 mins., acc. no. 1986-0090, no. VI 8602-0082; WLGP, MG32 B44, vol. 32, file 15, "Part 3," draft chap. for "Reflections on Canada and Its Future," 26 Jan. 1981; vol. 36, file 5, Gordon to M.G. Hurtig, 3 Feb. 1975.

103 WLGP, MG32 B44, vol. 36, file 11, speech to the University of Manitoba Conference on the Politics of Resource Development, 10 Mar. 1976; Gordon, "Regaining Control," 239–41.

104 Foster, *Self-Serve*, 12.

105 Rugman, "Foreign Ownership Debate," 174.

106 Brian Land interview.

107 WLGP, MG32 B44, vol. 32, file 13, "re Denis," 24 Mar. 1973.

108 Gordon, *Troubled Canada*, *Choice for Canada*, *Storm Signals*, *What Is Happening to Canada*.

109 Bashevkin, *True Patriot Love*, 85.

110 Bliss, *Right Honourable Men*, 270.

111 Walter L. Gordon, "An Open Letter to John Turner," *Toronto Star*, 7 Oct. 1986. See also Walter Gordon and Abraham Rotstein, "An Open Letter to the Prime Minister Re: Free Trade with the United States," *Toronto Star*, 23 Jan. 1986, A20.

112 Allan MacEachen interview.

113 James Coutts interview.

114 Confidential sources.

115 Newman, "Why Jean Chrétien Will Never be P.M.," 24.

116 Hughes, "Progress Report," 2.

117 Quoted in ibid.

118 Drummond, *Canadian Debate*, 24.

CHAPTER EIGHT

1 " 'I'm Not a Protectionist,' Gordon Says Expansively," *Vancouver Sun*, 27 Sept. 1966.
2 WLGP, MG32 B44, vol. 38, file 1, speech to the University of Toronto Teach-In on the Americanization of Canada, 6 Mar. 1970.

Bibliography

PRIMARY SOURCES

Archives

University of Alberta Archives
Andrew Stewart Papers

*Archives of the Anglican Diocese
   of Toronto*
Synod Journals

Bank of Canada Archives
Records of the Bank of Canada
Records of the Foreign Exchange
   Control Board
Louis Rasminsky Papers

Diefenbaker Centre Archives
John G. Diefenbaker Papers

Ernst & Young Archives
Clarkson Gordon Papers
Woods Gordon Papers
Woods Gordon Video Collection

Industry Canada
Corporate Reports filed under the
   Corporations and Labour Unions
   Returns Act

*Memorial University of Newfoundland,
   Centre for Newfoundland Studies*
Raymond Gushue Papers

National Archives of Canada
Records of Parliament
Records of Statistics Canada
Records of the Civil Service
   Commission
Records of the Department of
   Finance
Records of the Department of Industry,
   Trade and Commerce
Records of the Department of National
   Defence

Records of the Department of Trade and
Commerce
Records of the Privy Council Office
Records of the Royal Commission on
Administrative Classifications in the
Public Service
Records of the Royal Commission on
Canada's Economic Prospects
Records of the Royal Commission on
Customs and Excise
Records of the Royal Commission on
Price Spreads and Mass Buying
Records of the Tariff Board
Records of the Wartime Prices and Trade
Board

Gordon Blair Papers
Molly and Bruno Bobak Papers
Robert Bothwell Papers
Lionel Chevrier Papers
Brooke Claxton Papers
J.E. Coyne Papers
Robertson Davies Papers
Harold Alexander Dornan Papers
Donald Fleming Papers
Walter L. Gordon Papers
William and Maude Grant Papers
Arnold D.P. Heeney Papers
C.D. Howe Papers
Franc R. Joubin Papers
Henry Erskine Kidd Papers
Eric Kierans Papers
William Lyon Mackenzie King Papers
Judy LaMarsh Papers
Maurice Lamontagne Papers
Liberal Party of Canada Papers
Paul Martin Papers
Robin Mathews Papers
Mossom Boyd & Company Papers

Lester B. Pearson Papers
J.W. Pickersgill Papers
Abraham Rotstein Papers
Louis St Laurent Papers
Maurice Sauvé Papers
Peter Stursberg Papers
Robert Winters Papers

*National Archives of Canada, National
Film, Television and Sound Archives*
Canadian Broadcasting Corporation
Collection
Institute for Research on Public Policy
Collection
Joseph Schull Collection

*Department of National Defence,
Directorate of History*
Records of the Department of National
Defence

Archives of Ontario
Premier's Office Records, Leslie Frost
Administration
Records of the Committee on the
Organization of Government in
Ontario
Records of the Ministry of the Attorney
General

Library of Parliament
Tom Earle interviews
"Study Conference on National
Problems" (transcripts of speeches
and commentaries)
Peter Stursberg interviews

Privy Council Office
Cabinet Minutes, 1966–68

Queen's University Archives
W.C. Clark Papers
Committee for an Independent Canada Papers
T.A. Crerar Papers
John J. Deutsch Papers
Grant Dexter Papers
Donald Gordon Papers
Tom Kent Papers
Kenneth Taylor Papers

Royal Military College, Ex-Cadet Club
H.D.L. Gordon File
Walter Gordon File

University of Toronto Archives
Robert Bothwell Papers
A. Edward Safarian Papers

University of Toronto, Thomas Fisher Rare Book Library
Douglas LePan Papers

Other
Paul Hellyer Personal Papers, draft manuscript of memoirs
Denis Smith Personal Papers, various documents
David Stanley Personal Papers, various documents
Gerald Stoner Personal Papers, various documents
Gerald Wright Personal Papers, interview notes

Interviews

Alex Adamson
Rod Anderson
George Bain
John Bassett
Edwin Beament
Edgar J. Benson
Jack Biddell
Bernard Bonin
Peter Bosa
John Brunton
Marcel Caron
Stephen Clarkson
John Claxton
James Coutts
Marshall Crowe
Keith Davey
William Dimma
Richard Doyle

Gordon Edick
H. Edward English
David Ferguson
Douglas Fisher
Royce Frith
Douglas Fullerton
Kerr Gibson
Dorothy Gill
Alastair Gillespie
Jane Glassco
Eddie Goodman
Elizabeth Gordon
John Gordon
Russell Gormley
Charity Grant
Herb Gray
David Greenspan
Kathleen Griffin

Alvin Hamilton
Anthony Hampson
Walter Harris
Paul Hellyer
Alan Hockin
Beland Honderich
William Hood
Mel Hurtig
Claude Isbister
Tom Kent
William Kilbourn
Brian Land
Harvey Lazar
William Lecky
David MacDonald
Donald S. Macdonald
H.C. Thomas MacDougall
Allan MacEachen
Andrew MacKay
Michael Mackenzie
C.C.I. Merritt
Gildas Molgat
Hartland Molson
George Monk
Kyra Montagu
Hugh Morris
Peter C. Newman
Robert Nielsen
Martin O'Connell
B.B. Osler

Geoffrey Pearson
Doug Peters
J.W. Pickersgill
Michael Pitfield
Louis Rasminsky
Simon Reisman
Gordon Robertson
Mary Robertson
Abraham Rotstein
Edward Safarian
Donald Scott
Mitchell Sharp
S.J. Sinclair
Ross Skinner
David Slater
Arthur Smith
David Smith
Denis Smith
Guy Smith
Irene Spry
Richard Stanbury
David Stanley
G.G.E. Steele
James Steele
Gerald Stoner
Robert Douglas Stuart, Jr
John Turner
Helen Venables
Ian Wahn
Melville Watkins

Newspapers

Brandon Sun
Calgary Herald
Le Devoir (Montreal)
Edmonton Journal
Financial Post
Financial Times
Fredericton Gleaner

Globe and Mail (Toronto)
Halifax Chronicle-Herald
Hamilton Spectator
Kitchener-Waterloo Record
Moncton Times
Montreal Gazette
Montreal Star

New York Times
Ottawa Citizen
Ottawa Journal
La Presse (Montreal)
Regina Leader-Post
Toronto Star
Toronto Telegram

Vancouver Herald
Vancouver Province
Vancouver Sun
Victoria Times
Windsor Star
Winnipeg Free Press
Winnipeg Tribune

Church, School, and Association Publications

Canadian Churchman (Anglican Church)
College Times (Upper Canada College)
Independencer (Committee for an Independent Canada)
R.M.C. Review (Royal Military College)

Works by Walter L. Gordon

"Income Taxes, Succession Duties and Other Direct Taxes in Canada, the United States and Great Britain." *Canadian Chartered Accountant* (Apr. 1938): 261–89.

"Post-War Taxation." *Canadian Chartered Accountant* (Dec. 1944): 329–40.

China – 1959. Toronto: Toronto Daily Star 1959.

"The Challenge of Change." *Industrial Canada* (July 1960): 213–16.

Troubled Canada: The Need for New Domestic Policies. Toronto: McClelland and Stewart 1961.

"Service to Government by the Accounting Profession." *Canadian Chartered Accountant* (July 1961): 47–52.

"We Must Buy Back Canada." *Weekend Magazine*, 2 Mar. 1963, 18, 20–1.

Foreword to *Toronto: No Mean City*, by Eric Arthur. Toronto: University of Toronto Press 1964.

A Choice for Canada: Independence or Colonial Status. Toronto: McClelland and Stewart 1966.

Le Canada à l'heure du choix. Trans. Hélène J. Gagnon. Montreal: Éditions HMH 1966.

"Foreign Control of Canadian Industry." *Queen's Quarterly* 73 (Spring 1966): 1–12.

"The Need to Streamline Our Parliamentary Procedures." *Journal of Liberal Thought* 3 (Winter 1966–67): 161–6.

"Which Choice for Canada?" In Kenneth Bryden et al., *Continentalism vs. Nationalism.* Toronto: Ontario Woodsworth Memorial Foundation 1967.

"Canadian Nationalism." Review of *Nationalism in Canada*, ed. Peter Russell. *Canadian Forum* (Feb. 1967): 250–3.

"The Choice: 'A Free and Independent Canada or a U.S. Colonial Dependency.' "
Star Weekly Magazine, 8 July 1967, 2–4.

"The Future Politician." In Visions 2020: Fifty Canadians in Search of a Future,
ed. Stephen Clarkson. Edmonton: Hurtig 1970.

"The Right to Self-Determination." Canadian Forum (Apr.–May 1971): 27–8.

"Last Chance for Canada." Maclean's, Sept. 1972, 38, 68–70, 72.

"Walter Gordon on Giving Quebec Its Due." Maclean's, Sept. 1972, 72, 76–7.

"A Proposal for Rectifying the Present Situation." American Society of International
Law, Proceedings of the 68th Annual Meeting (1974): 17–20.

Storm Signals: New Economic Policies for Canada. Toronto: McClelland and Stewart
1975.

"Regaining Control of Canada's Resources." In The Big Tough Expensive Job:
Imperial Oil and the Canadian Economy, ed. James Laxer and Anne Martin. Don
Mills, Ont.: Press Porcepic 1976.

A Political Memoir. Toronto: McClelland and Stewart 1977.

"The Quebec Problem." In Divided We Stand, ed. Gary Geddes. Toronto: Peter
Martin 1977.

"There Is a Way to Prevent Canada's Disintegration. Is There a Will?" Maclean's,
30 May 1977, 9.

What Is Happening to Canada. Toronto: McClelland and Stewart 1978.

"Formidable Titan." Review of C.D. Howe: A Biography, by Robert Bothwell and
William Kilbourn. Canadian Forum (Mar. 1980): 31–2.

Foreword to Business Cycles in Canada: The Postwar Experience and Policy
Directions, by Maurice Lamontagne. Ottawa: Canadian Institute for Economic
Policy 1984.

Preface to Nuclear War: The Search for Solutions, ed. Thomas L. Perry and Dianne
DeMille. Vancouver: Physicians for Social Responsibility 1985.

"Epilogue: An Agenda for the 1990s." In Doing It Right: Eminent Canadians
Confront the Future, ed. John C. Munro. Toronto: James Lorimer 1987.

SECONDARY SOURCES

Adams, Eric G. Review of A Choice for Canada, by Walter L. Gordon. Our
Generation (Sept. 1966): 87–9.

Aitkin, Hugh G.J., et al. The American Economic Impact on Canada. Durham, NC:
Duke University Press 1959.

Anderson, Barry L. "Royal Commissions, Economists, and Policy: A Study of
the Economic Advisory Process in Post War Canada." PhD, Duke University
1978.

Anderson, Doris. *To Change the World: A Biography of Pauline Jewett*. Richmond Hill, Ont.: Irwin 1987.

Angus, Ian. *Canadian Bolsheviks: The Early Years of the Communist Party of Canada*. Montreal: Vanguard Publications 1981.

Arlen, Michael J. *Living-Room War*. New York: Viking 1969.

Armstrong, Alvin. *Flora MacDonald*. Toronto: J.M. Dent & Sons 1976.

Aronson, Lawrence Robert. "The Northern Frontier: United States Trade and Investment in Canada 1945–1953." PhD, University of Toronto 1980.

Atwood, Margaret. "Backdrop Addresses Cowboy." In *The New Romans: Candid Canadian Opinions of the U.S.*, ed. Al Purdy. Edmonton: Hurtig 1968.

Auld, D.A.L., ed. *Economics: Contemporary Issues in Canada*. Toronto: Holt, Rinehart and Winston 1972.

Austin, Barbara J. "Life Cycles and Strategy of a Canadian Company: Dominion Textile, 1873–1985." PhD, Concordia University 1985.

Axline, W. Andrew, et al., eds. *Continental Community? Independence and Integration in North America*. Toronto: McClelland and Stewart 1974.

Axworthy, Tom. "Innovation and the Party System: An Examination of the Career of Walter L. Gordon and the Liberal Party." MA, Queen's University 1970.

Axworthy, Thomas S., ed. *Our American Cousins: The United States though Canadian Eyes*. Toronto: James Lorimer 1987.

Azzi, Stephen. "'It was Walter's view': Lester Pearson, the Liberal Party and Economic Nationalism." In *Pearson: The Unlikely Gladiator*, ed. Norman Hillmer. Montreal and Kingston: McGill-Queen's University Press 1999.

Barber, Joseph. *Good Fences Make Good Neighbors: Why the United States Provokes Canadians*. Indianapolis: Bobbs-Merrill 1958.

Barkway, Michael. *Prosperity with Independence*. Toronto: Financial Post 1957.

– "The Fifties: An Ottawa Retrospect." *Waterloo Review*, no. 5 (Summer 1960): 28–39.

– "Why Coyne Was Asked to Resign." *Star Weekly Magazine*, 22 July 1961, 18–20.

Bashevkin, Sylvia B. "Does Public Opinion Matter? The Adoption of Federal Royal Commission and Task Force Recommendations on the National Question 1951–1987." *Canadian Public Administration* 31 (Fall 1988): 390–407.

– *True Patriot Love: The Politics of Canadian Nationalism*. Toronto: Oxford University Press 1991.

Beattie, Kim. *48th Highlanders of Canada, 1891–1928*. Toronto: 48th Highlanders of Canada 1932.

Beckman, Christopher C. *The Foreign Investment Review Agency: Images and Realities*. Ottawa: Conference Board of Canada 1984.

Bennett, S.G. *The 4th Canadian Mounted Rifles 1914–1919.* Toronto: Murray Printing 1926.

Benson, Eugene, and L.W. Conolly. *English-Canadian Theatre.* Toronto: Oxford University Press 1987.

Bercuson, David Jay. *True Patriot: The Life of Brooke Claxton, 1898–1960.* Toronto: University of Toronto Press 1993.

Berger, Carl. *The Sense of Power: Studies in the Ideas of Canadian Imperialism, 1867–1914.* Toronto: University of Toronto Press 1970.

Bird, John. "A Prophet in Ottawa." *Canadian Commentator* (Feb. 1957): 1–2.

– "Canadianizing the u.s. Subsidiaries." *Canadian Commentator* (Nov. 1957): 6–7.

Bissell, Claude. *Halfway up Parnassus: A Personal Account of the University of Toronto 1932–1971.* Toronto: University of Toronto Press 1974.

– *The Young Vincent Massey.* Toronto: University of Toronto Press 1981.

Black, Conrad. *A Life in Progress.* Toronto: Key Porter 1993.

Bliss, Michael. "Canadianizing American Business: The Roots of the Branch Plant." In *Close the 49th Parallel etc: The Americanization of Canada*, ed. Ian Lumsden. Toronto: University of Toronto Press 1970.

– *Years of Change 1967–1985.* Toronto: Grolier 1986.

– *Northern Enterprise: Five Centuries of Canadian Business.* Toronto: McClelland and Stewart 1987.

– *Right Honourable Men: The Descent of Canadian Politics from Macdonald to Mulroney.* Toronto: Harper Collins 1994.

Blyth, C.D., and E.B. Carty. "Non-Resident Ownership of Canadian Industry." *Canadian Journal of Economics and Political Science* 22 (Nov. 1956): 449–60.

Boland. F.J., ed. *Fourth Seminar on Canadian-American Relations at Assumption University of Windsor.* Windsor: Assumption University of Windsor 1962.

Bonin, Bernard. "M. Walter Gordon et l'investissement étranger au Canada." *Actualité économique* 42 (July–Sept. 1966): 345–53.

– *L'Investissement étranger à long terme au Canada.* Montreal: Les presses de l'École des hautes études commerciales 1967.

Booth, Amy. "Agglomerator Inc." In *Financial Post 500: The 1980 Ranking of Canada's 500 Largest Companies.* Toronto: Maclean-Hunter 1980.

Bothwell, Robert. *Nucleus: A History of Atomic Energy of Canada Limited.* Toronto: University of Toronto Press 1988.

– *Canada and the United States: The Politics of Partnership.* Toronto: University of Toronto Press 1992.

– *Pearson: His Life and World.* Toronto: McGraw-Hill Ryerson 1978.

Bothwell, Robert, Ian Drummond, and John English. *Canada since 1945: Power, Politics and Provincialism.* Rev. ed. Toronto: University of Toronto Press 1989.

Bothwell, Robert, and William Kilbourn. *C.D. Howe: A Biography.* Toronto: McClelland and Stewart 1979.

Bowen, Roger. *Innocence Is Not Enough: The Life and Death of Herbert Norman.* Vancouver: Douglas & McIntyre 1986.

Brecher, Irving, and S.S. Reisman. *Canada-United States Economic Relations.* Ottawa: Royal Commission on Canada's Economic Prospects 1957.

Breton, Albert. "The Economics of Nationalism." *Journal of Political Economy* 72 (June 1964): 376–86.

– *The Economic Approach to Nationalism.* Cambridge, Ont.: Collier-Macmillan 1972.

Brewster, Kingman, Jr. *Law and United States Business in Canada.* Washington, DC: Canadian-American Committee 1960.

Brimelow, Peter. *The Patriot Game: National Dreams and Political Realities.* Toronto: Key Porter 1986.

Brock, Thomas L. *The R.M.C. Vintage Class of 1934.* 3 vols. Victoria 1985.

– *"Fight the Good Fight:" Looking in on the Recruit Class at the Royal Military College during a Week in February 1931.* Montreal 1964.

Brossard, Philippe J. *Sold American!* Toronto: Peter Martin 1971.

Brunet, Michel. Review of *A Political Memoir* by Walter Gordon. *Revue d'histoire de l'Amérique française* 33 (June 1979): 83–6.

Bryce, R.B. "William Clifford Clark, 1889–1952." *Canadian Journal of Economics and Political Science* 19 (Aug. 1953): 413–23.

Bryden, P.E. *Planners and Politicians: Liberal Politics and Social Policy, 1957–1968.* Montreal and Kingston: McGill-Queen's University Press 1997.

Bullen, John. "The Ontario Waffle and the Struggle for an Independent Socialist Canada: A Study in Radical Nationalism." MA, University of Ottawa 1979.

Burns, R.M. *The Acceptable Mean: The Tax Rental Agreements 1941–1962.* Toronto: Canadian Tax Foundation 1980.

Cahill, Jack. *John Turner: The Long Run.* Toronto: McClelland and Stewart 1984.

Cameron, Colin. "Canada's Revolt against the United States." *Nation* (New York), 5 Dec. 1953, 460–1.

Cameron, Donald. "The Moral Passion of Economist Abraham Rotstein." *Maclean's,* Apr. 1973, 96.

Campbell, Robert Malcolm. *Grand Illusions: The Politics of the Keynesian Experience in Canada 1945–1975.* Peterborough: Broadview 1987.

– "The Discipline of Democracy: Prime Ministers and Economic Policy." In *Prime Ministers and Premiers: Political Leadership and Public Policy in Canada,* ed. Leslie Pal and David Taras. Scarborough, Ont.: Prentice-Hall 1988.

Canada. *Foreign Direct Investment in Canada* (Gray Report). Ottawa 1972.

Canada. Bank of Canada. *Annual Report of the Governor to the Minister of Finance.* Ottawa 1960–61.

Canada. Department of Labour. *Labour Organization in Canada.* Ottawa 1926.

Canada. Dominion Bureau of Statistics. *Canada's International Investment Position, Selected Years 1926 to 1949.* Ottawa: King's Printer 1950.

– *Canada's International Investment Position 1926–1954.* Ottawa: Queen's Printer 1956.

– *Trade of Canada 1957.* Vol. 1, *Summary and Analytical Tables.* Ottawa: Queen's Printer 1959.

– *Historical Catalogue of Dominion Bureau of Statistics Publications 1918–1960.* Ottawa 1967.

– *Inter-Corporate Ownership 1965.* Ottawa 1969.

Canada. House of Commons. *Debates.* 1945–75.

– Bill C-120: An Act respecting Banks and Banking. First Reading, 6 May 1965. Ottawa: Queen's Printer 1965.

– Bill C-222: An Act respecting Banks and Banking. First Reading, 7 July 1966. Ottawa: Queen's Printer 1966.

Canada. House of Commons. Special Committee on Price Spreads and Mass Buying. *Proceedings and Evidence.* Ottawa: King's Printer 1934.

Canada. House of Commons. Standing Committee on External Affairs. *Minutes of Proceedings and Evidence.* Ottawa: Queen's Printer 1956.

– *Eleventh Report of the Standing Committee on External Affairs and National Defence Respecting Canada–U.S. Relations* (Wahn Report). Ottawa: Queen's Printer 1970.

Canada. House of Commons. Standing Committee on Finance, Trade and Economic Affairs. *Proceedings: Decennial Revision of the Bank Acts.* Ottawa: Queen's Printer 1967.

– *Minutes of Proceedings and Evidence.* Ottawa: Queen's Printer 1972.

Canada. Privy Council Office. *Foreign Ownership and the Structure of Canadian Industry: Report of the Task Force on the Structure of Canadian Industry* (Watkins Report). Ottawa: Queen's Printer 1968.

– *Gaikoku shihon to kokumin keizai: Watokinsu hokoku.* Tokyo: Perikan sha 1969.

Canada. Royal Commission on Administrative Classifications in the Public Service. *Report.* Ottawa: King's Printer 1946.

Canada. Royal Commission on Canada's Economic Prospects (Gordon Commission). *Preliminary Report.* Ottawa 1956.

– *Final Report.* Ottawa 1957.

Canada. Royal Commission on Publications. *Report.* Ottawa: Queen's Printer 1961.

Canada. Royal Commission on the Automotive Industry. *Report*. Ottawa: Queen's Printer 1961.

Canada. Royal Military College. *Regulations and Instructions 1922*. Ottawa: King's Printer 1923.

Canada. Senate. *Debates*. 1965.

Canada. Statistics Canada. *Inter-Corporate Ownership 1969*. Ottawa 1971.

– *National Income and Expenditure Accounts: Annual Estimates 1926–1986*. Ottawa 1988.

– *Canada's International Investment Position: Historical Statistics 1926 to 1992*. Ottawa 1993.

– *The Consumer Price Index, May 1993*. Ottawa 1993.

– *Canadian Economic Observer, Historical Statistical Supplement 1993/94*. Ottawa 1994.

– *The Consumer Price Index, December 1994*. Ottawa 1995.

Canada. Tariff Board. *Report by the Tariff Board Relative to the Investigation Ordered by the Minister of Finance Respecting Cotton and Cotton Products*. Ottawa: Queen's Printer 1958.

Canadian-American Committee. *Recent Canadian and U.S. Government Actions Affecting U.S. Investment in Canada*. Washington, DC: Canadian-American Committee 1964.

Canadian Corporate Management. *Annual Report*. Toronto 1966–85.

"Canadians Feel American Influence Is Increasing." *Weekend Magazine*, 4 Feb. 1978, 3.

Canadian Public Figures on Tape. Audiocassettes. Toronto: Ontario Institute for Studies in Education 1973.

Carr, D.W. *Recovering Canada's Nationhood*. Ottawa: Canada Publishing 1971.

Carty, R. Kenneth, and W. Peter Ward, eds. *National Politics and Community in Canada*. Vancouver: University of British Columbia Press 1986.

Cayley, David. *George Grant in Conversation*. Concord, Ont.: House of Anansi 1995.

Chodos, Robert, Rae Murphy, and Eric Hamovitch. *The Unmaking of Canada: The Hidden Theme in Canadian History since 1945*. Toronto: James Lorimer 1991.

Christian, William. *George Grant: A Biography*. Toronto: University of Toronto Press 1993.

Clark, Marsh. "Why the First National City Bank Took the Rap in Canada." *Fortune*, Apr. 1967, 75, 78.

Clarke, Frank. "Divided Within: Economic Nationalism within the Liberal Party of Canada 1963–1968." MA, University of Waterloo 1992.

Clarkson, Stephen. "Anti-Nationalism in Canada: The Ideology of Mainstream Economics." *Canadian Review of Studies in Nationalism* 5 (Spring 1978): 45–65.

Clarkson, Stephen, ed. *An Independent Foreign Policy for Canada?* Toronto: McClelland and Stewart 1968.

Clement, Wallace. *The Canadian Corporate Elite: An Analysis of Economic Power.* Toronto: McClelland and Stewart 1975.

Clippingdale, Richard T. "J.S. Willison and Canadian Nationalism." Canadian Historical Association, *Historical Papers* (1969): 74–93.

Cole, Douglas L. "John S. Ewart and Canadian Nationalism." Canadian Historical Association, *Historical Papers* (1969): 62–73.

Cole, Taylor. *The Canadian Bureaucracy: A Study of Canadian Civil Servants and Other Public Employees.* Durham, NC: Duke University Press 1949.

Cook, Ramsay. "Not Right, Not Left, but Forward." *Canadian Forum* (Feb. 1961): 241–2.

– *The Politics of John W. Dafoe of the Free Press.* Toronto: University of Toronto Press 1963.

– "A Nationalist Intellectual behind Every Maple Tree." *Saturday Night*, Apr. 1970, 19–21.

– "Loyalism, Technology and Canada's Fate." *Journal of Canadian Studies* 5 (Aug. 1970): 50–60.

– *The Maple Leaf Forever: Essays on Nationalism and Politics in Canada.* Toronto: Macmillan 1971.

– "The Nationalism of Walter Gordon." Review of *A Political Memoir* by Walter Gordon. *Saturday Night*, Jan./Feb. 1978, 75–6.

– *Canada, Quebec, and the Uses of Nationalism.* Toronto: McClelland and Stewart 1986.

Cook, Terry. "George R. Parkin and the Concept of Britannic Idealism." *Journal of Canadian Studies* 10 (Aug. 1975): 15–31.

Copeman, W.S.C. *A Short History of the Gout and the Rheumatic Diseases.* Berkeley: University of California Press 1964.

Cottam, K. Jean. *Canadian Universities: American Takeover of the Mind?* Toronto: Gall Publications 1974.

Coyne, James E. *Living within Our Means.* Winnipeg Free Press pamphlet no. 64. Winnipeg: Winnipeg Free Press 1960.

– "Living within Our Means: The Goal of Economic Policy." *Vital Speeches of the Day*, 1 Apr. 1960, 356–61.

– "U.S. Trade, Capital Export Policies Don't Help Canada." *Commercial and Financial Chronicle*, 30 Mar. 1961, 3, 37–8.

The Crazy Twenties 1920/1930. Toronto: Natural Science of Canada 1978.

Crean, S.M. *Who's Afraid of Canadian Culture?* Don Mills, Ont.: General Publishing 1976.

Creighton, Donald G. "Towards the Discovery of Canada." *University of Toronto Quarterly* 25 (Apr. 1956): 269–82.
– "Presidential Address." Canadian Historical Association, *Report of the Annual Meeting* (1957): 1–12.
– "Decline and Fall of the Empire of the St. Lawrence." Canadian Historical Association, *Historical Papers* (1969): 14–25.
– *Canada's First Century*. Toronto: Macmillan 1970.
– "Reflections on the Americanization of Canada." *Laurentian University Review* 3 (Feb. 1971): 101–5.
– "Watching the Sun Quietly Set on Canada." *Maclean's*, Nov. 1971, 29–30, 83–4, 86, 89–90.
– "Canada and the Cold War." In *Towards the Discovery of Canada: Selected Essays*. Toronto: Macmillan 1972.
– *The Forked Road: Canada 1939–1957*. Toronto: McClelland and Stewart 1976.
– *Takeover*. Toronto: McClelland and Stewart 1978.
Creighton, Philip. *A Sum of Yesterdays*. Toronto: Institute of Chartered Accountants of Ontario 1984.
Cummings, H.R. *Early Days in Haliburton*. Toronto: Ontario Department of Lands and Forests 1962.
Dales, J.H. *The Protective Tariff in Canada's Development*. Toronto: University of Toronto Press 1966.
Daub, Mervin. *Canadian Economic Forecasting in a World Where All's Unsure*. Kingston: McGill-Queen's University Press 1987.
Davey, Keith. *The Rainmaker: A Passion for Politics*. Toronto: Stoddart 1986.
Dickey, John Sloan. "The Relationship in Rhetoric and Reality: Merchant-Heeney Revisited." *International Journal* 27 (Spring 1972): 172–84.
– *Canada and the American Presence: The U.S. Interest in an Independent Canada*. New York: New York University Press 1975.
Dimma, William Andrew. "The Canada Development Corporation: Diffident Experiment on a Large Scale." DBA, Harvard 1973.
"Disturbing Document." *Industry*, Mar. 1968, 1–2.
Dobbs, Kildare. "The Uniquely Cool Nationalism of Abraham Rotstein." *Maclean's*, Apr. 1973, 25–8.
Dobrzensky, Leopolda L. *Fragments of a Dream: Pioneering in Dysart Township and Haliburton Village*. 3rd. ed. Dysart, Ont.: Municipality of Dysart 1992.
Doern, G. Bruce, and Brian W. Tomlin. *Faith and Fear: The Free Trade Story*. Toronto: Stoddart 1991.
Doran, Charles F., and James Patrick Sewell. "Anti-Americanism in Canada?" *Annals of the American Academy of Political and Social Science* 497 (May 1988): 105–19.

Doran, Charles F., and John H. Sigler, eds. *Canada and the United States: Enduring Friendship, Persistent Stress*. Englewood Cliffs, NJ: Prentice-Hall 1985.

Drummond, Ian M. Review of *Troubled Canada* by Walter Gordon. *Canadian Forum* (Mar. 1962): 283–4.

– "Nationalists and Economists." *Canadian Forum* (Dec. 1964): 193–5.

– "Centennial Feelings and Economic Nationalism." *Canadian Forum* (Feb. 1967): 246–7.

– *The Canadian Debate about Foreign Investment 1945–1972*. Canada House Lecture Series no. 37. London: Canada House 1976.

– Review of *A Political Memoir* by Walter Gordon. *International Journal* 33 (Winter 1977–78): 265–6.

Dunn, Robert M., Jr. "Canada and Its Economic Discontents." *Foreign Affairs* 52 (Oct. 1973): 119–40.

Eastman, H.C. "Why the Economists Dislike Coyne." *Saturday Night*, 7 Jan. 1961, 24.

– "The Canadian Tariff and the Efficiency of the Canadian Economy." *American Economic Review* 54 (May 1964): 437–48.

Eayrs, James. *Canada in World Affairs, October 1955 to June 1957*. Toronto: Oxford University Press 1959.

– "The Neurotic Nationalism of Mr. Gordon's Budget." *Family Herald*, 18 July 1963, 26.

– "The Road from Ogdensburg." *Canadian Forum* (Feb. 1971): 364–6.

– "The Story of Walter and Mike." Review of *Gentle Patriot* by Denis Smith. *Saturday Night*, Dec. 1973, 37–8, 40.

Eden, Lorraine. "Foreign Direct Investment in Canada: Charting a New Policy Direction." *Canadian Foreign Policy* 2 (Winter 1994): 43–60.

Edmonds, Alan. *The Years of Protest 1960–1970*. Toronto: Natural Science of Canada 1979.

"Elizabeth Marjorie Leith Gordon." Ontario Gallery of Art *Journal*, Jan.–Feb. 1995, 15.

Emberley, Peter C. Foreword to *Lament for a Nation: The Defeat of Canadian Nationalism* by George Grant. Carleton Library New Edition. Ottawa: Carleton University Press 1995.

English, H. Edward. *Industrial Structure in Canada's International Competitive Position*. Montreal: Private Planning Association of Canada 1964.

– "Are these Jeremiahs Really Necessary?" *International Journal* 21 (Summer 1966): 354–65.

– "The Larger Issues of Foreign Ownership." *Canadian Banker*, Mar./Apr. 1970, 18–22.

English, John. *Years of Growth 1948–1967*. Toronto: Grolier 1986.

– *Shadow of Heaven. The Life of Lester Pearson*, vol. 1, *1897–1948*. Toronto: Lester & Orpen Dennys 1989.

– *The Worldly Years. The Life of Lester Pearson*, vol. 2, *1949–1972*. Toronto: Alfred A. Knopf 1992.

– "Speaking Out on Vietnam 1965." In *Canadian Foreign Policy: Selected Cases*, ed. Don Munton and John Kirton. Scarborough, Ont.: Prentice-Hall 1992.

English, John, and Norman Hillmer. "Canada's Alliances." *Revue internationale d'histoire militaire*, no. 51 (1982): 31–52.

Ex-Cadet. "The Royal Military College of Canada." *Canadian Defence Quarterly*, Apr. 1925, 239–46.

Fayerweather, John. "The Mercantile Bank Affair." *Columbia Journal of World Business* 6 (Nov.–Dec. 1971): 41–50.

– *Foreign Investment in Canada: Prospects for National Policy*. White Plains, NY: International Arts and Sciences Press 1973.

– *The Mercantile Bank Affair: A Case Study of Canadian Nationalism and a Multinational Firm*. New York: New York University Press 1974.

Ferguson, Barry. *Remaking Liberalism: The Intellectual Legacy of Adam Shortt, O.D. Skelton, W.C. Clark and W.A. Mackintosh, 1890–1925*. Montreal: McGill-Queen's University Press 1993.

Ferguson, G.V. "Likely Trends in Canadian-American Political Relations." *Canadian Journal of Economics and Political Science* 22 (Nov. 1956): 438–48.

Ferns, Thomas H. "John Leith Counsell." In *Dictionary of Hamilton Biography*, vol. 3, ed. Thomas Melville Bailey. Hamilton: W.L. Griffin 1992.

Fetherling, Douglas. "The Lion in Winter." *Saturday Night*, May 1983, 50–9.

– *Travels by Night: A Memoir of the Sixties*. Toronto: Lester 1994.

– *Way Down Deep in the Belly of the Beast*. Toronto: Lester 1996.

Financial Post. *Survey of Industrials 1959*. Montreal: Financial Post 1959.

"The First." *Last Post*, May 1972, 28–33.

FitzGerald, James. *Old Boys: The Powerful Legacy of Upper Canada College*. Toronto: Macfarlane Walter & Ross 1994.

Fleming, Donald M. *So Very Near: The Political Memoirs of the Honourable Donald M. Fleming*. 2 vols. Toronto: McClelland and Stewart 1985.

Fleming, R.B. *The Railway King of Canada: Sir William Mackenzie, 1849–1923*. Vancouver: University of British Columbia Press 1991.

Fletcher, F.J., and R.J. Drummond. *Canadian Attitude Trends 1960–1978*. Institute for Research on Public Policy Working Paper no. 4. Montreal: Institute for Research on Public Policy 1979.

"For Absent Friends." Committee for an Independent Canada. *The Independencer*, Nov.–Dec. 1977, 1, 4–5.

Forster, Donald. "The Economy." In *Canadian Annual Review for 1965*, ed. John
    Saywell. Toronto: University of Toronto Press 1966.
Foster, Peter. *Self-Serve: How Petro-Canada Pumped Canadians Dry*. Toronto:
    Macfarlane Walter & Ross 1992.
Foster, Tony. *Meeting of Generals*. Toronto: Methuen 1986.
Fox, Paul. "The Teach-In: Education or Propaganda? (1)" *Canadian Forum*
    (Nov. 1965): 172–3.
Fraser, Blair. "Will Ottawa Open The Cashbox?" *Maclean's*, 1 Oct. 1955, 9, 95.
–   "How Walter Gordon Has Recovered from Parliament's Biggest Pratfall."
    Maclean's, 25 July 1964, 2–3.
–   "The Sharp/Gordon Debate." *Maclean's*, 23 July 1966, 8–9, 36–8.
–   *The Search for Identity: Canada 1945–1967*. Toronto: Doubleday 1967.
–   *"Blair Fraser Reports:" Selections 1944–1968*. Ed. John Fraser and Graham
    Fraser. Toronto: Macmillan 1969.
French, William. "Walter Gordon: He's Changing Your Way of Life." *Globe
    Magazine*, 11 May 1957, 12–13.
Fulford, Robert. "The Angry Loser." *Canadian*, 22 Jan. 1966, 6–9.
–   "The Care and Feeding of Canadian Paranoia." *Saturday Night*, Feb. 1974, 7–8.
Fullerton, Douglas H. *The Dangerous Delusion: Quebec's Independence Obsession*.
    Toronto: McClelland and Stewart 1978.
–   *Graham Towers and His Times*. Toronto: McClelland and Stewart 1986.
Galbraith, John Kenneth. *A Life in Our Times*. Boston: Houghton Mifflin 1981.
–   *A View from the Stands*. Boston: Houghton Mifflin 1986.
Gallup, George H. *The Gallup Poll: Public Opinion 1935–1971*. New York: Random
    House 1972.
Gayn, Mark. "Walter Gordon: So Much Woe in So Little Time." *Star Weekly*, 20 July
    1963, 12, 14–15.
Gibson, Frederick W., and Barbara Robertson, eds. *Ottawa at War: The Grant Dexter
    Memoranda 1939–1945*. Winnipeg: Manitoba Record Society 1994.
Gibson, J.D. "The Changing Influence of the United States on the Canadian
    Economy." *Canadian Journal of Economics and Political Science* 22 (Nov. 1956):
    421–36.
Gigantes, Terry. Review of *A Choice for Canada* by Walter L. Gordon. *Our
    Generation* (Sept. 1966): 84–7.
Girard, Charlotte S.M. *Canada in World Affairs 1963–1965*. Toronto: Canadian
    Institute of International Affairs, n.d.
Giroday, Jean Boyer de la. *Canadian Taxation and Foreign Investment*. Toronto:
    Canadian Tax Foundation 1955.

Glassco, J. Grant. *Certain Aspects of Taxation Relating to Investment in Canada by Non-Residents*. Ottawa: Royal Commission on Canada's Economic Prospects 1956.

Glazebrook, G.P.deT. "Some Thoughts on Canadian Nationalism." In *Empire and Nations: Essays in Honour of Frederic H. Soward*, ed. Harvey L. Dyck and H. Peter Krosby. Toronto: University of Toronto Press 1969.

Godfrey, Dave. *Death Goes Better with Coca-Cola*. Toronto: House of Anansi 1967.

– "Man of Honour." Review of *A Political Memoir* by Walter Gordon. *Canadian Forum* (Feb. 1978): 31–3.

Godfrey, Dave, and Mel Watkins, eds. *Gordon to Watkins to You, A Documentary: The Battle for Control of Our Economy*. Toronto: new press 1970.

Godfrey, John F. Review of *A Political Memoir* by Walter Gordon. Liberal Party of Canada. *Dialogue*, Oct.–Nov. 1977, 14.

Gonick, C.W. "The Political Economy of Canadian Independence." *Canadian Dimension* (May–June 1967): 12–19.

Goodman, Eddie. *Life of the Party: The Memoirs of Eddie Goodman*. Toronto: Key Porter 1988.

Gordon, H.D. Lockhart. "Fifty Years Ago." *Canadian Chartered Accountant*, July 1961, 96–8.

Gordon, H. Scott. *The Economists versus the Bank of Canada*. Toronto: Ryerson 1961.

Grady, Patrick Michael. "The Canadian Exemption from the United States Interest Equalization Tax." PhD, Toronto 1973.

Grafftey, Heward. *Lessons from the Past: From Dief to Mulroney*. Montreal: Eden Press 1987.

– *Why Canadians Get the Politicians and Governments They Don't Want*. Toronto: Stoddart 1991.

Graham, Dominick. *The Price of Command: A Biography of General Guy Simonds*. Toronto: Stoddart 1993.

Graham, Michael R. *Canada Development Corporation: A Corporate Background Report*. Ottawa: Royal Commission on Corporate Concentration 1976.

Graham, W.R. "Liberal Nationalism in the Eighteen-Seventies." Canadian Historical Association, *Report of the Annual Meeting* (1946): 101–19.

Granatstein, J.L. *The Ottawa Men: The Civil Service Mandarins 1935–1957*. Toronto: Oxford University Press 1982.

– *Canada 1957–1967: The Years of Uncertainty and Innovation*. Toronto: McClelland and Stewart 1986.

– *How Britain's Weakness Forced Canada into the Arms of the United States*. Toronto: University of Toronto Press 1989.

– *The Generals: The Canadian Army's Senior Commanders in the Second World War.* Toronto: Stoddart 1993.

– *Yankee Go Home? Canadians and Anti-Americanism.* Toronto: HarperCollins 1996.

Granatstein, J.L., and Robert Bothwell. *Pirouette: Pierre Trudeau and Canadian Foreign Policy.* Toronto: University of Toronto Press 1990.

Granatstein, J.L., and Norman Hillmer. *For Better or For Worse: Canada and the United States to the 1990s.* Toronto: Copp Clark Pitman 1991.

Grant, George. *Lament for a Nation: The Defeat of Canadian Nationalism.* Toronto: McClelland and Stewart 1965. Carleton Library No. 50. Toronto: McClelland and Stewart 1970. Carleton Library new ed., with a foreword by Peter Emberley. Ottawa: Carleton University Press 1995.

– "Protest and Technology." In *Revolution and Response: Selections from the Toronto International Teach-in*, ed. Charles Hanly. Toronto: McClelland and Stewart 1966.

– *Technology and Empire: Perspectives on North America.* Toronto: House of Anansi 1969.

Grant, Judith Skelton. *Robertson Davies: Man of Myth.* Toronto: Viking 1994.

Grant, W.L. "Current Events." *Queen's Quarterly* 19 (Oct.–Dec. 1911): 170–80.

– "Truncated Imperialism." *Willisons Monthly*, Dec. 1927, 250–1.

Gray, Herb. "Good Fences: Controlling Foreign Investment." *Canadian Forum* (June 1975): 8–13.

– Review of *Storm Signals* by Walter Gordon. Liberal Party of Canada. *Dialogue*, Winter 1976, 21.

Grubel, Herbert G. *Citation Counts for Economists Specializing in International Economics: A Tribute to the Memory of Harry G. Johnson.* Burnaby: Simon Fraser University 1978.

Guenther, Victor J. *American Investment: Development or Domination?* Toronto: J.M. Dent & Sons 1971.

Gwyn, Richard. *The 49th Paradox: Canada in North America.* Toronto: McClelland and Stewart 1985.

"H.C. Hindmarsh Dies, Toronto Star President." *Editor and Publisher*, 29 Dec. 1956, 50.

Hackett, Robert. "Pie in the Sky: A History of the Ontario Waffle." *Canadian Dimension* (Oct.–Nov. 1980): 1–72.

Hahlo, H.R., J. Graham Smith, and Richard W. Wright, eds. *Nationalism and the Multinational Enterprise: Legal, Economic and Managerial Aspects.* Dobbs Ferry, NY: A.W. Sijthoff Leiden 1973.

Hanel, Petr, and Kristian Palda. *Innovation and Export Performance in Canadian Manufacturing.* Ottawa: Economic Council of Canada 1981.

Harkness, Ross. *J.E. Atkinson of the Star.* Toronto: University of Toronto Press 1963.

Hartle, Douglas G. *The Revenue Budget Process of the Government of Canada.* Toronto: Canadian Tax Foundation 1982.

Heeney, Arnold D.P. *The Things That Are Caesar's: The Memoirs of a Canadian Public Servant.* Ed. Brian D. Heeney. Toronto: University of Toronto Press 1972.

Heeney, Arnold D.P., and Livingston T. Merchant. *Canada and the United States: Principles for Partnership.* Ottawa 1965.

Heisey, Alan. *The Great Canadian Stampede: The Rush to Economic Nationalism – Right or Wrong.* Toronto: Griffin House 1973.

Helliwell, John F. "The Balance of Payments: A Survey of Harry Johnson's Contributions." *Canadian Journal of Economics* 11, suppl. (Nov. 1978): s55–s86.

Hellyer, Paul. *Damn the Torpedoes: My Fight to Unify Canada's Armed Forces.* Toronto: McClelland and Stewart 1990.

Hero, Alfred Oliver, Jr, and Louis Balthazar. *Contemporary Quebec and the United States 1960–1985.* Lanham, Md.: Centre for International Affairs, Harvard University 1988.

Hertzman, Lewis, John Warnock, and Thomas Hockin. *Alliances and Illusions: Canada and the NATO-NORAD Question.* Edmonton: Hurtig 1969.

Hillmer, Norman. "The Anglo-Canadian Neurosis: The Case of O.D. Skelton." In *Britain and Canada: Survey of a Changing Relationship*, ed. Peter Lyon. London: Frank Cass 1976.

– "The Canadian Diplomatic Tradition." In *Canadian Culture: International Dimensions*, ed. Andrew Fenton Cooper. Toronto: Canadian Institute of International Affairs 1985.

Hillmer, Norman, and J.L. Granatstein. *Empire to Umpire: Canada and the World to the 1990s.* Toronto: Copp Clark Longman 1994.

Hillmer, Norman, ed. *Pearson: The Unlikely Gladiator.* Montreal and Kingston: McGill-Queen's University Press 1999.

Hillmer, Norman, and Garth Stevenson, eds. *Foremost Nation: Canadian Foreign Policy in a Changing World.* Toronto: McClelland and Stewart 1977.

Hodgetts, J.E. et al. *The Biography of an Institution: The Civil Service Commission of Canada 1908–1967.* Montreal: McGill-Queen's University Press 1972.

Hollander, Paul. *Anti-Americanism: Critiques at Home and Abroad 1965–1990.* New York: Oxford University Press 1992.

Holmes, John W. "Merchant-Heeney Revisited: A Sentimental View." *America's Alliances and Canadian-American Relations*, ed. Lauren McKinsey and Kim Richard Nossal. Toronto: Summerhill 1988.

Horn, Michiel. *The League for Social Reconstruction: Intellectual Origins of the Democratic Left in Canada 1930–1942.* Toronto: University of Toronto Press 1980.

Horowitz, Gad. "Tories, Socialists and the Demise of Canada." *Canadian Dimension* (May–June 1965): 12–15.

Horton, Donald J. *André Laurendeau: French-Canadian Nationalist 1912–1968.* Toronto: Oxford University Press 1992.

Howard, Richard B. *Upper Canada College, 1829–1979.* Toronto: Macmillan 1979.

Hughes, Barry Conn. "Progress Report on *Our* War of Independence." *Canadian Magazine*, 1 Feb. 1975, 2, 4–5.

Hurtig, Mel. *The Betrayal of Canada.* Toronto: Stoddart 1991.

– *At Twilight in the Country: Memoirs of a Canadian Nationalist.* Toronto: Stoddart 1996.

Hutcheson, John. "Walter Gordon." *Canadian Forum* (May 1987): 5.

Hutchison, Bruce. *Canada: Tomorrow's Giant.* Toronto: Longmans, Green & Company 1957.

– "Why Canadians Are Turning Anti-American." *Harper's*, May 1958, 46–50.

– *The Far Side of the Street.* Toronto: Macmillan 1976.

Hymer, Stephen. *The Multinational Corporation, A Radical Approach: Papers by Stephen Herbert Hymer.* Ed. Robert B. Cohen et al. Cambridge: Cambridge University Press 1979.

Inglis, Alex I. "Loring C. Christie and the Imperial Idea: 1919–1926." *Journal of Canadian Studies* 7 (May 1972): 19–27.

Innis, Harold A. "Great Britain, the United States and Canada." In *Changing Concepts of Time.* Toronto: University of Toronto Press 1952.

Innis, Hugh. *Americanization.* Toronto: McGraw-Hill Ryerson 1972.

Irvine, Russell B. "Ottawa: the First Session." *Canadian Forum* (July 1963): 75.

Jackson, Eric, ed. *The Great Canadian Debate: Foreign Ownership.* Toronto: McClelland and Stewart 1975.

Jewett, Pauline. "The Wartime Prices and Trade Board: A Case Study in Canadian Public Administration." PhD, Harvard 1950.

– "The Menace is the Message." In *An Independent Foreign Policy for Canada?* ed. Stephen Clarkson. Toronto: McClelland and Stewart 1968.

Johnson, Harry G. "Canada's Economic Prospects." *Canadian Journal of Economics and Political Science* 24 (Feb. 1958): 104–10.

– "Problems of Canadian Nationalism." *International Journal* 16 (Summer 1961): 238–49.

– *The Canadian Quandary: Economic Problems and Policies.* Toronto: McGraw Hill 1963.

– "Economic Nationalism in Canadian Policy." *Lloyd's Bank Review* 74 (Oct. 1964): 25–35.

– "Canadian-American Economic Integration: A Time for Decision." *Journal of Canadian Studies* 1 (Aug. 1966): 31–6.

– "The Watkins Report." *International Journal* 23 (Autumn 1968): 615–22.

– *Technology and Economic Interdependence.* London: Macmillan 1975.

– *The Canadian Quandary: Economic Problems and Policies.* Carleton Library No. 106. Toronto: McClelland and Stewart 1977.

Johnson, Harry G., ed. *Economic Nationalism in Old and New States.* Chicago: University of Chicago Press 1967.

Jutras, Catherine. "Cancorp: A *Very* Canadian Company." *Canadian Business*, June 1980, 58–60, 65–6, 68, 70, 72.

Kearns, Lionel. "The Parable of the Seventh Seal." In *The New Romans: Candid Canadian Opinions of the U.S.*, ed. Al Purdy. Edmonton: Hurtig 1968.

Keeley, James Francis. "Constraints on Canadian International Economic Policy." PhD, Stanford 1980.

– "Cast in Concrete for All Time? The Negotiation of the Auto Pact." *Canadian Journal of Political Science* 16 (June 1983): 281–98.

Keenleyside, Terence A., Lawrence LeDuc, and J. Alex Murray. "Public Opinion and Canada-United States Economic Relations." *Behind the Headlines* 35, no. 4 (1976).

Keirstead, B.S. *Canada in World Affairs, September 1951 to October 1953.* Toronto: Oxford University Press 1956.

Kendle, John. *The Round Table Movement and Imperial Union.* Toronto: University of Toronto Press 1975.

Kent, Tom. *The American Boom in Canada.* Winnipeg Free Press Pamphlet no. 55. Winnipeg 1957.

– *Inside the Gordon Report.* Winnipeg Free Press Pamphlet no. 57. Winnipeg 1958.

– *Social Policy for Canada: Towards a Philosophy of Social Security.* Ottawa: Policy Press 1962.

– *A Public Purpose: An Experience of Liberal Opposition and Canadian Government.* Montreal and Kingston: McGill-Queen's University Press 1988.

Kettle, John. *The Big Generation.* Toronto: McClelland and Stewart 1980.

Kidd, Bruce. "Canada's National Sport." In *Close the 49th Parallel etc: The Americanization of Canada*, ed. Ian Lumsden. Toronto: University of Toronto Press 1970.

Kierans, Eric W. *Challenge of Confidence: Kierans on Canada.* Toronto: McClelland and Stewart 1967.

– "Towards a New National Policy." *Canadian Forum* (Jan.–Feb. 1972): 52–5.

– *Globalism and the Nation-State.* Montreal: CBC Enterprises 1984.

Kilbourn, William. *Toronto Remembered: A Celebration of the City.* Toronto: Stoddart 1984.

Kindleberger, Charles P. "All about United States Foreign Investment." *Economic Development and Cultural Change* 12 (Apr. 1964): 325–8.

– *The Life of An Economist: An Autobiography.* Cambridge, Mass.: Basil Blackwell 1991.

Knapp, Robert Whelan. "United States Direct Investment in Canada 1950–1960." PhD, University of Michigan 1963.

Knox, Frank A. "Canadian Capital Movements and the Canadian Balance of International Payments, 1900–1934." In Herbert Marshall et al., *Canadian-American Industry: A Study in International Investment.* Toronto: Ryerson 1936.

– "United States Capital Investments in Canada." *Papers and Proceedings of the American Economic Association* 47 (May 1957): 596–609.

Kostash, Myrna. *Long Way from Home: The Story of the Sixties Generation in Canada.* Toronto: James Lorimer 1980.

Krause, Lawrence B. "Discussion." *American Economic Review* 54 (May 1964): 471–9.

Kresl, Peter Karl. "The 'New Nationalism' and Economic Rationality." *American Review of Canadian Studies* 4 (Spring 1974): 2–19.

– "Before the Deluge: Canadians on Foreign Ownership 1920–1955." *American Review of Canadian Studies* 6 (Spring 1976): 86–125.

– "Nationalism and Economic Policy in Canada and Norway." In *Canada and the Nordic Countries*, ed. Jorn Carlsen and Bengt Steijffert. Lund: Lund University Press 1988.

LaMarsh, Judy. *Memoirs of a Bird in a Gilded Cage.* Toronto: McClelland and Stewart 1968.

"The Last Showdown." *Time*, 31 Dec. 1956, 57.

Laxer, Gordon. *Open for Business: The Roots of Foreign Ownership in Canada.* Toronto: Oxford University Press 1989.

Laxer, James. *The Energy Poker Game: The Politics of the Continental Resources Deal.* Toronto: new press 1970.

Laxer, James and Robert. *The Liberal Idea of Canada: Pierre Trudeau and the Question of Canada's Survival.* With a foreword by George Grant. Toronto: James Lorimer 1977.

Laxer, Robert M., ed. *(Canada) Ltd.: The Political Economy of Dependency.* Toronto: McClelland and Stewart 1973.

Layton, Jack G. "Capital and the Canadian State: Foreign Investment Policy, 1957–1982." PhD, York 1983.

Leacock, Stephen. "The Struggle to Make Us Gentlemen." In *My Remarkable Uncle and Other Sketches*. Toronto: McClelland and Stewart 1965.

Leacy, F.H., ed. *Historical Statistics of Canada*. 2nd ed. Ottawa: Statistics Canada 1983.

Lee, Dennis. *Civil Elegies*. Toronto: House of Anansi 1968.

Lemoine, B. Roy. Review of *A Choice for Canada* by Walter L. Gordon. *Our Generation* (Sept. 1966): 90–4.

LePan, Douglas. *The Net and the Sword: Poems*. Toronto: Clarke, Irwin 1953.

Lévesque, René. *Memoirs*. Toronto: McClelland and Stewart 1986.

Levin, Malcolm, and Christine Sylvester. *Foreign Ownership*. Don Mills, Ont.: General Publishing 1972.

Levitt, Joseph. *A Vision Beyond Reach: A Century of Images of Canadian Destiny*. Ottawa: Deneau 1982.

Levitt, Kari. *Silent Surrender: The Multinational Corporation in Canada*. Toronto: Macmillan 1970.

– "Towards Decolonization: Canada and Quebec." *Canadian Forum* (Mar. 1972): 2–11.

Leyton-Brown, David. "The Multinational Enterprise and Conflict in Canadian-American Relations." *International Organization* 28 (Autumn 1974): 733–54.

– "Extraterritoriality in Canadian-American Relations." *International Journal* 36 (Winter 1980–81): 185–207.

Lindeman, John, and Donald Armstrong. *Policies and Practices of United States Subsidiaries in Canada*. Montreal: Canadian-American Committee 1960.

Lipsey, Richard G. "Harry Johnson's Contributions to the Pure Theory of International Trade." *Canadian Journal of Economics* 11, supp. (Nov. 1978): S34–S54.

Litt, Paul. *The Muses, the Masses, and the Massey Commission*. Toronto: University of Toronto Press 1992.

Little, A.J. *The Story of the Firm, 1864–1964: Clarkson, Gordon & Co*. Toronto: University of Toronto Press 1964.

Litvak, Isaiah A., and Christopher J. Maule. *Cultural Sovereignty: The Time and Reader's Digest Case in Canada*. New York: Praeger 1974.

– "Interest-Group Tactics and the Politics of Foreign Investment: The Time-Reader's Digest Case Study." *Canadian Journal of Political Science* 7 (Dec. 1974): 616–29.

Litvak, Isaiah A., Christopher J. Maule, and R.D. Robinson. *Dual Loyalty: Canadian-U.S. Business Arrangements*. Toronto: McGraw-Hill 1971.

Litvak, Isaiah A., ed. *The Nation Keepers: Canadian Business Perspectives*. Toronto: McGraw-Hill 1967.

LoGalbo, John R. "The Time and Reader's Digest Bill: C-58 and Canadian Cultural Nationalism." *New York University Journal of International Law and Politics* 9 (Fall 1976): 237–75.

Lord, Barry. "'mericans." In *The New Romans: Candid Canadian Opinions of the U.S.*, ed. Al Purdy. Edmonton: Hurtig 1968.

Lower, Arthur R.M. *Canada: Nation and Neighbour.* Toronto: Ryerson 1952.

– *History and Myth: Arthur Lower and the Making of Canadian Nationalism.* Ed. Welf H. Heick. Vancouver: University of British Columbia Press 1975.

– "Nationalism and the Canadian Historian." *Canadian Historical Review* 66 (Dec. 1985): 541–9.

Lumsden, Ian, ed. *Close the 49th Parallel etc: The Americanization of Canada.* Toronto: University of Toronto Press 1970.

Lyon, Peyton. *Canada in World Affairs 1961–1963.* Toronto: Oxford University Press 1968.

McCall, Christina, and Stephen Clarkson. *Trudeau and Our Times.* 2 vols. Toronto: McClelland and Stewart 1990, 1994.

– "The Death of Liberal Nationalism." *Canadian Forum* (Nov. 1994): 25–8.

McCall-Newman, Christina. *Grits: An Intimate Portrait of the Liberal Party.* Toronto: Macmillan 1982.

McDougall, John N. *The Politics and Economics of Eric Kierans: A Man for All Canadas.* Montreal: McGill-Queen's University Press 1993.

McFetridge, D.G., and L.J. Weatherby. *Notes on the Economics of Large Firm Size.* Ottawa: Royal Commission on Corporate Concentration 1977.

MacIntosh, Robert. *Different Drummers: Banking and Politics in Canada.* Toronto: Macmillan 1991.

MacKay, Donald. *The People's Railway: A History of Canadian National.* Vancouver: Douglas & McIntyre 1992.

MacKenzie, David. *The Clarkson Gordon Story: In Celebration of 125 Years.* Toronto: University of Toronto Press 1989.

McKeown, Robert. "We Need *More* Truck and Trade with the Yankees." *Weekend Magazine*, 2 July 1966, 2–5.

– "John Kenneth Galbraith Says Yes." *Weekend Magazine*, 25 Mar. 1967, 26, 28–30, 32–3.

McKillop, A.B. *Contours of Canadian Thought.* Toronto: University of Toronto Press 1987.

Mackintosh, W.A. *The Economic Background of Dominion-Provincial Relations.* Ottawa: King's Printer 1939.

– "The Canadian Economy and Its Competitors." *Foreign Affairs* 34 (Oct. 1955): 117–27.

MacLaren, Roy. *Consensus: A Liberal Looks at His Party.* Oakville, Ont.: Mosaic 1984.

MacLennan, Hugh. "Can We Stay Canadian?" *Canadian Library*, May 1962, 242–4.

McLeod, John T. "Moses with a Maple Leaf: One Man's View of Walter Gordon." *Saturday Night*, July 1966, 21–4.

McMillan, Charles J. "After the Gray Report: The Tortuous Evolution of Foreign Investment Policy." *McGill Law Journal* 20 (July 1974): 213–60.

McQueen, Don. "The Waffle Lives On." *Commentator*, June 1971, 14–15.

Magder, Ted. *Canada's Hollywood: The Canadian State and Feature Films.* Toronto: University of Toronto Press 1993.

Mahon, Rianne. *The Politics of Industrial Restructuring: Canadian Textiles.* Toronto: University of Toronto Press 1984.

Marchak, M. Patricia. *Ideological Perspectives on Canada.* 3rd ed. Toronto: McGraw-Hill Ryerson 1988.

Marshall, Herbert, et al. *Canadian-American Industry: A Study in International Investment.* Toronto: Ryerson 1936.

Martin, Paul. *A Very Public Life.* 2 vols. Toronto: Deneau 1983, 1985.

Masters, Donald C. *Canada in World Affairs 1953 to 1955.* Toronto: Oxford University Press 1959.

Matheson, John Ross. *Canada's Flag: A Search for a Country.* Belleville, Ontario: Mika Publishing 1986.

Mathews, Robin. "Economics and Nationhood." *Canadian Dimension* (Apr.–May 1968): 16–18.

– "Whose Ancestors?" *Last Post*, Oct. 1971, 45–8.

– *Canadian Identity: Major Forces Shaping the Life of a People.* Ottawa: Steel Rail 1988.

Mathews, Robin, and James Steele, eds. *The Struggle for Canadian Universities.* Toronto: new press 1969.

"The Medicine-Man." *Saturday Night*, 3 Sept. 1955, 21–2.

Meisel, John. *The Canadian General Election of 1957.* Toronto: University of Toronto Press 1962.

Mellett, Edward Bruce. *From Stopwatch to Strategy: A History of the First Twenty-Five Years of the Canadian Association of Management Consultants.* Toronto: CAMC 1988.

Merchant, Livingston T. *Neighbors Taken for Granted: Canada and the United States.* New York: Frederick A. Praeger 1966.

Merriman, John M. "History, Growth and Progress of Canadian Cottons, Limited." *Canadian Textile Journal*, 4 Apr. 1958, 21–32.

Miller, John. "Bee Knew What He *Didn't* Like." *Content for Canadian Journalists*, Nov.–Dec. 1988, 30–1.

Moller, Herbert. "Youth as a Force in the Modern World." *Comparative Studies in Society and History* 10 (Apr. 1968): 237–60.

Molot, Maureen A. "The Elephant, the Mouse and the Financial Relationship." *Queen's Quarterly* 78 (Spring 1971): 71–82.

Moon, Barbara. "Finishing School for the Upper Class." *Globe Magazine*, 1 May 1965, 6–8, 23.

Morris, Peter. *Embattled Shadows: A History of Canadian Cinema, 1895–1939.* Montreal: McGill-Queen's University Press 1978.

Morton, W.L. *The Canadian Identity.* Toronto: University of Toronto Press 1961.

– "Nihilism Is Worse than Nationalism." Review of *The Maple Leaf Forever* by Ramsay Cook. *Globe Magazine*, 17 Apr. 1971, 13.

Mowbray, George. " 'Little Canadianism' and American Capital: What Price Economic Nationalism?" *Queen's Quarterly* 65 (Spring 1958): 12–21.

Murray, J. Alex, and Akira Kubota. "What Canadians Think of U.S. Investment." *International Review*, 12 Feb. 1973, 35–41.

Murray, Janice L., ed. *Canadian Cultural Nationalism: The Fourth Lester B. Pearson Conference on the Canada–United States Relationship.* New York: New York University Press 1977.

National Industrial Conference Board. *The Canadian Primary Textiles Industry.* Ottawa: Royal Commission on Canada's Economic Prospects 1956.

Neatby, Hilda, et al. "Canadianism – A Symposium." Canadian Historical Association, *Report of the Annual Meeting* (1956): 74–82.

Nelles, H. Viv. "Mike and Walter: Reconciled at the End." *Canadian Forum* (Aug. 1974): 25–9.

Nelles, H. Viv, and Abraham Rotstein, eds. *Nationalism or Local Control: Responses to George Woodcock.* Toronto: new press 1973.

Newman, C.J. "1966." In *The New Romans: Candid Canadian Opinions of the U.S.,* ed. Al Purdy. Edmonton: Hurtig 1968.

Newman, Christina. "The True Compromise: Good and Sane – How Mel Watkins Brought Socialism to the NDP." *Saturday Night*, Sept. 1970, 23–7.

– "An Unemotional, Resolutely Unjingoistic Guide to the New Canadian Nationalism." *Chatelaine*, Oct. 1970, 22.

– "The Short Life and Premature Death of Canadian Nationalism." In *Their Turn to Curtsy – Your Turn to Bow*, ed. Peter C. Newman and Stan Fillmore. Toronto: Maclean-Hunter 1972.

– "Growing Up Reluctantly; How a Political System Failed: The Birth and Brutal Death of the New Nationalism." *Maclean's*, Aug. 1972, 21–2, 56, 58–60.

Newman, Peter C. "Who *Really* Owns Canada?" *Maclean's*, 9 June 1956, 11, 13, 90, 92–6.

- "James Coyne and the Great Debate: Is Canada Possible?" *Maclean's*, 1 July 1961, 14, 41–4.
- *Renegade in Power: The Diefenbaker Years.* Toronto: McClelland and Stewart 1963.
- "What Really Happened to Walter Gordon." *Maclean's*, 19 Oct. 1963, 22, 76–9.
- "Despite the Budget Gordon Is Still an Economic Nationalist – and the Cabinet Is Still with Him." *Maclean's*, 18 Apr. 1964, 4–5.
- "The Great Money Panic of 1963." *Maclean's*, 16 May 1964, 20, 53–5.
- "What – If Anything – Is Wrong with U.S. Ownership?" *Maclean's*, 6 June 1964, 16, 33–5.
- *The Distemper of Our Times: Canadian Politics in Transition 1963–1968.* Toronto: McClelland and Stewart 1968.
- "The Thawing of Canada." *Saturday Review*, 13 Mar. 1971, 15–18, 88.
- *Home Country: People, Places, and Power Politics.* Toronto: McClelland and Stewart 1973.
- *The Canadian Establishment.* 2 vols. Toronto: McClelland and Stewart 1975, 1981.
- "The First to Fight." Review of *A Political Memoir* by Walter Gordon. *Maclean's*, 3 Oct. 1977, 72, 74.
- "Still Preaching in the Wilderness." *Maclean's*, 2 May 1983, 42.
- "Gordon's Bold Quest." *Maclean's*, 6 Apr. 1987, 36.
- *Sometimes a Great Nation: Will Canada Belong to the Twenty-first Century?* Toronto: McClelland and Stewart 1988.
- "Why Jean Chrétien Will Never be P.M." *Maclean's*, 22 Feb. 1993, 24.
Newman, Peter C., and Stan Fillmore, eds. *Their Turn to Curtsy – Your Turn to Bow.* Toronto: Maclean-Hunter 1972.
Nowlan, D.M. "The Love Song of Walter L. Gordon." Review of *A Choice for Canada* by Walter Gordon. *Canadian Forum* (Aug. 1966): 112–13.
Oliver, Peter. *Public and Private Persons: The Ontario Political Culture 1914–1934.* Toronto: Clarke, Irwin 1975.
- *G. Howard Ferguson: Ontario Tory.* Toronto: University of Toronto Press 1977.
"Once Again, Here's Walter." *Monetary Times*, May 1966, 46.
Ontario. *Report of the Interdepartmental Task Force on Foreign Investment* (Honey Report). Toronto: Department of Treasury and Economics 1971.
Ontario. Committee on the Organization of Government in Ontario. *Report.* Toronto 1959.
Ontario. Legislative Assembly. Select Committee on Economic and Cultural Nationalism. *Preliminary Report.* Toronto 1972.
- Select Committee on Economic and Cultural Nationalism. *Final Report on Cultural Nationalism.* Toronto 1975.

– Select Committee on Economic and Cultural Nationalism. *Final Report on Economic Nationalism*. Toronto 1975.

Osbaldeston, Gordon F. *Organizing to Govern*. 2 vols. Toronto: McGraw-Hill Ryerson 1992.

Owram, Doug. *The Government Generation: Canadian Intellectuals and the State 1900–1945*. Toronto: University of Toronto Press 1986.

– *Born at the Right Time: A History of the Baby-Boom Generation*. Toronto: University of Toronto Press 1996.

Page, Robert J.D. "Canada and the Imperial Idea in the Boer War Years." *Journal of Canadian Studies* 5 (Feb. 1970): 33–49.

Panet, H.A. "The Royal Military College." *Canadian Geographical Journal* 2 (June 1931): 441–54.

Parizeau, Jacques. "Les Investissements américains: sont-ils devenus une menace?" *L'Actualité économique* 32 (Apr.–June 1956): 140–56.

Park, L.C., and F.W. Park. *Anatomy of Big Business*. Toronto: Progress Books 1962.

Peacock, Don. *Barefoot on the Hill: The Life of Harry Hays*. Vancouver: Douglas & McIntyre 1986.

Pearson, Lester B. *Words and Occasions*. Toronto: University of Toronto Press 1970.

– *Mike: The Memoirs of the Right Honourable Lester B. Pearson*. 3 vols. Toronto: University of Toronto Press 1972–1975.

Pelletier, Gérard. *Years of Impatience, 1950–1960*. Toronto: Methuen 1984.

– *Years of Choice, 1960–1968*. Toronto: Methuen 1987.

Penlington, Norman. *Canada and Imperialism, 1896–1899*. Toronto: University of Toronto Press 1965.

Penner, Rudolph G. "The Inflow of Long-Term Capital and the Canadian Business Cycle 1950–1960." *Canadian Journal of Economics and Political Science* 28 (Nov. 1962): 527–42.

– "The Benefits of Foreign Investment in Canada 1950 to 1956." *Canadian Journal of Economics and Political Science* 32 (May 1966): 172–83.

Perry, Robert L. *Galt, U.S.A.: The 'American Presence' in a Canadian City*. Toronto: Maclean-Hunter 1971.

Petryshyn, Jaroslav. "A.E. Smith and the Canadian Labour Defence League." PhD, University of Western Ontario 1977.

Pickersgill, J.W. *The Liberal Party*. With an introduction by L.B. Pearson. Toronto: McClelland and Stewart 1962.

– *My Years with Louis St. Laurent: A Political Memoir*. Toronto: University of Toronto Press 1975.

– *The Road Back, by a Liberal in Opposition*. Toronto: University of Toronto Press 1986.

– *Seeing Canada Whole: A Memoir*. Toronto: Fitzhenry & Whiteside 1994.

Pilisuk, Marc. "The Evolution of the Teach-in." *Canadian Forum* (Nov. 1965): 176–7.

Pizer, Samuel, and Frederick Cutler. *U.S. Business Investments in Foreign Countries: A Supplement to the Survey of Current Business.* Washington: Department of Commerce 1960.

Plumptre, A.F. Wynne. "Special Trade Deal with U.S.A. Is Step towards Annexation." *Saturday Night,* 25 Dec. 1948, 18–19.

– *Three Decades of Decision: Canada and the World Monetary System 1944–75.* Toronto: McClelland and Stewart 1977.

Pope, Arthur. "Teach-in as Institution." *Canadian Forum* (Nov. 1965): 178.

Pope, W.H. *The Elephant and the Mouse: A Handbook on Regaining Control of Canada's Economy.* Toronto: McClelland and Stewart 1971.

Porter, John. *The Vertical Mosaic: An Analysis of Social Class and Power in Canada.* Toronto: University of Toronto Press 1965.

Potvin, Rose, ed. *Passion and Conviction: The Letters of Graham Spry.* Regina: Canadian Plains Research Centre 1992.

Prang, Margaret E. "Some Opinions of Political Radicalism in Canada between the Two World Wars." MA, University of Toronto 1953.

– "Nationalism in Canada's First Century." Canadian Historical Association, *Historical Papers* (1968): 114–25.

Prest, Alan. "Harry Johnson." *Economist,* 14 May 1977, 121.

Preston, Richard Arthur. *Canada's RMC: A History of the Royal Military College.* Toronto: University of Toronto Press 1969.

– "The New Nationalism Viewed from across the Border: Chauvinism or Survival?" *American Review of Canadian Studies* 5 (Autumn 1975): 48–65.

Purdy, Alfred. *The Cariboo Horses.* Toronto: McClelland and Stewart 1965.

Purdy, Alfred, ed. *The New Romans: Candid Canadian Opinions of the U.S.* Edmonton: Hurtig 1968.

"The Quarter's Polls." *Public Opinion Quarterly* 10 (Spring 1946): 104–39.

Quigley, Carroll. "The Round Table Groups in Canada 1908–1938." *Canadian Historical Review* 43 (Sept. 1962): 204–24.

Redekop, John H., ed. *The Star-Spangled Beaver: 24 Canadians Look South.* Toronto: Peter Martin 1971.

Reid, Escott. *Radical Mandarin: The Memoirs of Escott Reid.* Toronto: University of Toronto Press 1989.

Reid, Timothy E., ed. *Foreign Ownership: Villain or Scapegoat?* Toronto: Holt, Rinehart and Winston 1972.

Resnick, Philip. "Canadian Defence Policy and the American Empire." In *Close the 49th Parallel etc: The Americanization of Canada,* ed. Ian Lumsden. Toronto: University of Toronto Press 1970.

– *The Land of Cain: Class and Nationalism in English Canada 1945–1975*. Vancouver: New Star Books 1977.

Reuber, G.L. Review of *Troubled Canada* by Walter Gordon. *Queen's Quarterly* 69 (Autumn 1962): 471–2.

Reynolds, Nial. *In Quest of Yesterday*. 3rd ed. Minden, Ont.: Provisional County of Haliburton 1973.

Richardson, Alan J. "Canada's Accounting Elite: 1880–1930." *Accounting Historians Journal* 16 (June 1989): 1–21.

Ritchie, Charles. *Storm Signals: More Undiplomatic Diaries 1962–1971*. Toronto: Macmillan 1983.

Robertson, Heather. "The New Patriots: Pierre Trudeau and the Liberal Party Have Discovered That Nationalism Is Sexy Politics." *Today Magazine*, 25 Apr. 1981, 8–11.

Rodney, William. *Soldiers of the International: A History of the Communist Party of Canada 1919–1929*. Toronto: University of Toronto Press 1968.

Rohmer, Richard. *Ultimatum*. Toronto: Clarke Irwin 1973.

– *E.P. Taylor: The Biography of Edward Plunket Taylor*. Toronto: McClelland and Stewart 1978.

Ross, Alexander. "Joel Bell." *Energy*, Nov.–Dec. 1981, 15–17, 19, 21, 54–6.

– "Where Industry Gets Captains." *Canadian Business*, Jan. 1993, 40–5.

Ross, Douglas A. *In the Interests of Peace: Canada and Vietnam 1954–1973*. Toronto: University of Toronto Press 1984.

Rotstein, Abraham. Review of *The Canadian Quandary: Economic Problems and Politics* by Harry Johnson. *Canadian Forum* (July 1964): 80–2.

– "Canadian Affluence." Review of *A Choice for Canada* by Walter Gordon. *Tamarack Review* 40 (Summer 1966): 88–91.

– "Pearson's Choice." *Canadian Forum* (July 1966): 76.

– "Foreign Ownership of Industry: A New Canadian Approach." *Round Table* (London), no. 231 (July 1968): 260–8.

– "The Search for Independence." *Canadian Forum* (Oct. 1969): 146–8.

– Intro. to *Reclaiming the Canadian Economy: A Swedish Approach through Functional Socialism*, by Gunnar Adler-Karlsson. Toronto: House of Anansi 1970.

– "Sixties Myopia: The Great Canadian Sellout." Review of *Gordon to Watkins to You*, ed. Dave Godfrey and Mel Watkins. *Globe Magazine*, 13 June 1970, 15.

– "Foreign Control of the Economy." In *Read Canadian: A Book about Canadian Books*, ed. Robert Fulford, David Godfrey, and Abraham Rotstein. Toronto: James Lewis & Samuel 1972.

– "Déjà Vu." *Canadian Forum* (May 1972): 2–3, 14.

– *The Precarious Homestead: Essays on Economics, Technology and Nationalism*. Toronto: new press 1973.

– "Canada: The New Nationalism." *Foreign Affairs* 55 (Oct. 1976): 97–118.

Rotstein, Abraham, and Melville H. Watkins. "Communication is a New Key." *Canadian Forum* (Nov. 1965): 174–5.

Rotstein, Abraham, ed. *The Prospect of Change: Proposals for Canada's Future.* Toronto: McGraw-Hill 1965.

– *An Industrial Strategy for Canada.* Toronto: new press 1972.

Rotstein, Abraham, and Gary Lax, eds. *Independence: The Canadian Challenge.* Toronto: Committee for an Independent Canada 1972.

– *Getting it Back: A Program for Canadian Independence.* Toronto: Clarke, Irwin 1974.

Royal, Margaret V. "Canadian-American Relations: The Last Option. A Study of the Third Option in Canadian Foreign Policy." PhD, Queen's University 1984.

"The Royal Commission Report." *Civil Service Review* 19 (Summer 1946): 108–11.

Rugman, Alan M. "The Foreign Ownership Debate in Canada." *Journal of World Trade Law* 10 (Mar.–Apr. 1976): 171–6.

Russell, Peter, ed. *Nationalism in Canada.* Toronto: McGraw-Hill 1966.

Rutan, Gerald F. "Doctrinal Folly in the Name of Canadianism: Doctrines of the 'New' Nationalism in Canada." *American Review of Canadian Studies* 4 (Spring 1974): 37–53.

Ryan, Gerald C. "Trends in Capital Investment in Canada." *Canadian Chartered Accountant*, Aug. 1951, 43–7.

Safarian, A.E. "Dilemma of Foreign Investment." *Canadian Forum* (Feb. 1956): 246–7.

– "The Exports of American-Owned Enterprises in Canada." *American Economic Review* 54 (May 1964): 449–58.

– "Foreign Ownership and Control of Canadian Industry." In *The Prospect of Change: Proposals for Canada's Future*, ed. Abraham Rotstein. Toronto: McGraw-Hill 1965.

– *Foreign Ownership of Canadian Industry.* Toronto: McGraw-Hill 1966.

– "Approaches to Foreign Investment." *Commerceman* (1968): 13–19.

– "The Multi-national Corporation and the Communication of Values." *Explorations*, June 1968, 75–80.

– "The Task Force Report on Foreign Investment." *Journal of Canadian Studies* 3 (Aug. 1968): 50–7.

– *The Performance of Foreign-Owned Firms in Canada.* Montreal: Canadian-American Committee 1969.

– "Benefits and Costs of Foreign Investment." In *Canadian Economic Problems and Policies*, ed. Lawrence H. Officer and Lawrence B. Smith. Toronto: McGraw-Hill 1970.

– *Foreign Direct Investment: A Survey of Canadian Research*. Montreal: Institute for Research on Public Policy 1985.

Safarian, A.E., and E.B. Carty. "Foreign Financing of Canadian Investment in the Post-War Period." American Statistical Association, *Proceedings of the Business and Economic Statistics Section* (1954): 72–9.

Satin, Mark, ed. *Manual for Draft-Age Immigrants to Canada*. Toronto: House of Anansi 1968.

Saul, John Ralston. *Voltaire's Bastards: The Dictatorship of Reason in the West*. Toronto: Viking 1992.

Saunders, Richard M. Presidential Address. Canadian Historical Association, *Historical Papers* (1967).

Saywell, John, ed. *Canadian Annual Review*. Toronto: University of Toronto Press 1961–79.

Schindler, F.F. *Responsible Government in Ontario*. Toronto: University of Toronto Press 1969.

Schwartz, Mildred Anne. "Canadian National Identity as Seen through Public Opinion Polls 1941–1963." PhD, Columbia University 1964.

– *Public Opinion and Canadian Identity*. Scarborough, Ont.: Fitzhenry and Whiteside 1967.

– *The Environment for Policy-Making in Canada and the United States*. Montreal: C.D. Howe Institute 1981.

Sears, Val. *Is Canada For Sale?* Toronto: Toronto Star 1967.

Sharp, Mitchell. "Canada-U.S. Relations: Options for the Future." *International Perspectives*, special issue, Autumn 1972.

– *Which Reminds Me ... A Memoir*. Toronto: University of Toronto Press 1994.

Sharp, Ross. "Tribute to Walter Gordon." Liberal Party of Canada. *Dialogue*, Winter 1976, 10.

Sigler, John H., and Dennis Goresky. "Public Opinion on United States-Canadian Relations." *International Organization* 28 (Autumn 1974): 637–68.

"The Sixty-Day Blues." *Time*, 28 June 1963, 20.

Skinner, Ross M. "Research Contributions to Canadian Standards: A Retrospective." *Research in Accounting Regulation* 3 (1989): 197–217.

Slater, David W. "Gordon's New Book." Review of *A Choice for Canada* by Walter Gordon. *Canadian Forum* (June 1966): 49–51.

– "The Watkins Report." *Canadian Banker*, Summer 1968, 5–16.

Slater, David W., and R.B. Bryce. *War, Finance and Reconstruction: The Role of Canada's Department of Finance, 1939–1946*. Ottawa 1995.

Smiley, Donald V. "Canada and the Quest for a National Policy." *Canadian Journal of Political Science* 8 (Mar. 1975): 40–62.

Smith, A.E. *All My Life*. Toronto: Progress Books 1977.

Smith, David C., and David W. Slater. "The Economic Policy Proposals of the Governor of the Bank of Canada." *Queen's Quarterly* 68 (Spring 1961): 106–27.

Smith, Denis. *Bleeding Hearts ... Bleeding Country: Canada and the Quebec Crisis.* Edmonton: Hurtig 1971.

– *Gentle Patriot: A Political Biography of Walter Gordon.* Edmonton: Hurtig 1973.

– *Rogue Tory: The Life and Legend of John G. Diefenbaker.* Toronto: Macfarlane Walter & Ross 1995.

Smith, J.M. "Foreign Investment in Canada." *Behind the Headlines* 18, no. 2 (1958).

Smith, R. Guy C. *As You Were! Ex-Cadets Remember.* 2 vols. Kingston: R.M.C. Club of Canada 1984.

Smith, Ray. "Cape Breton is the Thought-Control Center of Canada." *Tamarack Review* (Autumn 1967): 39–53.

Souster, Raymond. "Death Chant for Mr. Johnson's America." In *The New Romans: Candid Canadian Opinions of the U.S.*, ed. Al Purdy. Edmonton: Hurtig 1968.

Stacey, C.P. *Canada and the Age of Conflict.* 2 vols. Toronto: Macmillan 1977, 1981.

Stairs, Denis, and Gilbert R. Winham, eds. *The Politics of Canada's Economic Relationship with the United States.* Toronto: University of Toronto Press 1985.

Starowicz, Mark, and Rae Murphy, eds. *Corporate Canada: 14 Probes into the Workings of a Branch-Plant Economy.* Toronto: James Lewis & Samuel 1972.

Steed, Judy. *Ed Broadbent: The Pursuit of Power.* Markham, Ont.: Penguin 1988.

Steele, James, and Robin Mathews. "The Universities: Takeover of the Mind." In *Close the 49th Parallel etc: The Americanization of Canada*, ed. Ian Lumsden. Toronto: University of Toronto Press 1970.

Stevenson, John A. "J.E. Coyne: Bank Governor Stirs a Tempest." *Saturday Night,* 29 Mar. 1958, 14–15, 39–40.

Steward, Hartley. "O Canada, the CIC is Standing Here on Guard for Thee." *Toronto Life,* July 1971, 31–5.

Stewart, Walter. "Canada – A U.S. Colony." *Star Weekly,* 5 Feb. 1966, 2–4.

– "The Canadian Firsters March on to Ottawa." *Maclean's,* Dec. 1970, 1–3.

Stursberg, Peter. "Ottawa Letter." *Saturday Night,* Aug. 1963, 31–2; Sept. 1964, 9–10.

– *Diefenbaker: Leadership Gained 1956–1962.* Toronto: University of Toronto Press 1975.

– *Lester Pearson and the Dream of Unity.* Toronto: Doubleday 1978.

– *Lester Pearson and the American Dilemma.* Toronto: Doubleday 1980.

Stykolt, Stefan, and Harry C. Eastman. "Disturbing Prospects." *Canadian Forum* (Feb. 1957): 246–7.

Swift, Jamie. *Odd Man Out: The Life and Times of Eric Kierans.* Vancouver: Douglas & McIntyre 1988.

Sykes, Philip. *Sellout: The Giveaway of Canada's Energy Resources.* Edmonton: Hurtig 1973.

Taylor, Charles. *Radical Tories: The Conservative Tradition in Canada*. Toronto: House of Anansi 1982.

Teeter, Michael. "A Group and an Issue: The Case of the Committee for an Independent Canada." BA, Carleton University 1976.

Templeton, Charles. *An Anecdotal Memoir*. Toronto: McClelland and Stewart 1983.

Thompson, Dale C. *Louis St. Laurent: Canadian*. Toronto: Macmillan 1967.

Thoradson, Bruce. Review of *Gentle Patriot* by Denis Smith. *International Journal* 29 (Spring 1974): 299–301.

Thorburn, H.G. "Mr. Gordon's Questions Answered." *Canadian Forum* (Mar. 1968): 269–70.

Thorp, Willard L. "Canada-United States Economic Relations." *Canadian Journal of Economics and Political Science* 26 (May 1960): 326–34.

"Three Businessmen Who Sell 'Buy-Canada-Back.'" *Maclean's*, Feb. 1970, 5.

Tighe, Melanie T. "Petro-Canada: Mandate Considerations since Its Creation." MA, Dalhousie University 1988.

Tinker, Frank A. "I'm Leaving Canada ... And I'm Glad." *Maclean's*, 1 Dec. 1954, 20–1, 48, 50–1, 54–5.

"Triangle at Ottawa." *Saturday Night*, 12 May 1956, 5.

Trudeau, Pierre Elliott. "A propos de 'domination économique.'" *Cité libre* (May 1958): 7–16.

– *Memoirs*. Toronto: McClelland and Stewart 1993.

Turnbull, W.J. "Development of Decentralization in the Post Office." In *Canadian Public Administration*, ed. J.E. Hodgetts and D.C. Corbett. Toronto: Macmillan 1960.

Turner, Susan, ed. "Gordon to Watkins to You: Press Conference." *Canadian Forum* (July–Aug. 1970): 158–60.

Underhill, Frank H. "Edward Blake and Canadian Liberal Nationalism." In *Essays in Canadian History*, ed. R. Flenley. Toronto: Macmillan 1939.

– Foreword to *Nationalism in Canada*, ed. Peter Russell. Toronto: McGraw-Hill 1966.

Urquhart, M.C., and K.A.H. Buckley, eds. *Historical Statistics of Canada*. Toronto: Macmillan 1965.

Vandercamp, J. "Harry G. Johnson: a Brief Tribute." *Canadian Public Policy* 3 (Summer 1977): 267.

Vernon, Raymond. *Sovereignty at Bay: The Multinational Spread of U.S. Enterprises*. New York: Basic Books 1977.

– *Storm over the Multinationals: The Real Issues*. Cambridge, Mass.: Harvard University Press 1977.

Viner, Jacob. "The Gordon Commission Report." *Queen's Quarterly* 64 (Autumn 1957): 305–25.

Vipond, Mary Jean. "National Consciousness in English-Speaking Canada in the 1920s: Seven Studies." PhD, University of Toronto 1974.

– "Canadian Nationalism and the Plight of Canadian Magazines in the 1920s." *Canadian Historical Review* 58 (Mar. 1977): 43–63.

– "The Canadian Authors' Association in the 1920s: A Case Study in Cultural Nationalism." *Journal of Canadian Studies* 15 (Spring 1980): 68–79.

– "The Nationalist Network: English Canada's Intellectuals and Artists in the 1920s." *Canadian Review of Studies in Nationalism* 7 (Spring 1980): 32–52.

– "Nationalism and Nativism: The Native Sons of Canada in the 1920s." *Canadian Review of Studies in Nationalism* 9 (Spring 1982): 81–95.

– *The Mass Media in Canada*. Toronto: Lorimer 1989.

Vokes, Chris. *Vokes: My Story*. Ottawa: Gallery Books 1985.

Waddell, Christopher Robb. "The Wartime Prices and Trade Board: Price Control in Canada in World War II." PhD, York University 1981.

"The Waffle: A Gentle Tip in Search of an Iceberg." *Last Post*, June 1970, 6–7.

Wahn, Ian. "Toward Canadian Identity – The Significance of Foreign Investment." *Osgoode Hall Law Journal* 11 (Dec. 1973): 517–35.

Wainwright, Andy, ed. *Notes for a Native Land*. Toronto: Oberon 1969.

Waite, P.B. *Lord of Point Grey: Larry Mackenzie of UBC*. Vancouver: University of British Columbia Press 1987.

Walker, Dean. "An Angry Economic Nationalist Hits Out at Ottawa, Too." *Executive*, Sept. 1976, 36–7.

Wallace, Robert. *Producing Marginality: Theatre and Criticism in Canada*. Saskatoon: Fifth House 1990.

"Walter L. Gordon: He's No Stranger to Royal Commissions." *Canadian Business*, Oct. 1955, 66.

"Walter Lockhart Gordon." *Canadian Chemical Processing*, July 1955, 18–19.

Walton, Richard J. *Canada and the U.S.A.: A Background Book about Internal Conflict and the New Nationalism*. New York: Parents' Magazine Press 1972.

Warnock, John W. "Why I Am Anti-American." *Canadian Dimension* (Nov.–Dec. 1967): 11–12.

– "All the News It Pays to Print." In *Close the 49th Parallel etc: The Americanization of Canada*, ed. Ian Lumsden. Toronto: University of Toronto Press 1970.

– *Partner to Behemoth: The Military Policy of a Satellite Canada*. Toronto: new press 1970.

Watkins, Melville H. Review of *The Canadian Quandary: Economic Problems and Politics* by Harry G. Johnson. *Canadian Forum* (July 1964): 79–80.

– "Canadian Economic Policy: A Proposal." In *The Prospect of Change: Proposals for Canada's Future*, ed. Abraham Rotstein. Toronto: McGraw-Hill 1965.

– "Is Gordon's Game Worth the Candle?" *Canadian Forum* (July 1966): 77–8.
– "Economic Nationalism." *Canadian Journal of Economics and Political Science* 32 (Aug. 1966): 388–92.
– "Economics and Mystification." *Journal of Canadian Studies* 4 (Feb. 1969): 55–9.
– "Learning to Move Left." *This Magazine Is about Schools*, Spring 1972, 68–92.
– "The Trade Union Movement in Canada." In *(Canada) Ltd.: The Political Economy of Dependency*, ed. Robert M. Laxer. Toronto: McClelland and Stewart 1973.
– "In the End, Not a Gut Nationalist." Review of *Gentle Patriot* by Denis Smith. *Last Post*, May 1974, 42–4.
– "Gordon's Nationalism and Quebec." Review of *A Political Memoir* by Walter Gordon. *Last Post*, Jan. 1978, 42–4.
– "The Economics of Nationalism and the Nationality of Economics: A Critique of Neoclassical Theorizing." *Canadian Journal of Economics* 11, supp. (Nov. 1978): s87–s120.
– "Walter Gordon 1906–1987." *This Magazine*, May–June 1987, 29–30.
– "Once Upon a Time: The Waffle Story." *This Magazine*, Mar.–Apr. 1989, 28–30.
– *Madness and Ruin: Politics and the Economy in the Neoconservative Age*. Toronto: Between the Lines 1992.
– "Foreign Ownership '94 – Buy, Bye Canada." *This Magazine*, Apr./May 1994, 30–2.
– "Architect of the Social Safety Net." *Toronto Life*, Nov. 1996, 111.
Wearing, Joseph. "Foreign Ownership: The True North Strong and Fettered." *Journal of Canadian Studies* 7 (Feb. 1972): 51–8.
– *The L-Shaped Party: The Liberal Party of Canada 1958–1980*. Toronto: McGraw-Hill 1981.
Weaver, Emily P. "Upper Canada College." *Canadian Magazine*, Mar. 1920, 407–16.
Welbourn, Patricia. "Made in u.s.a." *Weekend Magazine*, 22 Mar. 1969, 2–4, 6.
Westhues, Kenneth. "Inter-Generational Conflict in the Sixties." In *Prophecy and Protest: Social Movements in Twentieth-Century Canada*, ed. Samuel D. Clark, J. Paul Grayson, and Linda M. Grayson. Toronto: Gage 1975.
Whitaker, Reg. "A Nationalist Outcast, Spurned by His Own Class." Review of *Gentle Patriot* by Denis Smith. *Canadian Dimension* (Mar. 1975): 56–7.
– Review of *A Political Memoir* and *What Is Happening to Canada* by Walter Gordon. *Canadian Journal of Political Science* 11 (Sept. 1978): 665–7.
White, W.L., R.H. Wagenberg, and R.C. Nelson. *Introduction to Canadian Politics and Government*. Toronto: Holt, Rinehart and Winston 1972.
"Whither Waffle?" *Canadian Dimension* (Apr. 1971): 24–5.
"Who Will Own Canada?" *Star Weekly Magazine*, 16 Feb. 1957, 47.

"Who's Who in Foreign Business." *Fortune*, Mar. 1962, 62.

"Why Just Hewers of Wood?" *Star Weekly*, 11 Feb. 1956, sec. 1, p 11.

Wilbur, Richard. *H.H. Stevens, 1878–1973*. Toronto: University of Toronto Press 1977.

Wilkinson, B.W. *Canada's International Trade: An Analysis of Recent Trends and Patterns*. Montreal: Canadian Trade Committee 1968.

Williamson, J. Peter. *Taxation of U.S. Private Investment in Canada*. Toronto: Canadian Tax Foundation 1963.

Wilson, V. Seymour. *Canadian Public Policy and Administration: Theory and Environment*. Toronto: McGraw-Hill Ryerson 1981.

Wise, S.F. "The Origins of Anti-Americanism in Canada." In *Fourth Seminar on Canadian-American Relations at Assumption University of Windsor*, ed. F.J. Boland. Windsor: Assumption University of Windsor 1962.

Wolfe, David A. "Economic Growth and Foreign Investment: A Perspective on Canadian Economic Policy 1945–1957." *Journal of Canadian Studies* 13 (Spring 1978): 3–20.

Wright, Gerald. "Persuasive Influence: The Case of the Interest Equalization Tax." In *Continental Community? Independence and Integration in North America*, ed. W. Andrew Axline et al. Toronto: McClelland and Stewart 1974.

– "Cooperation and Independence: Canada's Management of Financial Relations with the United States 1963–1968." PhD, Johns Hopkins University 1976.

– Review of *A Political Memoir* by Walter Gordon. *Canadian Historical Review* 60 (Dec. 1979): 519–21.

Young, A.H. *The War Book of Upper Canada College, Toronto*. Toronto: Printers Guild 1923.

Young, A.H., ed. *The Roll of Pupils of Upper Canada College, Toronto, January 1830 to June 1916*. Kingston, Ont.: Hanson, Crozier and Edgar 1917.

Young, John H. *Canadian Commercial Policy*. Ottawa: Royal Commission on Canada's Economic Prospects 1957.

Ziedenberg, Jason. "Canada's Vietnam Legacy." *Canadian Dimension* (Oct.–Nov. 1995): 24–8.

Index

Abell, Sinc, 104
Adler-Karlsson, Gunnar, 172
Anderson, David, 165
Anderson, Rod, 97–8
Anglican Church, 9
Anti-Americanism, 7, 9, 10, 34, 36–7, 41, 44–5, 57–8, 64, 136–8
Argue, Hazen, 56
Arlen, Michael J., 135
Armstrong, Bill, 110
Armstrong, Donald, 140
Arnold, F.L.M., 13
Association of Canadian Publishers, 179
Association of Canadian Television and Radio Actors, 179
Association of Professional Engineers of Ontario, 43
Atkinson, Joseph E., 68
Atkinson Charitable Foundation, 68–9
Atwood, Margaret, 136, 137
Automotive industry, 19–20, 124–5
Auto Pact, 122, 124–5, 131
Axworthy, Lloyd, 177
Axworthy, Tom, 82

Baby boom, 133
Balcer, Léon, 45

Ball, George, 114
Ball, Gordon, 114
Bank Act, 117–18, 149, 152–5
Bank of Canada, 20
Barkway, Michael, 37, 43, 50, 75–7, 162
Bashevkin, Sylvia, 186
Bassett, John, 69, 173
Bell, Joel, 180
Bennett, R.B., 19
Bennett, Robert, 15
Bennett, W.A.C., 56
Benson, E.J. "Ben," 99, 148, 150, 153–5
Berton, Pierre, 177
Bilborough, W.H., 10
Bissell, Claude, 136
Bladen, Vincent, 124
Bland, Charles, 24
Bliss, Michael, 134, 186
Bobak, Bruno, 86
Bobak, Molly, 86
Bonin, Bernard, 77, 144, 158, 164
Bonnycastle, Larry, 25, 26
BP Canada, 186
Branch plants: see Foreign-owned firms
Brecher, Irving, 59
Brimwell, George, 79
British Columbia Trade Union Congress, 43

Broadbent, Ed, 136
Brunton, John, 67
Bryce, Robert, 22, 56–7, 96
Budget: (1963), 95–111, 113–14, 115, 119, 131, 139, 158; (1964), 114; (1965), 115
Burpee, Nancy, 97

Canada Assistance Plan, 131
Canada Development Corporation, 97–8, 114, 164, 180, 187; and CIC, 178–9; and Gordon, 111, 114–17, 132, 139, 143, 147; Liberal policy on, 114–15, 147; and Sharp, 143; and Wahn Report, 175; and Watkins Task Force, 162, 165
Canada Land and Emigration Company, 4
Canada Pension Plan, 97, 128, 131, 187
Canada Student Loans, 187
Canada Studies Foundation, 179
Canadian Arctic Resources Committee, 179
Canadian Club, 36, 44
Canadian Corporate Management Co. Ltd.: auto-parts manufacturing, 20, 124;

supports CIC, 180; creation of, 25; electronics company, sale to U.S. buyer, 67–8; Gordon president of, 28, 67; objectives, 25–6; paper companies, sale to U.S. buyer, 67–8, 139; profits, 68; sale of, 29; textiles manufacturing, 26

Canadian Cottons, 26, 190

Canadian Council of Film Makers, 179

Canadian Expeditionary Force (CEF), 6–8

Canadian Federation of Independent Business, 179

Canadian Forum, 18, 180, 201n93

Canadian Institute for Economic Policy, 179

Canadian Institute of International Affairs, 38

Canadian International Paper: *see* International Paper Company

Canadian Labour Defence League, 17

Canadian Management Company: *see* Canadian Corporate Management Co. Ltd.

Canadian Motorola Electronics, 67

Canadian National Railways, 67

Canadian Pulp and Paper Association, 42

Canadian Radio-Television Commission, 180

Canadian Vegetable Parchment, 67

Canadian Wheat Board, 56

Cassels, Kathleen: *see* Gordon, Kathleen

Cassels, Sir Walter G.P. (grandfather), 4–5

Castleden, George, 46

"Cell 13," 72

Centennial celebrations, 134

Charitable Gifts Act (Ontario), 68–9

Chevrier, Lionel, 82, 107, 108

Child, Art, 32

Citibank, 117–18, 149, 152–5

Civil rights movement (U.S.), 134–5, 163, 171, 174, 192

Civil Service Commission, 23–4

Clark, Clifford, 21–3, 24, 32

Clarkson, Adrienne, 177

Clarkson, G.T., 5, 16, 20

Clarkson, Stephen, 184

Clarkson & Cross, 4, 5

Clarkson Gordon: and banks, 117; creation of, 5; becomes Ernst & Young, 187; Gordon with firm, 15–16, 19–21, 23, 28, 31, 66; Colonel Gordon as senior partner of, 8, 15–16, 23; government contracts, 8, 16, 18–20, 25; growth of, 8, 31, 66; and *Toronto Star*, 68; creation of Woods Gordon, 21

Claxton, Brooke, 24

Claxton, John, 59

Cold War, 34

Coldwell, Major, 35, 44, 46, 56

Committee for an Independent Canada (CIC), 176–80, 183, 186, 193

Committee on Price Spreads: *see* Royal Commission on Price Spreads

Committee on the Organization of Government in Ontario, 71

Communist Party of Canada, 17

Connolly, John, 80, 82, 150

Conway, Geoff, 97–9

Couchiching Conference, 36

Counsell, Elizabeth: *see* Gordon, Elizabeth Marjorie Leith

Counsell, John Leith, 17

Counsell, Marjorie, 17

Coutts, James, 27, 29–30, 31, 187

Coyne, James, 89–90

Crean, Susan, 134, 168

Creighton, Donald, 36, 45, 173

Croll, David, 35

Cross, W.H., 5

Culture: American influence on Canada, 11, 33, 86, 168; CIC on, 178; Gordon's attitude, 33, 85–6, 124, 155, 168, 169, 191–2; *see also* Magazines

Currie, Sir Arthur, 13

Dales, John, 142

Davey, Keith, 165, 177; on Gordon, 131, 152; with Liberal party, 72, 82, 91

Davies, Robertson, 12, 86

Davis, Jack, 39–40, 57

Denison, George, 10

Deutsch, John, 52, 56

Dexter, Grant, 54–5

Diefenbaker, John: on Canadian-American relations, 36, 45, 46, 58; election campaign (1963), 91; Gordon on, 71; government of, 63, 110, 114, 126; oratorical power, 108; critical of public servants, 97

Dilworth, R.J., 5

Doern, Bruce, 179–80

Dominion Bureau of Statistics (DBS), 44–6, 47

Dominion Forge, 202n108

Douglas, T.C., 160, 165

Drew, George, 24, 44, 46

Drummond, Ian, 79, 84, 158, 180, 188

Drury, Charles M. "Bud," 97, 152

Dryden, Gordon, 72

Dunton, Davidson, 79

Eastman, Harry, 53

Eaton, Cyrus, 68

Eaton's, 18, 19

Edick, Gordon, 31, 72, 165–6

Eighth Canadian Reserve Battalion, 7

Eisenhower, Dwight, 58

Elderkin, C.F., 117
Election: (1957), 58, 114; (1958), 70–1; (1962), 90–1, 93; (1963), 91–2, 93; (1965), 129–30
Ellis, David, 187
Ellis, Winfield, 25
English, H. Edward, 39–40, 78, 140, 164
English, John, 51, 165
Ernst & Young, 187
Exchequer Court of Canada, 5
Expo '67, 134
Extraterritoriality: Gordon on, 83, 84, 139–40, 191; Wahn Report on, 175; Watkins Task Force on, 158, 161–2, 163, 164, 175

Ferguson, Dave, 18, 31, 82, 131
Fetherling, Doug, 68, 136
First National City Bank of New York: see Citibank
First World War, 5–8
Fisher, Douglas, 70, 173
Flag, 124, 131
Fleming, Donald, 47, 90, 96, 114
Flemming, Hugh John, 56
Folkestone, England, 6–7
Ford Motor Company, 83
Foreign Direct Investment in Canada: see Gray Report
Foreign Exchange Control Board, 20, 22
Foreign investment: in 1920s, 11; in 1940s and 1950s, 35; in 1960s, 139; in banks, 49; public opinion of, 47, 88–9, 172–3; see also Bank Act; Extraterritoriality; Foreign-owned firms; Mercantile Bank; Tariff, relation to foreign investment
Foreign Investment Review Agency (FIRA), 181, 182–3, 187
Foreign-owned firms: export policies, 42, 76, 84, 103, 140; hiring practices, 48, 50, 52, 83, 84, 161; imports by, 42, 48, 76, 84, 103, 140; minority Canadian ownership of, 48–9, 52, 53–4, 55, 85, 87, 103, 191; professional firms, use of non-Canadian, 33, 42, 48, 50–1, 52, 76, 84, 103; research and development by, 42, 76, 84, 140, 161
Forster, Donald, 117
Foster, Peter, 185
Fourth Canadian Mounted Rifles, 6, 9
Fowler, Robert, 42–3, 67, 78
Free trade, 78–9, 187
Frith, Royce, 72, 91
Frost, Leslie, 24, 68–9, 71
Fullerton, Douglas, 29, 39–40
Fulton, E. Davie, 45, 46
Functional socialism, 172

Galbraith, John Kenneth, 9, 86
Gardiner, Sir Thomas, 23
Gelber, Lionel, 11
General Agreement on Tariffs and Trade, 142
Gibbons, Sir George, 17
Gillespie, Alastair, 68, 70
Ginsberg, Allen, 136
Glassco, Jane (daughter), 33, 86
Godfrey, Dave, 136
Goforth, Wallace, 36
Gonick, Cy, 177
Goodman, Eddie, 177–9, 183
Gordon, Duncan Lockhart (brother), 5, 82
Gordon, Elizabeth Marjorie Leith (wife), 17–18, 33, 107, 185
Gordon, Emily Gordon (grandmother), 4
Gordon, Col. Harry Duncan Lockhart (father), 4–9, 12, 15–16, 22, 23, 29
Gordon, H. Scott, 39, 90
Gordon, Hugh Lockhart (brother), 5, 6, 7
Gordon, Isabelle (sister): see Wright, Isabelle Lockhart
Gordon, Jane (daughter): see Glassco, Jane
Gordon, Kathleen (mother), 4–5, 6–7, 12
Gordon, Kathleen "Kitty" (sister): see Griffin, Kathleen "Kitty" Lockhart
Gordon, Kyra (daughter): see Montagu, Kyra
Gordon, Walter Lockhart: Asian trip, 36–7, 70; birth, 5; budget (1963), 99–110, 119; budget (1964), 114; budget (1965), 115; as businessman, 25–6, 66–8; and Canada Development Corporation, 111, 114–17, 132, 139, 162, 180; with Canadian Corporate Management, 20, 25–6, 28, 67–8, 124; Canadian Forum part-owner, 18, 201n93; character, 3, 14, 27, 28–32, 130–1; A Choice for Canada, 86, 133, 138–45, 155, 186; with Clarkson Gordon, 15–16, 19–21, 23, 28, 31, 66; chairs Committee on the Organization of Government in Ontario, 71; and CIC, 176–7, 179–80, 193; and communism, 17–18; on culture, 33, 85–6, 119, 124, 155, 168, 169, 191–2; on Diefenbaker, 71; economic knowledge, 22, 30–1, 40, 189; in England during First World War, 6–7; on extraterritoriality, 83, 139–40, 191; appointed finance minister, 92; with Foreign Exchange Control Board, 20, 22; foreign-investment policies, 48–9, 73–4, 76, 83–4, 103, 139, 145, 148–9, 175, 184, 186, 191; and Foreign Investment Review Agency (FIRA), 183; on performance

of foreign-owned firms, 48–9, 83–4, 140–1, 159, 161, 190–2; on foreign ownership of banks, 117–18, 149, 152–5, 191; gout, 20, 23, 28, 73; at Grange Preparatory School, 6, 7; impact, 166, 167, 175, 180, 185–8, 192–3; impatience, 23, 29–30, 32, 49, 94, 95, 97, 99, 159; interventionist approach to economy, 22, 32, 170, 189; considers seeking Liberal leadership, 165–6; Liberal campaign chair, 91–2, 129; tries to influence Liberal policy, 37, 66, 72–6, 81–2, 87–8, 93, 114–15, 132, 145–7; reorganizes Liberal party, 28, 31, 66, 71–2, 81–2, 92, 93, 103, 192; management consultant, 21, 24–5; supports Marchand for leader, 166; marriage, 17–18; military service, 20, 202n108; nationalism reflects personal experience of, 3–4, 33, 141, 189–92; in New York City, 17; and oil industry, 185, 186; organizational skills, 27, 31–2, 92, 93, 129, 192–3; in Parliament, 91, 148; Pearson friendship developed, 19, 26–8, 70, 74–5, 95, 192, 201n100; Pearson friendship weakened, 92, 108–9, 130–1; and Pearson leadership campaign, 70; personality, 3, 14, 16, 18, 27, 29–32, 192; philanthropy, 29, 141; polio, 7; *A Political Memoir*, 185–6; urged to enter politics, 28, 70; sense of privacy, 3, 12; protectionism of, 19–20, 41, 59–62, 142, 169, 186–7, 189–90; as public servant, 20–3, 32, 189; on Quebec, 169–70; religion, 9; resignation

130–1, 166; resignation offered, 107; resignation threatened, 147–8, 153; chairs Royal Commission on Administrative Classifications in the Public Service, 23–4; chairs Royal Commission on Canada's Economic Prospects, 37–65, 142, 191, 193; with Royal Commission on Customs and Excise, 16, 49; with Royal Commission on Price Spreads, 18–19, 189; at Royal Military College, 3–4, 13–15, 28, 31, 105; social conscience, 18, 29, 33, 189; social policies, 22, 80, 110; *Storm Signals*, 86, 184, 186; with Tariff Board, 19–20, 124; and *Toronto Star*, 66, 68–70, 93, 150, 173, 192, 193; *Troubled Canada*, 82–7, 114, 186; supports Trudeau for leader, 166; and U.S., 7, 17, 32–3, 36–7, 74, 141, 155–6, 174–5, 190; at Upper Canada College, 9–12, 197n33; on Vietnam War, 138–9, 155–7, 174; and Wartime Prices and Trade Board, 22; and Watkins Task Force, 149–51, 158–60, 164, 193; *What Is Happening to Canada*, 186; with Woods Gordon, 21, 23, 24–5, 28, 30, 31, 66–7
Gordon, W.H. Lockhart (grandfather), 4–5, 9
Gordon & Dilworth, 5
Gordon Commission: *see* Royal Commission on Administrative Classifications in the Public Service; Royal Commission on Canada's Economic Prospects
Gordon Report: *see* Royal Commission on Administrative Classifications in the Public Service; Royal Com-

mission on Canada's Economic Prospects
Gouzenko affair, 34
Granatstein, J.L., 15
Grange Preparatory School, 6–7
Grant, Alison: *see* Ignatieff, Alison Grant
Grant, Charity, 12
Grant, George Munro, 10, 125
Grant, George Parkin, 125–7, 132, 136, 139, 166, 174, 177
Grant, Leroy F., 15, 41
Grant, William Lawson "Choppy," 10, 12, 125
Grauer, A.E. "Dal," 38, 50, 60
Gray, Herb, 179, 180
Gray Report, 180–3, 186
Great Depression, 18, 45, 189
Griesinger, William, 56
Griffin, Kathleen "Kitty" Lockhart (sister), 5, 7, 9, 12, 14, 17
Gualtieri, Roberto, 180
Gulf Oil Canada, 185
Gushue, Raymond, 38, 50, 60
Gwyn, Richard, 156

Haig, Sir Douglas, 6
Hamilton, Alvin, 114, 128, 177
Hampson, Anthony, 39–40
Harris, Walter, 38, 118
Hawthorn Publishing, 69
Hays, Harry, 177
Hébert, Jacques, 87
Heeney, Arnold, 27, 41, 58, 127–8
Heeney-Merchant Report, 127–8, 132
Heisey, Alan, 173
Hellyer, Paul: on budget (1963), 102, 106, 108, 109; on Gordon, 129, 150, 156; and Liberal party, 72, 82
Herbert, Charles, 20
Hockey, 167
Hockin, Alan, 115
Hodgetts, J.E., 24
Hollander, Paul, 135
Holmes, John, 128

Holton, Richard, 110
Honderich, Beland, 69–70, 109, 177
Honey, Peter, 182
Honey Report, 182
Hood, William, 39–40, 76
House of Anansi Press, 136–7
Howe, C.D.: on foreign investment, 35, 45–6, 47, 50–1, 64; Gordon consults, 28; on Gordon Commission, 38, 55, 57; on Liberal party changes, 71, 80; role in St Laurent government, 28, 35, 37
Howland, Robert, 39–40
Hughes, Barry Conn, 188
Hurtig, Mel, 177–8, 179
Hush, 16
Hutchison, Bruce, 55, 147
Hydro-Electric Power Commission of Ontario, 8, 16, 24
Hymer, Stephen, 158
Hythe, England, 7

Ignatieff, Alison Grant, 12, 198n51
Ilsley, James, 21, 22
Imperialism, 9–10, 166
Imperial Oil, 185
Innis, Harold, 158
Interdepartmental Task Force on Foreign Investment (Ontario): *see* Honey Report
Interest equalization tax (U.S.), 111–14, 131
International Paper Company, 67–8, 139
Investment Canada, 187
Irwin, James, 4
Isbister, Claude, 95, 98–100, 103, 110

Jackman, Henry R., 26
J.D. Woods & Co. Ltd.: *see* Woods Gordon
Jewett, Pauline, 122, 158, 177
Johnson, Harry, 77–8, 85, 135, 142, 172; on Gordon Report, 53–4, 78; on Watkins Report, 164–5
Johnson, Lyndon, 127

Kaplan, Robert, 183
Kearns, Lionel, 138
Keirstead, B.S., 36
Kennedy, John F., 111, 134
Kennedy, Robert, 134, 155
Kent, Tom, 80, 82, 97, 115, 125; on budget (1963), 102, 106, 109–10; on Gordon, 27, 80, 93; as Gordon ally, 80–1; on Gordon Report, 53, 55, 57, 63–4, 85; on Gordon's resignation, 131; on Howe, 38; at Kingston Conference, 79–90; and Liberal policy on foreign investment, 87, 88; on magazines, 119, 120, 121; on Pearson, 27
Kent State University, 174
Keynes, John Maynard, 84
Kidd, Henry Erskine "Bob," 71–2
Kierans, Eric, 105, 138–9, 143, 164, 168–9
Kilbourn, William, 12, 77
Kindleberger, Charles, 158
King, Martin Luther Jr, 134
Kingston Conference, 75–80, 87

Laidlaw, R.A., 25
Laing, Arthur, 156
LaMarsh, Judy, 72, 95, 107–9, 150, 177, 185
Lament for a Nation: *see* Grant, George Parkin
Lamontagne, Maurice, 82, 87, 148, 177; with Gordon Commission, 39–40, 61; at Kingston Conference, 79–80
Land, Brian, 96, 98–9, 109, 160
Lang, Dan, 72, 91
Laurin, Cy, 119, 121
Lax, Gary, 173
Laxer, James, 127, 170, 176, 177

Laxer, Robert, 173
Lazar, Harvey, 180
Leacock, Stephen, 10, 12
League for Social Reconstruction, 18
Lee, Dennis, 136, 169
LePan, Douglas, 39, 157, 177; with Gordon Commission, 39–40, 49, 51, 57, 62
Lévesque, René, 145
Levitt, Kari, 168, 169, 173
Liberal party: election campaign (1963), 91–2; election campaign (1965), 129–30; Gordon reorganizes, 28, 31, 66, 71–2, 81–2, 92, 93, 192–3; Harrison Hot Springs meeting (1969), 175; Leader's Advisory Committee, 82; leadership campaign (1968), 165–6; National Rally (1961), 81, 91; Pearson becomes leader of, 70; policies, 37, 72–81, 87–8, 93, 114–15, 145–7; policy conference (1966), 133, 145–7
Lindeman, John, 140
Little, A.J., 31
Lloyd, Glen, 25
Long, Marcus, 36
Lord, Barry, 138
Low, Solon, 22
Luce, Henry, 122
Lumsden, Ian, 168, 173
Lussier, Omer, 38, 49
Lynch, Charles, 128

McArthur, Jack, 115, 176, 181
McCall-Newman, Christina, 3, 110, 177, 184
McCarthy, Joseph, 35, 36, 44, 58, 64, 88, 192
McClelland, Jack, 177
McCutcheon, Wallace, 69
Macdonald, Donald, 96, 146
MacDonald, Flora, 177
Macdonald, Mary, 71, 102
McDougald, J.A. "Bud," 69

MacEachen, Allan, 82, 101, 150, 164, 186, 187; on Gordon, 31; on Gordon Commission, 56
McGovern, George, 155
MacIntosh, Alex, 115
Mackasey, Bryce, 153
MacKay, Andrew, 39–40, 41–2
Mackenzie, Michael, 30, 39–40
Mackie, Victor, 146
Mackintosh, W.A., 38, 60
MacLennan, Hugh, 86, 177
McLeod, John, 138
McNaught, Kenneth, 177
MacPherson, R.B., 79
Magazines: in 1920s, 11; and CIC, 178; and Diefenbaker government, 118–19; Gordon's policy on, 111, 118–24, 131, 155, 191–2; and St Laurent government, 118; and Trudeau government, 185; and Wahn Report, 175
Malcolm X, 134
Malenkov, Georgy, 36
Mao Tse-tung, 36
Marchand, Jean, 27, 156, 166
Marler, George, 71
Martin, Paul, 70, 98, 107, 109, 150: on Gordon's reorganization of Liberal party, 82; on Heeney-Merchant Report, 128; on Kingston Conference, 80; and magazine issue, 122; on Vietnam War, 155–6
Massey, Vincent, 8, 24
Masson, Claude, 158
Mathews, Robin, 126, 167, 177
Matthews, Bruce, 82
Medicare, 128, 131, 187
Mercantile Bank, 117–18, 149, 152–5
Merchant, Livingston, 127–8
Merchants Bank, 5
Mid-West Paper, 67
Molgat, Gildas, 145, 147
Molson, Hartland, 18, 25, 69

Monk, George, 13
Montagu, Kyra (daughter), 17, 33
Morton, Desmond, 15
Morton, W.L., 177
Motorola Inc., 67
Mount Sorrel, Battle of, 6
Mowat, Farley, 177
Mulroney, Brian, 187
Murdoch, James, 25
My Lai massacre, 174

Nash, Albert, 16, 18–19, 20
National Energy Program, 186, 187
National Film Board, 24
National Liberal Federation: see Liberal party
NATO, 74, 76, 91, 167
Nelson, Stanley, 24
New Democratic Party (NDP), 170–1, 176
Newman, Christina: see McCall-Newman, Christina
Newman, C.J., 137
Newman, Peter C., 70, 98, 138, 162; on Gordon, 7, 30, 31, 93, 108, 147, 156, 188; angered by Gordon's magazine policy, 123–4; CIC co-founder, 176–7
New nationalism, 167–74, 176–80, 182–3, 185–6, 188, 193
Nielsen, Bob, 70
Ninth Mississauga Horse Regiment, 6
Nixon surcharge, 174
NORAD, 73, 74, 91
Norman, Herbert, 58, 64, 88, 138, 192
Nowlan, George, 56

O'Connell, Martin, 97–8
October Crisis, 177
O'Hagan, Richard, 82
Oil industry, 185, 186
O'Leary, Grattan, 118, 122–3
Oliphant, Peter, 97
Order of Canada, 124, 131

Organization for Economic Co-operation and Development, 112
Osler, B.B., 17

Parkin, George, 10, 125
Pearson, Geoffrey, 88, 102
Pearson, Lester B. "Mike": on Auto Pact's connection to magazine issue, 122; and Bank Act, 152–4; and budget (1963), 101–2, 107–8; on CDC, 116; on communism, 34; economic knowledge, 26, 27, 88, 95, 101–2; on foreign investment, 44, 75, 87–8; on Gordon as Liberal leader, 165; Gordon friendship develops, 19, 26–8, 201n100; Gordon friendship weakens, 108–9, 130–1, 151–2; accepts Gordon's help with party reorganization, 70–2, 81–2, 92, 95, 103, 192–3; uneasy about Gordon in finance, 92, 109, 129, 130; invites Gordon back into Cabinet, 148–50; on Heeney-Merchant Report, 128; indecisiveness, 26–7, 72, 74, 129; and Kingston Conference, 75, 80; and Leader's Advisory Committee, 81–2; becomes Liberal leader, 70–1; target of McCarthyism, 36; nationalism of, 88, 124; Nobel Prize, 51, 70; nuclear policy, 91; organizational skills, 27; personality, 26–7, 205n163; and sixty days of decision, 91–2; nominates Towers as commission chair, 38; defends U.S. ambassador, 46; on Vietnam War, 156–7
Pearson, Maryon, 92, 109
Pelletier, Gérard, 145
Pennell, Lawrence, 147, 154
Periodicals: see Magazines

Petro-Canada, 185, 186
Petrofina Canada, 186
Phillips, W.E., 69
Pickersgill, J.W., 22, 82, 109, 150; on budget (1963), 101, 104–5, 107–8; on CDC, 116; on Liberal foreign investment policy, 87
Pipeline debate, 47, 64
Plumptre, A.F. Wynne, 10, 90, 113, 197–8n38; and budget preparation (1963), 96, 98–9, 103; on magazines, 119; on Vietnam War, 157
Pope, W.H., 168, 173
Port Hope Conference (1933), 75
Pratt, Irving, 25
Presgrave, Ralph, 21
Public Petroleum Association of Canada, 179
Purdy, Al, 136, 138, 173, 177

Quebec: views of foreign investment, 87, 144–5, 162, 163–4, 181–2; nationalism, 169–70, 181–2

Rasminsky, Louis, 100–1, 111–12
Reader's Digest: see Magazines
Reid, Escott, 136, 157
Reisman, Simon: on Auto Pact, 125; and budget preparation (1963), 96, 98–9; on Gordon, 60, 110; with Gordon Commission, 39–40, 57, 59–62, 96; and Watkins Task Force, 159
Reuber, G.L., 84
Richardson, H.A., 13
Ritchie, Charles, 110, 113
Ritchie, Edgar, 113
Robertson, Gordon, 121, 151
Rockefeller, Godfrey, 25
Rohmer, Richard, 173
Rosenbluth, Gideon, 158
Ross, Douglas, 156
Rotstein, Abraham, 173, 187; CIC co-founder, 176–7; on

FIRA, 182–3; on Gordon, 117, 143–4; publishes leaked version of Gray Report, 180; leader of new nationalism, 166, 168, 176–7, 193; on Vietnam War, 135–6, 156; differs with Watkins, 171–2, 176; and Watkins Task Force, 158, 166
Rowe, Russell, 182
Royal Commission on Administrative Classifications in the Public Service, 23, 24
Royal Commission on Canada's Economic Prospects: created, 38–40; Final Report, 62–4, 117, 186; on foreign ownership, 41–3, 47–9, 52–5, 62–4; hearings, 41–3, 47, 114; impact, 43–4, 47, 49, 57, 64–5, 88, 192, 193; Preliminary Report, 49–57, 59, 62, 191; research work, 39–40, 57, 59–62; on tariff, 51–5, 60–3
Royal Commission on Customs and Excise, 16, 49
Royal Commission on National Development in the Arts, Letters and Sciences, 24
Royal Commission on Price Spreads, 18–19, 189, 192
Royal Commission on Publications, 118–20
Royal Commission on the Automotive Industry, 124
Royal Military College (RMC), 4, 5, 13–15, 27, 28
Rugman, Alan, 185
Rusk, Dean, 122
Ryan, Claude, 177, 181–2

Safarian, A. Edward, 29; with Gordon Commission, 39–40, 59; research on foreign investment, 103, 140–1, 159, 164; with Watkins Task Force, 158–9, 165

St Laurent, Louis, 24, 27, 37, 70; on Gordon Commission, 55; invites Gordon into Cabinet, 28, 92; government of, 37, 45
Saul, John Ralston, 96
Sauvé, Maurice, 39–40, 81
Scott, Anthony, 39
Scott, James, 72
Securities and Exchange Commission (U.S.), 16
Sedgewick, George, 19
Select Committee on Economic and Cultural Nationalism (Ontario), 182
Sharp, Mitchell, 50, 130, 182–3; and Bank Act, 149, 152–4; and budget (1963), 107; on CDC, 116, 143; on foreign investment, 129, 143, 146; on Gordon, 32, 125, 156; on Gordon Commission, 57; and Gordon's return to Cabinet, 148–9, 150; and Kingston Conference, 75; on Liberal foreign investment policy, 87; at Liberal policy conference (1966), 146–7; and third option, 183–4; and Wahn Report, 175–6; and Watkins Task Force, 151, 159, 160
Shell Canada, 185
Sinclair, Jimmy, 55
Sixty days of decision, 91–2, 93, 97, 102, 110
Skinner, Ross, 31
Slater, David, 60, 77; on foreign investment, 146; on Gordon, 59, 144; with Gordon Commission, 39–40, 57
Smith, David, 156, 187
Smith, Denis, 30, 169, 173, 177
Smith, Emily Gordon: see Gordon, Emily Gordon
Social Science Federation of Canada, 179
Somme, Battle of the, 6
Sommerville, Norman, 18

Souster, Raymond, 137
Spry, Graham, 201nn93–4
Stanbury, Richard, 72
Stanfield, Robert, 56
Stanley, David, 97–9, 101, 115, 116
Steele, G.G. Ernest, 98–9, 110
Steele, James, 156, 167, 243n150
Stevens, H.H., 19
Stewart, Alastair, 58
Stewart, Andrew, 38, 50
Stoner, Gerald, 159, 160
Strong, Maurice, 115
Stuart, R. Douglas, 25, 46
Student Union for Peace Action (SUPA), 134–5
Study Conference on National Problems: see Kingston Conference
Stursberg, Peter, 114
Stykolt, Stefan, 53
Suez Crisis, 51, 64

Takeover tax, 97, 99–102, 104, 106, 132, 139, 191–2
Tariff: relationship to foreign investment, 11, 46, 53, 73–4, 76, 142, 168, 190; see also Free trade; Gordon, protectionism of
Tariff Board, 19–20, 26, 124
Tarragon Theatre, 86
Task Force on the Structure of Canadian Industry: see Watkins Task Force
Tax rental agreements, 22
Taylor, Charles, 127
Taylor, E.P., 69, 109
Taylor, Ken, 38, 96, 99
T. Eaton Company: see Eaton's
Templeton, Charles, 69
Third Canadian Division, 6
Third option, 183–4
Thompson, Roy, 68
Time: see Magazines
Tinker, Frank, 37
Tomlin, Brian, 179–80

Toronto Star, 160; supports Gordon, 68–70, 93, 168, 173–4, 192, 193; Gordon helps, 66, 68–70, 173, 192
Towers, Graham, 20, 22, 38, 109
Trans-Canada Pipeline, 47
Trent, John, 179
Trudeau, Pierre, 179–80; on foreign investment, 145, 176; Gordon disagrees with, 170; Gordon supports for leadership, 166; on Watkins Report, 166
Turner, John, 143, 164

Underhill, Frank, 77, 134
United Nations, 74
United States: neutrality in First World War, 7, 190; see also Civil rights movement; Culture; Foreign investment; Interest equalization tax; Vietnam War
University Club (Toronto), 187
University of Toronto, 15, 17, 136
Upper, Boyd, 72
Upper Canada College (UCC), 4, 9–12, 198n53

Vancouver Pacific Paper, 67
Vandercamp, J., 77
Vietnam War, 163, 174, 187; Canadian reaction to, 134–8, 157, 158, 166, 174, 192; Gordon's opposition to, 139, 155–7; and Waffle group, 171; Watkins' opposition to, 158, 165
Vimy Ridge, Battle of, 6
Viner, Jacob, 53

Waffle group, 169, 170–2, 177–8, 186
Wahn, Ian, 175–6
Wahn Report, 175–6, 181
Walker, Jimmy, 148

Walker Metal Products, 124
Walter Gordon Circle, 187
Warnock, John, 167, 173
Wartime Prices and Trade Board, 22–3
Watergate scandal, 174, 187, 192
Watkins, Melville, 165, 169, 172, 187, 193; on Gordon, 103, 142, 158; leader of new nationalism, 165, 166, 168, 193; on Vietnam War, 135–6, 165; and Waffle group, 170–2, 176, 177; and Watkins Task Force, 158–60, 162, 165
Watkins Task Force, 166; creation, 149, 151, 158, 193; report, 160–5, 168, 175, 182, 186; workings of, 158–60
Wilson, Harry, 109
Wilson, Tuzo, 136
Wilson, W.A., 29
Winters, Robert, 56, 129–30, 150, 156, 160
Withholding tax on dividends, 49, 52, 99–101, 114, 131
Wolfson, Harry, 77
Woodfine, William, 158
Woods, J. Douglas, 21
Woods Gordon: creation of, 21; becomes Ernst & Young, 187; government contracts, 23, 24–5, 67; growth of, 23, 24, 67–8
Wright, Gerald, 113
Wright, Isabelle Lockhart (sister), 5

York Club (Toronto), 109
York Knitting Mills, 21
Young, John H., 39, 59–62, 76, 78

Zimmer, David, 187